Israel's Higher Law

Israel's Higher Law

Religion and Liberal Democracy in the Jewish State

Steven V. Mazie

LEXINGTON BOOKS

A division of
ROWMAN & LITTLEFIELD PUBLISHERS, INC.
Lanham • Boulder • New York • Toronto • Oxford

LEXINGTON BOOKS

A division of Rowman & Littlefield Publishers, Inc.
A wholly owned subsidiary of The Rowman & Littlefield Publishing Group, Inc.
4501 Forbes Boulevard, Suite 200
Lanham, MD 20706

PO Box 317
Oxford
OX2 9RU, UK

British Library Cataloguing in Publication Information Available

Library of Congress Cataloging-in-Publication Data

Mazie, Steven V. 1971-
 Israel's higher law : religion and liberal democracy in the Jewish state / Steven V.
Mazie.
  p. cm.
 Includes bibliographical references and index.
 ISBN-13: 978-0-7391-1259-5 (cloth : alk. paper)
 ISBN-10: 0-7391-1259-7 (cloth : alk. paper)
 ISBN-13: 978-0-7391-1485-8 (pbk. : alk. paper)
 ISBN-10: 0-7391-1485-9 (pbk. : alk. paper)
 1. Judaism and state--Israel. 2. Judaism and politics--Israel. 3. Democracy--Religious
aspects--Judaism. 4. Liberalism--Religious aspects--Judaism. 5. Israel--Politics and
government--Philosophy. 6. Liberalism--Israel. 7. Democracy--Israel. I. Title.
BM538.S7M39 2006
322'.1095694--dc22   2005034577

Printed in the United States of America
 ™
⊖ The paper used in this publication meets the minimum requirements of American
National Standard for Information Sciences—Permanence of Paper for Printed Library
Materials, ANSI/NISO Z39.48–1992.

for Renanit and Amarya

Contents

Preface
Snapshots of Israel

Can a religious polity be a liberal democracy? Diving into Israel's Jewish-democratic conundrum demands both tapping into traditional sources of political philosophy and stretching beyond them. In these pages, I heed David Hume's admonition that "in all questions with regard to morals . . . there is really no . . . standard, by which any controversy can ever be decided" other than "an appeal to"—and I would add, a critical engagement with—"the general opinion."[1]

This book explores the relationship between Israel's Jewish and democratic foundations by paying close attention to "the general opinion"—the points of view of diverse, ordinary Israeli citizens. These voices illustrate with clarity and passion the tensions between Judaism and liberal democracy in terms that are more raw, more honest and less strategic than those of political or religious leaders. And they add numerous personal notes to the story of state and religion in Israel that ruffle the crisp concepts of political philosophy: how a Jewish woman's feelings about her secretive relationship with a Palestinian man relate to her stance on the "Jewish state"; the link between a Jewish man's journey in and out of ultra-orthodoxy and his views on religious freedom; a Muslim woman who cried throughout her first year in university among primarily Jewish students but now leads Arab-Jewish discussion groups; a religious Jew who supports the rabbinate's monopoly over Jewish marriage procedures but bristles at the callous manner in which they exercise this control. These interview subjects and twenty-seven others, featured in chapters 3-9, add much-needed color and nuance to a debate often mischaracterized as one that simply pits the religious against the secular, or the Arab against the Jew.

Before embarking on this exploration, it seems fitting to give a sense of the *experience* of Judaism in the Israeli state, of Israel's Jewishness as it is observed by the interviewer and author. Here, then, is a bit of personal ethnography—a composite journal recounting a single day in the life of a Jewish American researcher in Israel:

6:00 am: This morning, like every morning, the radio broadcast on the state-owned radio station is prefaced by the recitation of the *Shema,* the central article of faith in Jewish prayer. *Shema Yisrael: Adonai Eloheinu, Adonai Ehad.* ("Hear O Israel: The Lord is Our God, the Lord is One" [Deuteronomy 6: 4-9].) According to Jewish law *(halacha),* Jews must recite the Shema twice daily, in the morning and at bedtime. But there is no *halachic* requirement that the Shema be *heard* at any time, let alone on the radio. So why is it broadcast by the Israel Broadcasting Authority, under the auspices of the state's Ministry of Education?

6:01 am: The Shema is followed on this April morning by the Counting of the Omer, an obligatory ritual (according to Leviticus 23:15) in which Jews count the forty-nine days between the festivals of Passover (commemorating the exodus from Egypt) and Shavuot (commemorating the giving of the Torah at Mount Sinai). It's especially odd to hear the Omer counted at this time, given that the practice among observant Jews is to count it, after saying a blessing, during *evening* prayers. So if Orthodox Jews already know they need to count the Omer, and that they need to do so during the *ma'ariv* service, and if secular Jews eschew this and most other religious rituals, what purpose does the Israel Broadcasting Authority find in playing the Omer recitation at six in the morning? The government of Israel is under no biblical obligation to count the Omer: the religious duty pertains to individuals, not states (even Jewish ones). For the many Israeli Jews who fall in the middle of the pack—traditionally minded Jews who might say the Omer when they remember, but lack the religious rigor to perform every commandment—the announcement may provide a valuable reminder. The broadcast seems to be, too, an assertion of affiliation with Israel's Jewish religious heritage and a reflection of a kind of civil religion.[2] When the stentorian voice pronounces "Shema Yisrael," it speaks not only to a Jewish audience but to Israeli citizens, inhabitants of the modern polity called Israel. It thus fuses religion and nation via one short prayer. The Omer seems to be another connection with that Jewish heritage, which, like numerous elements of Israel's symbology, may be interpreted by various Jewish Israelis in very different ways. After the religious rituals have ended, *"Boker Tov Yisrael"* ("Good Morning Israel"), the daybreak news program, begins.

8:30 am: Waiting for the #9 bus in my central Jerusalem neighborhood of Talbieh, home to Israel's prime minister and president and a mixed population of secular and religious, though not ultra-Orthodox, Jews, I notice an advertisement on the bus-stop wall. A plastic bottle is pictured underneath the following statement, in large type: "A head covering is a duty, but flakes are not." (*Kisui rosh ze hova, aval kashkashim zeh lo.*) It takes me a moment to decipher the Hebrew (I had to look up the word for "flakes"), and another to grasp the meaning. A head-covering is mandatory? What? What exactly are they trying to sell? It was an ad for a dandruff shampoo, but one that would be indecipherable to someone ignorant of the Orthodox Jewish custom according to which both men and married women must cover their head (men wear a *yarmulke*, known in Hebrew as a *kippa*; women wear a wig, beret, scarf or hat, depending on the community, covering all or most of their hair). So while it may be a duty to cover your head, the ad goes, you don't have to have a head covered in dandruff flakes. Buy our shampoo. This sign of the Jewish state comes not from the Jewish state itself—that is, from political institutions, legislation or symbols. Nor does it come from an official agency like the Israel Broadcasting Authority. This sign comes from what we call civil society: from a bath product company choosing to play on notions of duty and of head coverings to sell a product. And they do it in a neighborhood in which a distinct minority of men and women actually wear head coverings, in which only roughly a quarter of those seeing the ad will regard themselves as bound to don a *kippa* or a hat. Still, the currency of the ideas is strong enough, and the practice widely known enough, that the ad will speak to nearly everyone who sees it, religious and secular alike. Dandruff is something all Israeli Jews can have the misfortune of sharing, whether they cover their heads for religious reasons or not. Now if this ad (suitably translated) were to appear at a bus stop in Boise or Rome or Buenos Aires, it would baffle the onlooker. It would even confuse the average Jewish resident of Manhattan. But in Israel it makes sense, and that fact signals the pervasiveness of Jews and of Judaism in Israel's public ethos.

9:00 am: I board a rush-hour bus on my way to Mount Scopus, site of the Hebrew University. The bus is already very crowded when I get on, and at the next stop passengers squeeze in through both the front and back doors to fill every available cubic centimeter. Then something remarkable happens. The passengers who have boarded in the back, prevented from approaching the driver by a throng of bodies, fish coins or bills for the three-odd shekel bus fare out of their purses or pockets, hand them to a rider in front of them with a head-and-eyebrow gesture toward the front, and the fares make their way through at least a dozen hands up to the driver. Then, after receiving and depositing the shekels, the driver rips a few wispy tickets off his pad, thumbs out the correct change for each passenger and holds the tenuous bundles out for nearby passengers to collect. Silently, everyone knows what to do: passengers take the ticket and money from the driver and pass them to someone behind them, she to another, and so on back to the waiting passengers. The transaction takes several minutes. It relies not only on the honesty of everyone in the chain not to pocket the cash, and the dexterity not to drop a stray ten *agora* coin, but on an unspoken principle that is never questioned: everyone pays a fare, even when it's near-impossible to accomplish that task, and everyone has a role in seeing to it that the fare is paid and ticket and change returned to the rider. You get the sense this operation runs itself, as it might in a particularly tight family. This phenomenon is very far removed from any official manifestation of public Judaism; it doesn't even have any explicit Jewish content, as did the shampoo ad. Something like this cooperation on the bus might be found in a small Midwestern town where everyone knows one another, but in a city of a half-million residents personal familiarity is not the explanation. Instead, it seems to be a quiet implication of the state's Jewish communitarian ethos. Do they have a sense that, for better and worse, everyone on the bus belongs to a big Jewish family?

9:20 am: The crowd on the bus continues to grow, so I take the opportunity to jump off in the ultra-Orthodox (or *haredi*) neighborhood of Geula, near Mea Shearim. I wander around for a couple of hours, talking to black-hatted men with long beards and severe gaits, looking at graffiti and stopping to read the ubiquitous signs, issued by community rabbis, that are plastered on public bill boards. These posters alone envelop the onlooker in a sea of *haredi* life. One notice, signed by Rabbi Karelitz (a prominent leader in the ultra-orthodox community), warns followers of a butcher shop that didn't properly separate meat and milk products during the previous week, in violation of the laws of dietary laws of *kashrut*; another announces a massive prayer rally at the Western Wall; another reminds followers that it is forbidden to leave the Land of Israel (even temporarily) without permission from a rabbi. Around the corner, a placard condemns watching or showing films—even documentaries—on the grounds that this may lead to the viewing of more illicit movies. Many signs eulogize recently departed community leaders and residents; dozens ask locals to donate to various charity funds:

> *Jew, Jew, Jew, Jew*—how can you stand by as the eleven orphans of the Gaon Tsadik Rabbi Nissim Yagen, of Blessed Memory, the Head of Kehillat Ya'akov Yeshiva, who devoted his life to the Community of Israel for decades, call out for help? Give! Sign up to give ten dollars a month, for at least thirty months!

Appeals for charity are everywhere. On a busy street corner, a glossy poster is pasted on the back of a phone booth featuring an alluringly golden roasted chicken at the center of a family table: "Mama, why can't we have chicken for Shabbes?" goes the pitch; the request is for families who cannot afford to buy meat for Friday night dinners. A dark-skinned man of Middle Eastern descent, wearing a white *kippa*, is selling "shoes for Shabbat" on the street. He accosts a pedestrian, motioning to his scuffed black loafers: "How can you walk around in those?!" A *haredi* Jewish man approaches me, clearly an outsider in this sea of ultra-Orthodoxy with my short-sleeved shirt, tan jeans and knit *kippa* I wear to soften my otherness. "Shalom, Ahi," (Hello, my brother) he says. "Have a good shabbat." Another man, with a *shtreimel* (fur lined hat), a black-and-white striped coat and a long white beard, engages me in conversation about his son's approaching Bar Mitzvah, turning away occasionally to chat in Yiddish with passersby, and requests a donation for his family of thirteen. In this enclave of ultra-Orthodoxy near Jerusalem's center, the signs of a totalistic mode of Jewish life are everywhere. The irony is that most of these residents do not believe that the fact of Israel's existence, or the questions about how Jewish it ought to be, or in what ways, have anything to do with their Jewish lives. Many of them contend, as did ultra-Orthodox leaders before and since 1948, that the Jewish state should not exist.

12:00 pm. After having a felafel and fresh-squeezed orange juice at a corner stand, I catch another bus up to Mount Scopus. The #9 ambles through more black-hat neighborhoods, then enters the large Jewish enclave in the otherwise Arab-dominated eastern side of Jerusalem. Dozens of neighborhoods populated by Palestinian Arabs abut the Hebrew University campus and the adjoining Jewish neighborhood of French Hill. Later, I take the #23 bus from campus back to the center of Jerusalem. This line whisks passengers to downtown more quickly by passing through the heart of the Arab neighborhoods on the eastern side of Nablus Road. Most riders eschew the shortcut, however, in favor of a longer ride through Jewish Jerusalem—even the special bulletproof windows on the #23 are not invitation enough to take the short trip through what looks and feels like another country. Part of the experience of Jewish life in Israel is the constant stream of reminders that a significant non-Jewish population shares the city and the land. Most of the Arab residents of East Jerusalem are not Israeli citizens—only a fraction exercise their right to apply for citizenship. But their presence, often avoided, is never completely hidden. The city's sharply segregated neighborhoods, largely separate bus lines and jobs mean that Jews seldom encounter Arabs except when hiring cleaning help, a handyman or construction worker.

12:15 am. Watching late-night television on Israel's Channel One, I stay up for the nightly ritual. First is *"pesuko shel yom,"* the Torah portion of the day. The image of a page from the Torah scroll fills the screen, and a *yad*, the traditional silver pointer, rests on the first word in the upper-right hand corner. Now the *yad* begins to move to the left as a deep Middle Eastern-accented voice slowly reads the biblical selection, more faithful to the guttural *hets* and *ayins* than those who speak European-inflected Hebrew. The brief Bible reading ends without commentary and fades into the closing segment of the broadcast day: a symphonic rendition of Israel's national anthem, "Hatikva," with the lyrics superimposed on an Israeli flag flapping against a blue sky. The day closes as it opened, this time with two signs of Israel's religio-national affiliation—one derived from an ancient religious text, another from a nineteenth-century nationalist movement. Both signify Israel's fundamental link with, and commitment to, a particular faith community.

*   *   *

These sketches of Jewish life in Israel convey a narrow slice of the Israeli experience. They capture, however, something of the nuance and grit of Judaism as lived in the Jewish state. While only the radio and television broadcasts stem an institutional relationship between religion and state, each moment is, in an important sense, made possible and nourished by the state. Israel has provided the framework through which this richly Jewish civil society could develop and thrive. It has brought together a population of broad ethnic, geographic and religious diversity; it has established national symbols that stir most of its Jewish citizens with one kind of patriotism or another; it has set aside space—both physical and spiritual—for its ultra-religious minority to realize its own conception of the righteous life; it has embraced certain aspects of its religious tradition in shaping a national ethos. Along the way, however, Israel has stumbled in failing to accord equality to its Arab minority and to the dissenting voices within its Jewish majority. In the pages to come, I use Israelis' voices to understand these successes and failures and to point the way to a more nuanced, more contextual account of the status of religion within liberal democracy.

Notes

1. David Hume, "Of the Original Contract," in *Hume's Political Essays*, ed. Knud Haakonssen (Cambridge: Cambridge University Press, 1994), 200.
2. Charles Liebman and Eliezer Don-Yehiya explore a similar theme in *Civil Religion in Israel: Traditional Judaism and Political Culture in the Jewish State* (Berkeley: University of California Press, 1984), where they isolate three historical periods in the development of an Israeli civil religion.

Acknowledgments

This book has profited from the help and support of many people. I am grateful, first, for my Ph.D. advisors at the University of Michigan who oversaw the development of the project. Arlene Saxonhouse encouraged me to do more serious and extensive field research than I had originally planned and challenged me at each step to confront the larger questions of political theory underlying the work. Noga Morag-Levine pushed me to address not only intra-Jewish but also Jewish-Arab conflicts in Israel, helped me prepare better interview questions and provided penetrating typed comments on chapter drafts. Conversations with Elizabeth Anderson were always enlightening, and I thank her for the suggestion to use qualitative research analysis software to turn my interview transcripts into chapters 3-9. Don Herzog, my chair, offered incisive critique alongside generous dollops of moral support and encouragement.

I express thanks to Mark Brandon who engaged me in conversations that led to the proposal and whose comments helped improve early drafts of the first three chapters. Marek Steedman's critical readings of the first and tenth chapters made me think especially hard. Thanks also to Dennis Hoover, for his insights, and to Sam Sokolove, who read and commented on the entire manuscript. At Bard High School Early College, my eager and talented "God and Caesar" students were uncommonly discerning in their readings of chapters 2 and 10; I only wish I could have responded adequately to all of their concerns in these pages. My editors at Lexington Books—Laura Roberts, Robert Carley, Joseph Parry, Katie Funk and Molly Ahearn—were cheerful and skillful in helping to bring the book to light.

The field research in Israel would not have been possible without a Doctoral Dissertation Improvement Grant in Political Science from the National Science Foundation (Grant No. SES-9910903). The research trip would not have been as comfortable or successful without the Kfar Saba hospitality of the Shochats, my cousins-in-law. For crucial help in connecting me with interview subjects, I owe debts of gratitude to Rachel Arbel, Idit Avidan, Hope Levav, Gabriel Margalit, Rachel Misrati, Noga Morag-Levine, Jeff Seidel and—most of all—to Liat Mayberg and Emily Shochat. Thanks also to the staff of the Israel Religious Action Center and to Rabbi Uri Regev for access to IRAC's fine archives; to the kind librarians at the Knesset archives; to Patricia J. Woods for leads, questions and collaboration; to Penina Morag for renting me the Disraeli flat and for introducing me to other generous people; to Hebrew University faculty Dan Avnon, Emmanuel Gutmann, Moshe Halbertal (also of the Shalom Hartman Institute), Moshe Lissak and the late Ehud Sprinzak, who shared their time, ideas and sources.

In addition to the grant from the National Science Foundation, a number of institutions have provided financial support during the research and writing. Thanks to Michigan's Rackham School of Graduate Studies for several key fellowships and travel grants; Michigan's Frankel Center for Judaic Studies for two research grants from the Weinberg/Berman fund; the National Foundation for Jewish Culture for the Beverly and Arnold C. Greenberg Doctoral Dissertation Fellowship in Judaic Studies in 2000-2001; the Institute for Humane Studies for both fellowship and travel grant support in 2000-2001; the Woodrow Wilson National Fellowship Foundation for a Charlotte W. Newcombe Doctoral Dissertation Fellowship in 2001-2002; and to Bard High School Early College for several generous FIPSE research grants.

I presented papers based on earlier drafts of chapters 1, 4 and 10 at annual meetings of the American Political Science Association, Midwest Political Science Association, Southern Political Science Association and Northeastern Political Science Association; thanks to fellow panelists, discussants and audience members for their instructive comments and questions. A passage from chapter 7 was previously published in "Consenting Adults? Amish 'Rumspringa' and the Quandary of Exit in Liberalism," *Perspectives on Politics* 3, no. 4 (December 2005): 745-59. Chapter 9 originally appeared, in slightly different form, as "Importing Liberalism: Brown v. Board of Education in the Israeli Context," *Polity* 36, no. 3 (April 2004), pp. 389-410. Portions of chapter 10 appeared as "Rethinking Religious Establishment and Liberal Democracy: Lessons from Israel," *The Review of Faith and International Affairs* 2, no. 2 (Fall 2004), pp. 3-12, archived at www.cfia.org.

I express particular appreciation to each of my thirty-one interview subjects, who invited me into their homes and volunteered to engage in fascinating discussions on the contours of their state. Their warmth, candor and fervor made escaping the theorist's armchair a richly rewarding experience both professionally and personally.

Deepest thanks to Mom and Dad, to dear Renanit, Amarya and my whole family, who love, encourage and inspire me in countless ways.

Introduction

In the October 2003 issue of *The New York Review of Books*, Tony Judt declared the State of Israel an "anachronism." According to Judt, "the very idea of a Jewish state—a state in which Jews and the Jewish religion have exclusive privileges from which non-Jewish citizens are forever excluded—is rooted in another time and place."[1] Judt's proposed solution to the Israeli-Palestinian conflict, which calls for the end of Israel as we know it, has its heart in a conception of the state that rejects any linkage between religion and constitution. Whatever its boundaries, Israel is illegitimate as a Jewish state *because* it is a Jewish state. Israel should abandon its illusory aspiration to be a "Jewish and democratic state" (as its basic legislation declares) and transform itself into a secular, bi-national state that embraces all the territory and all the people of historic Palestine.

According to this political philosophy, the ethnic or religious unity of the traditional nation-state is outmoded. Emerging in its stead is "a world of individual rights, open frontiers, and international law." This trend leaves no room for nation-states like Israel—polities with a national character shaped by a particular religious tradition. Nor does it leave room for the development of other democracies in the Middle East entertaining forms of religious establishment. The nascent regimes in Iraq and Afghanistan are illegitimate, on this view, unless they completely divide mosque from state.

Despite its sweeping scope, the kernel of Judt's argument may resonate with Americans who prize their First Amendment religious freedoms. But even a cursory survey of comparative politics reveals a host of states that challenge this view: Costa Rica, Great Britain, Bahrain and Denmark, for example, all maintain institutional or symbolic connections with a particular religion and yet provide their citizens with various elements of liberal governance, including religious freedom for minorities. Israel is another prime example—a state that regards itself both as Jewish and as liberal-democratic.

But is a Jewish and democratic state possible? Can *any* sort of religious establishment be reconciled with a liberal democratic framework?

As a theory of the social order built on basic human rights, a democratic form of government and the rule of law, liberalism is concerned above all with finding just institutional and political solutions to problems of pluralism. This book argues that while connections between religion and state are often antithetical to liberal aims, they are not necessarily so. A Jewish and democratic state *is* possible: the challenge is to sort out which elements of establishment are compatible with liberal democracy and which are not.

My argument grows out of the results of a research study in Israel in which I conducted extensive interviews with Israeli citizens concerning conceptual and practical matters related to their polity's religion-state arrangement.[2] The insights into liberalism and religion developed here owe great debts to these respondents and may prove useful not only to refining Israel's higher law but to thinking through similar questions in other countries, including the developing regimes in Iraq and Afghanistan. Rethinking religious establishment is a matter of practical necessity: it is wildly unrealistic to expect today's highly religious societies to abandon all vestiges of establishment overnight, when it took Americans several hundred years to even partially achieve this. With due reflection on the diversity of ways in which nations around the world handle religion in public life, it becomes apparent that the present-day American model may not be the one size that fits all.

Part I, "Foundations," sets the stage for a detailed inquiry into the justifiability of Israel's Jewish nature. Chapter 1 outlines the way that contemporary liberal theory handles the question of religion, situates Israel's religion-state relationship in a broader context, and points the way to a pliable theory of liberalism that includes more room for religion in politics and takes greater account of political culture in specifying appropriate arrangements for particular societies. Chapter 2 analyzes the "status quo" agreement that set up a modus vivendi between Israel's secular and religious parties at the dawn of statehood, sketches the Jewish dimensions of the state and introduces the debate over Israel's identity as "a Jewish and democratic state." Turning from elites to ordinary citizens, I then investigate how major segments of the Israeli public view the relationship between Israel's liberal and Jewish faces. Chapter 3 includes a discussion of my qualitative research methodology and narrative introductions of each of the thirty-one Israeli subjects I interviewed under a study funded by the National Science Foundation. In chapter 4, I analyze the subjects' revealing arguments about the nature of Israel as a Jewish state and as a democratic state and explore their ideas concerning two slogans urging change in Israel's religion-state arrangement: "separation of religion and state" (heard most often from Israeli Jews on the left) and "a state of all its citizens" (the phrase favored by Israel's Arab minority).

Part II, "Controversies Among Israeli Jews," and Part III, "Controversies Between Israeli Arabs and Jews," consider several specific elements of Israel's religion-state union. First, in chapter 5, I discuss linkages of religion and state that are seen as only moderately problematic (Sabbath laws) or as non-controversial (kosher state kitchens and government funding for religious education) among the vast majority of Arabs and Jews alike. Chapters 6 and 7 move on to address two matters that provoke the anger of liberal sectors of Israeli Jews: the rabbinate's monopoly on marriage between Jews and exemptions of ultra-orthodox youth from military service. In chapters 8 and 9 I discuss facets of the Jewish state that pose particular problems for Arabs: symbolic inequality, political exclusion and unequal access to land.

Part IV, "Conclusions," returns from the trenches to look anew at liberalism in light of what the Israeli case has to teach us. Chapter 10 begins by describing a serious dilemma for policymakers seeking to clarify or reconstitute Israel's higher law: Jews' and Arabs' prescriptions for reconstituting Israel's relationship with religion are, despite some points of overlap, often at odds. While the vast majority of Jews favor the symbolic and cultural trappings of a Jewish state, most Arabs reject this vision; and while many left-leaning Jews resist institutional connections between religion and state, most Arabs support these relationships as necessary to the protection of Muslim, Christian and Druze autonomy. With this challenge in mind, I develop a series of guidelines for re-thinking the role of religion in liberal democracies. I argue that religion and polity may legitimately relate to each other on a symbolic level, and that the state may, with proper justification and oversight, provide funding on an evenhanded basis for religious institutions. When religious bodies seek to forcibly impose religious law on unwilling citizens, however, I argue that the two spheres must be kept separate. This nuanced appraisal proposes that while mixing politics with religion is fraught with potential dangers, some religion-state connections in some societies serve genuinely liberal purposes. The picture from Israel suggests that religion may play certain kinds of roles in public political life that are—contrary to claims of Judt and others—utterly consistent with liberal ideals.

Notes

1. Tony Judt, "Israel: The Alternative," *The New York Review of Books*, vol. 50, no. 16 (23 October 2003).

2. Although the Israeli-Palestinian conflict certainly figures into Israel's internal Jewish-democratic debates, I directly treat only the latter in this book. Israel's religion-state questions took a back seat to peace and security matters after the Camp David summit collapsed in July 2000 and Palestinian-Israeli violence surged the following September. Aside from former Prime Minister Ehud Barak's short-lived effort in October 2000 to divert attention from the failed peace efforts by proposing a "secular

revolution" to significantly change the nature of the Jewish state, the religious-secular rifts in Israel have been overshadowed by debates about national security and the fate of Jewish settlements in Gaza and on the West Bank. Nevertheless, the internal debates are always simmering and are likely to heat up in the aftermath of Israel's withdrawal from the Gaza Strip, especially if the peace process continues to progress.

Part I
Foundations

Chapter 1
Beyond Separation

One of the most familiar ideas of contemporary liberal thought is this: state and church must remain separate. Whatever the virtues or vices of religion—whether varieties of religious faith and practice are good or bad for individuals, conducive to or destructive of healthy society, or based on true or faulty metaphysics—members of liberal states are asked to seek their salvation (if they decide to) as private individuals. In liberal polities, the story goes, we are free to believe what we like; we are free, within reasonable limits, to worship as we choose; and we are free to congregate with like-minded believers. But private associations in civil society are the proper place for this kind of thing; when we approach the public square, and participate in defining the constitution and policies of our government, we should leave our prayer shawls, prayer mats and rosaries at the gate that separates public from private.[1]

This prescription for separating church from state has emerged in the United States and elsewhere as an answer to the question of how to define the proper relationship between politics and religion. Debates rage over how exactly to interpret the Establishment Clause of the First Amendment—the constitutional hook for what Thomas Jefferson termed a "wall of separation"[2] between religious institutions and the federal government[3]—but it is commonly seen as the best approach to securing religious liberty. Some regard it as the only real choice. But as we learn in studying the origin of religious freedom, and the various approaches states employ today, strict separation isn't necessarily the heart of the matter, or the only approach worth considering.

Consider the standard story of how the liberalism of toleration first emerged in sixteenth and seventeenth century Europe. John Locke, reflecting on over 150 years of religious conflict in his hemisphere, put forward a prudential argument for religious freedom in his *Letter Concerning Toleration* of

1689. Religious diversity itself is not to blame for the wars of religion, Locke claimed. Instead, it is the attempts by governments to *oppress* religious groups and prune this diversity that have "produced all the Bustles and Wars, that have been in the Christian world, upon account of Religion."[4] In order to quell the fighting, states need to lift the oppressive yoke. Social harmony and stability require toleration of multiple religious beliefs and traditions.

What form should this toleration take? Although many read him otherwise, Locke never argues that the state must disestablish itself entirely from religion.[5] His central claim is that civil government should do nothing to coerce its citizens in matters of salvation. "The Care of Souls does not belong to the Magistrate," Locke writes. "The Care... of every man's Soul belongs unto himself, and is to be left unto himself."[6] Locke's toleration was neither as deep nor as broad as that which liberal states practice today. First, he famously excluded three classes of people from religious toleration: the intolerant (who would use their rights only to try to seize power and oppress others); Catholics and Muslims (in Locke's terms, those who, by "deliver[ing] themselves up to the Protection and Service of another Prince," hold religious ties to the Pope or the Caliph that eclipse their civic obligations); and atheists (who, having no heavenly father to answer to in the afterlife, could not be trusted to fulfill civic oaths and duties in this life).[7] Second, the motivations behind Locke's suggestions should not be confused with those of modern multiculturalists: his toleration seems to have been born of necessity and not of a desire to celebrate diversity. That we see clearly throughout the *Letter*, particularly where he writes that Jews' and Heathens' beliefs are "false and absurd" and notes that, while force is illegitimate as a method of changing men's minds, "Exhortations and Arguments" against wrong-headed believers are fair game, and to be applauded.[8]

This is hardly the description of a state that is neutral on religious questions; it is, rather, a state that is free to hold and even attempt to spread religious truths—as long as it sets up no legal impediments for those citizens who believe otherwise. Context suggests this as well. When Locke wrote his *Letter*, he was living in Holland, a tolerant state that nevertheless had an established church. And twenty years earlier when he and the Earl of Shaftesbury drafted a constitution for the English colony Carolina in the 1660s, provision was made for extensive religious liberty alongside an official, tax-supported state church.[9]

Whatever Locke's views on this question,[10] separation is ripe for renewed consideration. Given the number of societies in the world that combine religion and state to some degree, and the aspiration of new societies in Iraq and Afghanistan to couple democratic rule with religious influences, it is time to push toward a new set of "living truths" (in J.S. Mill's terms) with regard to separation of church and state.[11]

Religion and State: A Typology

Listening to many liberals, one would think there are only two possibilities for state-religion arrangements: separation (the legitimate approach) and integration (the illegitimate approach). John Rawls, for instance, uses a seductively simple syllogism to establish his argument that states must organize themselves around strictly "political" values—values that do not stem from controversial moral or religious beliefs. First, Rawls argues, a diversity of religious, moral and philosophical views will come to exist, and will persist, in democratic regimes with free institutions. Second, organizing a polity around one of those doctrines requires the "oppressive use of state power," and will ultimately fail, since a successful democratic regime must enjoy the support of a large majority of its citizens. Therefore, third, a state ought to avoid organizing principles that derive from a particular worldview, or as he terms it, a "comprehensive doctrine."[12]

This syllogism does most of its work in the second premise, which Rawls calls the "fact of oppression." But this step leaves open a host of questions that throw the conclusion into some doubt: Are all religious infusions into politics illegitimate? Some? Which ones? What constitutes "oppressive use" of state power, as opposed to non-oppressive use? Do citizens whose comprehensive views are ignored by the state necessarily (in fact) feel oppressed? Should we think of them as oppressed if they themselves do not? Do they have legitimate cause for complaint? Under what circumstances? On what grounds? Does the *nature* of the "reasonable pluralism" make a difference in deciding whether a particular state is justified in propounding one comprehensive doctrine (or several)? Does it matter if the state is home to a majority sect with several minority sects rather than dozens of small sects, for instance?

To approach these questions, it would be helpful to have a sense of how, very broadly speaking, political societies in the twenty-first century negotiate their relationship with religion and with religious institutions. Five models of religion-state interrelation suggest themselves to illustrate the dominant approaches used today. As these models show, there are more than a few ways to integrate religion and state, and more than one way to separate them.

Several considerations determine where a regime fits onto this typology: provisions for freedom of religious exercise; sources of public state law; funding of religious organizations; nature of state symbols drawn from religion; and degree of discrimination against minority religions. These factors may be grouped into two: (1) nature of *state affiliations with religion* and (2) degree and scope of *religious toleration*. Note that these loosely map the two religion clauses of the First Amendment. The first asks whether an "establishment" of religion exists, and what its character is; the second inquires into legal protections for religious liberty, both freedom of worship and freedom from discrimination based on religious identity.

The models I identify are: (1) separation of church and state (unaffiliated/highly tolerant); (2) institutionalized religious pluralism (loosely affiliated/tolerant); (3) anti-religious (unaffiliated/intolerant); (4) theocratic (strongly affiliated/intolerant); and (5) established religion (affiliated/tolerant).[13] A few words about each:

First, according to the model of separation of religion and state, the polity professes no religion as its own, declares itself neutral on religious questions, gives no priority to particular religions over others, and tends to avoid actions in which the state would be seen as endorsing religion. States on this model, which include the contemporary United States, post-communist Russia and some other members of the Commonwealth of Independent States (not including Uzbekistan or Turkmenistan, which often mistreat Muslims), Chile, Jamaica, France, India, Ireland and, as of January 1, 2000, Sweden[14], couple their non-establishment principles with significant protection of religious liberty and guarantees against discrimination for minority believers.

The second model, institutionalized religious pluralism, comprises states that identify particular religions for recognition, protection or promotion. These states are similar to those in the first model in that they protect religious liberty to some degree, maintain (for the most part) a separation of state from the institutions of particular religions and are officially neutral with regard to (most) religious questions. However, these states endorse the concept of religion generally, or at least show official recognition of particular faiths, by providing them with public support. Examples of this model include Germany (which collects taxes from citizens who choose to identify as Catholic, Protestant, Anglican, Jewish or Muslim, and distributes the funds to each religion's community organization), Hungary (which recognizes twelve "traditional" religions and relegates others to the status of "Confessional Communities" until they satisfy certain membership and time thresholds)[15] and Indonesia (which recognizes Islam, Catholicism, Protestantism, Hinduism and Buddhism, and requires its citizens to profess a belief in God).[16] Additional examples are Poland and Mexico.

Third, the model of anti-religious states includes communist regimes such as China, North Korea and the former Soviet Union. Here we find separation of religion from state, as in the first model, but a separation that views religion with hostility rather than respect. In pre-1989 Albania, Mongolia, and the USSR, for example, the state propounded not secularism but atheism, and prohibited religious organizations and religious worship. Similar religious persecution is found, in varying degrees, in North Korea and China today.

At the other extreme we find the fourth model, theocracy. In states such as Saudi Arabia, Sudan, Iran and Afghanistan under the deposed Taliban regime, religion serves as the basis of the state in nearly every way. Religious law constitutes or strongly informs the law of the state and freedom of religion is curtailed sharply, if not entirely. Public and private life alike is subject to strict regulation by religious-political norms. Religious clerics exercise significant control over the policies and operations of the government, and where institutions of representative democracy exist (as in Iran), may have the power to nullify legislation or rule candidates for office ineligible on religious grounds.

Fifth is perhaps the most frequently seen model of religion-state interaction today: established religion. This model shares elements with several of the others. Like theocracy, this model establishes a single religion as the official state creed, preferring (in some sense) one faith to all others. Unlike the theocratic model, however, the linkage between polity and religion is looser, has narrower implications for public policy and does not entail a wholesale denial of religious liberty. In fact, many states with established churches protect the rights of religious minorities to a significant degree, often as strongly as states in the separation or institutionalized religious pluralism models. Among the polities in this established religion yet tolerant mold are England (affiliated with the Anglican Church), Denmark, Norway, Iceland and Finland (Evangelical Lutheran Church) Greece and Bulgaria (Eastern Orthodox Church), and Liechtenstein, Monaco and Malta (Catholic Church).

Like any typology, the one I have just sketched glosses over many important distinctions between states within each category in order to keep the list of models manageable and useful conceptually. I should add that few if any states fit any of the models perfectly; instead, many possess attributes of several of the models. In the United States, for example, a host of familiar factors suggest that state and church are not entirely separate: the national motto "In God We Trust" appears on every piece of currency; state legislatures and both Houses of Congress employ religious chaplains who offer public prayers; religious organizations enjoy tax-exempt status; and references to God are sprinkled liberally in official documents and government employees' oaths of office.

In Iran, a theocracy whose official religion is Islam of the Twelver Shi'a Ja'fari school[17], Sunni Muslims face discrimination, and members of the Baha'i faith endure wide persecution.[18] Nevertheless, as in the institutionalized pluralism model, limited toleration for certain sects exists and, at least officially, "no one may be molested or taken to task simply for holding a certain belief."[19] In addition to granting other Sunni Islamic schools jurisdiction over their adherents in religion, education and matters of personal status such as marriage and divorce, Iran's constitution names Zoroastrianism, Judaism and Christianity as "recognized religious minorities" whose proponents are "free to perform their religious rites and ceremonies, and to act according to their own canon in matters of personal affairs and religious education."[20] China, too, provides some legal protection to five faiths—Daoism, Catholicism, Protestantism, Islam and Buddhism—while banning the public worship of all others.

The religious-political roots of the State of Israel lie in four apparently inconsistent traditions: liberal democracy, Judaism, Zionism and the Ottoman millet system. While it is sometimes hailed as the only democracy in the Middle East, Israel is not a model of liberal separationism (it conceives of itself a Jewish state; allows Orthodox rabbis a monopoly on matters of Jews' personal status, including marriage and divorce; and harbors an exclusivist immigration policy that favors Jews). But on the other hand, Israel is far from a Jewish theocracy (equal civil and political rights are guaranteed to non-Jews; public law is formulated by a democratically elected parliament; and a secular judiciary protective of individual rights interprets that law). Moreover, Israel has inherited from its pre-state, pre-British Mandate days in the Ottoman Empire a system by which various religious communities conduct their own affairs. The Jewish, Muslim, Christian and Druze religious communities in Israel thus maintain separate religious court systems and receive state funding for cultural, educational and religious projects.[21]

Is this mélange of political traditions tenable? Can religion play a role in the higher law of a liberal state? Before embarking on a detailed analysis of the Israeli case, further theoretical ground must be cleared. The case for moving beyond separation as liberalism's sole position on questions of religion and state is latent in the theory of the political philosopher who has come to define contemporary liberalism: John Rawls.

Rawls on Reason and Religion

In Rawls's first two books, *A Theory of Justice* (1971)[22] and *Political Liberalism* (1993), "religion" did not even appear as a listing in the index. In the years since *Political Liberalism* was published, however, the question of how liberalism treats religion has received a great deal of attention from both critics and supporters of Rawls's project. In the last two chapters of his *Collected Papers* (1999)[23], Rawls responds to these commentators with a fresh exposition of his idea of "public reason," a concept that aims to specify the role that religion may play in deliberation over public policy.

Because citizens in modern democracies are deeply divided about the ultimate values in life, no single religious or philosophical view "is appropriate as a political conception for a constitutional regime."[24] Rawls nevertheless hopes that all citizens can find a footing within their diverse value systems for affirming a single political conception of justice. Christians may find the principle of toleration underwritten by the fundamental tenets of their faith; Kantians may derive the principles of justice from an appropriately applied categorical imperative procedure; utilitarians may see Rawls's basic structure as conducive to the well being of society as a whole. Individuals will affirm the shared conception of justice on *intrinsic* grounds (from within their beliefs and traditions), not on grounds *extrinsic* to their values (such as those prescribing the necessity of an agreement to disagree).[25] Whereas a modus vivendi holds together only as long as it remains in the interests of each party to maintain it, and risks collapse the moment one group gains an advantage over another, what Rawls calls an "overlapping consensus" is resilient in the face of political change. Because individuals affirm it for intrinsic reasons and not only to alleviate irresolvable conflicts, the overlapping consensus "does [not] depend on happenstance [or] a balance of relative forces."[26]

Rawls acknowledges that this may sound too rosy for a society wrought by profound differences of moral and religious belief, so he has a story to tell about how something close to an overlapping consensus might (in fact) develop.[27] This story (as we will see in chapter 2) is interesting in juxtaposition to Israel's development, where dissensus is still the norm nearly six decades after its founding. Most societies, Rawls says, begin as a network of mere modus vivendi relations and then develop into (first) a "constitutional consensus"—in which agreement is reached on principles of democratic procedure and basic political rights—and (finally) an overlapping consensus. In these transitions, the "looseness" found in individuals' deeply held views gradually leads them to embrace political arrangements they may have only reluctantly accepted originally. This takes place in tandem with a transformation of people's religious views. The political conception of justice itself, Rawls says, "tend[s] to shift citizens' comprehensive doctrines" and makes them more reasonable, enabling a move from "simple pluralism to reasonable pluralism."[28]

The fuel of an overlapping consensus is its mode of political discourse: public reason.[29] In his initial account of public reason, Rawls argued that it is never appropriate to bring religiously inspired arguments into political discussions.[30] Citizens should put aside their sectarian views when debating their polity's constitution and focus on the proper object of political justice: "the good of the public."[31] Rather than consider what is good for me—as, say, an Orthodox Jew, a fundamentalist Christian, or a Millian individualist—when I discuss crucial matters of state or enter the voting booth I should think about what is good for my political society as a whole. I should act in accordance with the interests of a diverse citizenry united not by a single comprehensive view of life but by a principled political consensus among individuals holding many conflicting religious and non-religious views.

Rawls modified his theory, adopting an "inclusive view" of public reason, upon considering two historical cases of religious political discourse that ultimately served (or even saved) liberal democracy: Martin Luther King, Jr.'s critique of segregation in the South and the abolitionists' religious appeals against slavery as early as the 1830s. Whereas King put forward both religiously based and thus nonpublic reasons (a Thomist definition of an unjust law as "a human law that is not rooted in eternal law") *and* public reasons (e.g., a constitutional argument drawing on the 1954 *Brown v. Board of Education* decision), the abolitionists were compelled to turn to nonpublic reason to make their argument. "In this case," Rawls asserts, "the nonpublic reason of certain Christian churches supported the clear conclusions of public reason," including the priority of individual liberty for all. Use of nonpublic reason is acceptable and even laudable, then, when it is necessary in order to bring about the conditions of legitimate government. But once a well-ordered society is established, religious arguments should recede from the public forum and the highly limiting view of public reason should take hold.[32]

In the late 1990s, Rawls's thinking again evolved in favor of greater leniency toward religiously based political argumentation. Moving beyond his "inclusive view" to a yet-more-inclusive "wide view," Rawls invited citizens to provide arguments and other kinds of input (such as Gospel stories and bits of Biblical or philosophical exegesis) that are specific to their own comprehensive views of the good life under any and all circumstances. However, this invitation comes with a "proviso":

> Reasonable comprehensive doctrines, religious or nonreligious, may be introduced in public political discussion at any time, provided that in due course proper political reasons—and not reasons given solely by comprehensive doctrines—are presented that are sufficient to support whatever the comprehensive doctrines introduced are said to support.[33]

Under this proviso, a congresswoman may cite Leviticus in support of a bill criminalizing sodomy, as long as she also, at some point, gives a sufficient public policy reason for this action. A judge is justified in looking to the Talmud or to Ronald Dworkin's writings for help in adjudicating a hard case, but she must eventually give publicly accessible reasons from precedent or from other sources deemed acceptable in public law.[34]

Rawls leaves many details open as to how this proviso would be satisfied.[35] The central demand, though, is clear: those wishing to voice religious, philosophical and moral perspectives in public political discussions (concerning any issue) are welcome to do so as long as they *also* provide good reasons that are independent of their sectarian beliefs. This provisional invitation to bring religious talk into political discussions, Rawls hopes, will strengthen social cohesion and lead to greater civility and mutual respect among citizens. By laying their full views on the table and providing arguments consistent with public reason, citizens will understand one another better and develop greater trust in those with different opinions.[36]

With these arguments, Rawls again tries to stake out middle ground. This time he aims between those like Stephen Carter and Richard Neuhaus who welcome full-blown religiously motivated arguments in politics[37] and those like Richard Rorty who condemn all such talk as a "conversation-stopper."[38] But, at least on first glance, he is unlikely to satisfy either side. Those who are skeptical about the value of any religious talk in politics will note that Rawls fails to show why this talk *itself*—the reasoning that springs from a speaker's sectarian beliefs—is valuable in public debate. On the other side, some religiously devout citizens will complain that the proviso still fails to welcome them or their views into public debate. By requiring "public reasons" alongside religiously motivated reasons, Rawls maintains the epistemic authority of secular rationality while denigrating the value of religious speech. For in the end, public reasons are both a necessary and sufficient ingredient in legitimate political debate, while religiously based appeals are neither: You need not give a religious reason to support your proposal, but whether or not you choose to, you must come prepared with public reasons. This may trivialize the believers' most strongly held arguments—marginalizing them as offensive (at worst) or irrelevant (at best)—while elevating the revered status of public reason even more highly.

The Pliability of Public Reason

Although neither secularists nor religious activists would be entirely happy with Rawls's proviso, its basic proposition is sound: citizens need some common language and common understandings to debate their polity's guiding principles. If this language is to serve its function, it cannot be limited to purely secular rationality in societies where religious sensibilities play a major role in informing citizens' political views. It cannot be based on a single, inflexible standard universal to all democracies. Instead, it must reflect the particular political culture of the state in which it is spoken. This means that public reason, in practice, must be pliable. Rawls seems to appreciate this pliability in his sole published reference to Israel:

> While democratic societies will differ in the specific doctrines that are influential and active within them—as they differ in the western democracies of Europe, the United States, Israel and India—finding a suitable idea of public reason is a concern that faces them all.[39]

This passage suggests, sensibly, that the content of public reason will depend on the nature of the society it addresses. Countries such as Israel (a Jewish state) and those of western Europe (many of which fall into the "established church" model discussed above) should develop conceptions of public reason that suit their societies.

In *The Law of Peoples*, Rawls argues that "decent" societies, not only "liberal" ones, are worthy of toleration in the international arena.[40] Rawls speaks of decent societies as "acceptable" (p. 83); as at least somewhat, though not "perfectly" "just" (78); and—least flatteringly—as "not fully unreasonable" (74). He characterizes liberal regimes as more "reasonable and just" (83) and as "superior" (62) to decent regimes. A decent people, Rawls claims, may establish a state religion. The official faith "may, on some questions, be the ultimate authority within society and may control government policy on certain important matters." But there are limits on the uses of religion in a decent society. The state religion may not be used as pretext for interference with other states; it cannot launch holy wars in an attempt to conquer or convert other peoples. And it must permit "a sufficient measure of liberty of conscience and freedom of religion and thought, even if these freedoms are not as extensive nor as equal for all members of the decent society as they are in liberal societies."[41]

The links and contrasts between liberal and non-liberal decent regimes become a bit sharper when Rawls discusses the contours of an imaginary republic called Kazanistan. This hypothetical case study—a rare departure for Rawls—involves a society that proclaims Islam the favored faith and prohibits non-Muslims from holding high-level political or judicial positions and from influencing the development of government policy. Kazanistan does, however, provide religious toleration for minority sects and "encourages them to have a flourishing cultural life of their own and to take part in the civic culture of the wider society."[42] Seeking to fortify their ties to the state, Kazanistan also allows members of religious minorities to join the army and to serve as military officers. Finally, Kazanistan takes all groups' needs and perspectives into account by consulting with representatives of each and by considering their ideas in light of Kazanistan's "special priorities," one of which is "to establish a decent and rational Muslim people respecting the religious minorities within it."[43]

Is Kazanistan Israel in Muslim garb? No, not quite, but there are a number of similarities.[44] It is reasonable to conclude that Rawls would probably classify Israel as a "decent but nonliberal" society that deserves toleration and inclusion in military alliances but should not be regarded as fully just or as deserving the adjective *liberal*. This initial take, though, merely restates the common idea that state religions are incompatible with liberalism. It does not present an argument for this contention.

Several comments Rawls makes in his discussion of the law of peoples suggest that his line between liberal and decent regimes is fuzzier than he claims. While some commentators have attacked Rawls from the opposite perspective—criticizing his law of peoples for being overly tolerant and thus insufficiently liberal[45]—I propose that Rawls's extension of political liberalism to the international arena presses in the right direction. It just doesn't press quite far enough.

Rawls introduces the concept of decency in order to argue that liberal peoples have reason to tolerate, and cooperate with, more than just other liberal peoples. He bases this point on a bit of tautological reasoning: "If liberal peoples require that all societies be liberal and subject those that are not to politically enforced sanctions, then decent nonliberal peoples—if there are such—will be denied a due measure of respect by liberal peoples."[46] The problem is, we can't know antecedently what "measure of respect" is "due" a decent nonliberal people; we have to know what decent peoples *are* before we can determine what we owe them. Why, as Charles Beitz asks, "should decency by regarded as on a par with liberal justice" for the purposes of international order?[47] Rawls responds by trying to assuage liberals as to the acceptability of decent regimes. Such polities, he writes, respect basic rights, incorporate something akin to democratic government and permit dissent and social change.[48]

Given these redeeming features of decent states, Rawls argues that intolerance "may wound the self-respect of decent nonliberal peoples" and fail to provide enough room for "the idea of a people's self-determination."[49] Further, international sanctions or trade barriers would embitter a decent regime and limit its potential to "recognize the advantages of liberal institutions and take steps toward becoming more liberal on its own."[50] Although it stands to reason that a society cannot become "more" liberal without first being at least somewhat liberal (the March Hare's carping notwithstanding[51]), the semantics, by themselves, are of little consequence. Whatever labels we use, the differences between a "liberal" and a "nonliberal decent" society appear to be less fundamental than Rawls maintains.[52] Their similarities point toward a looser and more pliable theory of politics that embraces some states with limited religious establishments.[53]

But what would a legitimate public ethos *be* for such a society? If it should be based on the polity's self-conception (as revealed through its founding documents), we face the odd conclusion that some varieties of religious reasoning are not merely admissible but essential to public discussions. That is, since Israel defines itself, in part, according to a particular religion, an Israeli citizen who rejects Israel's Jewish character in important political discussions and voting may—ironically—violate the spirit of public reason in her state. At the very least, engaging in public reason in Israel is different from engaging in public reason in the United States (or other polities that separate religion from state), and the polity's Jewish identity would mark the major distinction.

Religious reasons of a certain sort can be public reasons—but not all religious reasons, and not in all societies. In the American context, separation between religious and civil authority is a political value enshrined by the Establishment Clause of the First Amendment; Americans still differ heatedly over what separation entails and how strong it should be. In Israel, the vast majority of Jews favor the idea of a Jewish state and see a role for the state in promoting Jewish values; there are searing debates, however, over what those values are and how they should be pursued. (And there is a significant non-Jewish minority that is opposed to the concept of a Jewish state.) Agreement on an ideal, in other words, does not entail agreement on what course of action should be taken. Far from muffling debate and cabining controversy, public reason seems to fuel wide-ranging and revealing discussions for non-religious and religious participants in liberal democratic societies of all types. This introduces a vexing question, however: what kinds of religious considerations are legitimate?

Public reason bends to fit various political societies; it is deeply contextual. It gives voice to considerations that participants in a polity find to be appropriate considerations. The debate proceeds on the assumption that public (not merely sectarian) values are on the table, but it invites myriad arguments and perspectives on the nature of those values as well as the best ways of realizing them and balancing them with competing values.

Though it is both open to creative analysis and adaptable to the ideas and political cultures of different societies, public reason should not legitimize every argument simply because it is uttered or finds support in the public ethos. These limits on its pliability stem from what Rawls terms the "content of public reason." Although this content too is in a sense pliable—with different liberalisms and different societies reaching different conclusions—the following three baselines apply:

> First, a list of certain basic rights, liberties and opportunities (such as those familiar from constitutional regimes);
>
> Second, an assignment of special priority to those rights, liberties and opportunities, especially with respect to the claims of the general good and perfectionist values; and
>
> Third, measures ensuring for all citizens adequate all-purpose means to make effective use of their freedoms.[54]

Basic constitutional liberties and the means for citizens to realize them are nonnegotiable. While some religious reasoning should be welcomed, any argument that seeks to deprive other citizens of their basic rights is ethically out of bounds. This, however, is seldom the case. Religious argument rarely constitutes an implicit appeal to coerce others. Jeremy Waldron gets the latter point exactly right:

> Rawls writes as if each comment that is made in public debate is nothing more than a proposal to use public power to forcibly impose something on everyone else so that what we have to evaluate, in each case, is an immediate coercive proposal. That is seldom what we are faced with. Instead, a religious doctrine is likely to be put forward as one contribution among others in a debate about how political power is to be used. In that context, it is much less clear whether there is anything unfair or unreasonable about such an intervention. A contribution may be put forward as something for one's fellow citizens to ponder and consider along with other views that they are listening to, something for them to take into account. What they make of it may be left up to them.[55]

Waldon is correct that we shouldn't judge religious contributions *a priori*. We could, however, use some standards for evaluating religious reasons when they are aired and for developing them when we speak in the public realm ourselves. Here are my guidelines for what we should make of religion in public debate:

> (i) Public reason should not only allow but welcome a broad range of arguments, including many apparently religious arguments, when they are suitably connected to a public political value;

> (ii) The precise range of acceptable arguments will vary according to the political society in question; and

> (iii) Public reason should reject proposals that deny citizens fundamental rights or liberties.

The first two guidelines reconceive the idea of public reason along wider lines—bringing more religion of a certain kind into the public sphere—while the third employs Rawls's characterization of the "content" of public reason to impose a limit on the ways in which religion may function in that sphere. A few comments on each guideline:

The first principle holds that arguments of all kinds, including religiously based proposals, are acceptable in public debate as long as they can be related to a value applicable to the wider society. Like Rawls's "proviso," this would allow religiously inspired contributions a role in public debate. Unlike Rawls's formula, though, this principle asks a participant in a debate to show why her religious argument is *itself* a public reason rather than to supply a public reason "in due course." It asks for the political value *in the* religious point, not for a public reason that sits *separately* from the religious point. A legislator who seeks to expand federal funding for faith-based charities on the grounds that it will save Christian souls meets Rawls's proviso if at some point he also claims that the plan will improve drug rehabilitation programs in the inner city. According to my principle, the legislator's first reason is, by itself, irrelevant and thus inadmissible in public debate.[56] On the other hand, if the same legislator cites the parable of the Good Samaritan to argue that churches will do a better job of serving drug addicts than secular institutions, her contribution—even though religiously inspired—is welcome. Unlike Rawls's proviso, which untenably finds value in airing arguments that are both inaccessible and nonpublic, my principle is receptive only to religious arguments which themselves purport to have some connection to a public good.[57] In practice, there may be only a subtle difference between Rawls's proposal and mine. But such a norm may have the benefit of leading religious participants to critically evaluate the relationship between their religious doctrines and public policy preferences more closely. It may lead some to reconsider the nexus between their political and religious views and spur them to revise one or the other.

The second principle—the pliability of public reason across cultures— holds that what counts as a public reason in one society might not qualify in another. In Israel, an appeal to the Jewish character of the state is both routine and, considering its unique history and circumstances, legitimate. Israel was founded as a Jewish state and defines itself as a Jewish state in its quasi-constitutional legislation. It represents itself with countless Jewish symbols. In the United States, however, an appeal to a supposed Christian basis of the state is not legitimate, although it is not infrequently heard (even today). Unlike Israel, the United States is governed by a constitutional requirement providing that "Congress shall make no law respecting an establishment of religion." Whatever the Establishment Clause means—and no consensus yet exists on that question, even among Supreme Court justices—it certainly precludes an identification of the state with Christianity, official preference for Christian causes or the establishment of a Christian church. (Appeals to America's more general religious or "Judeo-Christian" values, while problematic and in some ways inaccurate, are less worrisome. States might give expression to certain values while not officially affirming them in their laws and constitutions.)

The third principle is in some ways the most important for political theory in that it addresses not individual ethical duties (whether one ought or ought not to use religious arguments) but legitimate political outcomes. This, strangely, is an area into which debates over religion and liberalism seldom enter. According to this principle, it is the nature of the proposal that matters most, not the reasoning or motivations behind it. Regardless of whether the considerations on which a political decision is made are legitimate, then, certain proposals stand no chance for acceptance in a liberal state. Even appeals based on common values hold no weight if the proposals they suggest threaten basic individual liberty. No policy that contravenes basic individual rights—including a religiously based petition—is admissible in a liberal state. However, some religiously based appeals in support of *non-coercive* proposals may qualify as public reasons, even if they are intended to serve only a single segment of society. This is true in religiously diverse polities like the United States (where a commitment to multiculturalism could give minority groups certain dispensations unavailable to others[58]) or in ethno-religious nation-states like Israel (where, in addition to accommodating minorities via cultural rights, the state recognizes and protects certain interests of its Jewish majority[59]). As I argued above, a religious reason ("the state should give citizens religious school vouchers in order to advance the cause of Christianity") can become a public reason ("the state should give citizens private school vouchers in order to assist parents in affording the kind of education that they consider best for their child") with a change of pitch and a recognition that public policies must serve public goods.[60]

These three principles, of course, do not put an end to the difficulties. They do not resolve the vexing questions of political justification in Israel we are about to tackle. They do, however, draft a blueprint for addressing those questions that moves beyond the liberal dogma that *any* linkage of religion and state—and any religious talk in political debate—is illegitimate. The guidelines I have suggested leave open the possibility that some interactions between religion and state in some political societies may be legitimate or even attractive. My project in the rest of the book is to examine the particular ways in which Israel combines religion and state. By looking at the complexities of Israel's dual identity from the perspectives of diverse Israelis, we will find new insights into the proper place of religion in the higher law of a liberal-democratic state.

Notes

1. Many contemporary liberal theorists and most contemporary civil liberties activist groups hold this position, whether implicitly or explicitly; a passionate account is found in Isaac Kramnick and R. Laurence Moore, *The Godless Constitution: A Moral Defense of the Secular State* (New York: W.W. Norton & Company, 2005).

2. Jefferson borrowed the phrase from James Burgh, a Scottish dissenter, but Roger Williams seems to have coined it in 1644 when he lamented the opening of "a gap in the hedge or wall of separation between the garden of the church and the wilderness of the world...[.]" (Quoted in David M. O'Brien, *Constitutional Law and Politics, Volume Two: Civil Rights and Civil Liberties* [New York: W.W. Norton & Company, 1991], 637.) Justice Hugo Black later revived the wall image in Everson v. Board of Education, 330 U.S. 1 (1947).

3. Since the Bill of Rights originally applied only to the national government (against James Madison's objections), the Establishment Clause left the states free to maintain the churches they had established in the 1770s. (Only colonies Rhode Island, Pennsylvania, Delaware and New Jersey never had a state church; Massachusetts barred Jews from public office until 1828 and disestablished entirely only in 1833.) With the incorporation of the Establishment Clause into the 14th Amendment in 1947 (via the Everson case), the proscription was formally extended to the states. See O'Brien, *Constitutional Law*, 636-40 and Noah Feldman, *Divided by God: America's Church-State Problem—And What We Should Do About It* (New York: Farrar, Straus and Giroux, 2005), 47.

4. John Locke, *A Letter Concerning Toleration* (Indianapolis, In.: Hackett Publishing Co., 1983), 55.

5. For a similar interpretation of Locke's *Letter*, see Philip Hamburger, *Separation of Church and State* (Cambridge, Mass.: Harvard University Press, 2002), 53-55.

6. Locke, *Letter*, 35.

7. Locke, *Letter*, 49-51

8. Locke, *Letter*, 27, 35, 46-47.

9. § 96 of Carolina's Constitution reads: "As the country comes to be sufficiently planted and distributed into fit divisions, it shall belong to the parliament to take care for the building of churches, and the public maintenance of divines, to be employed in the exercise of religion, according to the Church of England; which being the only true and orthodox, and the national religion of all the king's dominions, is so also of Carolina; and therefore it alone shall be allowed to receive public maintenance by grant of parliament." See David Wooton, ed., *Political Writings of John Locke* (New York: Penguin Books, 1993), 228.

10. David Wooton notes that Locke may have objected to the establishment of the Church of England as Carolina's official church and included it in the Constitution only to comply with the colony's charter. See the Introduction in Wooton, ed., *Political Writings of John Locke*, 41-42, and Feldman, *Divided by God*, 259 n33.

11. John Stuart Mill, *On Liberty* (Indianapolis, Ind.: Hackett Publishing, 1978), 34.

12. John Rawls, *Political Liberalism* (New York: Columbia University Press, 1993), 37, 38.

13. These categories are informed by Shimon Shetreet, "State and Religion: Funding of Religious Institutions—The Case of Israel in Comparative Perspective," *Notre Dame Journal of Law, Ethics and Public Policy* 13 (1999): 424-27. A similar account is found in Benyamin Neuberger, "Religion and Democracy in Israel" (Jerusalem: The Floersheimer Institute for Policy Studies, 1997). Neuberger refers to the institutionalized pluralism model as the "recognized communities" approach. Stephen Monsma and J. Christopher Soper call it the "structual pluralist" model. See Monsma and Soper, *The Challenge of Pluralism: Church and State in Five Democracies* (Lanham, Md.: Rowman & Littlefield, 1997), 10-12.

14. Carol J. Williams, "Sweden Ends Designation of Lutheranism as Official Religion," *Los Angeles Times*, 1 January 2000, 2.

15. E. Kenneth Stegeby, "An Analysis of the Impending Disestablishment of the Church in Sweden," *Brigham Young University Law Review* (1999): 703.

16. Seth Mydans, "In Indonesia, Islamic Politics Doesn't Mean Religion," *New York Times*, 24 October 1999, Week in Review, 4.

17. See Constitution of Iran, Article 12, <http://www.iranonline.com/iran/iran-info/Government/constitution-1.html> (15 July 2005).

18. S.I. Strong, "Law and Religion in Israel and Iran: How the Integration of Secular and Spiritual Laws Affects Human Rights and the Potential for Violence," *Michigan Journal of International Law* 19 (Fall 1997): 152-54.

19. See Constitution of Iran, Article 23, <http://www.iranonline.com/iran/iran-info/Government/constitution-1.html> (15 July 2005).

20. See Constitution of Iran, Articles 12 and 13.

21. Michael Walzer, *On Toleration* (New Haven: Yale University Press, 1997), 41.

22. John Rawls, *A Theory of Justice* (Cambridge, Mass.: Harvard University Press, Belknap Press, 1971).

23. John Rawls, *Collected Papers,* ed. Samuel Freeman (Cambridge, Mass.: Harvard University Press, 1999). The first and more important essay, "The Idea of Public Reason Revisited," is also reprinted in Rawls's *The Law of Peoples* (Cambridge: Harvard, 1999), 129-180. Page references below refer to the chapters in *Collected Papers.*

24. Rawls, *Political Liberalism,* 135.

25. This is why Rawls speaks of not a consensus *simpliciter* but an *overlapping* consensus.

26. Rawls, *Political Liberalism,* 148.

27. He supposes that "a full overlapping consensus is never achieved but at best only approximated[.]" Rawls, *Political Liberalism,* 165.

28. Rawls, *Political Liberalism,* 164. Interestingly, Aristotle analyzes friendship in an analogous way, and discusses the concept's political uses. "Friendship," he writes, "would seem to hold cities together, and legislators would seem to be more concerned about it than about justice . . . .if people are friends, they have no need of justice." Those friendships based on "utility" and "pleasure" are "incomplete" friendships (contingent, derivative, akin to a modus vivendi) while the friendship of "virtue" is the sole "complete" form (closer to an overlapping consensus?). Usefulness may wane, and erotic passion may dwindle as quickly as it is stirred up, but "virtue is enduring." See Aristotle, *Nicomachean Ethics,* trans. Terence Irwin (Indianapolis: Hackett Publishing Company, 1985), 1155-56.

29. Rawls, *Political Liberalism,* 215.

30. Public reason does not ask citizens to abandon their Orthodox Judaism, fundamentalist Christianity or Millian individualism, Rawls claims. It asks them to put aside considerations that stem from those controversial views only when they are participating in the public political realm and fundamental questions are at stake. The limits "do not apply to our personal deliberations and reflections about political questions," whether those questions involve fundamental questions or not.

31. Rawls, *Political Liberalism,* 213.

32. Rawls, *Political Liberalism,* 247-52.

33. Rawls, *Collected Papers,* 591.

34. Interestingly, Rawls quarrels with Ronald Dworkin's contention that "political morality" is one such accessible source. He worries that such references to morality are "too broad" and likely to lead a judge to an illegitimate judicial decision if its source is not found within a particular society's political conception of justice. See Rawls, *Political Liberalism,* 236n23.

35. He does not specify, for instance, when the publicly accessible reason must be provided (on the same day or on some later day), on whom the duty to fulfill the re-

quirement falls or in what mode the religiously based argument is to be delivered (as a central point or as an aside). In keeping his account quite general, Rawls argues that the rules cannot be worked out in advance. Instead, they depend on "the nature of the public political culture" in question. Different societies, then, may choose to satisfy the proviso in very different ways. See Rawls, *Collected Papers*, 592.

36. Rawls, *Collected Papers*, 592-94.

37. Stephen Carter, *The Culture of Disbelief: How American Law and Politics Trivialize Religious Devotion* (New York: Anchor Books, 1994); Richard Neuhaus, *The Naked Public Square: Religion and Liberal Democracy in America* (Grand Rapids, Mich.: Eerdmans Press, 1986).

38. See Richard Rorty, "Religion as Conversation-Stopper," *Common Knowledge* 3, no. 1 (1994): 1-6.

39. Rawls, *Collected Papers*, 574 (italics added).

40. Rawls, *Law of Peoples*, 59.

41. Rawls, *Law of Peoples*, 74.

42. Rawls, *Law of Peoples*, 76.

43. Rawls, *Law of Peoples*, 77.

44. Israel, like Kazanistan, is affiliated with a particular religion and gives official preference to that religion. Israel is also associationist and tolerant: it sees its citizens as belonging to religious communities and gives each religious authority limited autonomy to conduct the affairs of its community. And just as Kazanistan aspires to be a "decent and rational Muslim regime" that nevertheless respects all its citizens, Israel defines itself as a "Jewish and democratic state" in its Basic Laws and pledges (in its Declaration of Establishment) to "foster the development of the country for the benefit of all its inhabitants." Whereas Kazanistan limits the formal equality of its minorities by banning them from official leadership positions, however, no rule has prevented Israeli Arabs from serving in the Knesset, on the judicial bench (even of the Supreme Court) or as a government minister. Still, representation of Arabs in the highest political positions is thin and reflects a level of social discrimination against minorities apparently not found in Rawls's idealized Kazanistan. Moreover, while Kazanistan welcomes non-Muslims into the highest ranks of the military, Bedouin and Druze are the only minorities allowed to serve in the Israel Defense Forces. Unlike Kazanistan's consultation hierarchy (the details of which are unspecified), Israel gives full democratic rights of speech, press and voting for all citizens, Jewish and Arab alike.

45. See, for example, Charles R. Beitz, "Rawls's Law of Peoples," *Ethics* 110, no. 4 (July 2000): 669-96; Fernando Teson, *A Philosophy of International Law* (Boulder: Westview, 1998); and Andrew Kuper, "Rawlsian Global Justice: Beyond *The Law of Peoples*," *Political Theory* 28 (October 2000): 640-74.

46. Rawls, *Law of Peoples*, 61.

47. Charles R. Beitz, "Human Rights as a Common Concern," *American Political Science Review* 95 (June 2000): 275.

48. Rawls, *Law of Peoples*, 61.

49. Rawls, *Law of Peoples*, 61.

50. Rawls, *Law of Peoples*, 62.

51. "Take some more tea," the March Hare said to Alice, very earnestly. "I've had nothing yet," Alice replied in an offended tone, "so I can't take *more*." "You mean you

can't take *less*," said the Hatter. "It's very easy to take more than nothing." (Lewis Carroll, *Alice in Wonderland*, chapter 7.) Thanks to Marek Steedman.

52. Jonathan Riley makes a similar point: "What Rawls calls decent nonliberal societies may better be viewed as at least minimally liberal, to emphasize continuities between advanced democratic Western societies and nondemocratic societies (including pre-democratic versions of Western societies themselves) that honor some minimum of human rights." Jonathan Riley, "Interpreting Berlin's Liberalism," *American Political Science Review* 95, no. 2 (June 2001): 293fn14.

53. For an argument criticizing what I am characterizing as Rawls's new, looser liberalism on grounds of socio-economic equality, see Allen Buchanan, "Rawls's Law of Peoples: Rules for a Vanished Westphalian World," *Ethics* 110, no. 4 (July 2000): 697-721.

54. Rawls, *Collected Papers*, 581-82.

55. Waldron, "Religious Contributions," 841.

56. An important reminder: we are talking about ethical norms, not legal rules. I am not proposing that a legislative body should adopt rules punishing its members for irrelevant religious comments. I claim only that the legislator ought not make such a point, and if she does, that other legislators should disregard it in their deliberations.

57. Some might prefer Rawls's proviso to my principle on the grounds that it is receptive to more religious talk and thus more conducive to free speech. But it must be remembered that neither Rawls nor I propose any legal limits on speech. The question is, given freedom of speech, which arguments ought to *matter* politically. I think religious arguments that point to a political good ought to matter, but see no compelling reason for including in this category sectarian arguments that contain no reference to a public value.

58. Consider, for example, exemptions from public education for the Amish (upheld by the U.S. Supreme Court in Wisconsin v. Yoder, 406 U.S. 205 [1972]) or tax-exempt status for religious organizations (upheld by the Court in Walz v. Tax Commission of City of New York, 397 U.S. 664 [1970]).

59. Some accommodations might involve protecting the interests of Orthodox Jews, who constitute a minority inside the Jewish majority: limited exemptions of Haredi youth from military service, for example. Other policies might appeal to (the majority of) Jews generally, such as legislating a national Holocaust memorial day or referencing the "Jewish longing for Zion" in the national anthem.

60. This claim is allied with the "equal treatment" interpretation of the First Amendment's religion clauses. According to this position, public funds may be distributed to religious and nonreligious organizations on an evenhanded basis when used for public purposes. See Stephen V. Monsma and J. Christopher Soper, eds., *Equal Treatment of Religion in a Pluralistic Society* (Grand Rapids, Mich.: Eerdmans Publishing Company, 1998).

Chapter 2
The Jewish State

The Declaration of the Establishment of the State of Israel, signed on May 14, 1948, proclaimed that the new nation in Palestine "will ensure complete equality of social and political rights to all its inhabitants irrespective of religion, race or sex [and] will guarantee freedom of conscience, language, education and culture."[1] Alongside this statement of equal democratic freedoms was a unique premise: Israel will be the state of a particular religious group. It will be "open for Jewish immigration and for the Ingathering of the Exiles"; it will be "a Jewish State in Eretz-Israel."[2]

The twin commitments embodied in the Israeli Declaration—embracing Judaism (and Jews) and protecting the rights of religious and ethnic minorities—imply that a liberal, religious state is a possibility. But the two adjectives have posed many challenges as the secular yet avowedly Jewish state has grappled with questions of how to include its non-Jewish Arab citizens and how to deal with conflicts among its diverse Jewish communities. These tensions were present from the beginning, in the founding document of the state, when signatories placed their faith in "*tzur Yisrael*," the Rock of Israel. Religious signers thought this term to represent God, while the secular signatories regarded it as symbolizing the heritage of the Jewish people.[3] A Hobbesian, for whom the state must immediately settle the meanings of words in order to consolidate power, might condemn this openness to multiple interpretations as destabilizing to a new commonwealth.[4] Indeed, although the "Rock of Israel" compromise allowed groups with contradictory world views to work past their disagreements, at least for one historic moment, it did not put an end to their competing notions of what the Jewish state ought to become.

Zionism, Religious Zionism, Anti-Zionism

Israel's story begins with Zionism, the movement for the national redemption of the Jewish people in the Land of Israel, which had begun as an essentially secular project. Viennese Jewish writer Nathan Birnbaum coined the term in 1885; eleven years later, in 1896, Theodor Herzl published *The Jewish State*.[5] In this book Herzl famously concluded that the only solution to the incessant risks of anti-Semitism (the "Jewish problem" left unresolved even after the political emancipation of Jews in most of Western Europe) was the establishment of an independent Jewish nation-state, preferably in the Jews' ancient homeland of Palestine or Eretz Yisrael (the land of Israel).[6]

Most Jewish religious leaders balked at the suggestion. Jewish sovereignty in the Land of Israel, according to the traditional Jewish line, will become possible only after the ingathering of the exiles, the coming of the messiah and the construction of the third temple on Mount Moriah in Jerusalem, the spot where both ancient temples of Israel once stood. Zionism was interpreted by religious leaders as a disingenuous and premature messianism fueled by the Enlightenment thinking of secular-minded Jews and as the movement through which the secular Jew attempted, in one historian's words, to "adapt to the modern world without ceasing to be a Jew."[7] So Zionism became associated with "a collective form of assimilation; for Jews to have their country—territorially, not just spiritually—is to become 'like all other men,' in having a country like other countries."[8] This interpretation, together with the fear that a false messianism fueled the movement, led most Orthodox Jewish leaders to repudiate Zionism.[9]

There were exceptions, however. Not all Orthodox thinkers condemned the Zionist mission. Two rabbis of the mid-1800s offered theologies that linked settlement of the land of Israel with the path of redemption: Rabbi Yehuda Alkalai (1798-1878) of Sarajevo and Rabbi Zvi Hirsch Kalischer (1795-1874) of Thorn in eastern Germany.[10] Building from medieval Jewish sources, Alkalai envisioned a forerunner to the messiah (the Son of Joseph) who would conquer the Land of Israel and establish Jewish political leadership there. "The Redemption," Alkalai wrote, "will begin with effort by the Jews themselves: they must organize and unite, choose leaders and leave the land of exile."[11] Assuming a leadership role himself, Alkalai toured the capitals of Europe where he spread his ideas and established a committee for settlement in Palestine.[12]

Kalischer prophesied an incremental redemption that would unfold as Jews moved to the Holy Land, and spearheaded a project to build an agricultural school for Jewish pioneers.[13] These ideas found similar expression in the mid-1800s in the teachings of the Polish Rabbi Samuel Mohilever, a disciple of Rabbi Kalischer. Mohilever argued that it was incumbent upon religious Jews to join ranks with the secular Zionists, since the campaign to settle the Land of Israel would hasten the messianic redemption. Rabbi Isaac Jacob Reines of Belorussia, a disciple of Mohilever, shared this view, emphasizing the importance of Palestine as a center for the revitalization of traditional Jewish learning. Coming to Herzl's support shortly after he founded the World Zionist Organization in 1897, Reines launched *Hamizrahi*, the Religious Zionist movement of Eastern European Jewry, in 1902. This organization, whose name is a combination of the Hebrew words *mercaz ruhani* ("spiritual center") adopted the following as its motto: "The Land of Israel for the People of Israel according to the Torah of Israel."[14]

Hamizrahi, along with Hapoel Hamizrahi (the labor wing of the movement which emerged in 1922), would become Israel's National Religious Party (NRP) in 1956. It advanced three fundamental ideas. First, in opposition to the non-Zionist Orthodox, Hamizrahi preached the importance of human action in history. The party argued that Jews should not simply wait for redemption but must actively settle the land to hasten the dawn of the messianic age. Second, also *contra* traditional Orthodoxy, Hamizrahi claimed that redemption is a community-wide project and demands the cooperation of all Jews, religious and secular alike. And third, nudging the secular-minded Zionist movement back to its Jewish roots, the group insisted that spirituality and education are necessary to bring all Jews closer to traditional Judaism and Torah.[15]

The Chief Rabbi of pre-state Israel, Rabbi Avraham Yitzhak Kook, saw the secular state—which would be founded thirteen years after his death—as the foundation for an eventual Torah state and an essential stage on the road to the world to come. He viewed the secular Zionist leaders as unwitting participants in the project of messianic redemption.[16] The secularists were religious despite themselves: "Even those Zionists who were divorced from Jewish religious tradition had nevertheless been motivated by the 'inner divine spark' in their soul, although they were not yet ready to admit or acknowledge this fact."[17]

There was a sizeable faction of Orthodox Jews who resisted this political theology, however. Vehemently rejecting the linkage of traditional Judaism with Zionism, Agudat Yisrael was established in 1912 by a group of ultra-religious German Jews who split from Hamizrahi. Despite their similar commitments to fulfilling the commandments of traditional Judaism, the Agudah's political platform contrasted sharply with that of its parent party: No human attempt should be made to hasten the messianic age, since redemption will occur only through the will of God. No Jewish sovereignty should be established in the Land of Israel (although settlement there is a *mitzvah* [religious commandment] and should be pursued). No Orthodox Jews should join the secular Zionist project.[18]

The "Status Quo"

In the years leading up to the establishment of the State of Israel, David Ben-Gurion (the political leader of the *Yishuv*, or pre-state settlement) sought ways to achieve a compromise according to which Israel could develop a Jewish character while accommodating its secular Zionist, Religious Zionist and ultra-Orthodox anti-Zionist Jewish fragments. The compromise that emerged, which became known as the "status quo" agreement between the secular and religious parties, had its roots in a consensus that evolved earlier in the century, before Israel became a state.

The modus vivendi was built upon two foundations: the millet arrangement of granting autonomy to religious groups that had prevailed under Ottoman rule and during the British Mandate, and a spirit of grudging accommodation that marked even the early relations between secular and Religious Zionist movements. In 1920 the World Zionist Organization gave Hamizrahi license and funding to operate an autonomous religious educational system separate from both the Yishuv's secular Zionist system and the Agudah's religious system. (The latter was independent of the Yishuv and, for the most part, funded itself.) In 1921, the Chief Rabbinate was established by the mandatory government to oversee a system of religious courts handling marriage, divorce and burial among Jews. The Knesset Yisrael gave this body further shape in 1928 by designating both an Ashkenazi Chief Rabbi and a Sephardi Chief Rabbi, and in 1935 by instituting a system of elections for the posts. Finally, at the Nineteenth Zionist Congress in 1935, Mapai and Hamizrahi agreed that both *kashrut* (the Jewish dietary laws) and *Shabbat*, the Jewish Sabbath, would be honored in public life and public institutions.[19]

Each aspect of this arrangement seemed to be confirmed nearly a year prior to statehood in a letter that Ben-Gurion and other leaders of the Jewish Agency sent to the Executive Committee of Agudat Yisrael on June 19, 1947.[20] Writing in his capacity as the chairman of the Jewish Agency, Ben-Gurion made four promises to the leadership of the Agudah: (1) Saturday would be publicly observed as the day of rest for the Jewish population; (2) *kashrut* would be observed in all government kitchens; (3) religious courts would maintain exclusive jurisdiction over matters of family status, including marriage, divorce and burial; and (4) the full autonomy of the religious educational system would be preserved.[21]

There is some question, however, as to whether this letter truly represents an agreement on the entrenchment of status quo. According to Menahem Friedman, the text of the letter does not convey any actual commitment on the part of the Jewish Agency to the four elements listed above.[22] On the matter of *kashrut*, for instance, the letter pledges that "in every state kitchen intended for Jews there will be kosher food"; it contains no promise, Friedman observes, "that the state institutions will serve *exclusively* kosher food."[23] And concerning matters of personal status, the letter reads: "The leadership appreciates the seriousness of the problem...and will do everything possible...to prevent, God forbid, the division of the House of Israel into two."[24] Friedman asks, "If the intention was in fact to preserve the status quo, why the hesitant formulation? Why not say simply that...marriages and divorces for Jews will be conducted in the Jewish state according to Torah only?"[25] In explaining the intentions of the Jewish Agency leaders, Friedman highlights the importance of the opening paragraphs of the letter, which read as follows:

> The leadership of the Jewish Agency has considered your request in the matter of guaranteeing personal status issues, Shabbat, education and kashrut in the Jewish state that will soon be established.

> As the chairman of the leadership indicated to you, neither the Jewish Agency nor any other body in Israel is authorized to determine from the beginning the constitution of the Jewish state to be established. The establishment of the state requires the authorization of the United Nations, and that is not possible if freedom of conscience for all the state's citizens is not guaranteed and if it is not clear that there is no intention of establishing a theocratic state. In the Jewish state there will be non-Jewish citizens as well— Christians and Muslims—and it is clear that it will be essential to guarantee full equal rights to all citizens and to prevent coercion or discrimination in matters of religion.[26]

On Friedman's re-telling, the Jewish Agency's letter to the Agudah leadership was drafted to assuage the ultra-Orthodox on a few issues of concern to them; it was not meant as a proposition that the *de facto* status quo arrangement should be legally entrenched in the emerging state. Whether or not it was so intended, however, the substance of the Yishuv's status quo on matters of religion did in fact survive statehood, and has persisted in its essential form through the first six decades of Israel's existence.

Why would Ben-Gurion, the powerful, intensely secular leader of the Zionist project, agree to the conditions of the status quo? Why would he concede these four important issues, abandoning the hope to forge a truly secular Zionist state? Perhaps, as Friedman suggests, he never really thought he was conceding anything. But even if he did regard the arrangement with some distaste, Ben-Gurion's motives seem pragmatic: the future prime minister's immediate aim was to secure the participation or at least non-obstruction of the religious parties in the incipient Jewish state.[27] Nissim Rejwan quotes Ben-Gurion's frank words: "I knew that we required the widest possible political backing to carry out the gigantic tasks that I envisaged....I was prepared to limit my program to the basic urgencies and offer concessions on what I regarded as subsidiary issues."[28] Beyond that, Ben-Gurion seemed to believe that the religious Jews were a remnant from the exile, a dying breed, a quiet and insular community that would seldom be heard among a society of robust secular Jewish pioneers. The most effective way to control the religious, Ben-Gurion reasoned, was to welcome them into the state and to let them have a hand in setting the terms of their involvement. The late Yeshayahu Leibowitz, the iconoclastic Orthodox scholar who argued for a secular Israeli state, often reported a conversation he had with Ben-Gurion in the mid 1950's:

> He said to me: "I understand very well why you demand the separation of religion from the state. You want the Jewish religion to be reinstated as an independent factor with which the political authority will have to contend. Therefore I shall never agree to the separation of state and religion. I want the state to hold religion under its control."[29]

Leibowitz was dismayed by the religious parties "being 'kept' by the secular government"; he claimed that Orthodoxy would thrive, and recapture its true values, by refusing state funding and becoming a more independent force in Israeli society.[30]

The leaders of the Agudah, whom Leibowitz criticized along with the Religious Zionists, received Ben-Gurion's status quo letter with some ambivalence. On one hand, they were happy to find what they perceived to be written confirmation of the pre-state arrangement.[31] On the other, they regretted what seemed to be a pact with an ideological enemy. Moshe Ona reports that the organization "was not completely satisfied with the [provisions of the letter] but regarded the four promises as a meaningful achievement on the most important matters of principle, an achievement which established its role in shaping the character of the coming generations of the Jewish people in its land."[32] Upon presenting a list of candidates for the First Knesset, the Agudah made clear that their participation in the Jewish state did not imply approval of the Zionist project. The State of Israel, they said,

> is not only a desecration of God and a desecration of the holiness of our land, but an organized public rebellion against God and his Torah, and it is forbidden to let this pass in silence. . . . We have decided, the leaders of Agudat Yisrael in Israel, with the agreement of the Council of Torah Sages, to participate in the election for the First Israeli Parliament ("Knesset"). There is a difference . . . between a Zionist organization, from which the Haredim have separated themselves, and a sovereign state, of which every resident and citizen within its borders is a member by necessity. It is impossible to ignore it, or to prohibit it; rather, it is possible only to fight from within over the shape of its character, . . . to influence

the content of the Basic Laws of the New State and the manner of its leadership.[33]

So according to the "status quo," toleration runs both ways: the secular parties tolerate (some of) the demands of the religious parties and the religious parties tolerate the secular parameters of the State of Israel. On the latter point the NRP and the Agudah differ: the former sees the secular Israeli state as a step along the path to the messiah while the latter reluctantly tolerates it as a structure within which the material and religious interests of their community may be secured. The picture is a classic modus vivendi: a practical compromise that bypasses rather than confronts disagreement. The three Jewish perspectives towards Zionism and the Jewish state—secular, religious and rejectionist—cohabit in an agreement to vehemently disagree. As Gary Schiff puts it, "Each party, consistent with its distinctive ideology and history, viewed the rise of the state of Israel through its own particular lens."[34] And each regards the value of participating Israeli politics in different and even mutually incompatible ways.

Jewish Dimensions of the State

The status quo agreement set the stage for Israel to become a Jewish state in a number of respects. As I argued in chapter 1, however, these features do not qualify Israel as a theocracy, a state governed by clerics applying religious law. Israel's religion-state linkages are milder and fewer than those of Saudi Arabia, Sudan or Afghanistan under its former Taliban government. The freedoms Israel grants its citizens are much wider than they are in these rigorously religious societies, and Israel's legal system is, by and large, independent of religion. Still, there has been and is today significant controversy over the justifiability of certain aspects of Israel's incorporation of religion into the state that do bear theocratic markings.

We can begin by distinguishing three nodes of official religion-state interaction in Israel: symbols, institutions and legislation.[35]

In the first category, we find innumerable symbols that relate to or are drawn from Judaism or Jewish history. These testify to Israel's connection with a particular religion and a particular people with much greater specificity and emphasis than symbols such as "In God We Trust" display the religious roots of the United States. Take the Knesset, for example. Casting this modern-day legislative body as a post-exilic institution of Jewish sovereignty, the name "Knesset" (held over from the pre-state "Knesset Yisrael") was chosen for its connection to Haknesset Hag'dolah (the Great Assembly), established in Jerusalem in the fifth century BCE upon the return of the Jews from their exile in Babylonia. The number of Knesset members, 120, also

matches that of its ancient namesake.[36] The Knesset chamber's seats are arranged in the shape of the seven-branched *menorah* (candelabrum), which is
also the state's official emblem.

At the Israel Museum, across the street from the Knesset building in Je-
rusalem, the Shrine of the Book prominently displays the Dead Sea Scrolls
(Hebrew bible texts dated to the Second Temple era, from the second century
BCE to 70 CE) and exhibits can be found on such topics as the Jewish life
cycle. The Holocaust plays a major role in Israeli public life, with Yom
Hashoah (Holocaust Remembrance Day) as a national holiday and Yad
Vashem (the Holocaust Memorial Museum) as the state landmark most visited by foreign dignitaries. The Kotel, also known as the Western or Wailing
Wall, symbolizes Israel's historical connection to ancient Israel and the temples that once stood in the Old City. Additional examples of symbolic linkages of Judaism and state are biblical verses that are worked into public officials' speeches, imprinted on postage stamps and engraved into public
buildings; the national anthem describing the "Jewish soul's" two thousand
year longing to return to Zion; and the state flag's Star of David.

Moving to the second category—institutions—Israel's religion-state arrangement gets more complicated and enters territory that appears to involve clear violations of the nonestablishment principle of the U.S. Constitution (a provision which finds no similar expression in Israeli law). Israel provides both legal status and financial support for several Jewish institutions,
including the chief rabbinate and the chief rabbis and religious councils of
localities around Israel. The religious councils distribute funds to local synagogues, control Jewish holy sites, oversee the food industry's *kashrut* practices and pay local religious officials.[37] The national and local chief rabbis
serve as spiritual leaders, possessing little if any formal authority. Many pay
attention to their rulings in matters of *halacha* (Jewish law), especially those
of political significance. Former Chief Rabbi Avraham Shapira, for example,
ruled in 2000 that the Golan Heights (a territory in northeast Israel captured
from Syria in the 1967 war) "was bequeathed to the tribes of Israel by divine
command as stated in our holy Torah" and cannot be returned to Syria in a
peace agreement. It is "forbidden to uproot settlements from Eretz Yisrael,"
he wrote.[38] Shapira and another former chief rabbi, Mordechai Eliyahu, issued a similar ruling that forbade Israeli soldiers from participating in Israel's evacuation of nine thousand Jewish settlers from the Gaza Strip and
several West Bank outposts in August 2005.[39] Only a handful of soldiers
heeded these instructions.

Until December 2003, the main governmental unit to deal directly with
overseeing and funding religious community practices was the Ministry of
Religious Affairs, although additional points of contact were found in the
Ministry of Education and Culture and in the Ministry of Interior. On
Christmas Eve 2003, following several months of political wrangling, the

Knesset voted to dismantle the Ministry of Religious Affairs. In an unusual alliance, the secular Shinui and Religious Zionist NRP—two parties that usually sit on opposite sides on religion-state questions—joined forces to accomplish this change. Shinui leader Yossi Lapid took primary credit and noted that Israel was now "one step closer to a liberal, civil society."[40] Zevulun Orlev, NRP Knesset member and Minister of Social Affairs at the time, claimed the vote as an "historic achievement of the NRP." How could a National Religious Party member, who wants to see closer integration of religion and state in Israel, view the dismantling of this body as a historic achievement? Very little changed in the day-to-day details of religion and state as a result of the disappearance of the Ministry of Religious Affairs, despite the hyperbole from a representative of the ultra-Orthodox Shas party who claimed the change would amount to a "spiritual Holocaust for the Jewish people."[41] The various tasks that the ministry handled have been folded into other governmental divisions. The Prime Minister's office, for example, now houses the state's Chief Rabbinate; the Justice Ministry oversees the rabbinical courts. Part of the NRP's satisfaction lies in the toothless oversight role the secular authorities play in the new arrangement. The Sephardic Chief Rabbi retains the power to choose judges for the religious courts; the Justice minister's only responsibilities, in MK Orlev's words, are to "take out the trash and clean the courts."[42]

The Jewish community is not the only group in Israeli society that factors into the institutional connections between religion and state. Under the terms of the millet system held over from the Ottoman and British Mandate periods, Israel gives Jewish, Muslim, Christian and Druze religious courts various degrees of autonomy to regulate matters of personal status among their respective communities.[43] Muslim courts, applying to all Muslims residing in Palestine and covering all aspects of personal status, have the widest jurisdiction. Christian courts' exclusive jurisdiction is limited to marriage, divorce and alimony among Christian Israeli citizens. The extent of Jewish and Druze courts' jurisdiction lies between that of the other two groups. They handle matters of marriage and divorce for community members who are either Israeli citizens or permanent residents. In all other areas of personal status law (such as succession, property of legal incompetents and guardianship), the Jewish, Christian and Druze courts hold concurrent jurisdiction along with the secular state courts.[44] (Generally, cases concerning concurrent-jurisdiction matters may be adjudicated in religious courts if both parties consent.) Israel also provides funding for Jewish, Muslim and Druze religious services (Christian groups decline the aid, seeking to preserve greater autonomy from the state) and education.[45]

The third juncture of religion and the Israeli state—legislation—is most contentious when it overlaps with the institutional aspect of the polity's religion-state arrangement. Little criticism is heard of the millet system from

Muslim, Christian and Druze communities. Criticism is much stronger and more often voiced from the majority of Israeli Jews who do not share the religious beliefs and practices of the Orthodox chief rabbis or the Orthodox members of their local religious councils, and who suffer from what they call *kefiah datit* (religious coercion). Legislation, and sometimes a lack thereof, contribute to this perceived oppression in a number of ways. Under Israeli law, for example, there is no provision for civil marriage. Any Israeli couple wishing to marry or divorce in the country must do so within their religious community and within the rules set by the religious courts to which they are subject. This is one of the terms of the religious-secular status quo agreement, as are Shabbat restrictions which include abridged public bus service in most of the country, closed roads in religious neighborhoods and regulations against the operation of businesses on Saturdays. Non-Orthodox Jews and non-Jews sometimes complain that such legislation impinges on their mobility and freedom. Even with these principles realized in legislation, however, Jewishly inspired legislation entails little direct interference with Israelis' private lives or their religious observance. Unlike Iran and the former Taliban regime in Afghanistan, Israel lacks a morality police that enforces individual compliance with religious scruples. Aside from the significant limitations of family law, there is no requirement that private individuals observe Jewish commandments. You may keep kosher or observe the Sabbath if you so choose, but the state does not bind you to adhere to *halacha*.[46]

Constituting a Jewish and Democratic Israel

The status quo has evolved as an agreement under which neither side is especially happy and each constantly attempts to gain a bit of ground on the other. (The religious push for more restrictive Shabbat legislation, say, while the secular ask for legal provisions for civil marriage.) As we found in the last chapter, Rawls believes that political arrangements often begin modestly—with a modus vivendi akin to the one just described—but evolve over time into a more principled overlapping consensus. Along the way, the polity develops a way of talking about fundamental political questions that unites every reasonable person in that society, no matter the content of her religious, moral or philosophical views. So although people will continue to subscribe to mutually incompatible world views, and will continue to disagree politically, they will be able to find agreement on the terms for discussing their political disagreements. They will find reconciliation not on ultimate metaphysical questions, but on the proper sorts of considerations for resolving fundamental political questions. Or so Rawls says.

But the conflict between Judaism and secularism that spurred the state's status quo agreement seems to have been built upon a clash of worldviews and very different conceptions of public reason. It paved the way not for less but for more conflict in the debate over the constitution that raged in Israel's first years and continues to this day. The U.N. General Assembly had approved the establishment of Israel on the condition that it would quickly draft a constitution, and the Declaration of Establishment required that a constitution be drawn up by the Constituent Assembly "not later than October 1, 1948." Israel's first legislative assembly, however, enacted the Transition Law of 1949, transforming itself from Constituent Assembly into an ordinary parliamentary body without first settling on a constitution.[47] The First Knesset deliberated on the constitutional question through the first half of 1950.[48]

David Bar-Rav-Hai, a member of left-wing Mapai[49], held that Israel should not shackle itself or its revolutionary spirit too quickly. He claimed that Israel was still in its infancy and lacked the requisite maturity to commit to a formal constitution; anyway, he observed, even the Americans took "eleven difficult years" to adopt their constitution after winning independence.[50] Another Mapainik, Ben-Zion Dinaburg, advanced the opposite view. The constitution should be adopted now, Dinaburg claimed, in order to give Israelis—many of whom brought little knowledge of active political life from their home countries—a detailed account of the rights and duties of citizenship. Only with a constitution modeled on the French Declaration of the Rights of Man and Citizen, according to Dinaburg, will the new state assimilate its diverse immigrants (olim[51]) and forge a new, flourishing society.[52] Menachem Begin, leader of the right-wing Herut (which would become Likud in 1973), as well as leaders of the far-left Mapam, also supported a constitution that would protect the rights of minorities and rein in the power of the dominant Mapai.[53]

But Mapai leader David Ben-Gurion, along with the religious parties, led what turned out to be a successful campaign against a constitution. Ben-Gurion argued that constitutionalism was appropriate for bringing freedom to an absolutist regime (as in eighteenth century Europe) or for setting the parameters of a federal system (as in the United States), but would be superfluous in Israel, where democracy and freedom were already the norm. "In a free country like Israel," he proclaimed, "there is no need for a declaration of freedoms."[54] Most commentators agree, however, that democracy wasn't Ben-Gurion's primary concern. In advancing the interests of the majority party, and in preserving the power of the state from constitutional curtailments, his position was at least as politically savvy as it was principled.[55]

Ben-Gurion, as we saw above, also had an interest in placating the religious parties with whom he hoped to forge a lasting parliamentary coalition. For the Orthodox, opposition to an Israeli constitution was a matter of deep principle. Jews, according to the religious view, should be governed by only one "higher law"—the divine law stemming from the Torah and Talmud. To entrench any secular series of laws as Israel's constitution was tantamount to sacrilege. Instead, Israel should look to traditional Jewish law—including the commandments laid out in the Hebrew Bible and interpreted in rabbinical commentaries—as its sole source of constitutional value. Rabbi I.M. Levin of the ultra-Orthodox United Religious Front urged this point in his contribution to the debate of 1950. In addressing the question of "how this people [will] organize its life in its state," Levin concluded that the Jews should resist the impulse to become like other nations—in settling for a "normal" state—and return to its ancient organizing principles of the Torah.[56]

Bowing to Prime Minister Ben-Gurion's position, and in order to avoid a religious-secular *kulturkampf* in the fragile new state, the Knesset voted on June 13, 1950, to adopt the compromise Harari proposal.[57] According to this resolution, the Knesset assigned its Constitution, Law and Justice Committee the task of drafting a constitution made up of a series of Basic Laws; these laws were to be presented to the Knesset and incorporated into the state's constitution after further debate over sensitive questions of a preamble, the constitution's degree of flexibility, its supremacy over other laws and the date for its completion.[58] The Knesset officially put the constitutional issue on hold. Rather than draft a complete constitutional text all at once, the Knesset decided to allow the constitution to emerge gradually through a patchwork of Basic Laws that would one day form a single constitution.[59] This approach effectively side-stepped a religious-secular cultural war in Israel.

More than a half-century later, Israel's Jewish-democratic divide has grown and the state still lacks a formal and complete written constitution. Israel's nine Basic Laws passed before 1992, for the most part, lack entrenched status and can be changed by a simple majority vote in the Knesset.[60] These laws define the operations of the Knesset and judiciary, create a presidency, establish Jerusalem as Israel's capital and so on.[61] But, notably, the pre-1992 Basic Laws contain nothing resembling a bill of rights. Nor do they confer a power of judicial review on Israel's Supreme Court. Since 1992, the onset of what Chief Justice of Israel's Supreme Court Aharon Barak and others have called a "constitutional revolution,"[62] the picture has changed significantly.[63] With the adoption of two new Basic Laws in that year—Basic Law: Freedom of Occupation and Basic Law: Human Dignity and Liberty—Israel's Supreme Court has powerful new tools at its disposal. The two laws, passed in the waning hours of the Twelfth Knesset (1988-1992), codify for the first time protected human and civil rights for Israeli citizens and nationals.[64]

As Barak points out, 1992 did not mark the beginning of the Israeli Supreme Court's human rights doctrine. Indeed, in the style of the English legal system, the Court had been protecting certain rights through judge-made law since the first days of statehood.[65] As early as 1953, in the case *Kol Ha'am v. Minister of Interior*[66], the Court invalidated an executive branch order to suspend publication of two communist newspapers that had criticized the government's foreign policy. In the decision, Justice Agranat cited open deliberation and the rights of free speech and a free press as values inherent in Israeli democracy (and guaranteed by implication in the Declaration of Establishment) that may not be suspended by the government in all but the most exceptional circumstances.[67] Indeed, since *Kol Ha'am* the Supreme Court has "supposed, in light of the democratic character of the state, that our normative world is full of human rights."[68]

Prior to 1992, however, the Supreme Court "established human rights by way of interpreting laws, and with a change in the laws came a change in the rights."[69] The two new Basic Laws, in Barak's words, "comprised a revolution in the legal and constitutional status of fundamental human rights in Israel. ...The rights ceased to be 'not written in the books' and became rights 'written in the books' that enjoy a preferred constitutional status."[70] With the switch from judge-made to legislated constitutional law came a "deep internal shift" in the "normative status" of the rights.[71] The new legislation, Barak writes, "removed Israel from its isolation [as a country without a formal written constitution], and established us in the great camp of nations in which human rights are anchored in a written and entrenched constitution—in a document of supremacy and normative priority."[72]

The specific rights guaranteed in the two new Basic Laws are broad and wide ranging, but subject to limitation and not fully entrenched. Basic Law: Freedom of Occupation ensures that "every Israel national or resident has the right to engage in any occupation, profession or trade."[73] Basic Law: Human Dignity and Liberty stipulates that "there shall be no violation of the life, body, or dignity or any person as such," no violation of "the property of a person" and no "deprivation or restriction of the liberty of a person by imprisonment, arrest, extradition or otherwise"; holds that all persons are free to leave Israel and that any Israeli national has the right to enter Israel; creates for all persons a "right to privacy and to intimacy" and a right against unconsented searches and surveillance.[74] According to section 8 of this Basic Law, however, any of these rights may be restricted by a law "befitting the values of the State of Israel, enacted for a proper purpose, and to an extent no greater than is required, or by regulation enacted by virtue of express authorization in such law." All courts (with the Supreme Court as the highest court of appeal) are entrusted with the responsibility of deciding whether a law restricting rights meets these standards; in other words, the courts now have the power to exercise judicial review over legislation passed by the Knesset.[75]

The rights that these recent Basic Laws provide have provoked less attention from the public and the courts than might be expected. Instead, judges and commentators have riveted on the "purpose" clause common to both that re-introduces, in a subtle and seemingly innocuous way, the debate over Israel's Jewish and democratic character. In Basic Law: Human Dignity and Liberty, this clause (section 1a) reads:

> The purpose of this Basic Law is to protect human dignity and liberty, in order to anchor in a Basic Law the values of the State of Israel as a Jewish and democratic state.[76]

The conflict between Jewish and democratic values that we first encountered in the Declaration of the Establishment has returned, this time stated in a way that finesses the possibility of conflict. The phrase "Israel as a Jewish and democratic state" suggests harmony rather than internal contradiction. Also, the wording of the purpose clause sets out the "values of the State of Israel" as the ultimate goal to which the rights of human dignity and liberty are a means. That is, the specific rights enumerated in this Basic Law (privacy, dignity, bodily integrity), appear not to be valued in themselves but in light of their ability to anchor the State of Israel's values as a "Jewish and democratic state" in constitutional legislation.

The Knesset members who drafted and supported this purpose clause divided sharply over its meaning. Religious parties viewed the clause as a religious foundation for an otherwise liberal list of rights that codified the importance of Israel's Jewish values; left-wing parties saw it as a victory for liberal democratic values over religious principles and presumed (correctly, as it has turned out) that the courts would tend to read the clause their way.[77] The meaning of "Israel's values as a Jewish and democratic state," then, was sharply but silently contested (by members of the Knesset acting as Constituent Assembly) long before it was handed to the courts as an adjudicative tool. So while in theory the Knesset provided the courts with a coherent constitutional text, Dan Avnon notes, in effect it "subordinat[ed] specific rights to a fuzzy normative framework" and "transferred to the judiciary the responsibility and authority to determine an extremely divisive social, political and cultural issue."[78]

The new basic legislation gave the courts little guidance in answering a number of important questions. What are the State of Israel's democratic values? Are they simply the rights as found in this Basic Law? If so, why bother citing the normative background? How does that help a judge trying to apply the law? And, more significantly, what are Israel's Jewish values? Are they the religious values of the Orthodox communities? Secular humanist or cultural Jewish values? Jewish values as broadly expressed in the Declaration of Establishment? How are the courts to decide which Jewish values the Knesset intends (if it intends any specific values at all)? And how are the courts to decide which combination of Jewish and democratic values is relevant? How are they to handle the cases in which Jewish and democratic principles collide?

Employing a revealing but perhaps impolitic metaphor to describe the Knesset's passage of the 1992 Basic Laws, Chief Justice Aharon Barak has likened the new authority granted to the courts to a "non-conventional weapon."[79] The "new constitutional rules of the game," Barak writes, "enable judges to invalidate a piece of legislation that does not meet the demands of the Basic Laws."[80] The Knesset, acting as a Constituent Assembly, thus "expressed its faith in the judges of Israel."[81] According to Barak, "the judges are worthy of this faith, and will prove it justified. The use of authority that has been given to them will be exercised with exceptional care, with attention to the heavy responsibility lain upon them."[82] So, for Barak, the Knesset had entrusted a powerful tool—comparable to nuclear weaponry—in the hands of Israel's judges. But what is required of an Israeli judge attempting to elucidate the meaning of "Israel's values as a Jewish and democratic state" with "exceptional care"?

Barak's solution comes in two parts: the strategy of abstraction and the test of what he calls the "enlightened public." First to the strategy of abstraction. As a first pass on the meaning of the purpose clause of the Basic Laws, Barak says, a judge needs to find common ground between Jewish values and democratic values and to discover how they cohere.

> In my opinion, the phrase "Jewish and democratic" constitutes not two competing principles but a notion of consonance and harmony. The content of the expression "Jewish state" must be determined at an appropriate level of abstraction. In my opinion, it is necessary to give meaning to this expression at a high level of abstraction that will bring together every segment of society and find what is common among them. We need to employ a level of abstraction that is high enough to put [Jewish values] onto a single scale with the democratic character of the state. Surely, the state is Jewish not in the *halacha*-religious understanding of the term, but instead in the sense that Jews have a right to immigrate to Israel, and the Jewish national ways of life are the ways of life of the state. The fundamental values of Judaism are the fundamental values of the State of Israel.[83]

Which values are those? Barak lists a handful—love of man, the sanctity of life, social justice, honest and good business, protection of the dignity of human beings, the rule of law—to be understood at their "abstract, universalist level" such that they "match the democratic character of the state."[84] We should not forget, Barak says, that Israel is home to a "considerable non-Jewish minority"—Israeli Arabs, who comprise nearly a fifth of the Jewish state's population. In light of this fact, according to Barak, "the values of the State of Israel as a Jewish state are the same common universalist rights of democratic society that developed in Jewish tradition and history."[85] Once he has determined what Israel's values are, the judge should compare the purpose of a piece of legislation to his conception of Israel as a Jewish and democratic state, in order to determine whether it meets the test. Barak says that this comparison "is not technical...it demands sensitivity and understanding." The jurisprudential task involves not a formalistic method of adjudication but a judicious sensibility and a "healthy dose of judicial discretion."[86]

Sometimes, though, even the highest level of abstraction isn't abstract enough. Sometimes, Barak says, Jewish and democratic values will conflict despite a judge's most imaginative effort to make them cohere. Here is where the second stage of Barak's strategy—the test of the "enlightened public" (ha'tsibur ha'naor)—enters the picture. If there is no way to square democratic with Jewish principles, "this resolution has to be made according to the perceptions of the enlightened public in Israel. This is an objective test that directs the judge to the overall values that form the image of the modern Israeli."[87]

Who constitutes the enlightened public? And how are its values to be "objectively" determined? Barak speaks of the concept in both metaphorical and tangible terms. In his less enlightening moments of metaphor, Barak calls the enlightened public "the judicial ethos and basic social principles that make a society just and worthy."[88] Near the end of his article on the constitutional revolution, Barak uses the phrase this way:

> [The judge] gives expression to the fundamental principles and values rooted in [Israel's] national identity, and reflects the "I believe" of the enlightened public, the historical development, tradition and yearning of the nation.[89]

In his more concrete moments, Barak identifies the kinds of people he means to call "enlightened": members of the legal community such as judges, lawyers and academics. In Barak's eyes, a judge must take account of the perspectives of the following when deciding how to exercise his discretion: (1) members of the legislative and executive branches; (2) judges; (3) lawyers and advocates; (4) legal scholars; and (5) the enlightened public. Barak places particular emphasis on this fifth element: "The judge has special interest in the position of the enlightened public, which—while it does not have a formal role in the branches of government and is not expert in law—reflects the wisdom and the restraint required of the judge.... This enlightened public—of which the judge generally sees himself a part—greatly influences the society's fundamental conception of judicial discretion."[90]

Thus we see the unity of Barak's two accounts of the enlightened public. The concept describes both a set of fundamental principles of social justice and the individuals who are privy to those principles—members of the legal community, broadly conceived. It is both in their official or professional roles (as judges or legislators or scholars) *and* in their private roles (as enlightened citizens) that these individuals' views on Israel's Jewish and democratic values are relevant to judicial interpretation.

Does Barak do violence to the "Jewish" part of the picture by bringing the concept of Jewish values to a high level of abstraction and subordinating them to a democratic framework? Does he implicitly shun the views of traditional Jews by referring to the enlightened beliefs of the "modern Israeli"? Is his very term "enlightened" inclined toward liberal notions introduced in the Enlightenment—and away from traditional Jewish sources that preceded the Age of Reason? Is Barak's use of the term "enlightened public" anything more than a projection of his own values—his own particular perspective on what makes society "just and worthy"—onto the public-at-large? Is Aharon Barak—with a resume that includes Professor of Law and Dean of Faculty at the Hebrew University, Lecturer at the New York University, Michigan, Harvard and Yale law schools, Attorney General, Israel Prize recipient in legal sciences, President of the Supreme Court—not the *embodiment* of the enlightened public? Indeed, he has been a member of the executive branch, a lawyer, a scholar, a judge, a professor—and thus fits into every category that he says judges should consult when exercising their discretion. Is Barak's enlightened public test just a convenient method to rationalize his considered beliefs about law?

Former Israeli Supreme Court Justice Menachem Elon pursued some of these questions in a 1993 commentary on Basic Law: Human Dignity and Liberty.[91] Elon writes that Barak's strategy is misguided because it considers the values "that Judaism has imparted to the world-at-large" by "looking at the values the world-at-large has received 'at a universalist level of abstraction,' and not by studying the roots from which those values were created, from within the sources of Judaism and the traditions of Israel!"[92] Further, Elon writes that the "legislative intent" of the Basic Law is "to find the common denominator and the synthesis" between the dual values of a Jewish and democratic state and that this must be interpreted as directing judges to not one but *two* sources" of note—not to construe democratic ideals as central and to consider Jewish values as "superfluous." Perhaps given the order in which the two adjectives "Jewish" and "democratic" are presented (Jewish coming first), Elon argues, it is the Jewish values that should fix the meaning of democracy and not the other way around.[93] And he gives an example, showing how the meaning of section 5 of Basic Law: Human Dignity and Liberty (concerning imprisonment of the accused) might be read as a fortification of a ruling from Jewish law.[94]

Barak's jurisprudential methods on the question of Jewish values have been attacked not only by fellow jurists but by many Orthodox Jews in Israel. *Yated Ne'eman*, the newspaper of the ultra-Orthodox United Torah Party, editorialized in August 1996 that Barak "is stronger than any government. He overshadows the police, the legislature, and also the executive. He has arrogated for himself the right to decide for me and for you what we are permitted to think and what we have the right to fight for."[95] Another religious paper, *HaShavua*, opined that "Aharon Barak is the driving force behind a sophisticated campaign against Jewish life in Israel."[96] And Rabbi Avraham Ravitz, an influential Knesset member from the United Torah Judaism party, took specific issue with Barak's "enlightened public" test: "What's at stake is values, and when values are at stake, the court's position is no stronger than the fishmonger's in the market—or a member of Parliament. [The Supreme Court justices'] Friday night parties with their friends in nice suits doesn't make them more enlightened than anyone else."[97]

These sentiments illustrate that the clash of values isn't quite as simple as "Jewish versus democratic." The very nature of democracy is also contested. According to Barak, "a regime in which the majority denies the basic rights of the minority is a regime of majority rule. Yet it is not a democratic regime. Democracy cannot be maintained without human rights."[98] This is a fair point few democrats would dismiss (though some will prefer "civil rights" or "democratic rights" to "human rights").

But any conception of democracy that sacrifices the element of free public discussion—and the basic principle of government by discussion—might likewise be inadequate. If the values of significant elements of the Israeli public diverge significantly from those of Barak's enlightened public, perhaps his standard could stand some reshaping for both pragmatic and principled reasons. Political institutions, after all, cannot maintain legitimacy without the support of the people they serve. As Barak himself wrote in 1989, several years before Israel's judiciary was entrusted with the elaboration of Israel's Jewish and democratic values, "the problem of judicial discretion arises with full force when the fundamental values are not sufficiently anchored in legislation, but rather must be fashioned."[99]

A renewed attempt to anchor Israel's higher law in writing was launched in May 2003, when the Knesset's Constitution, Law and Justice Committee began holding hearings to draft a "constitution by broad consensus."[100] The effort is more reflective and serious than earlier attempts, and draws on the work that several organizations, including the Israel Democracy Institute and the Israel Policy Center, have devoted to the question. It is reasonably broad-based as well, with input being solicited from all sectors of the Israeli public and the Jewish diaspora. The committee, headed by Likud MK Michael Eitan, has completed the first stage of the process and plans to submit the document to the full Knesset in 2006. If it passes three readings in the Knesset, the Israeli electorate will vote on the draft constitution in a national referendum.[101]

Even as it aims for ratification of a full constitution, the committee seems to appreciate the difficulties involved in achieving the "broad consensus" it seeks. In addressing "why a constitution is necessary," the lawmakers assert that "the constitution embodies the shared values of society." But then the committee hedges, setting expectations rather low:

> The constitutional process will have significant value even if the current project ultimately fails. Deliberating [on] the basic commitments that Israeli citizens share as a community may contribute to national unity and help to reduce social rifts and tensions, as well as reduce feelings of hostility and alienation that exist between the various sectors of Israeli society. Israel is a divided and polarized society where a sense of unity and solidarity, and the willingness to cooperate and compromise are low, while the potential for conflict and even violence is high. Under such circumstances, there is great value in a constitution that gives all groups a sense of belonging to the political community, and a sense of security that their basic interests will be respected. A constitution by broad consensus has the potential to bridge gaps, be a source of political and democratic solidarity and unity, and constitute a strong foundation for the continued existence of the state. Finally, even if this project should fail to produce a formal constitution, many sections are likely to be adopted as individual laws.[102]

It is likely, even apparently by the committee members' own estimation, that this iteration of an Israeli constitution will founder as previous attempts have. Israel's deepening social divisions make consensus more and more elusive, and in the wake of Israel's withdrawal from the Gaza Strip in 2005, the fissure between religious and secular Jews may widen, at least in the short term.

The ambiguity over the meaning of the "Rock of Israel" in Israel's Declaration of Establishment resurfaces continually in the Knesset's attempts to lay the groundwork for Israel's higher law. As everyone involved learns anew with every step, the question of Israel's official Jewishness never recedes. Few people doubt that Israel is, in a basic sense, a Jewish state. But as we will now begin to hear from Israelis themselves—members of the wider public, not only the enlightened elite—no general agreement exists, nearly six decades after the state's birth, as to what precisely that means.

Notes

1. See Daniel J. Elazar, ed., *Constitutionalism: The Israeli and American Experiences* (Lanham, Md.: University Press of America, 1990), 211-12.

2. See Elazar, *Constitutionalism: The Israeli and American Experiences,* 211.

3. Charles S. Liebman and Eliezer Don-Yehiya, *Religion and Politics in Israel* (Bloomington: Indiana University Press, 1984), 17. The late Orthodox scientist and philosopher Yeshayahu Leibowitz calls this compromise Israel's "original sin" reflecting "a fraudulent agreement between two sectors of the public, which is to the credit of neither." In his view, using the transcendent term to refer to human values and aspirations distorts the meaning of the "Rock of Israel" and leads to the sacralization of political aims—with dangerous consequences. It is, he thinks, a violation of the commandment against using "the name of the Lord thy God in vain." Leibowitz, *Judaism, Human Values, and the Jewish State,* ed. Eliezer Goldman (Cambridge: Harvard University Press, 1992), 190.

4. See Thomas Hobbes, *Leviathan,* ed. Edwin Curley (Indianapolis: Hackett Publishing, 1994), chap. 4, §12; chap. 26, §21.

5. Howard M. Sachar, *A History of Israel: From the Rise of Zionism to Our Time,* vol. 1 (New York: Alfred A. Knopf, 1979), 38.

6. The Zionist movement did not focus its aspirations on the land of Palestine until the Seventh Zionist Congress in 1905, when the "Uganda Plan" to establish a Jewish state in British-controlled Kenya was rejected. See David Vital, "The Afflictions of the Jews and the Afflictions of Zionism: The Meaning and Consequences of the 'Uganda' Controversy," in *Conflict and Consensus in Jewish Political Life,* ed. Stuart A. Cohen and Eliezer Don-Yehiya (Jerusalem: Bar Ilan University Press), 79-91 and Susan Hattis Rolef, ed., *Political Dictionary of the State of Israel* (New York: Macmillan Publishing, 1987), 344.

7. Conor Cruise O'Brien, *The Siege: The Saga of Israel and Zionism* (New York: Simon and Schuster, 1986), 48.

8. O'Brien, *Siege,* 48-49.

9. O'Brien, *Siege,* 48-49.

10. O'Brien, *Siege,* 48-49.

11. Quoted in Shlomo Avineri, *The Making of Modern Zionism: The Intellectual Origins of the Jewish State* (London: Weidenfeld and Nicholson, 1981), 51.

12. Ben Halpern and Jehuda Reinharz, *Zionism and the Creation of a New Society* (Oxford: Oxford University Press, 1998), 43-45; David Vital, *The Origins of Zionism* (Oxford: Clarendon Press of the Oxford University Press, 1975), 234n2; Mendell

Lewittes, *Religious Foundations of the Jewish State* (Northville, N.J.: Jason Aronson, Inc., 1977), 164.

13. Vital, *Origins of Zionism*, 12; Lewittes, *Religious Foundations*, 164; O'Brien, *Siege*, 50.

14. Lewittes, *Religious Foundations*, 165-66.

15. Halpern and Reinharz, *Zionism*, 109-13.

16. Menachem Friedman, "Jewish Zealots: Conservative versus Innovative" in Laurence J. Silberstein, ed., *Jewish Fundamentalism in Comparative Perspective: Religion, Ideology and the Crisis of Modernity* (New York: New York University Press, 1994), 158; Mordechai Marmorstein, *Derekh hadashah yeshana* (Religious Zionism: a reappraisal) (Tel Aviv: Mapik, 1993), 85-94 [Hebrew].

17. Eliezer Don-Yehiya, "Jewish Messianism, Religious Zionism and Israeli Politics: The Impact and Origins of Gush Emunim," *Middle Eastern Studies* 23 (April 1987): 226.

18. David Hartman, *Conflicting Visions: Spiritual Possibilities in Modern Israel* (New York: Schocken Books, 1990), 41-42; Hattis Rolef, *Political Dictionary*, 12-13.

19. Liebman and Don-Yehiya, *Religion and Politics in Israel*, 32-33.

20. Liebman and Don-Yehiya, *Religion and Politics in Israel*, 32.

21. Liebman and Don-Yehiya, *Religion and Politics in Israel*, 32.

22. Menahem Friedman, "Ve-eleh toldot ha-status-quo" (And these are the origins of the status quo: religion and state in Israel), in *The Transition from Settlement to State 1947-1949: Continuity and Change*, ed. Varda Pichavsky (Haifa: Herzl Institute of Haifa University, 1990) [Hebrew], 47-77.

23. Friedman, "Origins of the Status Quo," 52.

24. Text of the letter quoted in Friedman, "Origins of the Status Quo," 66-67.

25. Friedman, "Origins of the Status Quo," 52.

26. Letter quoted in Friedman, "Origins of the Status Quo," 66-67.

27. Ervin Birnbaum, *The Politics of Compromise: State and Religion in Israel* (Rutherford, NJ: Fairleigh Dickinson University Press, 1970), 27.

28. Quoted in Nissim Rejwan, *Israel in Search of Identity* (Gainesville, Fla.: University Press of Florida, 1999), 105.

29. Leibowitz, *Judaism, Human Values, and the Jewish State*, 216.

30. Leibowitz, *Judaism, Human Values, and the Jewish State*, 216-21.

31. Harry M. Rabinowicz, *Hasidism and the State of Israel* (East Brunswick, NJ: Associated University Presses, 1982), 268.

32. Moshe Ona, *Be-derakhim nifradot* (On separate paths: the religious parties of Israel) (Gush Etzion: Yad Shapira Press, 1983) [Hebrew], 132.

33. Ona, *On separate paths*, 130.

34. Gary Schiff, *Tradition and Politics: The Religious Parties of Israel* (Detroit: Wayne State University Press, 1977), 51.

35. These categories and some of my analysis in the paragraphs to follow are informed by Liebman and Don-Yehiya, *Religion and Politics in Israel*, ch. 2.

36. See Lewittes, *Religious Foundations*, 58 and the entry "Knesset" by Netanel Lorch in Hattis Rolef, ed., *Political Dictionary of the State of Israel*, 180.

37. Liebman and Don-Yehiya, *Religion and Politics in Israel*, 36.

38. Quoted in Nadav Shragai, "Rabbis: Golan is Eretz Yisrael," *Ha'aretz*, 5 January 2000.

39. Quoted in Ya'akov Katz, "Former Chief Rabbis Forbid Participating in Gush Katif Closure," *Jerusalem Post*, 17 July 2005.

40 Nina Gilbert, "Religious Affairs Ministry Dismantled," *Jerusalem Post*, 25 December 2003.

41 Gilbert, "Religious Affairs Ministry Dismantled."

42 Gilbert, "Religious Affairs Ministry Dismantled."

43. Judges in the religious courts are state officials whose salaries are paid by the state. *Qadis* (Muslim judges), for example, are selected by a nine-member Nominations Committee (three Members of Knesset, two *qadis*, two lawyers and two government ministers), at least five of whom must be Muslim. Martin Edelman, *Courts, Politics and Culture in Israel* (Charlottesville: University Press of Virginia, 1994), 78.

44. Asher Ma'oz, "Enforcement of Religious Courts' Judgments Under Israeli Law," *Journal of Church and State* 33, no. 3 (Summer 1991): 474-75.

45. Liebman and Don-Yehiya, *Religion and Politics in Israel*, 19.

46. One mild exception to this rule is the Hametz Law, which officially prohibits the sale or public display of bread products during the festival of Passover. In the days leading up to Passover 2005, Prime Minister Ariel Sharon asked Interior Minister Ophir Pines-Paz to apply this seldom-enforced law. Pines-Paz refused. See Attila Somfalvi and Ilan Marciano, " 'Enforce Pesach Law': Sharon Instructs Interior Minister to Enforce Law Banning Bread Displays During Holiday," *Ynet News*, 28 March 2005.

47. Sachar, *A History of Israel*, 356.

48. For more detail on various aspects of the constitutional question, see Emanuel Rackman, *Israel's Emerging Constitution 1948-51* (New York: Columbia University Press, 1955), esp. chaps. 3, 8.

49. Mapai, a Socialist Zionist party established in 1930, merged with other left-wing parties to form the Israel Labor Party in 1968. Under the initial leadership of David Ben-Gurion, Mapai dominated Israeli politics from the early days of the Yishuv (the Jewish settlement in pre-state Palestine) to 1977, when the right-wing Likud party won a Knesset majority for the first time. Likud and Labor represent the two largest blocs of Israeli voters; since 1977 they have traded electoral victories and have shared power several times under National Unity Governments.

50. George Gross, "The Constitutional Question in Israel," in *Constitutionalism*, ed. Elazar, 61.

51. This is the Hebrew term for immigrants to Israel (*oleh* and *olah* are the masculine and feminine singular forms). *Olim* stems from *aliyah*, the term for immigration to Israel, which means "ascent."

52. Gross, "Constitutional Question," in *Constitutionalism*, ed. Elazar, 67-68.

53. Daphna Sharfman, *Living Without a Constitution: Civil Rights in Israel* (Armonk, N.Y.: M.E. Sharpe, 1993), 42-43.

54. Quoted in Sharfman, *Living Without a Constitution*, 44.

55. Sharfman, *Living Without a Constitution*, 43-45.

56. Gross, "Constitutional Question," in *Constitutionalism*, ed. Elazar, 64.

57. Sachar, *A History of Israel*, 357.

58. Gross, "Constitutional Question," in *Constitutionalism*, ed. Elazar, 58-59.

59. Dan Horowitz and Moshe Lissak, *Trouble in Utopia: The Overburdened Polity of Israel* (Albany: SUNY Press, 1989), 157.

60. Only select provisions of the Basic Laws are entrenched. Section 4 of Basic Law: The Knesset, which requires an absolute majority of Knesset members (61 MKs, rather than a simple majority of those voting) for any change to the nature of Knesset elections, is one example. Others found in the same Basic Law are Section 9a (a majority of eighty necessary to extend a Knesset's term), Section 34 (an absolute majority necessary to dissolve the Knesset), 44 and 45 (a majority of eighty necessary to permit a change or suspension of the Basic Law as a result of emergency regulations).

61. Basic Law: The Knesset (1958, most recently revised 1987) establishes national direct elections for parliament members and sets legislative procedure and rules; Basic Law: Israel Lands (1960) prohibits the transfer of ownership of Israeli land to private parties; Basic Law: The President of the State (1964) describes the powers and functions of the president and election by the Knesset; Basic Law: The Government (1968, most recently revised 2001) specifies executive powers and describes the role of cabinet ministers; The Basic Law: State Economy (1975, most recently revised 1983) provides for state taxes, a state budget, a national currency and inspection by the State Comptroller; Basic Law: Israel Defense Forces (1976) subordinates the army to the government's authority, provides for a Chief of General Staff and a duty of citizens to serve; Basic Law: Jerusalem—Capital of Israel (1980) includes protection of Holy Places for all religions and assigns special priority to the economic development of the city; Basic Law: The Judiciary (1984) provides for the state's secular court system including a eleven-member Supreme Court, establishes a Judges' Election Committee for judicial appointments and grants judicial independence; and Basic Law: The State Comptroller (1988) enumerates the election, role and duties of the state auditor.

62. Aharon Barak, "Mehaipcha hukatit: zechuiot yesod muganot" (A constitutional revolution: fundamental rights protected," *Mishpat U'Memshal* 1, no. 1 (August 1992) [Hebrew]: 9-35.

63. The 1992 Basic Laws accelerated a trend toward an expanding role for Israel's judiciary. See Shimon Shetreet, *Justice in Israel: A Study of the Israeli Judiciary* (Boston: Martinus Nijhoff Publishers, 1994), 449-96.

64. Dan Avnon, "Legislative Rights Talk in Israel: The Supreme Court as Interpreter of Israel's Jewish and Democratic Values," Paper prepared for delivery at the Second Workshop of Parliamentary Scholars and Parliamentarians, Oxfordshire, England, August 3-4, 1996, 1.

65. Daphne Barak-Erez, "From an Unwritten to a Written Constitution: The Israeli Challenge in American Perspective," *Columbia Human Rights Law Review* 26 (Winter 1995): 311.

66. Kol Ha'am v. Minister of Interior, H.C. 73/53, 87/53 (1953) 7 P.D. 871. An English translation of the case may be found in Itzhak Zamir and Allen Zysblat, eds, *Public Law in Israel* (Oxford: Oxford University Press, Clarendon Press, 1996), 55-73.

67. See Pnina Lahav, "Rights and Democracy: The Court's Performance," in Larry Diamond and Ehud Sprinzak, eds., *Israeli Democracy Under Stress* (Boulder: Lynne Rienner Publishers, 1993), 133-39. The Kol Ha'am decision drew heavily upon American jurisprudence and free speech doctrine. See Pnina Lahav, *Judgment in Jerusalem: Chief Justice Simon Agranat and the Zionist Century* (Los Angeles: University of California Press, 1997), 108.

68. Barak, "Constitutional Revolution," 11.

69. Barak, "Constitutional Revolution," 11.

70. Barak, "Constitutional Revolution," 12.

71. Barak, "Constitutional Revolution," 12.

72. Barak, "Constitutional Revolution," 13.

73. See <http://www.mfa.gov.il/mfa/go.asp?MFAH00hj0> (3 December 2005).

74. See <http://www.knesset.gov.il/laws/special/eng/basic3_eng.htm> (3 December 2005).

75. This power of judicial review was first formally declared by the Supreme Court in its decision in United Bank Mizrahi Bank Ltd. v. Migdal Assoc. Village, 49(4) P.D. 221 (1995). See Menachem Hofnung, "The Unintended Consequences of Unplanned Constitutional Reform: Constitutional Politics in Israel," *American Journal of Comparative Law* 44 (Fall 1996), 596.

76. An amendment added in 1994 further sets out the "basic principles" of the Basic Law: "Fundamental human rights in Israel are founded upon recognition of the value of the human being, the sanctity of human life, and the principle that all persons are free; these rights shall be upheld in the spirit of principles set forth in the Declaration of the Establishment of the State of Israel." See Israel Ministry of Foreign Affairs website.

77. Avnon, "Legislating Rights Talk," 7-8.

78 Avnon, "Legislating Rights Talk," 2-3.

79. Barak, "Constitutional Revolution," 34.

80. Barak, "Constitutional Revolution," 34.

81. Barak, "Constitutional Revolution," 34.

82. Barak, "Constitutional Revolution," 34.

83. Barak, "Constitutional Revolution," 30.

84. Barak, "Constitutional Revolution," 31.

85. Barak, "Constitutional Revolution," 31.

86. Barak, "Constitutional Revolution," 31.

87. Aharon Barak, "Basic Law: Freedom of Occupation," Address delivered on December 26, 1993 at a conference organized by The Israeli Center for Management, 14. Cited in Avnon, "Legislating Rights Talk in Israel," 14.

88. Barak, cited in Avnon, "Legislating Rights Talk in Israel," 16.

89. Barak, "Constitutional Revolution," 34.

90. Aharon Barak, *Judicial Discretion* (New Haven: Yale University Press, 1989), 207-209.

91. Menachem Elon, "Derech hok ba-huka" (The way of law in the constitution: the values of a Jewish and democratic state in light of the Basic Law: Human Dignity and Freedom), *Iyyunei Mishpat* (Tel Aviv University Law Review) 17 (1993) [Hebrew]: 659-688.

92. Elon, "The Way of Law in the Constitution," 687.

93. Elon, "The Way of Law in the Constitution," 687-88.

94. Elon, "The Way of Law in the Constitution," 688.

95. Quoted in Serge Schmemann, "Israeli High Court Under Attack by Religious Jews," *New York Times*, 28 August 1996, A3.

96. Schmemann, "Israeli High Court Under Attack," A3.

97. Schmemann, "Israeli High Court Under Attack," A3.

98. Barak, *Judicial Discretion*, 195-96.

99. Barak, *Judicial Discretion*, 197.

100. The committee maintains an extensive website with historical background, briefs on major constitutional issues and summaries of meetings and debates. See <http://www.cfisrael.org//home.html> (25 August 2005).

101. See <http://www.cfisrael.org//timetable.html> (25 August 2005).

102. See <http://www.cfisrael.org//why_constitution.html> (25 August 2005).

Chapter 3
Thirty-One Israelis

...Israel is woefully unprepared to confront the next fifty years conceptually...with regard to the Jewishness of the Jewish state....When I speak of 'Israel' or 'Israelis,' I refer to the community of opinion-molders in the state, including its governing establishments as well as its academic and intellectual leaders. (The ordinary folk are usually far wiser in such matters, although they are often misled by the former.)

—Daniel Elazar[1]

We now turn to what Israel's "ordinary folk," a diverse, well-informed, politically astute population, have to say about the Jewish and democratic aspects of their polity.[2] Since Chief Justice Aharon Barak declared the dawn of Israel's "constitutional revolution" in 1992, jurists, academics, philosophers, political scientists, yeshiva heads, rabbis (including Israel's Chief Rabbis), legislators and social commentators have taken up the question of what constitutes a "Jewish and democratic state," where the tensions lie in this formulation, and which adjective ought to take precedence in the case of contradiction.[3] But none of this scholarship investigates the views of average Israelis.

In the Spring of 2000, I spoke to thirty-one Israeli citizens about the relationship between religion and their state. In all, I interviewed twenty-six Jews (six Haredim, seven Religious Zionists, six secular, seven traditional) and five Arabs (three Muslim, one Christian and one Druze) in a study funded by the National Science Foundation.* I also found a host of illuminating sources as I traveled through the country: newspapers, party newsletters, graffiti, placards and pamphlets. I went to political rallies and the First Is-

---

* As an alternative to reading straight through the next three chapters, some readers may prefer to skim the respondents' biographical sketches below and flip back to them periodically when encountering their political views later in the book.

raeli Zionist World Congress, visited yeshivot, sat in on religious-secular dialogue groups, traveled in Jewish towns on the West Bank and Arab villages in the Galilee and attended Jewish religious services. I witnessed, sometimes as an outside observer, sometimes as a participant-observer, just how deeply religious Israel's politics are, and how politicized Israeli religion can be.

Aims and Methodology

The nearly one thousand pages of transcripts generated by the interviews serve as primary texts for investigating Israel's wrenching questions about religion and liberalism. In the chapters to come, I try to take the comments in each interview seriously. I pay close attention to the arguments made on behalf of various positions, evaluate them for both internal consistency and coherence with the views of other subjects, and mine them for insights regarding liberalism's commitments vis-à-vis religion. In line with my conclusions from chapter 1, I treat the arguments presented by my subjects as potentially "public reasons" in Rawls's sense—reasons that fellow Israelis may be expected to reasonably accept, even if they stem from religious considerations. But not every argument considered here qualifies as a public reason, and I have no illusions that all of my subjects will feel equally "taken seriously" after reading my conclusions in later chapters. I do hope, however, that they will find their views accurately represented and fairly analyzed even if they disagree with my arguments.

Israel is, of course, full of people—over six million citizens in 2000—and I couldn't attempt to "read" them all. Nor did I seek to generate statistically significant data about their views. I sought, instead, to find a diversity of ideas, to leave no major perspective out of the study, and to select individuals who were thoughtful enough (and, in most cases, educated enough) to reflect critically on Israel's *nomoi*. So although I sketch below certain basic data about my subjects (their ages, hometowns, professions, genders, among other factors), I provide these bits of information only as background, to help the reader get to know each subject holistically and to have a sense of the pool collectively. I do not present them as an implicit argument that the sample is representative of Israeli society as a whole.

Bearing the particular aims of this project in mind, four principles guided my selection of subjects. First, I sought individuals whose thoughts bore a significant resemblance to those of at least a portion of one of the five groups (Haredim, Religious Zionists, traditional Jews, secular Jews and Arabs). In other words, I did not, with one or two possible exceptions, interview those who would be regarded as untenable *from the point of view of most members of that group.* Note that this principle did not exclude individuals who may be characterized as extreme—or even beyond the pale—by members of *other* groups (an ultra-Orthodox man living in Jerusalem's pious Mea Shearim neighborhood, say, may be typical of a portion of his religious grouping even though viewed by a secular or Reform Jew as on the fringes of society). The second principle for selection was to locate, where plausible and relevant, heterogeneity in views. Where there were important differences of opinion inside the five groups I mentioned (and not merely a handful who opposed the general view), I looked for individuals who represented those opposing camps. I was particularly interested in finding some observant Jewish subjects—in the Haredi and Religious Zionist sectors—whose political perspectives challenged those of the standard bearers. This strategy admittedly skews the sample, but it carries the benefit of introducing lesser-heard and potentially fresh and interesting views into the mix that may prove helpful in the project of political theory that frames these interviews. Third, and less crucially, I sought a reasonable geographic mix, a representation of different ethnic groups, genders, ages and socio-economic classes. Subject diversity along these lines was a subordinate aim; diversity of religious perspective and views based on those perspectives was much more important. When seeking appropriate and representative subjects in a sector of the population that would be difficult for me to penetrate, for instance, I compromised on gender diversity in favor of authenticity of ideas for that group.[4] So the first and second principles trumped the third, where a conflict was unavoidable. Finally, my fourth guideline was to find articulate, generally well-educated individuals with some perspective on the questions I wanted to ask, who were willing to spend two to three hours with me speaking candidly about their religious and political views.

To meet this goal, I employed a combination of availability sampling (also called convenience sampling), purposive sampling and snowball sampling, rather than a version of probability sampling.[5] In other words, I used subjects who were readily available to me, or who were referred to me by acquaintances; chose them on the basis of how useful they would be for my study; and requested referrals from subjects for other potential subjects they knew who might also serve as good respondents. I took this course for two reasons. First, I sought subjects who came from particular religious groupings to discuss their views on Israel's religion-state arrangement primarily in order to help me think through the logic and structure of Israelis' arguments on these matters, not to achieve quantitative precision in specifying what percentage of which segments of the population believe what. Second, a number of surveys querying Israelis' attitudes on religion-state matters have been conducted previously. My project draws on the results of those studies, but seeks to delve more deeply into citizens' reasoning processes, their thinking behind their positions, their stories, their experiences, and their attitudes toward other groups in Israeli society. A small, focused group of subjects was the obvious choice over a large, randomized pool.

As mentioned above, I sought out representatives from two groups—Haredim and Religious Zionists—in greater proportion than their representation in Israeli society.[6] I suspected at the outset, and my suspicions were confirmed, that the greatest diversity of opinion is to be found in these circles, and that the ideas held by these deeply religious Jews are worthy of particular attention, since they pose the challenge to typical theories of liberalism with particular poignancy.[7]

The Respondents: An Overview

To set my subjects' political views in the context of their daily lives and levels of religious observance, this section sketches each respondent's personal background, stance toward religion and attitudes toward other groups in Israeli society. I introduce each subject here one by one in order to reveal from the outset the personalities and individual lives that lie behind the political views analyzed later in the chapter. These personal details are important both for evaluating the range of political opinions expressed and for learning something about the religious attitudes that motivate them.[8]

The interviews were semi-structured, in-depth conversations that lasted between one and three hours; the average length was just under two hours. I used a different set of questions for Jewish subjects and Arab subjects, though the instruments overlapped significantly. (See Appendix.) I asked most questions of most subjects, but I left some out and added others as each interview developed. To try to get more of a sense of their personal and family lives, I met most of the subjects (seventeen) in their homes. Other interviews took place in the respondent's place of work (eight) or in public areas (in a park or restaurant). Twenty-one of the interviews were conducted in Hebrew, ten in English.[9]

I guaranteed confidentiality and anonymity to twenty-eight of the subjects introduced below, although most said they didn't mind if their names were used. These subjects are identified below with aliases (first names only). The remaining three subjects, who lead organizations in Jerusalem, are Jonathan Rosenblum (Haredi), Rabbi Uri Regev (traditional) and Rabbi Mickey Rosen (Religious Zionist). I present these subjects' names—with their permission—in order to allow a fuller discussion of their professional lives and the institutions they represent. I tape-recorded each interview, hired an Israeli transcriber to transcribe the Hebrew interviews, and transcribed the English interviews myself. I did not fully translate the Hebrew interviews into English. Instead, I worked from the original Hebrew transcripts and translated selections as necessary for inclusion in the text. All of the quotes appearing below that come from the Hebrew interviews are my translations.

First, a snapshot of the entire pool. I interviewed ten women and twenty-one men between the ages of nineteen and fifty-nine; their median age was thirty-three and their average age was thirty seven Of the twenty-six Jews, fourteen come from Jerusalem, two from Jerusalem suburbs on the West Bank, four live in Ra'anana (a northern suburb of Tel Aviv), and one each lives in Tel Aviv, Bat Yam (south of Tel Aviv), Beit Shemesh (between Jerusalem and Tel Aviv), Haifa (on the northern Mediterranean coast) and Rehovot (south of Tel Aviv and inland); one lives on a kibbutz in the north. The five Arab subjects come from five different places: Beit Hanina in Jerusalem, Qualansuwa, Umm Al-Fahm, Mrar, and Ilabun. Twenty-one of the twenty-six Jewish subjects are Ashkenazi Jews with roots in Europe or the West; four (two Religious Zionist, one Haredi and one traditional) are Mizrahim (one immigrated from Tunis, while the other three are of Moroccan and/or Yemenite origin); and one is Ethiopian. Eighteen of the subjects (including all five Arabs) were born in Israel. The remaining thirteen are originally from the United States (six), the former Soviet Union (two), England (one), South Africa (one) and Tunis (one). With one exception, all of the secular, traditional, Religious Zionist and Arab respondents hold advanced degrees (with a B.A. or higher), are working toward an advanced degree, or plan to embark on university study within a year. Of the Haredi Jews, one holds a B.A. and a law degree; the other five do not, concentrating their studies in *yeshivot* or other institutions offering exclusively religious education.

Secular Jews

I interviewed six Jewish Israelis who define themselves as secular, five women and one man ranging in age from twenty-four to fifty-three. Included in the sample are two Russian-born women (one recent immigrant, one who came to Israel as a toddler), three Sabras (native-born Israelis) and one Ethiopian immigrant. The two youngest subjects are finishing studies in preparation for entering university, while the other four all hold advanced degrees. One lives in Bat Yam (a town south of Tel Aviv on the Mediterranean coast), one in Ma'ale Adumim (the first and largest Israeli settlement on the West Bank), one on a kibbutz; three live in Jerusalem. Five of these six interviews were conducted in Hebrew; the exception is the interview with Shulamit, whose English is equivalent to that of a native speaker from her several years working in the United States. Here is an overview of each subject in this group:

Since **Mina**, forty-three, made aliya from Russia with her mother and daughter in 1992, she has "never regretted it, not for a second." She is divorced, lives with a partner in Bat Yam, and has a grown daughter who is married with a child. Mina's employment is in a prominent museum at Tel Aviv University, handling all issues having to do with new immigrants, "primarily Russian speakers but also new immigrants from other countries," and she serves as a tour guide for Russian groups. Mina earned a degree in pedagogy in Moscow, concentrating in general world history, and is a certified history teacher. Our interview takes place in the busy, disheveled office she shares with three or four co-workers. Speaking quickly in thickly accented but fluent Hebrew, Mina says that religion is "important" to her, but that she "does not observe the tradition." Instead, she defines her Judaism as "to feel and to live in a framework." "On Shabbat I always work because I am a tour guide. Lately, though, I have been trying to celebrate the holidays, Passover and others...so that the family would be together, be united, be in a common framework." Mina grew up in a "pretty highly assimilated" family in Russia that nevertheless always held a Passover Seder and spoke Yiddish inside the house. They showed respect to her grandparents, whom she says were "very religious, kept the commandments, and never once touched pork." As a result, Mina feels a connection with Israel's Haredi population, whom she says her grandparents resembled.

At fifty-three, **Shulamit** is a gregarious, carefully coiffed single woman, born to Israeli *halutzim* (pioneers) the year before the state was founded. "For me," she says, "to be Jewish is to live in a Jewish, Zionistic state. And that's about it." Although she does not keep the commandments ("I like shrimp, what can I do?") and avoids synagogue as much as possible, attending only for friends' weddings and Bar Mitzvahs, Shulamit always spends holidays with her parents on a kibbutz near Netanya and she "keeps" Yom Kippur in her own style ("I rarely fast, but I stay at home and don't drive the car"). Shulamit earned a B.A. in English and theater studies, did master's work in comparative religion and got an M.B.A. in executive leadership at the Hebrew University. Working in a series of jobs at her alma mater, Shulamit spent two years in New York directing the overseas students' admissions office. She now works as the director of a preparatory program on Jerusalem's Mount Scopus campus. Having recently expanded and renovated her flat, transforming it into a veritable museum bursting with ornate décor and faux antique furniture, Shulamit mocks her "Shasnikim" (Mizrahi ultra-Orthodox) neighbors who have "perhaps twelve kids" living in two bedrooms. She compares the Shas spiritual leader, Rabbi Ovadia Yosef, to the late Ayatollah Khomeni of Iran. Reflecting on the visit Pope John Paul II made to Israel in March 2000, Shulamit remarks, "We were hoping that by mistake they would take Ovadiah back and leave the Pope here!"

Naomi, a focused, energetic twenty-four year-old who lives on the secular Kibbutz Gesher on the northern Mediterranean coast, wants to enter university to study medicine or veterinary sciences. After serving her required two years in the army, at twenty-one she traveled for six months in South America, then spent another few months in the United States and Europe. For Naomi, as for Shulamit, "to live as a Jew in Israel is simply to live in the Land of Israel." Naomi describes herself as "totally Jewish, but for me Judaism is different from the Judaism of a religious person." She says that she, her Sabra mother and father of Peruvian origin "love being Jewish" and celebrate all the holidays "in the manner we choose, and not in the manner religious people demand." She regards such religious observances as wearing *kippot*, not eating pork and marrying through the rabbinate as "not a duty" and "irrelevant." Naomi feels no connection with Haredim; little with Religious Zionists; has only scant contact with Israeli Arabs, although she resents them for not serving in the army or performing national service; and knows no Reform or Conservative Jews in Israel. She has a very positive view of American Reform Judaism, however, as a result of her work as a counselor at a Reform camp in Georgia. She says she will not return to her kibbutz after university studies, preferring the less collectivist atmosphere of a coastal moshav.

Another young Israeli, **Yoram**, came to Israel with his family from Ethiopia in 1984. At age eight, he was one of 6,500 Beta Israel (Ethiopian Jews) who were airlifted to Israel in a rescue operation known as "Operation Moses." ("Operation Solomon" brought fourteen thousand more in 1990.) At twenty-four, proud of his native Israeli accent and hesitant to talk about his Ethiopian roots, Yoram says that Judaism is important to him as a matter of "tradition and background" and helps to "unify and consolidate" the Jewish people. He describes his religious upbringing as "traditional" (his parents keep kosher and Shabbat). Since high school and the army, however, he has become non-observant. Yoram speaks advanced English with little accent (although the interview was conducted in Hebrew). He wants to study law in university next year. Like the other secular subjects, Yoram associates mainly with other secular Jewish Israelis. He has no contact with Israeli Haredim, few Religious Zionist friends and knows nothing of the Reform and Conservative movements. He has some Arab friends, he says, but none that he would ever go out for the evening with.

Tanya, fifty, was born in Lithuania, moved to Poland when she was six, and immigrated to Israel with her parents and five brothers and sisters in 1958. Tanya's mother was the sole Holocaust survivor in her family; her father, a Shomer Ha'tzair (Zionist youth movement) trainee, fought in the Red Army and was a captain in the Russian army during World War II. Since coming to Israel, Tanya has worked her way from the top of the country (Naharia), down the northern coast (Kiryat Haim and Haifa), down further and across to the center of the country (Modi'in), to Jerusalem. Today, a single mother, Tanya lives in Jerusalem's fashionable, secular Greek Colony neighborhood, works as a registrar at the Hebrew University, and raises her twelve year-old daughter. In her office are half a dozen photographs of her daughter, shots of Pope John Paul II, a drawing of doves and a set of Russian dolls. With a B.A. in Russian studies and contemporary Jewish thought, Tanya defines her Judaism as "only historical, not religious in any way." Like her parents but unlike her grandparents, who were "Orthodox religious," Tanya's Judaism centers upon "language, a common fate and a common history." All religion, in Tanya's eyes, from Catholicism to Protestantism to Islam to Judaism, is "the mother of sin," producing "war, confrontations between people, hate, jealousy, inflexibility." And although she celebrates certain holidays, such as Passover, she tries to be out of the country for Rosh Hashana and Yom Kippur. "I am a *Haredi* (ultra-Orthodox) secular woman!"

Another single leftist secular woman at fifty-one, with a B.A. in educational counseling and philosophy, **Ronit** has a hard time describing her Judaism. "It's difficult to say, because it isn't something that occupies me. I was born Jewish, but I don't feel any different from non-Jews. I don't feel that I'm any better than non-Jews." Ronit's immediate family is purely secular, but she "strives not to travel abroad on Rosh Hashana or on Passover Eve" because her mother prefers to have the children at home for the holidays. Her father's father's uncle and offspring constitute "almost an entire tribe living in Mea Shearim" with whom the secular side of the family has no contact. In contrast to each of the other twenty-five Jewish subjects, who associate only marginally with non-Jews, Ronit says that "many of my closest friends are not Jewish." Ronit (who votes Hadash, an Arab-Jewish party to the left of Meretz) has few kind words for mainstream Israeli secularism, the condescending "Telavivis" who strut on Tel Aviv's Sheinkin Street as if to say, " 'We are progressive, we know better and the light is with us; the other side represents the forces of darkness.' Let's just say that's not the way to build a state. That will only cause an explosion." In contrast, Ronit has "nothing against Haredim," aside from their "lack of individualism," and she finds admirable their willingness to help one another. As for Religious Zionist Jews, Ronit admits: "I can't stand them. That's my racism." During our interview in her tastefully cluttered, French-, Israeli-, Native American-, Arab- and Turkish-themed home—featuring museum posters, throw pillows, Persian rugs, *hamsas* and a large pot full of bulbs of garlic near the tiny TV set—the phone rings. "That was one of my very best friends, from Bethlehem. I feel a common language with her more than with many Jewish American women, for example." Almost whispering with the tape recorder turned off, Ronit adds that she has a serious Israeli Arab boyfriend, but she refuses to give details or even tell me where he lives. The relationship is a closely guarded secret in both her family and his.

Haredim (Ultra-Orthodox Jews)

Because this group of Israeli Jews generally lives in isolation from non-Haredi communities, and because they commonly view secular culture and outsiders with various degrees of suspicion, this was by far the most challenging community for me to penetrate. My first attempt to recruit a Haredi subject followed a recommendation from Jeff Seidel, a well-connected *ba'al teshuva* (born-again ultra-Orthodox) man who moved from Chicago to Jerusalem's Old City in the 1980s and arranges Shabbat meals and Jewish learning for Jewish students from abroad. Jeff suggested I call the patriarch of one of his host families, a man affiliated with the small, extremist Neturei Karta group in Jerusalem's Mea She'arim neighborhood. "He may talk to you," Jeff told me, "and he may not." When I phoned **Moshe**, my request was immediately but politely declined. As an outsider, he told me, my own beliefs and experiences would "twist the truth and reality." But that was not the end of the phone call. Moshe, after inquiring into my own religious practice, offered an untempered critique of my project and career path:

> Pardon me for saying it, but I do not see any value in your project. It's worthless. It's all politics. Politics? Don't get involved in politics! The rabbis say that "politic" is the same as "Amalek" in *gemmatriah* [Jewish numerology]. A frum yid [religious Jew] doesn't *want* to be in politics. That's for the Greeks. It's galus [exile]. It's what the goyim do. Forget your Ph.D. Sit in the Torah world— that's what you should do—sink yourself into Torah. The university world is all fake, it's all *sheker* [lies], it's all about power and money. It's all a fake. Wake up and get out of that! Take your Ph.D., put it in the fire and start to live.

And upon finding out that I am married, in my late twenties, and have no children, he offered a few more words:

> You are a *murderer!!* Any rabbi would say...you're not allowed to use contraceptives except in very specific circumstances. But you are a murderer! A murderer! Get into Torah and get into yiddishkeit!

Over the forty-five minutes Moshe had me on the phone, I learned that he had become ultra-Orthodox thirty years earlier (after completing a degree in philosophy and English literature at the University of Manitoba) and now proudly has eleven children and thirty-five grandchildren. And after further impassioned entreaty to leave academia, give up my murderous lifestyle and delve into yeshiva study, I declined his offers to come to his home for Shabbat dinner and a Passover seder. Sounding uncannily like Cephalus in Book One of Plato's *Republic*, who chooses piety over philosophy when his notions of justice come under scrutiny, [10] Moshe left me with the following words:

> Well, you got your interview after all. This is what it is like talking to a Haredi. The title of the interview can be, "Politic is the same Gematria as Amalek." Now I'm sorry I must go. I have to go off for afternoon prayers. Everything good for you, may you be successful and happy and blessed. Be in touch, Steven.

He gave me an interview, indeed, one that I kept in mind when recruiting and talking to Haredi Jews over the remainder of my research trip. I knew that the type of Haredi who was likely to agree to be interviewed would probably be on the milder side of the spectrum, less extreme politically (if not necessarily religiously) than Moshe, for whom engagement in politics is equivalent to cavorting with Amalek, the eternal enemy of the Jews.

My second call to a potential Haredi subject met with greater success. **Yehuda** granted the interview, he told me later, only because I prefaced my request by telling him that Gavriel, his wife's second cousin (and my wife's great uncle), had suggested I call. It didn't matter that he rarely saw this common in-law, or that the in-law lived several worlds away in Givatayim, an upscale Tel Aviv suburb and hub of Israeli secularism. As Yehuda put it, "Since Gavriel sent you, I felt obligated to do it. You tell him that." As Gavriel, who is in his mid-seventies, put it, "They still have hope that I will become Orthodox!" Walking down the narrow dusty street to the interview, a troika of Haredi girls, maybe eleven or twelve years of age, glance at me and snicker. I had put on long pants and shirt for the interview, despite the ninety-five-degree heat, and donned a knit *kippa*, but I stand out in this Haredi enclave as clearly as Yehuda would stand out in Givatayim.

At forty-five, Yehuda's long white beard adds at least fifteen years to his appearance. He dresses in black (hat, shoes, pants, belt) and white (his shirt) and wears the thickest glasses I have ever seen, making his eyes appear like pinpricks through the lenses. He and his family live in a small, sparkling clean, extremely modest apartment deep in Jerusalem's Beit Yisrael neighborhood. The front living room/kitchen where we sit is free of all decoration—except for a certificate proving his son's graduation from yeshiva—and lined, floor to ceiling, on all walls, with the imposing bindings of *sifrei kodesh* (Jewish holy books). Yehuda tells me I was lucky to catch him this afternoon, since he is on Passover break from his teaching at a local Talmud Torah, a school for boys.

A Jerusalemite since birth, Yehuda describes his life in few words: "I learn and I teach." And his Judaism? "Original Judaism, authentic Judaism, true Judaism. With no distortions, nothing fake, no cosmetics. Just the original Judaism that we received from our teacher Moses, from Mount Sinai."

How important is Judaism to Yehuda? "Extremely. Like life itself. Like life itself." Yehuda and his wife have twelve children, age one to age twenty-five. "We were educated on the good path and on the basis of the Shulhan Aruch, and that's how we educate our children. Every generation bequeaths the heritage to the next generation. That is how we teach and wait for the Messiah. We feel ourselves still in exile and we await the Messiah, he should come quickly." Yehuda's political views he admits are "extreme," even within ultra-Orthodoxy, but he maintains that they are demanded by Judaism. He regards Religious Zionists as *treif* (non-kosher); they may be "observers of the tradition," but they have an "invalid perspective [*hashkafa pesula*]." Yehuda does not "hate" secular Jews but "pities" them and "prays they will return in repentance." In contrast, he rejects Reform and Conservative Judaism as "distortions" and "a tragedy to the people of Israel" similar to the Holocaust. "A secular Jew *knows* he isn't behaving according to the Jewish religion. The Reform Jews *think* that they are Jews. They have a rabbi. They have a synagogue. But they don't keep the Torah. They come to synagogue on Shabbat in their cars!"

Oren, at twenty-four, is the youngest of my six Haredi subjects and the only one who is unmarried. I met him, a yeshiva student since age fourteen, at a secular-religious dialogue group that meets biweekly at Gesher, an organization designed to bridge gaps between Israel's rifted Jewry.[11] When I asked him for an interview, he warned me he was an atypical Haredi; in the interview itself, he repeated that caveat and called himself "pretty liberal— for a Haredi." Unbearded, with no black hat or coat but wearing a pressed white shirt and elegant black dress slacks, socks and shoes, exposed *tzizit* (fringes) and a medium-sized black felt *kippa*, Oren says he "strives to observe all the *mizvot* [commandments]," and "of course" dons *tefillin* (prayer phylacteries), keeps Shabbat and *kashrut*, "but in practice it isn't easy." The cell phone attached at his belt is a sign of his relatively welcoming approach to modernity, and to an "openness" that does not characterize Yehuda's world view. Oren describes himself as the most religious of six children, coming from a family that straddles Haredism and Religious Zionism. On one hand, Oren studied in state national-religious schools before entering yeshiva; his father served in the army; and the home in which he grew up embraced "diverse forms of literature" in addition to Jewish holy texts, entertained "any topic of conversation" at their Jerusalem dinner table and fits in the "*kippa seruga*" category—that of knit head-coverings usually associated with Religious Zionists—rather than the black *kippot* and black hats of the Haredim. On the other hand, his parents both studied in a "more Haredi" educational framework and his family both rejects the idea of the holiness of the greater land of Israel and eschews National Religious Party demonstrations against land transfers. Oren plans a career in real estate, figures that he will, "at some stage" serve in the Israeli army after he leaves yeshiva, and embraces opportunities like the Gesher dialogue group because "there is no reason that people should hate each other" and because "many secular people identify Judaism with politics, and that's a problem." In his opinion, Religious Zionism is too busy "sanctifying" things such as the land, the state, the national anthem; secular culture is impoverished; and Conservative Judaism may serve a role outside of Israel, but in Israel it is otiose, and Reformism should not be called "Judaism."

Nosson, another Haredi I met at the Gesher group, claims that all the other "Haredim" at the discussion "are not true Haredim." With a very long brown beard, long black coat and a black hat, and with his particularly biting comments for the secular Jews at the dialogue table, Nosson both looks and sounds like a Haredi who's worth his salt. Born in Israel and raised in the United States by modern Orthodox parents (his father was raised in an orphanage; his mother was a Holocaust survivor) from age six to seventeen, Nosson returned to Israel, where he studied in yeshivot in Bnei Brak—Israel's only exclusively Haredi town, near Tel Aviv—and Jerusalem. Today, Nosson (that's the Yiddish-inspired Ashkenazi pronunciation of his pseudonym—it would be "Natan" in modern Hebrew) studies in yeshiva and works part-time as a *mekarev*, one who tries to bring non-observant Jews closer to traditional Judaism. Nosson is only thirty-two, but comes across as quite a bit older. He is married to a native Israeli woman, has four children (he betrays a hint of regret at this modest number, given his thirteen-year marriage), and lives in the Jerusalem suburb of Givat Ze'ev, just across the 1967 border into Samarian desert on the West Bank—only a few minutes' drive from the Palestinian city of Ramalla. Yiddish, not Hebrew, is spoken in the home. Nosson's parents supplement his living in rather grand style: Their apartment is large and attractive, with a modern kitchen and a huge, expensively furnished dining room featuring gads of silver Judaica. Photographs of his Hasidic grandparents and great-grandfather hang in the entranceway. For Nosson, being Jewish is "to be a member of the chosen people," a status he clarifies at great length as "not racist, not haughty," but based on "a spiritual difference" that gives Jews "more potential." Because God holds Jews to "much higher standards than the rest of humanity...we must strive to be a light unto the nations [or *lagoyim*]." Truth is absolute for Nosson: "Extremism is a good thing when it comes to truth. With values you do not and cannot compromise." Because he lives over the Green Line, he is technically a settler, but Nosson believes that most Religious Zionists do not sufficiently observe religious law and err in mixing with the secular world. He regards secular Jews as basically "empty" and hostile (and aggressively so in his neighborhood), and he opposes Reform and Conservative Judaism as "forgeries."

Yeshayahu, also raised in the United States for part of his childhood, presents a much more accommodating tone than does Nosson. One of thirteen children of a "very Chassidic" family (his father is a "very big important rabbi") from Baltimore, Yeshayahu "didn't so much love the framework in the United States" and moved to Israel by himself when he was fourteen. Standing alone among my Haredi subjects—and admitting that Zionism "is something usually not found in Haredi families"—Yeshayahu expresses his and his family's "love, tons and tons of love for the Land of Israel and the State of Israel." (When he first visited Israel at age seven, he says, "I got off the airplane and I kissed the ground.") The winding religious path that followed his teenage *aliya* (immigration to Israel) took Yeshayahu from yeshiva to yeshiva (in the Har Nof neighborhood of Jerusalem, to Petah Tikva, to Rehovot); led him for two years away from traditional Judaism to "consider everything" ("I flirted with mysticism, philosophy, Buddhism, all sorts of beliefs....the Koran"); and circled back to ultra-Orthodoxy. Today, at twenty-five, Yeshayahu is married, has a little girl, and is the rabbi of a synagogue in Jerusalem's Rehavia neighborhood, "Ahdut Yisrael" (The Unity of Israel), which embraces Orthodoxy with a kind of Jewish universalist spin. "Here we strive to create an environment where there are no differences between Ashkenazim and Sephardim, Yemenite, American, Israeli, French. The congregation is very diverse: some are Haredim and some are not even religious. We unite everyone." Judaism for Yeshayahu? "A lot of love and a lot of spirit, that's my Judaism. But I don't sacrifice anything. When it comes to a matter of *halacha* [Jewish law], I do not compromise." Like Nosson, Yeshayahu seeks to bring Jews closer to what he perceives as the true Judaism. But the strategy is different: "Judaism is not by coercion. The moment you coerce someone, he doesn't hear and Judaism becomes dirty. Judaism is accepted much more readily via the ways of pleasantness [*darchei noam*]." Accordingly, Yeshayahu thinks the struggle against Reform and Conservative Jews is "uncalled for" since it only pushes them away from Judaism.

Nehama, the sole woman I was able to interview from the Haredi sector, is a mother of three, thirty-three years old, and of Yemenite descent. Nehama's upbringing was traditional (*masorti*)—her family always kept Shabbat and kashrut, went to synagogue, and celebrated the holidays—but she gradually became more religious and, by age twenty, was no longer eating off her parents' dishes. Her Haredi life involves "a stricter observance of commandments, greater knowledge, more study" and changes in "dress, education, values and outlook." Our discussion takes place on the patio of the house her grandfather built upon arriving in Israel from Yemen in the 1920s, a structure that is home to her family (on the main floor), her parents (in the upstairs apartment), her brother (across the way on the first floor), and her husband's office in the basement. The quarters are tight, but the family is too. Every Friday evening everyone eats together upstairs, in the parents' apartment. But Nehama and her husband, whose observance of the dietary laws is much stricter than her parents', cook their own food in their tiny downstairs kitchen, lug up their own plates, and make their own kid-dush over the Sabbath wine. Nehama has nothing positive to say about Ar-abs, "pities" secular Jews for their lack of education, and believes that Reli-gious Zionists err in making the state part of their religion.

When **Jonathan Rosenblum** (his real name) came to Israel on his hon-eymoon after earning his B.A. from the University of Chicago and his law degree from Yale, he planned to study for a summer before beginning rab-binical school at the Jewish Theological Seminary in New York. His plans quickly changed. The Conservative Jew, who had "never met someone wear-ing a kippa until [he] was twenty-eight" and whose parents always told him "the most important thing was being Jewish," ended up in Ohr Sameah ("The Happy Light")—a Haredi yeshiva whose aim is to attract non-Orthodox Jews and cultivate ba'alei teshuva. Feeling comfortable there, he stayed and learned, abandoned plans to study Conservative rabbinics, and established a home in Har Nof, an Anglo-dominated black-hat neighbor-hood in western Jerusalem. (As it happens, four of his brothers also came to Israel and became ultra-Orthodox.) On the wall in Jonathan's office—he writes a weekly column for the *Jerusalem Post*, contributes to other Jewish publications and runs Am Ehad, an advocacy organization for Haredim—hangs a crowded family photograph (featuring eight kids), impressionistic paintings of Mea She'arim and a framed certificate of a Yale Moot Court of Appeals prize signed by, among two other judges, Thurgood Marshall. On his desk a new Palm Pilot rests atop Tractate Nidda of the Babylonian Tal-mud. With a big black velvet *kippa*, and a full, but not long, beard, Jonathan tells me of the elite *heder* (day school) that his seven boys attended. Although he laments that his "kids at thirteen stopped any secular education," and won't reach Phi Beta Kappa (or even, most likely, go to college) he "knows the cost of giving them some other kind of education." Religious Zionist thought leads to "all kind of silliness," and its educational system leads most youth away from observance. But Zionism in any form is preferable to post-Zionist secularism, in Jonathan's mind, because it is based on the "idea of life as having a purpose." "The hardest thing is to live with people who don't see life as ultimately purposeful."

Religious Zionist Jews

Of the seven Israelis I interviewed who described themselves as Reli-gious Zionists (or, to translate the more commonly used Hebrew term, "na-tional religious" Jews), five were born outside of Israel. Three made *aliya* from the United States (two as young children, one as an adult), while one came from Tunis and one from England. Three of the interviews (those with the English immigrant and two of the Americans) were conducted in English, the other four in Hebrew. Three subjects live in Jerusalem, and one apiece lives in Tel Aviv, Ra'anana, Beit Shemesh and Rehovot. None of the subjects are settlers currently living on the West Bank, and only one is a woman.

Richard and his family came to Israel in 1983 in order "to live a normal Jewish life." Seeking an environment in which "the calendar is a Jewish calendar, the society is a Jewish society, the problems are Jewish problems, and the future is a Jewish future," and which would allow his family of six to "fulfill our traditions and observances in an efficient way," Richard left Toronto, where he was a Conservative rabbi, and moved to Jerusalem. "I try to live the traditional Jewish life," he says, and he defines himself as "Orthoprax—Orthodox in observance, not necessarily in theology." So although he wears a knit kippa and keeps the commandments, he "accepts the idea of biblical criticism and the development of Jewish law and custom." His pleasant home in an outlying Jerusalem neighborhood contains the ingredients of a modern, Religious Zionist family. In the living room, a wall of Jewish books (including a full set of the Babylonian Talmud), silver candlesticks, Jewish art and tzedakah boxes co-exist with sheet music from "Camelot" and "Cabaret" by the piano, "Thelma and Louise," "Platoon" and three dozen more videos next to the TV, and Art Nouveau books on the coffee table. Atop the TV sits a scroll that keeps track of the Omer, so they won't miss a day.[12] Three large Israeli flags lie draped over the railing of their porch, and a "The People are With the Golan" sign[13] graces their refrigerator. Richard looks boyish at fifty-five in his button-down shirt and khaki pants. In his work as a writer in Jewish fields, he has "considerable" contact with Haredim and respects their commitment to Jewish observance, large families and "care for the sick and innocent"—"without which the country would be in very serious trouble"—but their "neglect of the total needs of the state, [lack of] recognition of the state, and exploitation of state funds bother" him. Richard admires "the ultra-nationalists' tenacity to live anywhere and everywhere in this country" but believes "they have not effectively communicated their message to the country as a whole." He generally gets along with secular Jews, noting that at times they are "intolerant or abusive to the religious population"; wishes that Reform and Conservative rabbis would stop encouraging couples to get married abroad; and thinks that Arabs "are not bad."

Avi was also born in the United States (in Teaneck, New Jersey), but he came to live in Israel with his parents and two sisters when he was four and "feels like a Sabra." (Another sister was born in Israel.) Raised in Rehovot, an immigrant-heavy city south of Tel Aviv, Avi attended a state-religious elementary school, a B'nei Akiva (Religious Zionist youth movement) yeshiva and a military boarding school. Full of questions and doubts about religion at 18, he spent a year studying in a yeshiva in the West Bank settlement of

Eli, where he confirmed his Orthodoxy before entering the army. Then he served in the Israeli Defense Forces as an officer in an elite fighting unit (he asked me to turn off the tape recorder before telling me the name) for 4 ½ years, eighteen months longer than required. Avi says that his perspective on Judaism stems from his family's: "It is an inseparable part of my life. I live it on a daily basis." Now, at twenty-five, Avi is preparing to enter university and hoping to be accepted into a B.A. program in medicine. Avi's clean-shaven face, T-shirt, jeans, sandals and shaggy hair are indistinguishable from those of his secular classmates. Only his blue knit *kippa* marks him as religious. Avi has "many very good secular friends." He thinks, however, that secularism has contributed to a loss of Jewish culture and has made the Jewish nation "more and more like the other peoples of the world." Avi has many complaints about Haredim, ranging from their failure to perform army service to disapproval of their perspective on Judaism; and he criticizes those "fanatics" within Religious Zionist ranks—"people like Yigal Amir or Baruch Goldstein"[14]—who "simply took something [from Judaism] and twisted it." It bothers Avi that Reform rabbis "agreed to permit homosexual marriages"; in his view, these new streams of Judaism "have taken the *halacha* and the religion and distorted it into another religion." Avi says he has Arab and Druze friends, but demands that Arab citizens of Israel must be "genuine" and offer "support" to the state.

Zvi, a small, very bright and inspired twenty-four year-old from Tel Aviv, has an interesting religious history. Hanging on the wall of his room is a tapestry from his travels in India as well as photos of Rabbi Schneerson (the late Lubavitcher rebbe) and the centenarian guru of the Shas party, Rabbi Yitzchak Kaduri. Coming from a "traditional-religious" family that "watched television after making Friday night kiddush"[15] (his father's parents came from Aden, a former British colony that became part of Yemen in 1967, and his mother immigrated from Morocco when she was five), Zvi began to veer away from religion ("*hazar be'sheala*") at thirteen when he was away from home at a "completely secular" boarding school for the gifted. After having a "crisis in faith in God" in twelfth grade, he nevertheless heeded his parents' request to lay tefillin as a soldier in the occupied territories. Zvi then gradually became more and more religious. Today he calls himself "Mizrahi Orthodox religious nationalist," avoiding the adjective "Zionist" because of its secular connotations. An avid dancer, it still "pains" him to give up mixed dancing at the discotheques, but "when you compromise on something, you gain something else." The same principle applies more widely for Zvi: "that's my micro-perspective, but often it holds in the macro too...in the state of Israel there is often conflict between two" competing goals. Zvi "dreams" of practicing medicine, where he can be "God's messenger [*shaliah*]" in helping to heal the sick. He quotes to me the famous

Talmudic principle: "saving one soul of Israel is like saving the entire world."

Another young Religious Zionist, **Yoel**, moved from Queens, New York to Israel with his parents when he was six. The oldest of eight children, Yoel is twenty-three, married with a young child, and studying accounting and economics at Bar Ilan University while working in an accounting firm. He lives in a middle-class apartment in the mixed secular-religious town of Ra'anana, a northern suburb of Tel Aviv. Dressed in a grey polo shirt and jeans with *tzitzit* (fringes of a traditional garment) hanging out, Yoel tells me "I don't believe there is any aspect of our life that has nothing to do with religion." Coming from a religious home, Yoel became stricter in his observance as he learned more in the state-religious schools and yeshivas where he studied. (He brought his knowledge home, informing his mother, for instance, that using a sponge on Shabbat falls into a forbidden category of work). In the year before he entered the army, he spent another year studying in a yeshiva in the West Bank town of Hebron (home to 150,000 Palestinian Arabs and a few hundred Jews). One of the reasons he went to yeshiva was to be able to "go out to the army and be with people who are not religious and show them what it's about." By being a model of good behavior, Yoel believed he could "create respect for religion" in a non-religious Israeli, produce greater tolerance and awareness, and maybe even lead him to light Shabbat candles or go to *shul* (synagogue). Yoel wishes Haredim would see the importance of doing the same and of leaving yeshiva after "eight or nine years of learning" and becoming a lawyer or a businessman. Referring to the lifetime of study most Haredim choose, Yoel says, "I don't think that's the way Hashem (God) wants us to live."

Nahman came to Israel from Tunis when he was seventeen along with his father, his brother, and one of his sisters. His mother (his parents are divorced) and another sister, who "didn't want to make *aliya*" stayed in Tunis. Raised as a religious Jew, Nahman attended the religious school of the Jewish community in Tunis and studied in a religious high school run by Chabad (an international Hasidic movement). Upon arriving in Israel, he immediately was called up to the army, first going to a religious kibbutz for a year where he polished his already fluent Hebrew and was introduced to his future wife, an immigrant from England. After finishing the army and doing a B.A. in Middle Eastern studies at Bar Ilan University, Nahman enrolled in a training course and worked as a police officer in Beit Shemesh, a town thirty minutes from Jerusalem where he and his family (his wife and four children) live. Now thirty-three, Nahman commutes to Jerusalem's police headquarters, where he is an investigator in a special unit that handles "minority" crimes—primarily those of Arabs, but also those of Christian groups with plans to stir trouble in the Holy Land around the millennium. (The official name of his unit is being changed to Matam: *Mehlak Tafkidim Meyuhadim*, or

"Department of Special Assignments" because "some people look askance at the word 'minority.' ") Nahman defines his Jewishness as "religious nationalist," adding that "although I don't wear black...in recent years, I have been attracted to Shas," the ultra-Orthodox Sephardic party, and in particular, to its spiritual mentor, Rabbi Ovadiah Yosef. "I have all his books. I follow his *halachot* [religious rulings]." Summing up his allegiances, Nahman says: "My head is with NRP,[16] but my heart is with Shas." Nahman and his wife maintain an "open" home, striving to "blend Torah with the modern world" in a way that he says Haredim do not. His brother was murdered by Palestinian terrorists in 1993, and he complains that "Arabs are so extreme that they are ready to kill," that "as Arabs become more learned more they get more extreme...scientists at Bir Zeit University all make bombs...with Jews it's the opposite"; that Arabs citizens of Israel "drink from the well and then spit in it, even educated ones."

Unlike the five subjects introduced above, **Ganit,** thirty-nine, represents the moderate-to-liberal wing of religious nationalism. She opts for the small Meimad party—an acronym standing for "Medinah Yehudit, Medinah Demokratit," or "A Jewish State, a Democratic State"—which ran together with the Labor Party in the elections of 1999 and 2003. Although Meimad is dismissed by many Religious Zionsts (Nahman derides it as "Meretz[17] with a *kippa*"), it has taken some small strides in recent years both politically (in gaining several Knesset seats and Ministry positions and serving as Barak's sounding board for his short-lived proposal for a "civil revolution"[18]) and ideologically (in beginning to influence Israeli public opinion and publishing a bi-monthly magazine dealing with issues of religion and state). Ganit works in the legal department of the Ministry of Labor and Social Welfare, focusing on issues related to the defense of children. Educated in Israel's state-religious schools in Jerusalem, Ganit pursued a legal education at the Hebrew University of Jerusalem after fulfilling her mandatory army stint. She is married with one daughter and two sons; her mother is an immigrant from Canada, her late father was a Sabra. Ganit's religious upbringing followed her into adulthood, in contrast to the turn away from observance that her sister took "during and after her army service." Although she is hatless during our interview, Ganit says that she always wears a head covering outside the home. Coming from a Hesder Yeshiva[19] background in the large Jewish settlement bloc of Gush Etzion on the West Bank, her husband is "more right-wing than I am" and now votes for the rightist National Religious Party. Despite their compatible levels of religious observance, Ganit and her husband "have many differences of opinion over politics."

Rabbi **Mickey Rosen** (not an alias) heads the Yakar Center for Tradition and Creativity, just a few blocks down from Ganit's home in the Old Katamon neighborhood of Jerusalem. A liberal Religious Zionist who favors Meimad, Rabbi Rosen says he feels "somewhat like a Dodo bird, belonging to another planet." Yakar, founded in 1992 when Rabbi Rosen arrived from England, focuses on "education, social concern and spiritual expression" for Jews of all backgrounds and beliefs. Its orientation, however, is Orthodox. Journalist Yair Sheleg notes that Yakar is part of Israel's "new spiritual religiosity," using the prayer melodies and inspiration of the late Rabbi Shlomo Carlebach (the hippie-ish "dancing rabbi" who popularized a neo-Hasidic spiritual Judaism in the 1960s and 1970s).[20] Many of the Yakar faithful are Jews from the United States who have made aliya or are spending a year living in Jerusalem. On Friday nights Yakar's raucous Shabbat services attract many devoted Reform rabbinical students—perhaps even more than Kol Haneshama, a nearby Reform synagogue. How does the rabbi reconcile his openness with his strict religious principles?

> I don't want to be at war with anybody!...I am ambivalent about Reform and Conservative in this country. I have two voices inside me, even though half the community in Yakar seems to be Reform, Reconstructionst and Conservative. I really don't want to be trapped into a mindset which delegitimizes the other. My sense is, Reform and Conservative have a much greater role to play in the Diaspora, where there chiefly wouldn't be signs of a Jewish world had it not been for that. I have always tried to build a consensus to allow them to participate to the extent that that does not offend any fundamental principle.

He considers himself politically and socially liberal, but Rabbi Rosen is no Leftist. "It's a major mistake," he says, "to imagine that the left wing are more tolerant and liberal than the right wing. The right wing might be fascist, but then the left wing is ideologically Stalinist."

Traditional Jews

Recent studies reveal an Israeli public that is, on the whole, much more observant of Jewish rituals than the widely held but misleading notion of a secular/religious split suggests.[21] The rituals with the highest rates of participation (having a Passover seder, lighting Hannukah candles, keeping at least some semblance of kosher in the home) are shared even by many of Israel's self-defined "secular" Jews, and that holds true for my secular Jewish respondents introduced above. The segment of the population between *hiloni* and *dati/Haredi*—between secular and religious/ultra-Orthodox—represents nearly 40 percent of Israel's Jewry. The subjects I interviewed in this section (known as *masorti* or "traditional" Jews) are quite diverse religiously. Included are three women and four men, three from Jerusalem, three from Ra'anana and one from Haifa. Each comes from a very different background.

What links them together is at least one of the following two criteria: self-identification as *masorti*, or a higher degree of ritual religious observance or synagogue attendance.

Rivka, fifty-six, with a liberal smile, a smoker's voice and dyed red hair, comes from purely secular stock. Her parents, whom she refers to as "*halut-zim*," or Zionist pioneers, came from Eastern Galicia to help found the state. Raised on a non-religious kibbutz, Rivka and her family did not keep kosher, her father worked on Shabbat, and there was no prayer book to be found in their home. Their observance of Judaism was Zionist in character, marking Passover, for instance, with a "*kibbutz haggada*" that told the story of Jewish redemption by downplaying the traditional liturgy describing the exodus from Egypt and emphasizing the establishment of the modern state of Israel. Today, though, Rivka "is a member of the Conservative community" in Kfar Saba, the town abutting hers, Ra'anana, and uses the traditional *haggada* on Passover. For twenty years, Rivka has been attending the Conservative synagogue, populated by many English-speaking immigrants, every Friday night. "My husband doesn't go," she says. "He has nothing to do with it." The children, however, do have some connection to the synagogue (two of her four children, now "all grown up," had Bar and Bat Mitzvahs) and "have a positive attitude toward religion." And her son, married in 1999, rejected the Orthodox rabbinate and was wed by one of the synagogue's rabbis (after having gone to Gibraltar for the wedding that made their union official in the eyes of the state). A curator at a museum of Jewish history, with degrees in Bible and History and Museology from Tel Aviv University, Rivka's affiliation with Conservative Judaism is not based on "faith at all" (she's not sure God exists) but on her "fondness for Jewish culture" and "nationality, which means a kind of belonging." Ritual observance has little to do with this for Rivka, so, she says, "I choose my *mitzvot* [commandments]," deciding not to keep kosher or Shabbat, but studying Talmud on a regular basis. On the scale of traditional Judaism, which spans a wide gap between secular and religious, Rivka leans heavily toward secularism and is the least observant of the seven *masorti* Jews I interviewed. But her affiliation with established Conservative Judaism and synagogue attendance distinguishes her from the secular respondents.

A forty-three-year-old professor of materials engineering at the Technion Institute in Haifa, Shmuel's brand of traditional Judaism is the mirror image of Rivka's. Never enamored of what he considers fast, meaningless worship, Shmuel last attended synagogue after his father's death when he went twice a day to say *kaddish*, the prayer of mourning; and he fulfilled this duty for one week, not the traditionally required full year. Shmuel's *masorti* life involves staying far from *shul* (synagogue) and observing Judaism in private with his friends and family (he has a wife and two sons, ages six and twelve). With a kosher kitchen, a *sukka* in the yard every Sukkot, and an incredibly detailed, hand-written family tree that is framed and prominently displayed in his office, Shmuel's home shows many signs of Jewish connection and observance. The family tree, which he presents to me with pride and a bit of remorse, traces Shmuel's lineage back to generations of important rabbis. "My great great grandfather was Yehuda, chief rabbi of Europe, and his fathers and grandfathers are all the dynasty of chief rabbis in Prague. One of the branches of Yehuda's family goes all the way back to Rashi," the leading biblical and Talmudic commentator of the eleventh and twelfth centuries. This weighty history, Shmuel sighs, "is a load on my shoulders. I think I am the first who went away from Orthodoxy. So I am to blame." But after having grown up in Sanhedria, a Haredi neighborhood in Jerusalem, Shmuel has "no positive feelings" towards Israel's ultra-Orthodox and doesn't want to be the type of Jew "who stopped developing two or three thousand years ago." On the other hand, he views secular Jews "who don't do any Jewish holidays and behave like someone who lives in Antarctica" as "mistaken," but he respects their choice. He "has positive feelings" for Reform and Conservative Jews, believing that their services are more meaningful than the Orthodox style, but chooses not to get involved.

Chaim, twenty-two, pauses before characterizing his Judaism. His mother "comes from an Orthodox home" and his father was raised on a secular kibbutz; Chaim "emerged as something in the middle." A volunteer at a Conservative-affiliated kibbutz in the hot Arava desert, half an hour north of Eilat, Chaim's dark mop of curly hair, baggy shorts and calloused feet give him the hip relaxed look of a real *kibbutznik*. Chaim associates his Jewishness with the fact that he lives in Israel and has Jewish parents, and keeps "part" of the commandments. In addition to observing the laws of *kashrut* (pretty strictly) and Shabbat ("a little"), Chaim goes to synagogue on the holidays. "Essentially I give respect to the history and tradition of the Jewish people. But religion itself is less important to me." Chaim finished his army term a few months ago and is working for another few in the *gan*, the place where the littlest members of the kibbutz spend their days. Haredim, in Chaim's eyes, are "industrious, diligent and studious" in Talmud and religious studies but they "lack tolerance," are too extreme ("that's never good, it's better to find something in the middle") and their treatment of women is "primitive." Secular Jews are more open, as long as they aren't extreme or anti-religious, but they have "fewer values." Although he "isn't sufficiently familiar with Arabs," he feels their "dual identity" makes it difficult for them to live as Israeli citizens.

Rotem, a graduate student pursuing simultaneous master's degrees in clinical psychology and Jewish education, is twenty-eight and lives in Jerusalem. The offspring of Anglo immigrants (her father is from South Africa, her mother from Canada), Rotem was born in South Africa and moved to Israel with her parents when she was four. As an affiliate of the Conservative movement, Rotem sees Judaism "as a framework for formulating my search about what it means to live a good life, what it means to live a righteous life" and as a "community that helps me define who I am." Because, she says, "I don't know if I believe in God," Rotem's fairly traditional observance ("*kashrut* obviously, the holidays obviously, I don't work, cook or study on Shabbat, but I do drive and watch TV") reflects her view of the commandments as "guides in moral behavior." Judaism's ethical precepts, such as giving charity and caring for animals, are thus very important to Rotem. She hopes to pursue a Ph.D. that combines psychology with Jewish studies, and perhaps to teach someday. In the meantime, she is preparing for her wedding to a religious "but very Leftist" former yeshiva student and working with the rabbi to add certain elements that are generally missing form traditional Jewish ceremonies (such as the bride giving the groom a ring under the wedding canopy). Rotem has many positive feelings about both Religious Zionists and Haredim (the former are "loyal" and have "family-oriented values"; the latter "really try to be moral" and have "really wonderful ideas of how to deal with raising ten kids at once") but she disapproves of the "missionary" zeal of Haredim and the "relatively fascist" education that "brainwashes" Religious Zionist youth. Israeli secular culture, in contrast, is "more intellectual" and "much more aware of human rights" but is missing values such as "volunteering in society, giving of yourself and being neighborly" that once characterized it. Engaging in a bit of self-criticism, Rotem notes that Reform and Conservative Jews can at times seem "wishy-washy"; on the flip side, however, they "tend to see reality as complex."

I meet **Rita** in her comfortable Ra'anana home on a Friday afternoon as she prepares for Shabbat. A forty-nine-year-old immigrant from Morocco who "observes the tradition but isn't very religious," Rita represents by far the largest segment of Israel's *masorti* Jewish population: *Mizrahi* (eastern) traditionalists. Taking a break from peeling potatoes for the Sabbath evening meal, Rita tells me that she "doesn't drive on Shabbat, separates meat and milk and doesn't eat non-kosher food." Her husband, a Yemenite Jew, "lays *tefillin*" every morning, prays in synagogue regularly and comes from a somewhat more observant home where Shabbat was more closely kept. But, she says, in her sleeveless white shirt, white pants and sandals which set off her dark complexion, "we aren't totally totally strict—I watch television, listen to the radio (on Shabbat). We aren't fanatic. I am in the middle—not secular but traditional." With four children, ages sixteen to twenty-five, Rita and her husband have created a family half the size of their birth families (Rita has eight brothers and sisters). Rita grew up in Jaffa, a small town directly south of Tel Aviv that is home to a substantial Arab population. A high school graduate, she has held a number jobs ranging from legal secretary to accounting clerk to child care professional. Today, they rely on her husband's salary (he's the director of a marketing firm) and she "takes care of the children." Socially, Rita has virtually no contact with Haredim or Religious Zionists; she sees the former as "embedded within themselves" and seeking to "build a ghetto" separate from the rest of Israeli society, while she "doesn't understand the point" of the latter's way of life. She thinks that Reform and Conservative Judaism are "very nice" and is happy that a new Conservative synagogue is opening next door to their home; she plans to check it out. Israeli Arabs arouse Rita's suspicion. Even her gardener, the only Arab she knows personally, "frightens" Rita. She doesn't know if he comes from the occupied territories or from somewhere within Israel, and does not want to ask.

Aaron, an American who made *aliya* in 1976, lives a few blocks from Rita's home in Ra'anana. An ordained Conservative rabbi who switched careers after eight years on the pulpit in two small midwestern cities, Aaron earned a Ph.D. in education from Ohio State University and decided with his wife to move to Israel. "We felt and still feel that we would like to live in a place where there's a Jewish majority, where we both take responsibility for our actions and have the ability in every way, politically and culturally, to contribute to the mainstream and not to be marginal." Now Aaron is a professor of education at Tel Aviv University, where he teaches courses on how to teach Jewish identity, Bible and Jewish philosophy. While his observance has not changed "at all" (he still keeps kosher, for instance, and is active in Ra'anana's small Conservative synagogue), Aaron's Jewish identity is now significantly shaped by his environment: "Judaism is an integral and essential part of my life. In Israel, it doesn't require the same kind of thought and planning as it does elsewhere. It is certainly part of the fabric, the rhythm of the year, of the holidays." Aaron and his wife confess to having had difficulty "transmitting" Conservative Judaism to their three children (ages nineteen, twenty-one, and twenty-nine). "It doesn't fit well with the Israeli environment." Aaron doesn't have any contact with Haredim, and has no Arab friends, but he associates with many Religious Zionists and secular Jews, and maintains a collegial relationship with Israeli Arab faculty at the university.

At the time of our interview, Rabbi **Uri Regev** (his real name) was head of the Israel Religious Action Center, the "legal and public arm" of Israel's Movement for Progressive Judaism, as Reform is known here. (He has since moved on to a bigger job: director of the World Union for Progressive Judaism.) Born in Israel to secular parents, Rabbi Regev participated in an exchange program at sixteen that introduced him to Reform Judaism in the United States. Inspired by what he saw, he collected degrees in law from Tel Aviv University and rabbinics from the Hebrew Union College. Then, in 1987, he "combined these two areas of interest" and founded IRAC "to promote the values of human equality, social justice and religious tolerance." Rabbi Regev, with no *kippa* on his head, a colorful short-sleeved button down shirt and a well-trimmed salt-and-pepper beard, is one of only a few handfuls of Israeli-ordained Reform rabbis. On the wall of Regev's office are his H.U.C. diploma; a framed saying ("Kindness is contagious—catch it!"); an old map of the Land of Israel; and a modern, stylized Star of David. On his modestly stocked bookshelves are several tractates of the Talmud, some in English; the Reform Union prayer book, and volumes on Jewish history and the Middle East. IRAC offers litigation services, public education, and "outreach to policymakers," mainly on religion-state matters. The Center challenges the Israeli status quo, for example, on the Orthodox rabbinate's monopoly on conversion, marriage and divorce. Regev emphasizes that IRAC is also a more general social action organization, aiding new immigrants in dealing with the trials of Israeli bureaucracy, but its main thrust is clearly the pursuit of religious freedom and pluralism.

Arabs

Jews make up about 76.5 percent of the Israeli population, while Arabs constitute most of the remaining fifth. According to 2003 estimates, Muslims (mostly Sunni) make up 15.9 percent of the total population, Christians 2.1 percent and Druze 1.6 percent.[22] Of the five Arab citizens of Israel I interviewed three are Muslim (one religious, one traditional, one secular), one is Christian and one is Druze. In introducing relevant background information about these respondents below, I present their conceptions of their national identity as Israeli citizens in addition to their religious identities. This distinction is a basic one in thinking about the role of Israeli Arabs as a minority in a "Jewish and democratic state," and sets the stage for the critique of Israel that is often heard from the Arab sector.

Nadia, twenty-eight, was born in Nazareth, a mixed Muslim-Christian city in the southern Galilee, and now lives in Beit Hanina, an Arab neighborhood in northern Jerusalem, with her Palestinian[23] husband and five-year-old boy. "I am not religious," Nadia says, dressed in jeans and a jean jacket, with uncovered hair, "but I don't disparage Islam. It is part of my culture, part of my life and my beliefs." Nadia thinks that Islam is "much more interwoven in daily life and in culture and mentality" than is Judaism, so she sees her secularism as less extreme than that of a secular Israeli Jew. Nadia has her B.A. and M.A. in sociology and works as the leader of discussion groups on Arab-Jewish relations and Jewish education. When she first entered the Hebrew University of Jerusalem, where she studied for both of her advanced degrees, Nadia experienced a great "culture shock." No one, she said, related to her "as an Arab or as a person." She struggled with the language and unfamiliar style of teaching, resented Jewish students who "were impolite, always shouting," disapproved of Jewish women "who dressed in the shortest, most see-through clothing," and felt strongly "from a national perspective" that students and professors alike were "racist." In short, she "cried non-stop the entire year." Although she is a citizen of the state, Nadia defines herself as "a Palestinian Arab living in Israel," eschewing the adjective "Israeli." She says the flag and the national anthem "don't belong to me" and remind her of her "alienation" from the state. Nadia has "a ton" of connections with Jews in her studies and work, and has a "very good Jewish friend" she even "tells secrets" to, but she "never" invites them into her home and does not visit Jewish friends' homes, either. Echoing the covenant of the Palestine Liberation Organization and a common charge against Zionism, Nadia insists that "Judaism is a religion, not a nationality. People who are here for religious reasons I can understand. But secular Jews who are here and claim a right to the land I do not understand. It is impossible to live in this country that way."

Muhammad, forty-five, meets me at our designated rendez-vous: a gas station on the edge of his village Qualansuwa, a few miles from the Israeli port city of Netanya. From there, he leads me to his home, over a dozen twists and turns on unmarked roads into the well-tended but dusty village. I had removed the Israeli flag flying from the backseat window of my borrowed car before setting out for this day trip, but I turned many curious heads anyway following Muhammad to and from his home; the presence of an outsider in this 16,000-person village doesn't go unnoticed. Greeting me with a wide smile and copious wishes and blessings ("Welcome. I am happy to give the interview, to help and to contribute. It is interesting and an experience also for me."), Muhammad's hospitality was easily the most gracious of any of my subjects. (During the two hours we spent together, his brother's wife brought me water, a platter of cold drinks, glorious strawberries, and, later, strong, sweet Arabic coffee and pastries.) Looking something like an American yuppie with his clean-cut appearance and his Polo button down shirt, jeans and sandals, Muhammad defines his Islam as "traditional" (*masorti*). He doesn't fulfill the Muslim obligation to pray five times daily, but he does pray once a day, and worships on Fridays, the Muslim Sabbath. He heeds prohibitions against eating pork and drinking wine; shields himself from the secular influences of nearby Israeli cities like Netanya and Tel Aviv; and finds beauty in Islamic customs such as "helping your family, respecting others, loving your fellow as yourself, and volunteering." Muhammad proudly defines himself as an "Arab Israeli," comparing his identity to a "Jewish American"; notably, he is the only one of my five Arab subjects who avoids the label "Palestinian," saying "I don't live on the West Bank." Muhammad is anxious to represent himself as a loyal citizen of the state[24]: On Holocaust Remembrance Day, Muhammad stands during the siren; he says that the national anthem, "represents me, because I am an Israeli"; and asserts that he "felt no discrimination as a student at Tel Aviv University," where he studied Hebrew literature and history. A Hebrew teacher and guide for Arab high school students at the Jewish Diaspora museum in Ramat Gan, Muhammad enjoys a "high standard of living" in the plumply furnished home he built himself for his family of six. He has many Jewish associates in his work and expresses disapproval only of what he calls "extremists" of any religion. He complains, for example, about the "Haredi Muslims" who burnt down a bar in his village that sold wine the day after it opened.

Majjed, a strapping twenty-one-year-old Druze from the village of Mrar in the lower Galilee, describes himself as a "totally secular" atheist Communist. "Religion isn't important to me at all." Granting that it may serve a purpose in "unifying people," Majjed mocks the idea that Moses could have waved his staff and separated the Red Sea. As a student completing prerequisites for a degree in law at the Hebrew University, Majjed laments that "people always look at me with suspicion," especially the university administration. The most prominent item in Majjed's dormitory room is a huge red banner of Che Guevarra ("Hasta la Victoria Siempre" is emblazoned above his image). There is also a *keffiye* (a traditional Arab men's headcovering) hanging on the back of his door ("it's not religious—it's for the rain in the winter"), stickers for the Hadash political party (an Arab-Jewish party represented by three Knesset members pushing for a bi-national, dejudaized state) and a couple dozen empty bottles of Carlsberg and Goldstar beer. Despite his apparent vigor, Majjed says he failed the army's physical exam and thus was exempt from his requirement as a Druze to serve in the IDF. His smirk, however, signals another motive for not serving: ideological opposition. Majjed's identity is "a Druze Palestinian Arab citizen of Israel." He has some Jewish friends, but when going out to drink beer, only Arab friends come along. To those Jews who justify de facto second-class status for Israeli Arabs by pointing out the two dozen Arab countries they could live in, Majjed says, "My good friend, I was born here, my father was born here, my grandfather was born here. You can sit down, get up, shout—I am here! If you kill me, my son is here; and if you kill him, my brother is here. I will not move from here. This is my land and I will not move from it."

Youssef, twenty, shares a room with Majjed at the Hebrew University's campus in Jerusalem. He comes from Ilabun, a village near Tiberias in the Galilee that is home to a mostly Arab Christian population of 3,500. As a youth, Youssef attended a school in his village "funded by Christians from abroad" in which Christian and Muslim children study everything together, including Christianity, but Muslims have separate classes in Islam as well. Youssef's non-religious Christian parents (his father works for the state as a traffic cop, his mother is a teacher) seldom go to church, "even on holidays." The exception is Christmas, when "Santa Claus comes and gives out presents...we pray in the church and then the whole family gathers and eats together." Youssef, like his roommate, defines himself as secular—"I am the farthest you can be from religion"—and as a "Palestinian Arab who lives in the state of Israel." He chooses this option because " 'Israeli' is not a nationality. My nationality is Arab....'Israeli' only represents belonging to the state." For Youssef, Israeli Independence Day is "Yom Ha-Nakba"—"Day of the Catastrophe": "In 1948, a Palestinian state was supposed to be established...but the Jews came here and took over these lands. Therefore it is a disaster for the Palestinian people." So even though his "first priority" is securing "peace between the two sides here" he would never think of "participating happily in Israeli Independence Day." He intends to begin a B.A. in the Hebrew University in the fall, to pursue a career in accounting, and eventually to start a family and build a home in Ilabun. Asked to comment on his relations with other Arab groups, Youssef refused: "I don't want to answer that question because for me there is absolutely no distinction between Muslim, Christian and Druze. We are all Arabs, we all have one nationality. There are no differences between us." And his relations with Jews? "I have met people from the entire population of Jews—Haredim, nationalists, *kibbutznikim*. I relate to each person as a person, not in terms of their religious or political identity."

Omer, my youngest subject at nineteen, is a gentle "religious-traditional" Muslim planning a career in computer science. Hanging on the wall above his bed, in a room down the hall from Majjed and Youssef's, is a giant color photograph of Jerusalem's Al-Aqsa mosque with thousands of Muslims prostrate in prayer during the holy month of Ramadan. A well-thumbed Koran bound in green leather lies on a shelf next to his bed. Tall, slim and serious, Omer takes an hour and a half out of his math studies (he has a test the next day) to talk to me, and engages me in another thirty minutes of conversation about my views on religion after the interview ends. Omer comes from the town of Umm Al-Fahm, home to 40,000 mainly Muslim residents, in the "Triangle" area of central Israel where many Israeli Arabs live. A devout Muslim, Omer prays five times daily, keeps Halal, the dietary laws, avoids sex, and "works for religion," trying to prove the truth of Islam to others. His parents, also religious, sent Omer to study Koran when he was small. Upon entering the preparatory program at the Hebrew University, Omer felt "strange" speaking Hebrew regularly; "it was as if I was leaving my society and entering a new one." He defines himself as a "Palestinian Arab living in Israel," a "foreign country." Omer feels somewhat of a connection, however, with Israeli Haredim and Religious Zionist Jews; "I must recognize them and respect them...since they are realizing their religious ideology." Omer believes that being tolerant and accepting is required by Islam, and that all religion serves valuable social goals in providing a "framework for good living." (In our discussion after the interview, however, Omer told me that according to Islam, the end of days will bring a holy war led by the returning prophet Mohammad in which all of the Muslim faithful destroy everyone else, non-believing Muslims, atheists and believers in other faiths alike.)

Notes

1. Daniel J. Elazar, Contribution to "The Jewish State: The Next Fifty Years (A Symposium)," *Azure* no. 6 (Winter 1999): 76-77.

2. My approach might be conceived as a more methodologically rigorous version of the discussions with Israelis found in Amos Oz, *In the Land of Israel*, trans. Maurie Goldberg-Bartura (San Diego: Harcourt Brace, 1983). It also shares an affinity with the techniques in Jennifer Hochschild, *What's Fair? American Beliefs About Distributive Justice* (Cambridge, Mass.: Harvard University Press, 1981).

3. See, for example, Yoram Hazony, *The Jewish State: The Struggle for Israel's Soul* (New York: Basic Books, 2000), a polemic warning of a rising tide of post-Zionism in Israel's academic and cultural elite; Yossi David, ed., *Medinat Yisrael: bein yahadut ve-demokratia* (The state of Israel: between Judaism and democracy) (Jerusalem: Israel Democracy Institute, 2000) [Hebrew], a collection of interviews and articles with academics and rabbis; Eliezer Weinryb, *Dat u'medinah: heibetim philosophim* (Religion and state: philosophical aspects) (Tel Aviv: Hakibbutz Hameuchad, 2000) [Hebrew], two imaginary Israelis, Orit (secular) and Yedidya (religious), debating separation of religion and state in Israel through Rawls, Sandel and Kymlicka; Ruth Gavison, *Yisrael ke-medinah yehudit ve-demokratit: metahim ve-sikuim* (Israel as a Jewish and democratic state: tensions and prospects) (Tel Aviv: Van Leer Jerusalem Institute, Hakibbutz Hameuchad Publishing, 1999) [Hebrew], an argument that Israel's dual character is both a conceptual possibility (under a thin, but not liberal, conception of democracy) and morally justified; Ron Margolin, ed., *Medinat Yisrael ke-medinah yehudit ve-demokratit* (The state of Israel as a Jewish and democratic state) (Jerusalem: The World Association for Jewish Philosophy with AVICHAI, 1999) [Hebrew], transcripts of participants' speeches at the 12th World Congress on Jewish Philosophy held in August, 1997, additional thoughts from each participant, and primary sources on Israel's basic laws, the Declaration of Human Rights, American Constitution, Israeli Supreme Court decisions, as well as sources in Jewish law and philosophy, Zionist thought and selections from Hobbes, Spinoza, Locke, Montesquieu, J.S. Mill and Isaiah Berlin; Aviezer Ravitsky, *Dat u'medinah ba-mahshevet Yisrael* (Religion and state in Jewish philosophy: models of unity, division, collision and subordination) (Jerusalem: Israeli Democracy Institute, 1998) [Hebrew], a study of four classic Jewish approaches to the question; Menachem Mautner, Avi Sagi and Ronen Shamir, eds., *Rav-tarbutiut be-medinah demokratit ve-yehudit* (Multiculturalism in a democratic and Jewish state) (Tel Aviv: Ramot, 1998) [Hebrew], a collection in memory of the late Ariel Rozen-Zvi; and Tel Aviv University Law School, *Medinah yehudit ve-demokratit* (A Jewish and democratic state) (Tel Aviv: Ramot, 1996) [Hebrew], a reprint of articles from *Iyyunei Mishpat* (the Tel Aviv University Law Review) vol. 19, no. 3 (July 1995).

4. In particular, I faced difficulties securing female interview subjects in the Haredi, Religious Zionist and religious Muslim sectors. In these communities, it is sometimes considered immodest for women to speak about politics and to hold pri-

vate conversations with males, especially unfamiliar ones. I interviewed one Haredi woman (Nehama) and one Religious Zionist woman (Ganit) but no religious Muslim women. (The Israeli Arab woman I interviewed, Nadia, is a secular-traditional Muslim). I did not insist on equal representation of female subjects in these groups (or, as I write above, in any other) because I was concerned that such a goal would lead to a left-leaning pool of religious respondents. My worry was not that women are more liberal than men in these communities, but that those who are *willing to be interviewed* are likely to hold exceptional views in their particular sub-group.

5. For a more extensive discussion of these methods, see Robert S. Weiss, *Learning from Strangers: The Art and Method of Qualitative Interview Studies* (New York: Free Press, 1994), 15-37; and Duane R. Monette, Thomas J. Sullivan and Cornell R. DeJong, *Applied Social Research: Tools for the Human Services*, 4th edn. (New York: Harcourt Brace, 1998), 140-54.

6. Secular Jews and traditional Jews each make up about 40 percent of Israeli's Jewish population, while Haredi Jews constitute only 5 percent and Religious Zionists 15 percent. See Gavison, *Jewish and Democratic State*, 11-12 and Shlomit Levy, Hanna Levinsohn and Elihu Katz, *Beliefs, Observances and Values Among Israeli Jews 2000* (Jerusalem: Israel Democracy Institute and AVI CHAI Foundation, 2002), 5.

7. For a more detailed account of the methodology behind some of this research, see Steven Mazie and Patricia Woods, "Prayer, Politics and the Women of the Wall: The Benefits of Collaboration in Participant Observation at Intense, Multi-Focal Events" *Field Methods* 15, no. 1 (February 2003): 25-50.

8. With the introductions below I hope to avoid a shortcoming in Robert N. Bellah, Richard Madsen, Anne Swidler, William W. Sullivan and Steven M. Tipton, *Habits of the Heart: Individualism and Commitment in American Life* (Berkeley: University of California Press, 1985). In drawing on transcripts of over two hundred interviews to find quotations supporting their proposition that the individualistic nature of white middle-class American discourse masks latent republican longings, Bellah et al. failed to convey a sense of the individuals behind the comments or the context in which they were expressed. (Chapter 1 of that book, which dwells on four archetypal case studies, is an exception.) See Joseph Gusfield, "I Gotta Be Me" (review essay), *Contemporary Sociology* 15 (January 1986): 7-9; and Robert E. Goodin, Review of *Habits of the Heart, Ethics* 96 (January 1986): 431-32.

9. I used English with six native English speakers (Richard, Yoel, Aaron, Rotem, Jonathan Rosenblum and Rabbi Mickey Rosen) and with four native Hebrew speakers whose English was particularly rich and fluent (Shulamit, Rivka, Shmuel and Rabbi Uri Regev). I used Hebrew in the remainder of the interviews, including those with two Haredi subjects (Nosson and Yeshayahu) who spent their childhoods in the States and speak fluent English but preferred to use Hebrew. All five of the interviews with Arabs were conducted in Hebrew, a fluent second language for the vast majority of Israeli Arab citizens.

10. Plato, *Republic*, trans. A.D. Lindsay, ed. Terence Irwin (London: Everyman, 1992), 331d.

11. See Gesher's website at <www.gesher.co.il>.

12. The Omer is a period of forty-nine days between Passover and the festival of Shavuot that Jews are obligated to count off daily with a special blessing.

13. This sign became ubiquitous in Israel in the early 1990s; it expresses opposition to returning the Golan Heights to Syria.

14. Yigal Amir assassinated Prime Minister Yitzhak Rabin on November 4, 1995; Baruch Goldstein massacred twenty-nine Muslims while at prayer in Hebron on February 25, 1994. Both committed their crimes out of religious nationalist zeal.

15. Under his influence, Zvi's parents have now become more religious. His four siblings have each pursued a different path: one "secular" sister lives in the United States; another "strongly traditional" sister keeps Shabbat but sometimes answers the phone on Saturdays; a third, who had become religious for her former husband, returned to wearing pants after the divorce. His "traditional-secular" brother, married with two daughters, is "like most of the traditional public in Israel: he'll be at our father's kiddush and come on Rosh Hashana or Yom Kippur to pray, but on Shabbat he watches TV, drives, and goes out with friends."

16. The National Religious Party (Mafdal in Hebrew) is the predominantly Ashkenazi mainstay of Religious Zionism in Israel.

17. Meretz is a leftist secular party, considered by some to be anti-religious.

18. See David Franklin, "Barak to Forge Ahead with Civil Reform Plan," *Jerusalem Post*, 12 September 2000. The One Israel coalition whip, Ophir Pines-Paz, proposed that Barak consult Meimad on the terms of his plans to bring changes to the religious-secular status quo. " 'Meimad represents the most advanced and moderate stream in Religious Zionism,' said Pines-Paz, 'and the borders of civil progress must be borders acceptable to Meimad.'"

19. Hesder Yeshivot offer programs combining Torah study with army service; they appeal to many of Israel's religious nationalist youth.

20. Yair Sheleg, *Ha-dati'im he-hadashim: mabat achshavi al ha-hevrah ha-datit beyisrael* (The new religious Jews: recent developments among observant Jews in Israel) (Jerusalem: Keter, 2000) [Hebrew], 255-56.

21. Debunking the myth that Israeli Jews are overwhelmingly secular, the 1993 Guttman Report concluded that "there are certain traditional attitudes, values and practices that embrace a vast majority of Israeli Jews." See Shlomit Levy, Hanna Levinsohn and Elihu Katz, *Beliefs, Observances and Social Interaction Among Israeli Jews* (Jerusalem: Louis Guttman Israel Institute of Applied Social Research, 1993); for a summary of the report, see *The Jewishness of Israelis: Reponses to the Guttman Report*, 1-38, ed. Charles S. Liebman and Elihu Katz (Albany, N.Y.: SUNY Press, 1997). An update of the 1993 survey conducted in 1999 shows very similar results. See Levy et al., *Beliefs, Observances and Values Among Israeli Jews 2000*. While the later study showed that levels of observance had remained similar (with 98 percent, for example, posting a *mezuza* scroll on their front door and 85 percent participating in some kind of a Passover *seder*), 7 percent fewer Jews identified themselves as "traditional" while five percent more preferred the term "non-religious."

22. See the online *World Factbook* published by the Central Intelligence Agency, <http://www.odci.gov/cia/publications/factbook/geos/is.html#People> (20 July 2005).

23. Against the grain of a growing trend, I use the term "Palestinian" here to denote an Arab who is not a citizen of Israel. Until recently, the term "Palestinians" referred only to Arab residents of Israel's occupied territories (the West Bank and Gaza) who lacked Israeli citizenship while "Israeli Arabs" identified Arab citizens of the state. Of late, many Arabs holding Israeli citizenship—including four of the five subjects discussed in this section—have begun calling themselves "Palestinian." In a Givat Haviva Institute for Peace Research survey from 2000—conducted *before* the

outbreak of the Al-Aqsa Intifada in September 2000—only 15 percent of Arab citizens of Israel chose to identify themselves with the adjective "Israeli" (11 percent called themselves "Israeli Arab", 4 percent "Israeli") while 80 percent labeled themselves "Palestinian" (46 percent described themselves as "Palestinians/Arab-Palestinians in Israel," 21 percent as "Palestinian Arabs," and 3 percent as "Palestinians"). This is a relatively recent phenomenon: in a similar poll from 1996, 46 percent used the adjective "Israeli" (38 percent "Israeli Arab," 8 percent "Israeli") and only 27 percent identified themselves using the term "Palestinian." David Rudge, "Poll: Israeli Arabs' Palestinian Identity Growing," *Jerusalem Post*, 31 March 2000.

24. Near the end of the interview, when I asked him if he thinks Israeli Arabs are "full citizens" (*"ezrahim mele'im"*) of the state, he thought I asked if they were *"ezrahim ne'emanim"*—loyal citizens.

Chapter 4
Israel in the Eyes of Israelis

This chapter discusses major concepts in Israeli debates over issues of religion and state by analyzing and critically examining thirty-one Israelis' views.
My subjects are not expert informants: although some are quite knowledgeable, few are specialists on the details of policy questions, Supreme Court
decisions or Israeli history. Nor are they statistically significant representatives of their communities or of Israeli society as a whole. Although my
sketches of the subjects in chapter 3 suggest the importance of understanding something of the subjects' religious beliefs, my primary aim is not to answer why they came to hold their political opinions and attitudes. I see my
subjects' arguments, rather, as vital resources for rethinking Israel's religion-
state arrangement and for reassessing liberalism's stance toward religion.

I begin with the two main pieces of the Israeli puzzle: "Israel as a Jewish
State" and "Israel as a Democratic State." First I consider why the notion of a
Jewish state might be odd or elusive and then look at the myriad ways in
which Israelis see their state as Jewish and approve or disapprove of its Jewish nature. The central debate emerging in the interviews concerns whether
Israel should be a largely secular "state of the Jews" or a religiously Jewish
state. Next I explore my subjects' understandings of Israel's democratic nature. The thirty-one Israeli interviewees tend to agree on something remarkable: democracy, they say, is concerned primarily with *liberty*. They divide,
however, over how democratic Israel is and how democratic it ought to be.

Following this conceptual analysis, I turn to widely used political slogans: "Separation of Religion and State" and "A State of All Its Citizens."
While both notions find support among both Jewish and Arab Israelis, the
first slogan is associated most with issues affecting Jews and the second with
matters related to the status of Palestinian citizens of Israel.[1] I observe that
although many Israeli Jews and most Israeli Arabs are united in seeking less
of a connection between religion and their state, the two groups' visions of

Israel's ideal religion-state arrangement are disparate and, on some issues, mutually exclusive. The consensus Jewish view in support of separation entails lifting the monopoly that religious courts enjoy on questions of Jews' personal status, rethinking yeshiva students' draft exemptions and limiting public observance of Judaism while preserving Jewish state symbols and funding for religious education. The Arab view concurs that all streams of religious education should be funded by the state, but it tends to be less exercised about civil marriage and not at all about kosher state kitchens or Haredi army service. The Arab call for separation is based on a vision of a "state of all its citizens" in which equality is realized not only with regard to formal rights and economic and social conditions but in terms of state symbols that are accessible to non-Jews. In some important ways, then, Jews and Arabs seeking to alter the religion-state arrangement in Israel are working at cross-purposes. This poses particular challenges to policymakers seeking a "constitution by broad consensus" to serve as Israel's higher law.[2]

After discussing their lives and religious beliefs, I asked my respondents several rather grand conceptual questions on the relationship between religion and state in Israel:

- Do you think Israel is a Jewish state? In what ways is it Jewish or not Jewish? Do you prefer the term "State of the Jews"?
- Do you think Israel is a democratic state? In what ways is it democratic or not democratic? What, in your eyes, characterizes democracy? Is democracy important to you?
- How do you interpret the phrase: "the values of Israel as a Jewish and democratic state"?[3] Do you see any conflict between Judaism and democracy? Or do these values go together?
- Some say that Israel needs to separate religion from state. Do you agree?
- Some say that Israel should be a "state of all its citizens." What does this phrase mean to you? Do you agree?

My plan was to explore subjects' interpretations of and attitudes toward certain expressions and ideas latent in Israeli public discourse in order to clarify the ways in which these often fuzzy concepts are used in debates over Israel's political philosophy. In questions later in the interview, I hoped to flesh out and examine respondents' views on which specific Jewish attributes of the Israeli state they believe are justified, which unjustified, and why. There is often a wide gulf between the kinds of positions many Israelis tend to support in principle and what traditional liberal theorists would take to be the required implications that flow from those positions. The most interesting and relevant disjuncture occurs in the notion of separating religion and state. While a significant majority of my respondents support this policy (despite the opposition of most Religious Zionists and some Haredim), both Arab and Jewish subjects also express support for many linkages between state and religion that liberals would typically consider incompatible with such a commitment. Jews and Arabs alike, for example, advocate direct government funding for religious education, while Jews also tend to support state recognition of a Chief Rabbinate and preserving exclusively Jewish state symbols. In later chapters I dwell on this puzzle, trying to understand and work with the ideas Israelis have about their own state in order to shed some light on both the justifiability of Israel's religion-state arrangement and the liberal position which says that any such arrangement is inherently suspect.

Rather than present each respondent individually, as I did in chapter 3, here I discuss their answers integratively, noting points of agreement and disagreement inside and among the five groups and identifying important trends.

Israel as a Jewish State

It was only at the suggestion of an advisor that I included the question, "Do you think Israel is a Jewish state?" in my interview guide. In earlier drafts of my questions, I planned to dive straight into particular aspects of the state's Jewishness and the tensions between Judaism and democracy. I had assumed, prior to considering the recommendation, that the answer is understood—and would be understood by Israelis—from the start.[4] I worried that Israeli subjects (not always known for their patient reserve) would stare at me incredulously as if I were asking them if they thought the sky is blue or if grass is green: "What do you mean?" I feared they'd say, "Of course it is! Are you kidding?!" Though most Israelis indeed believe strongly that the state is Jewish, my worries were misplaced: no one scoffed at the question. Many of the subjects, in fact, paused in reflection for a moment before answering; a few noted, "that's a great question!" No one considered the inquiry ridiculous, and that's an essential point. No one thought that the fact of Israel's Jewishness was somehow beyond question.

Is Israel a Jewish state? I suggested in chapter 2 that the answer is a qualified yes, citing the Declaration of Establishment's clear assertion to that effect ("[Israel will be] a Jewish State in Eretz-Yisrael"); noting three dimensions on which Israel's Jewishness might be seen—in most of its symbols, in much of its legislation and in some of its institutions; and describing a few of the everyday details of public Judaism. Nevertheless, applying the adjective "Jewish" to a state is problematic, even leaving aside questions of justice for a moment. What does it mean for a state to be Jewish?

The term "Jewish" is linked to "religion" to describe Judaism; it also describes individuals who are members of the religion. For Orthodox and most Conservative Jews, "Moshe is Jewish" means that Moshe was born to a Jewish mother or was converted to Judaism by a rabbi or panel of rabbis. (Reform Jews also consider children of Jewish fathers to be Jewish, even if the mother is not.) "Jewish" also is used, without undue conceptual difficulty, to identify things such as holidays, beliefs, teachings and values that derive from or are associated with Judaism. (People might disagree about *whether* a certain value is Jewish, but they understand what the stakes are: they aren't baffled by the idea that a value may or may not be associated with Judaism.) More abstractly (in a historical or metaphysical sense), some people refer to particular tracts of land as "Jewish" because they were purportedly given to the Jews by God, or are historically linked to the Jewish people or are, at present, populated by Jews.

But linking "Jewish" to "state" (even though far from baffling initially) is more complicated. It's not immediately clear why it makes sense to call a state Jewish. The modern pre-messianic state, unlike a holiday or a value, is ordinarily not central to or directly derivative of religious doctrine. That is, although some religions sometimes prefer state support for their institutions or state endorsement of their religious truths, most religions in most places today get along fine without a direct link to a particular state. Their doctrines do not expire with the fall of a regime. Many religions, in fact, prefer no connection to the state because they view the political realm as inherently corrupt and corruptible. The State of Israel is seen as central to Judaism by some religious adherents—notably Religious Zionists—but even for them it is a stand-in, a mostly secular shell to be scraped out and filled in with theocracy at the end of days.[5] Although many states maintain various connections with particular religions, it is seldom difficult to imagine states severing those connections and remaining recognizably, say, Sweden (which disestablished from the Lutheran church in 2000) or Iran (which was secular until the Islamic Revolution in 1979). That's because since the post-Reformation wars, it has not quite made sense to think of religion as the main quality providing identity to a state. States might be established or fundamentally transformed *in the name* of a religion, but unlike people, states are not born *members* of particular religions. Nor can they convert, even through revolution. The Weberian notion of a state as possessing a monopoly on the use of legitimate force within a given territory leaves little room for ascriptions of religious identity. And even if we think of the state as a moral person or, in Hegel's terms, as a universal embodiment of a community's collective will, it still seems incapable of what we usually think of as religious belief or observance.[6]

But, again, the idea that Israel is a Jewish state does not perplex us as would comments to the effect that one's stick of chewing gum is Jewish, or that leaf-cutter ants are Jewish, or that the Tropic of Capricorn is Jewish. Religion and politics are linked in myriad ways (both historically and conceptually) in ways that religion is seldom linked with chewing gum, with insects, or with imaginary lines around the earth. Ancient Judaism, notably, was intimately tied to the state, with monarchs from King Saul to King Solomon ruling in Palestine. It both makes some sense, then, to speak of a Jewish state and to be wary, from the outset, of thinking that there is a simple answer to the question of whether modern Israel *is* Jewish or not. There are *many* ways in which religion and state may possibly relate. The Jewishness of a state is something that cannot be confirmed or disproved simply by looking at its pedigree, or its people, or its laws, or its institutions, or its symbols, or its leaders. Since all of these considerations and more might be relevant, the question does not admit of an undifferentiated reply. Following from that insight, there is no single answer to the question of whether a "Jewish state" is justified or whether any given religion-state linkage is justified. The question must always divide into two parts: Which aspects of the Jewish state (or the religion-state linkage) are justified? Which are not?

Before getting ahead of ourselves, though, and before trying to sketch principles for distinguishing a religion-state relationship that is justified from one that is not justified, we should gain a clearer idea of the various ways Israel might be conceived as a Jewish state. In that effort, the thirty-one Israelis are a great help. In part, they are helpful in their ambiguity, for few of the subjects offer a straight "yes" or "no" answer. It seems that for many Israelis of all stripes, the question of Israel's Jewishness is far from black-and-white. Some of them aren't sure what a Jewish state is, or where to find evidence that the state is Jewish. Many of them, in Hegelian fashion, seem to identify the Israeli state with Israeli civil society, referring not to legislation and institutions—"official" elements of the state—but to the Jewishness of Israeli citizens or to the degree of religiosity among Israel's Jews. These diverse perspectives on the question suggest the notion is not only contested (Israelis locate their state's Jewishness in different places) but conflicted (they detect the pull from other sets of considerations: most notably, Israel's democratic character, Jewish law [*halacha*], or both).

Although all the secular Jews in my study think that the state is Jewish, some hesitate or qualify their answers. Consider Mina's tentative reply: "[Pause]. In some way, yes." Common among the secular respondents is a belief that at least some aspects of the current *way* in which the state is Jewish is problematic, but most nevertheless believe that a Jewish state ought to exist, and they embrace the notion. The seculars locate Israel's Jewishness in the Declaration of Establishment and the Law of Return (Mina); in the fact that religion and state were combined from the beginning by David Ben-Gurion (Shulamit, Ronit); and in its unjustifiably "religious" nature (Shulamit, Naomi and Tanya). Illustrating her uncertainty about just what counts as a Jewish state, Ronit says, "I find the formula of 'Jewish state' a little difficult, but it's clear that this is a state that is governed by Jews and they govern it for the Jews. If that's what you call a Jewish state, it's a Jewish state." Yoram notes that the state is Jewish owing to its Jewish society; he thinks this was diluted in the 1990s, however, by the secular Russian immigration and weakening Zionist ideology. Many of the secular respondents (four of the seven) react to the question with a quick denunciation of the kind of Jewish state that they regard as coercive—each saying that the state is "too Jewish" either in terms of how it treats non-Orthodox Jews or non-Jews, or both.

Each of the traditional Jews in my sample, like the secular Jews, concurs that Israel is a Jewish state. Many of their answers reflect a personal connection and attraction to the Jewish *avira* (air, environment) of the state that is lacking in the secular Jews' responses. Rivka notes that Judaism is "very, very important" and finds expression in the Law of Return, "many of the laws, the education system," and the fact that "the majority of citizens are Jewish." Chaim also mentions the fact that "Jews live in the state" as fundamental to its Jewishness. Others cite the definition of a "Jewish state" in the Declaration of Establishment (Shmuel), the feeling of peace on Shabbat and Yom Kippur (Rotem), the knowledge that "all Jews have a place to go" in the event of a crisis (Rita), and "the rhythm of the year, the weekly cycle from 'Shabbat Shalom' to holidays, the Hebrew language, the fact that the history of the state and of the Jewish people is taught to kids in school," along with "Hebrew literature, both classical and contemporary" (Aaron).

The level of enthusiasm for the Jewish state continues to swell when we turn to the Religious Zionist subjects. Each of these individuals treats the question as an invitation to wax nostalgic about her homeland. When asked if their state is Jewish, Religious Zionists do not pause. Rabbi Rosen, for instance, sees Judaism as the state's "raison d'etre" and the "reason why we're here"; Ganit says it "clearly" is Jewish because "every Jew here feels it is his home" (she thinks it should be a "state of the Jews" rather than a religious Jewish state, however—more on that distinction below); Richard says Israel is "certainly" Jewish because "its essential ethos and way of life are in very broad terms cognitive of Jewish tradition" and "its primary purpose is the well-being of the Jewish people." Yoel introduces the land as key: "the fact that it is *in* Israel" makes Israel Jewish, as do "the background and reasons for which it was founded, and by whom it was founded." Avi, too, notes that "Israel was founded as a Jewish state"; he adds that Israeli Independence Day and the fact that Israelis speak Hebrew express its Jewishness. Two members of this category are partisans of the Jewish state but lament its status at the turn of the millennium. Zvi notes the "worrying state of Judaism in Israel" that has developed in the past ten to fifteen years, particularly with regard to youth who "know nothing"—not even the Ten Commandments. Nahman thinks that a truly Jewish state must be based on Jewish laws, which are currently lacking, and that "most people here don't see it as a Jewish state."

Don't they? In referring to "most people" Nahman likely means secular and perhaps traditional Israelis. But as we saw above, all of these subjects see Israel as a Jewish state, and survey data show that non-observant and somewhat observant Jews (who together make up at least 70 percent of Israeli Jewry) strongly support some notion of a Jewish state.[7] So is Nahman simply wrong? Or is his conception of a Jewish state materially different from that of most Jews whose religious observance is less strict? There is strong support for the second explanation: Nahman's statement indicates his view that most Jewish Israelis do not see Israel as the kind of Jewish state he thinks it is—one that ought to be governed by religious Jewish legislation. And he is probably correct. A helpful phrase that frames the difference between secular/traditional and Religious Zionist conceptions of Israel's Jewishness has its root in interpretations of Theodor Herzl's writing: Israel as a "state of [or for] the Jews."[8] The internal debate over Israel's status has often focused on the difference between this concept—which usually implies a state that is a haven for a majority of Jews, with a government of, by and for Jews—and a religiously based Jewish state, one that not only belongs to Jews but aligns itself with Orthodox Judaism.

Among the Religious Zionists in my study, everyone but Ganit and Richard clearly prefers the term "Jewish state" to "state of the Jews." Ganit, the most politically liberal of the Religious Zionists, wavers between the two ideas and (like Richard) finds that the terms ultimately mean the same thing:

> I still think that this is a Jewish state but not *religious* Jewish—I don't think that saying a state is Jewish makes it a religious Jewish state. I do think a Jewish state is a state in which everyone who's Jewish—I never thought about these things, I'm thinking about them as I speak with you!—can come and practice the Jewish religion according to his own way of life.

Zvi reframes the issue as one of compromise between religious and nonreligious Israeli Jews, with secular Jews assenting to a mildly Jewish state while enjoying the freedoms of an otherwise liberal-democratic "state of the Jews":

> We'll take a compromise between the two, between religious and secular. At least let's go back to ten or fifteen years ago. I don't want more than that. At least let's have a situation where every person will do what he wants in his home. I can't come into a person's home and tell him: do this or that. But at least what we call the Jewish institutions should have a Jewish color, because we are still a Jewish state that's supposed to have a Jewish content. There should be not just secular but also holy studies in the schools, so that people will know what a page of the Gemarra [Talmud] is. No

one knows what a page of the Gemarra is today. They know how to solve hundreds of math problems but tell them to read a page of Gemarra, and people will stand in shock: "what's this?" So we must find the mid-point, the compromise between what we call a halachic state and a totally secular state, the compromise in the middle. That way I too as a religious person will be able to say: "O.K. I live in a Jewish state," and a secular person will say, "O.K., it's true that I live in a Jewish state, but it allows me to live as I wish" without starting to argue and to wrangle about every little thing. It's important to see the world relatively broadly.

Expanding on Zvi's analysis, which favors a Jewish state for its presumably greater religious content, Avi adds an important twist. His is the only comment from a Religious Zionist on this question that refers to Israel's non-Jewish Arab minority: "A state of the Jews," he argues, "means that only Jews can live here. A Jewish state is not only for Jews; it can be for all the various sectors. Personally I think that's very good."[9] Ultimately, though, he thinks Israel must be both Jewish *and* for the Jews:

Saying that it's a Jewish state doesn't mean that as a Jewish state Muslims and Christians will have exactly the same relationship to the state that Jews have—that would give the state a different character. It's clear that this is a state for the Jews but it is also a Jewish state in which those with other opinions can integrate within it. Maybe there is some kind of combination between the two expressions.

Circling back to Nahman's comment that most people don't see Israel as Jewish, we find a third possible reading of the Israeli state that transcends (or escapes) Judaism. Nahman believes there to be a significant difference between a Jewish state and a state of the Jews that maps a distinction between "Jews" and "Israelis":

When you say "Jewish state" people understand that it belongs to this Nation, belongs to us. But this thing that belongs to us is so bereft of value! The Jews here in Israel see themselves, in my opinion, more as Israelis than as Jews: "I live among the People and don't live somewhere else." A Jewish state must be based on something; a state of the Jews just means "I'm Jewish and I live here." What do you mean "I'm Jewish"? Everyone will interpret that differently.

Nahman's final sentence is not a celebration of religious or cultural diversity among Jews; it is a worry that permitting such a diversity of interpretations free rein in the state will lead to a valueless, content-free Jewish state that will come to be identified more with its name (Israel) than with its history and essence.

Even if they disagree over what the shape of Israel's Jewish nature ought to be, secular and traditional Jews are at one with the Religious Zionists over how to understand the differences between a "Jewish state" and a "state of the Jews" as those terms are used in Israeli public political debate. Aaron, the former Conservative rabbi from the United States, sees a state of the Jews as "a framework which gives Jews the right of a variety of expressions," while a Jewish state "is generally referred to as a legal, a Jewish legal religious state." He prefers the former term and finds it more compatible with the political philosophy of his native country: "I would attribute that in a strange kind of way to coming out of the American tradition where the state provides safety and in a way sets the tone in reality but the individuals work out the details the way they want." And echoing Yoram's prediction of an eventual separation of religion and state in Israel, Aaron offers this: "It will happen anyway, an open state. You can't stop that. I mean if you look at the linguistics and cultural anthropology and look into what's going on, it's an ever-evolving situation. If you want to use a heavy hand, you won't succeed."

Naomi, the secular *kibbutznikit*, agrees: "A state of the Jews is a state in which every Jew has the right to come and live, no matter if he's religious, secular, Reform, Conservative, whatever." She cites the principle of "live and let live," explaining that it means others "shouldn't try to coerce, shouldn't try to tell me what to do. That's why I think it should be a state of the Jews." But Naomi doesn't want to jettison the Religious Zionist's favored term, only to reinterpret it: "It's possible to call that a Jewish state too, as long as Judaism isn't involved in politics." This comment captures the attitude of many secular and traditional Jews who are proud to call Israel a Jewish state even as they object to various manifestations of its Jewishness. They turn away from the expression only when presented with an alternative that more closely matches their conception of the Jewish state. So it seems appropriate to view the "Jewish state" - "state of the Jews" debate as a dispute over competing conceptions of the Jewish state itself, not necessarily a dispute over whether Israel should be a Jewish state.

What do Arabs and Haredim think of the debate between a Jewish state and a state of the Jews? Not much. The Arabs, for the most part, find the state oppressive in its Jewish dominance regardless of whether the source of that domination is "Jewish" or "Jews." Omer and Youssef find no difference between the concepts: "it's the same thing," they both intone. Nadia agrees and is more critical: "It's a semantic game, and Jews are the kings of semantic games." The non-Zionist or anti-Zionist ultra-Orthodox Jews, similarly, generally do not want the state of Israel to be either a Jewish state *or* a state of the Jews. But their reasons couldn't be more different. The first term, for a Haredi Jew, implies that the secular state either is or can be given a religious basis prior to the messianic age; the second implies the legitimacy of diverse approaches to Judaism, which in turn threatens Haredi control over the state's religious establishment.

Among my Haredi subjects, only one strongly believes the state is Jewish. The rest, for one reason or another, begrudge Israel its religious nature. Yehuda expresses one of two versions of the classic ultra-Orthodox line on the question—the less widely held "rejectionist" position—while Nosson represents the second, "accommodationist" position that most of the Haredi world has adopted.[10] Yehuda refuses to "participate in elections" because "it is forbidden to have a state. I don't help them. Those who send Members of Knesset help them. I am of those extremists who believe that it is forbidden to vote...I have lived here for six generations. We lived here before the state arose. They came and established a state and I don't recognize them." Clarifying his position, Yehuda explains,

> We do not see the state as a Jewish state. The name "Israel" is a forgery. We think the state was illegitimate from the very beginning, because it is forbidden to take the state into our own hands. We believe that due to our sins the Second Temple was destroyed and the Holy One Blessed Be He[11] sent us into exile. We must wait until the messiah redeems us from the Goyim. To take the state in our own hands with our own power contradicts our belief.

Yehuda also cites the "secular majority who destroyed the religion," the fact that "only" 27 of the 120 Knesset seats are occupied by religious Jews, and the fact that Israeli law is "secular" as proof that no Jewish state exists in the land of Israel today. The true Jewish state will come about only when the messiah arrives.

But whereas Yehuda, an affiliate of the anti-Zionist "Eda Haredit," is "totally against the state" (as are Jews in the yet more extreme sect known as Neturei Karta[12]), Nosson (a supporter of the Agudat Yisrael party) distinguishes between Zionism—which he strongly opposes—and the state itself, which, he says, provides some good things for "Torah Judaism." Straddling these positions, he is reluctant to say whether or not Israel is a Jewish state:

> It could be just a semantic issue. What do you mean by a Jewish state? There is a Jewish majority here, that much is known. But the state is not administered in the way that Judaism dictates and that too is known without a doubt.

Turning to history, Nosson then explains his opposition to Zionism. "God told us we must not return to the Land of Israel by force," he says. "The 'ingathering of the exiles' is partial; the majority of Jews still live outside of Israel. And its independence is even partial; we all know that Israel isn't independent from an economic or from a political point of view—it depends on America. The only thing Zionism has succeeded in doing is to desecrate the People of Israel." Nosson traces the roots of the problem to the Enlightenment in Western Europe and notes that Zionists made "cynical use of religious motifs such as the Land of Israel, Zion, and the ingathering of the exiles" in an attempt to turn the religion on its head and present a new authentic Judaism. Up to this point, Yehuda would agree with Nosson's diagnosis. Nosson's view diverges from his over the significance of 1948: "The central stream of Haredi Judaism," Nosson says, engaged in only "passive opposition" after the establishment of the state, participating in legislative politics and seeking representation for Haredi interests. And despite its *treif* (non-kosher) roots, and the fact that things would have been "much much better without Zionism," the state has helped "Torah Judaism to flourish" and allowed tens of thousands of Jews to "live in security as they sit and study."[13]

One beneficiary is Oren, the young yeshiva student who describes himself as "pretty liberal." Oren argues that although it is written in the Declaration of Establishment that Israel is a Jewish state, "what has resulted over the past fifty years is not exactly a Jewish state, with everything that the term implies"; *halacha*, for example, does not form the basis of the laws. Echoing Nahman, he says: "This state is more Israeli than it is Jewish." Oren doesn't vote in elections, but this is a result of "disliking politics" and "not finding any party, religious or secular, that represents me"; he is not, like Yehuda, ideologically opposed to the state or to elections. Missing from Oren's position is any vitriol toward Zionism per se, or a reluctance to recognize the state. Nevertheless, he avoids celebrations and studies in yeshiva on Israeli Independence Day (sometimes he goes to a barbeque, but "it's like Christmas—everybody celebrates even though no one believes in Jesus") and does not see it as a special day, certainly not worthy of the special Hallel prayer[14] said by religious Jews on Passover, Shavuot, Hanukkah and Sukkot, and, by Religious Zionists, on Israeli Independence Day as well.

Nehama, the Yemenite *ba'alat teshuva* and Jonathan Rosenblum, the *ba'al teshuva* American-born columnist, agree that the state of Israel has little Jewish meaning. Identifying the state with society, Nehama says Israel is Jewish from the point of view of its population, but not from the point of view of its leaders. She then complains bitterly that Israel has "lost its purpose" in allowing in so many "goyim"—non-Jewish Russians and foreign workers from places like Thailand and the Philippines. "Half of the country we have already given to the Arabs, so where is the state for the Jews? The state *of* the Jews?" And taking issue with Religious Zionism, Rosenblum says "You can talk '*reishit tzmihat geulateinu*' ('the beginning of the flowering of our redemption') all you want, but it's harder and harder just looking around in this state to believe that this is the beginning of the redemption...When the state became interested in giving the land away, there was an unbearable tension. To me it leads to all kinds of silliness."

Finally, the idiosyncratic Yeshayahu (the one who calls himself a Zionist) is the only Haredi in my sample who believes unreservedly that Israel is a Jewish state. "The majority of the citizens are Jewish. And in my eyes, the majority of the public here in Israel behave and keep at least one little thing, or even in their hearts there is something Jewish. They are Jewish first of all by origin and secondly the state contains a spirit of Judaism through and through."

A majority of Arabs in the study (four of five) also believes that Israel is a Jewish state. (Three of the respondents sharply resent that fact, while one, Muhammad, "lives with it" though he would prefer a "state of all its inhabitants.") The one who does not quite agree, Omer, has the following reasoning:

> In a Jewish state all the citizens speak Hebrew and all the citizens are members of the Jewish religion. So if I look at the state of Israel now...not everyone is a member of the Jewish religion and there are Muslim Arabs and Christian Arabs and Druze. Therefore, Israel is 80 percent Jewish and 20 percent a non-Jewish state. Currently not everyone is Jewish.

In thus associating the character of the state with the religious and linguistic makeup of the citizenry, Omer believes there is little difference between the concept of a Jewish state and that of a Zionist state. On this point he is joined by each of his fellow Arab subjects, but Muhammad believes that Zionism is weaker today than it was fifty years ago, and both Majjed and Youssef point out that the Zionist character of the state is even more problematic than its Jewish character. (Youssef: "it seeks the Greater Land of Israel"; Majjed: "it's an great endangerment to my existence.") For his part, Youssef thinks "it doesn't matter if I think it's a Jewish state or not. It is a Jewish state with no connection to what I think or to what I believe. Every time I hear 'Hatikva' and every time I hear the racist things people say against Arabs, implying that they don't belong to this state...I *feel* that I don't belong to this state, despite the fact that I do belong to it." Majjed, too, both identifies and attacks national Jewish elements of the state:

> It's Jewish because the flag and the national anthem show that it's Jewish. The Law of Return shows that it's a Jewish state. Not giving the right of return to Palestinian refugees who fled in 1948 shows that it's a Jewish state. The mess with getting water to the Palestinians shows that it's a Jewish state. I could tell you about twenty-five more things that show that it's a Jewish state, easily. It shows just *how* Jewish it is.

Nadia agrees, saying the state is Jewish both "by definition" and "in action." It gives her "a feeling of estrangement from the state" because its "symbols and institutions belong to them (the Jews), and that's not fun." Muhammad, the eldest of my Arab subjects, is also the most well-off financially and the only one who owns his own home. For him, the Jewish state isn't the tragedy it is to the younger four Israeli Arabs. A long-time member of the mainstream, center-left and overwhelmingly Jewish Labor party (of its nineteen representatives in the Sixteenth Knesset elected in 2003, Ghaleb Majadla was the sole Arab)[15], he observes that "reality says it is a Jewish state, since most of its residents are Jewish." But in his village, which he says is always "improving, with everyone building his own home," he isn't influenced at all by the Jewish character of the state. At work, teaching Jewish history and Hebrew, Muhammad emphasizes the strong religious, linguistic and cultural connections between Jews and Muslims. "We are all children of Abraham," he says. "We are alike in so many ways."

Is Israel a Jewish state? How would we know if it is? And what kind of Jewish state is it? The thirty-one subjects clarify the confusion over these questions even as they raise difficult philosophical and theological problems. For our present political theoretical purposes, we need not enter Talmudic debates over the content of such a state vis-à-vis messianic potentialities. Nor is it necessary to conclude that Israel is or is not in fact a Jewish state—there are numerous complications that would either preclude such an announcement or render it trivial. Suffice it to say that the vast majority of Israelis see their own state as Jewish, which provides reason enough for us to proceed with that idea in mind. There is no consensus, however, as to what makes Israel a Jewish state today, what an ideal Jewish state would look like and whether Israel ought to be a Jewish state. The "state of the Jews" vs. "Jewish state" debate most clearly shows a division along intra-religious lines. Although the visions for an ideal Jewish state diverge markedly among those who advocate a Jewish state, we do not yet have a clear picture of which specific elements of the state might gain common affirmation from various groups in Israeli society.

Israel as a Democratic State

Democracy is a notoriously complex and nuanced idea, with many variations and justifications. Asking Israelis whether they think their state is democratic, however, involves surprisingly few difficulties. It certainly lacks the degree of conceptual confusion at play in asking whether their state is Jewish. For in contrast to the debate over Israel's Jewish character, the public debate over Israel's democratic nature rests on a readily identifiable and fairly consistent notion of democracy. When Israelis talk about democracy, I found, they have certain fundamentals in mind, but some ideas commonly associated with democracy rarely come up. None of my subjects, for example, refers to "government by the people" and only three mention majority rule, the feature Americans tend to associate most strongly with democracy. None of my subjects talks about political participation. No one highlights civic responsibility. What do they talk about? Rights of speech and of press, of the right to vote, of minority rights, of equality and, above all, of what Isaiah Berlin terms "negative liberty"—the absence of external constraints. When Israelis talk about democracy—no matter whether they are proponents or opponents of the idea—they are talking about a kind of liberalism.

Examining Israel's Zionist, socialist, collectivist roots might lead one to guess that its Jewish citizens would propound something of a communitarian notion of democracy, emphasizing the good of the whole over the part and staying away from ideas that exalt the individual and his rights of privacy. This pioneering Zionist ethic, it might reasonably be surmised, would both depend upon and lend support to a notion of positive liberty—one that gives the Jewish people a collective right to "be free in its own land" (as "Hatikva," the national anthem, puts it) rather than allow individual Jews to "do what they like" in their private lives (as many of my subjects put it). But the group orientation of early Zionism, it seems, has been at least partially supplanted—or some may say supplemented—by an ethic of liberal democracy.[16]

Why do Israelis see democracy in terms of liberal individualism? My goal here is not to psychoanalyze my subjects. But several features of the societal debate over "the values of Israel as a Jewish and democratic state" may shed some light on the way that democracy tends to be conceived among Israeli citizens. First, most Israelis (from elite commentators to the average educated citizens in my study) tend to regard the adjectives in that phrase as at least potentially conflicting, if not mutually exclusive. They tend to see "Jewish" as a code word for limitation and "democratic" as an indicator of freedom. So whenever something that might otherwise be attributable to democracy or the democratic process is seen as a restraint, it is shunted to the other concept (if connected in any way to Judaism) or (if unrelated to Judaism) is simply deemed anti-democratic. That is, Israelis would tend to regard a policy prohibiting the import of non-kosher meat as a *Jewish* law, not as a *democratic* policy that won the support of a large majority of Knesset representatives (eighty percent of whom are not members of religious parties). Similarly, they might regard a law that bans skateboarding in public as *anti-democratic* since it restricts Israelis' freedom to skate in certain areas. Democracy is stripped of much of its procedural content (according to which a policy is considered democratic if enacted in line with democratic procedures) and is often read as simply whatever conduces to greater freedom.

Second, a tension exists between two types of negative freedom that Israelis ascribe to a proper and well-functioning democracy. The first type of freedom has already been discussed: the freedom of individuals to do what they will. The competing notion—which in some cases Israelis hold together with the first—refers to the freedom of minority communities to preserve and practice their way of life. The latter idea adopts a group-based rather than an individualistic perspective, protecting the rights of minority religious groups rather than those of ontologically unconnected individuals. It stems from the experience of non-Jewish religious groups under Israel's inherited millet system, according to which each sector has jurisdiction over issues relating to its members' personal status and schooling.

However they define the concept, a large majority of all respondents agree that Israel is, at least to some extent, a democratic state.[17] The Arab subjects (with one exception, Muhammad) are most critical of Israel's democratic character, finding it incomplete and in need of significant improvement even as they favor the cultural autonomy associated with Israel's millet system. Many secular and traditional Jews share this sentiment, emphasizing different points. Haredim and Religious Zionists are mixed on the question, many of them noting that democracy is not a traditionally Jewish value.

The notion of equality is predominant among Israeli Arab subjects' interpretations of what counts as democracy. Equality, in the sense of equal treatment and equal rights, also plays the central role in Arabs' refusal to see Israel as fully democratic. Nadia is blunt: "The word democracy [used vis-à-vis the state] is one big bullshit. The state is democratic—I don't say it isn't. I mean in dealing with the Arab sector, it is not democratic." Omer concurs: "There is full democracy for Jews and partial democracy for non-Jews" owing to the fact that "some laws are connected to religion." According to Youssef, "from a legal perspective they *say* it's democratic, but if you look at what *happens* in this country," Jewish criminals who murder Arabs spend only "three or four years" in prison while Arabs who commit murder receive the full sentence. "What kind of democracy are we talking about?" Youssef thinks that "in voting there is democracy," since every citizen of Israel gets one vote. "But aside from that? Nothing. When you say 'Jewish state,' you prefer a particular population to another population. Where is the equality among all of the citizens?"

Majjed expands the critique of Israel's democracy beyond ill-treatment of Arab citizens, reflecting the leanings of his political party:

> Look at education and at everything else. The definition of a democratic state is to give equal rights to every citizen without discriminating based on religion, race or sex. Right? I'm not speaking only of Arabs. By the way, I told you that I am a member of a Jewish-Arab party [Hadash]. I don't say that all the Jews are rich and

all the Arabs are poor. Go down to the south, to Dimona, to Rahat, to Ofakim, to all those places. Their situation is also horrible. But these people don't have high political consciousness and they vote for people who screw them at the end of the day. These people vote for Likud.

Democracy is very important for all of the Arab subjects, but only Muhammad seems content with the status quo. In his words, "there is nothing that needs improvement" in Israeli democracy:

> Of course there is democracy here! We here have satellite dishes, so we see the TV channels from the Arab countries. There's no democracy there. Here we are able to say what we think; not so there. There, first of all, when a leader comes to visit you have to applaud, to act the way the authorities want you to. Here you have the opportunity every four or five years to vote for the Knesset, the government and the local councils. You can belong to political parties freely—Jewish, Arab or Zionist. You can also demonstrate. There is no limit. You can even write political articles in the Hebrew press, freely.

Muhammad adds that he "grew up on democracy," and that if someone took democracy away from him and tried to impose something on him, "it would be like someone ripped a limb off my body."

The freedom that Muhammad finds so appealing in Israeli democracy is a combination of individual and group liberty. As a traditional (though not strictly observant) Muslim, Muhammad finds it crucial that "we have religious autonomy. We have a Mufti," he says, "who tells us things that relate to religious issues. Sometimes we need to get an authorization or an order from the Mufti, but it's in coordination with the state authorities, because they work in the Ministry of Religion [which has since been disbanded and reorganized]." Omer, the religious nineteen-year-old, similarly speaks of "each sector having its own power, such as the Muslim courts and the Jewish courts enforcing the religious laws of each religion, separately." Nadia, too, cites "freedom for different groups to live in their own way" as the essence of democracy.

Many secular Jews sympathize with the plight felt by the dissatisfied Arab subjects, but they complain more loudly about the "religious coercion" that affects their own lives. Shulamit is a prime example. Defining democracy as freedom of speech, and having the right to vote and to choose, Shulamit says that Israel "wants to be democratic, but the Shasnikim [members of the ultra-Orthodox Shas party] won't let it be." Worrying that an even stronger representation of Haredim in the Knesset would lead to modesty laws similar to those in Iran and to rules mandating private Shabbat observance, she nevertheless notes that the religious-secular "status quo" has drifted in favor of the non-religious. "When I came to Jerusalem thirty years ago, you couldn't go to the movies on Friday night! There were no restaurants open. But today, many restaurants are open, many non-kosher restaurants—unheard of thirty years ago." Still, she fears that if Shas were in control they "would move the state back to the Middle Ages. . .Orthodoxy and democracy do not go together." Note that Shulamit is not inclined to reject the possibility of *Judaism* and democracy going together—recall that she defined her own Judaism as "living in a Jewish state." Instead, Shulamit rejects only that Orthodox political Judaism that seeks to enforce religious observance on non-observant Jews. "For me," she says, "Judaism and the state are the same thing."

Naomi, the *kibbutznikit* who is less than half Shulamit's age, has a very similar perspective motivated by an unconcealed anger toward Israel's religious establishment. The Haredim, she claims, withhold "the most important principles of democracy"—"equality, freedom of expression, freedom of speech, and freedom to do what you want to do"—by mandating religious marriage, say, and by burning down Russian-owned stores that sell pork. Shulamit argues that only a two-state solution modeled on the separation of the kingdoms of Israel and Judea in the tenth century B.C.E. will solve Israel's problems (one state for secular, one for ultra-Orthodox); Naomi invites "our Arab brothers to come live here in peace" and thinks Haredim should be "thrown out" to start their own country somewhere else.

Tanya, Ronit and Yoram share a somewhat less emphatic critique of Israeli democracy. Allowing that there are elections every four years, and that citizens are permitted to voice their opinions by voting, Tanya argues that "civil rights are very undeveloped here" and that Israel needs a constitution to correct the deficiency. Ronit's emphasis is on the lack of "equality between all citizens," referring specifically to Arabs; she thinks Israel is "democratic in comparison to her neighbors, but not fully democratic." Yoram, echoing Oren, thinks that the answer to whether or not Israel is democratic "depends on whom you ask." It's democratic for Jews, not for Arabs, and needs to devote more energy to ensuring equal conditions for all citizens.

Mina, the recent Russian immigrant, thinks Israel is "relatively" democratic. And although she, too, wants to see more democracy in Israel, Mina warns that "too much democracy is an illusion and can lead to communism." She finds a potential danger in too much freedom of expression, for example.

Rita, the only traditional Jew in my sample who seemed ambivalent about the fruits of democracy, built on Mina's critique in cautioning that "Israel is too democratic" in allowing unrestrained freedom of press. The others in this category generally side with most of the secular Jews in identifying the democratic attributes of the state—free elections, freedom of speech, and a general freedom "to choose to do what you want"[18] being the most frequently cited. Each also points out where Israeli democracy comes up short. Shmuel decried the influence of the Orthodox parties and the lack of a constitution providing "protection from the rule of the majority"; Rivka noted that Israel is "quite democratic," coming back to the point a few minutes later ("I forgot an important point") to discuss the deficiencies vis-à-vis both Arabs and non-Orthodox Jews.

Rotem and Aaron agree with many of the critical points, but they are both more supportive of the overall health of Israeli democracy. Aaron favorably cites University of Haifa sociologist Sammy Smooha's argument that Israel is not a liberal democracy but an "ethnic democracy," one that serves a "core ethnic nation" through democratic institutions but provides something short of full membership to those outside the nation.[19] Rotem employs a comparison with the West:

> It's more democratic than a lot of states, and it's certainly far, far
> away from being an ideal democratic state that I would like to see.
> But I don't think it's less democratic than the United States. I think
> the United States is not so democratic either.

Asked to clarify that remark, Rotem sounds indignant in mentioning "Indians that are living in reservations, blacks who are treated abysmally," among others, and detailing Israel's sins toward Palestinians and Israeli Arabs.

Religious Zionists also express worry about Israel's democratic system, but mostly from the opposite direction. That is, some of the subjects in this category view Israel as too democratic for its own good. And whereas every Arab, secular Jew and traditional Jew in the study says she is committed to democracy over Judaism, both personally and politically, every Religious Zionist expresses both a stronger personal commitment to Judaism than to democracy *and* a conviction that when Judaism and democracy conflict politically, the latter must bow to the former. (Ganit is the only one who hedged on the second question, but her responses to subsequent questions—and her favorable citation of former Supreme Court Justice Menachem Elon's view that the order of the adjectives in the phrase "Jewish and democratic state" means something—indicate her tilt toward what she calls the state's "wide Jewish outlook.")

A certain ambivalence toward democracy abounds in both the Religious Zionist and Haredi sectors. Take Richard, for example. Appearing to combine concepts found in Locke, Rousseau and Mill, he associates democracy with elections, accountability of public officials, citizen participation in "major decisions that affect the life of the nation," and the "American goals of the pursuit of life, happiness, freedom without abusing the rights of other people." But Judaism, to which Richard owes his first duty, "is not democratic" when it comes to the aristocratic method of determining the law (only "authorized interpreters of the tradition" take part) or the class system that "assigns status based on birth" to Cohens, Levites and Israelites (requiring, for example, Israelites to tithe to both Levites and to the Cohen priestly class).[20] Similarly with Zvi, who believes there must be compromise away from an "absolutely Jewish state" ("that can be but only with the coming of the messiah, not now"), but sees his first responsibility as toward Jewish law, not civil Israeli law.

For Yoel, "there is nothing in life that has nothing to do with religion." That includes the state. And that means that democracy must be sacrificed to preserve Israel as a Jewish state by excluding Arabs from major national decisions. "It's hard for me to say it because I have an American background and have the generally politically correct feeling that democracy is the best form of government," he says, "but I do *not* believe that Arabs have the right to determine the course that our country is to take." He thus proposes nullifying the votes of Arab Knesset members in votes of national fate, but allows that they should be able to participate in economic and other matters that affect them as a group or determine their towns' and villages' funding. From another perspective, Nahman believes that Judaism and democracy are compatible in that what some call "religious coercion" really isn't anti-democratic. The laws that prohibit work on Shabbat and the importation of non-kosher meat help to "connect secular Jews to Judaism"; religion "gives people a lot of things that the open, modern world does not give." So democracy is valuable, but within a Jewish framework.

Other than Yeshayahu, for whom it is "very important," none of the Haredi subjects express much of a longing for democracy. "Freedom," Yeshayahu's strongest association with the form of government, is Nehama's choice as well. She believes that "religion doesn't believe in democracy," however, because there is no principle in Judaism which says that "people can do whatever they want." Bringing up a radio broadcast she heard that morning indicating then-Prime Minister Ehud Barak's desire to introduce a constitution and abolish the Ministry of Religious Affairs (a move that would occur three years later under Prime Minister Ariel Sharon), Nehama ridicules the flexibility of civil law: "The laws of the Torah never change. In a million years, it will still be forbidden to eat milk with meat. So what is democracy? Change the law when you feel like it?!" Jonathan Rosenblum, the American born-again Haredi, agrees that "it would be hard to make the case that democracy is a Jewish value," since the ideal Jewish polity is a monarchy. Yehuda concurs: "According to the Torah there is no such thing as democracy, where everyone does what he wants. The Torah dictates what we do." Oren is less direct, but he also notes a fundamental difference between Judaism and democracy: "With democracy, you go according to the majority. Judaism has something like this too, but it doesn't operate according to a national referendum and it doesn't involve the choices of all the citizens." The Talmudic principle according to which halachic disputes should be settled by "leaning after the many" ("*aharei rabin lehatot*") applies to learned, authorized Torah scholars, not to the average Moyshe on the street.

Is Israel a democratic state? Most Israelis in my pool say yes, although many find their state to be less democratic than it ought to be and some consider it overly democratic. Arabs and many secular and traditional Jews fit in the first category, with the former finding problems of inequality and the latter decrying insufficient liberty. And Haredim and many Religious Zionists, who are suspicious of the value of democracy, constitute the second category. When substituting a term that most closely matches Israelis' conception of democracy—liberalism—we find a first take on one of the central questions of this book: Is Israel a liberal state? In a way, yes, and in a way, no. Much more needs to be said about the details. In the next two sections, we move down one rung in level of abstraction to consider political slogans that propose changes in Israel's religion-state arrangement.

Separating Religion and State:
Jewish Israelis' Views

Israelis have been debating whether to separate religion and state since the days before they had a state. They have not given up on the idea nearly sixty years after Israel's birth. It is not surprising that the debate has been so consistent and so heated, especially given the acknowledged tensions between Jewish and liberal democratic values and the role that each had—and still has—in constituting Israel. But as I discovered in my interviews, the debate takes on a character different from that which might be expected and suggests that "separation" is hardly the fixed or clear concept it might seem. The slogan "separation of religion and state" operates in Israel's Jewish sector *not* as a prescription for dismantling all or most of the Jewish character of the state but as place marker for another concept: the protection of individual religious liberty. To complicate matters, when Jewish Israelis advocate separating religion and state, they mean something very different from what Israeli Arabs intend by the same proposal. In the next section I present the views of Israeli Arabs on separation. Here I focus on how Jewish Israelis relate to the concept.

Israel's Basic Laws contain no provisions that clearly confer either a right to "free exercise of religion" or a requirement that the state avoid "establishing" religion, the First Amendment principles that constitute the American version of religious liberty. Neither of the two principles finds an analogue in Israeli law. The first, however, gains some *de facto* support in Israel's Declaration of Establishment and protection through Basic Law: Human Dignity and Freedom (1992, 1994). While free exercise of religion lacks explicit backing in Israeli law, however, a principle of nonestablishment is not only missing but implicitly precluded by several of the laws and institutions that make up the Israeli state.

In asking Israelis about separation of religion and state, I investigate the following: How widely supported is the principle among individuals in various religious groups? What reasons do individuals offer for or against separation? How compelling are those reasons? What do Israelis mean by separation of religion and state? How do other positions the subjects take relate to their stance on separation?

Of my thirty-one subjects, twenty-two express support for separating religion and state in Israel while nine oppose the idea. All but one Arab respondent supports separation. Among the Jewish respondents in my interview pool, the secular and traditional Jews are nearly unanimous in support of separation; the Religious Zionists are, with two exceptions, strongly opposed; and the Haredim are split down the middle, with two in support, two opposed, and two torn between the rival positions.[21]

Arguments in Favor of Separation Among Israeli Jews

Although their reasoning varies, the Jewish subjects' arguments in favor of separation of religion and state may be grouped into three often-overlapping categories. (1) *Liberal Freedom:* Religion is a private matter of conscience that a liberal democratic state (with its promise of negative liberty) has no legitimate charge to control. Separation will solve the problem of religious coercion in which the state requires citizens to mold their behavior to divine commandments of Judaism. (2) *Jewish Flourishing:* Integration of religion and state makes Judaism unattractive in the eyes of the non-Orthodox and pushes them away from religion. With separation, Israelis' interest in and attachment to Judaism will increase. (3) *Religious Autonomy:* The Israeli state is essentially secular and has only a fraudulent religious veneer. Nominal, partial integration of religion and state entails unjust state interference with religion, threatening the autonomy of religious groups and their doctrines.

Speaking roughly, the first argument is most frequently heard from secular and traditional subjects; the second from those Haredi and Religious Zionist respondents who support separation, as well as from many secular and traditional subjects; and the third from Haredim.

Liberal Freedom
Starting with the argument from liberal freedom, we find several dimensions of the idea that Israel ought to separate religion and state. Democratic theory founded on individual liberty, recognition of the pluralism of Israeli Jewry, mutual toleration and respect among secular and religious

Jews are major themes. Mina, the secular immigrant from Russia, ties this point to her vision of Israeli democracy: "If we say that we're a modern, democratic state, being tied to the Rabbinate and things like that is anti-democratic. It's important to respect religion, but everyone must have the option to choose for himself." Naomi, too, regards this freedom of choice as essential to Israel's "modernization" and to quell the religious-secular divisiveness in Israeli society:

> Just as the secular public doesn't want to force the religious public to do what secular Jews do, they should understand that they can't force us to do what they like. I think that [with separation] Israel could live with much greater internal peace than it has now. At present, there's no peace at all.

Asked how Judaism and state should be connected, the traditional Jew Shmuel says:

> They should be totally separated from each other, of course! The state is a secular product, not a religious product. And religion is a matter of preference of the people. I can believe, I don't have to believe—this is something that I have to choose. But if I live in the state, I have to obey its rules. Because otherwise, the state could not remain. And if I want to preserve the state, I have to make some kind of a plan where I play by the secular rules, but religion is a matter of belief; it's a matter between me and God. I don't want to give you any report of what I do or what I believe or what I do with God. I may join with you and others in a group where we believe in the same thing, but I don't enforce it on you. But if I live in the state, I have to let others do that too. So they should be totally separate. Like in the United States!

Shmuel's comparison of his prescription of separation of religion and state to the arrangement in the United States was matched by several other subjects, including Rivka (traditional) and Yeshayahu (Haredi). When we come to the details of what the subjects mean by separation later in this chapter, however, we see how different the conceptions are from American separation—even though they flow, in part, from similar liberal reasoning. This is significant not so much in showing that Israelis sometimes misconceive the vagaries of the U.S. Supreme Court's Establishment Clause jurisprudence (or misread Rawls) but in highlighting that the American version of separation of religion and state (or Rawls's political liberalism) is just that: a version. It may be an excellent model for some societies, but it is not the only model, and it may not be appropriate for a state such as Israel.

All of the subjects quoted in this section strongly support the idea of a Jewish state, even as they argue for separation of religion and state. What, on an initial reading, could this mean? Rotem is more aware than Shmuel and some other subjects in seeing her positions as potentially subject to a charge of contradiction; she vigorously defends her view from that critique:

> Q: Do you think that Israel ought to separate religion from state?
>
> A: Yes, a hundred percent. That doesn't mean that there wouldn't be a Jewish state though. It would mean that people could really choose to make it a Jewish state, not by some kind of force, government force, something like that. A real Jewish state is a state where every Jew in it would want it to express Jewish values, Jewish ideas, Jewish culture. It doesn't in any way have to be expressed in government power. It would be very well for the state to separate from religion.
>
> Q: So the distinction would be between a Jewish society and a Jewish state?
>
> A: Yes. That sounds right [laughs].
>
> Q: Between civil society and actual politics, government.
>
> A: Yes. For the Jews in the country, I would very much like to see them all eventually organized in small communities which are Jewish communities, which lead some form of Jewish lifestyle, some form of Jewish culture. Just because it makes life much more meaningful. But communities and the state are almost contradictions in some ways.
>
> Q: Communities and the state...?
>
> A: They don't go together. Because a community is on a voluntary basis and state orders—like you have to get married in a Jewish ceremony—is just exactly the opposite of voluntary.

Rotem's use of the argument from liberal freedom differs from Mina's. Consistent with what some subjects described as a "state of the Jews," she wants to separate religion and state not only to give individuals the right to choose, but to give various Jewish religious sub-groups—not only Haredim and Religious Zionists, but others (presumably including her fellow Conservative Jews)—the ability to establish communities of meaning with their own rules, own rabbis and own traditions.

Jewish Flourishing

Rotem's motivation behind the liberal freedom argument is clearly related to the second argument for separation, Jewish flourishing. According to the latter, the source of disillusionment with Judaism on the part of much of Israel's secular Jewish population is, perhaps ironically, Judaism's involvement in the state. Unlike the argument from liberal freedom—which is heard mainly from secular and traditional Jews—this claim is voiced by Jews across the religious spectrum of Israeli society. It is one of the dominant tropes of those who would like to see religion and state separated in Israel.

Start with Naomi, the secular kibbutz-bred twenty-four-year-old who came to appreciate Judaism only when she worked in a Reform camp in the United States one summer:

> American Jews knew how to sing *birkat hamazon* [grace after meals]! I didn't know anything. At the beginning I was embarrassed, but how would I know? Of course I wouldn't know. Because here in Israel they say it's such a requirement that you pray before every meal and after every meal—they *tell* me what to do. There, it was so fun to learn it, and to sing it at every meal. It was a different world! It sounds absurd that I need to fly to the United States to realize how much I love the Jewish religion. It's funny, because I do love the Jewish religion, but here in Israel I can't do it. Reform Judaism is a religion I really love. I had great fun spending four months there and doing *kabbalat shabbat* [Friday evening prayers] and seeing everyone on Shabbat stopping all activity, wearing all white, coming at the same time to eat dinner, singing Shabbat songs. It's a beautiful thing, the most beautiful thing there is in the world. But in Israel it couldn't happen.

Why not?

> I think it's possible to preserve the religion without involving it in politics. I think that if it were that way, many of us—even *kibbutznikim*, who are considered the biggest heretics that there are— will be able to enjoy religion just as every other religious Jew enjoys religion. But because it's mixed up inside politics, it turns religion into something disgusting, repulsive, hateful. We simply hate religion because it's so involved in politics.

But we still don't have a clear answer as to *why* the politicization of religion produces such loathing. Why, if she now sees Judaism in such a positive light, does Naomi avoid anything having to do with religion—even Reform Judaism—in Israel? For two reasons. First, for Naomi, simply "living in Israel" makes her a Jew, while American Jews need "to do something to feel Jewish." Second, turning the slightest bit away from secularism "will only help the religious politicians, and then they will be able to influence the government more and more." In the end, she says, "everyone will be religious, and we will have a totally black state [*medina shehora*—i.e., dominated by Haredim]. It doesn't pay."

Oren, the "pretty liberal" Haredi yeshiva student, agrees that removing religion from the state will bring Israelis to hold Judaism in higher regard and to choose to engage in its rituals:

> People will value Judaism more highly because they'll see it as an independent body. If you want it, take it; if you don't, then don't. I won't force you, for example, to marry via my Rabbinate, in my institutions. . .It will be a private body like any other body, like an H.M.O. [*kupat holim*] for example. I think that many people in the state want Jewish weddings and things like that. But as it is today, when you come to Judaism you come to something that forces you to do something—so people don't want to approach it. They abhor it, so they keep away.

If you separate Judaism from the state, the Jews will come. Or will they? Oren premises his argument on the sensible claim—supported by my interviews—that most of Israel's non-religious Jews see themselves as Jewish mainly through their connection to the State of Israel. "If there is a separation of religion and state," he then argues, "they'll have a problem seeing what their Judaism is expressed in. They'll miss it. Everyone will need to work personally on his own Judaism."[22]

Two more views from diverse perspectives reach the same conclusion. Yeshayahu worries that the Israeli right-wing has co-opted religion, leaving those on the Left bereft of Jewish feeling:

> With everyone today who feels that religion needs to be separate, the moment that they'll feel that the religion is outside the system—they'll *love* it. Religion is not something that belongs to the camp on the Right or the Left or the Center. Religion belongs to all the camps, but today it is found only on the Right. The Left distanced itself from religion because of the same religious people who supposedly represent religion, and they are on the Right. And that's a mistake. I'm not saying that non-religious people can't keep the religion. I'm saying the Torah shouldn't be presented as if it's the Torah of the Right. The Torah is with the Right and the Left together!

And Aaron notes that too much religious Judaism pushes Jews away:

> I heard somebody say having no separation of religion and state is like what happened under the Soviets. There was a lot of communism but by the end there were no communists left. You can have lots of Judaism, but I'm not sure how many Jews we're going to have left. It's alienating! It's absolutely alienating! For those people who are not part of it—who are not that 27 percent of the population, let's even stretch it to 30 (and there too for a great many peo-

ple)—this is a repressive thing. And what happens is this: what
they call the Jewish aspects, and which I would call ritual and
ceremony, becomes repugnant. Who would want to be part of it?

Religious Autonomy

The third approach to justifying separation, like the second, claims that
the politicization of religion sullies Judaism. Whereas the argument from
Jewish flourishing focuses on the negative light in which non-Orthodox Israelis regard a state-ordained Judaism, the third blames integration of religion and state for unjustly interfering with Orthodox Jewish practice and belief. According to arguments of this type—put forward by a portion of Israel's Haredi Jewry—the state's linkage with religion only sullies Judaism by
extracting a stamp of approval from religious authorities. Imparting religious legitimacy buys a hand in shaping political affairs, but it subjects the
Haredi community to the kinds of compromises and regulations that participation in secular politics inevitably entails. True Judaism is thus led
astray.

The rejection of state interference, however, is infrequently linked to an
outright rejection of *involvement* in politics. Some Haredim, like Yehuda, do
withhold recognition of the state and refuse to vote or otherwise participate
in politics. They, as I noted in Part I of this chapter, constitute the anti-
Zionist, anti-Israel rejectionist camp of Haredim.[23] Most ultra-Orthodox,
however, while anti-Zionist, provide *de facto* support to the Israeli state and
participate actively in the polity. Nosson, Nehama and Jonathan Rosenblum,
for example, fit into the accommodationist camp. Among those on the rejectionist side, of whom Yehuda is the sole representative among the Haredi
subjects, the argument from religious autonomy is central to the call for
separation. When I ask Yehuda for his view, however, he claims that his rejectionist stance prevents him from even stating an opinion:

> Q: Do you think there should be a separation of religion and state?
>
> A: Like in the United States?
>
> Q: Yes.
>
> A: I told you, I think the state is illegitimate [*p'sula*]. So I can't help
> you and tell you that I want a state and I want it to separate be-
> tween the religion and nationality. Because I'm totally against the
> state. On this question, though, there are those who believe that
> we must cease [associating religion with the state]. There is a con-
> troversy; there are two opinions on the question. I am absolutely
> opposed to the state, so how can I tell you I want to separate relig-
> ion and state? I am totally against the state.

In other words, it's not merely the combination of religion and state in Israel that Yehuda and his ilk reject: it is *any* state of Israel that comes to be not through messianic means but through the efforts of Jews prior to the end of days. After stating his caveat—wanting to be certain that I understand his fundamental position—Yehuda reveals his view:

> Q: So what do you think needs to be done with this state?

> A: I think that it is necessary to separate the religion from the state and for them not to meddle with religion. When there's no distinction between politics and religion, in the education realm they tell us what we should teach, which subjects to study. When there's a separation between religion and state it will be much better. But again, it [the state] is against my principles. I am answering you only in the context that *they* think there should be a state. I explain to you that then there should be a separation between religion and state in the future. Why? So that they won't get involved in religion. The Education Ministry dictates the curriculum to the children. They teach more than a million students for heresy! It would be preferable to make a separation between religion and state.

In this response Yehuda cites a primary concern among Israel's Haredi communities: education. Although the pre-state status quo agreement included a guarantee that the state would provide funds for a separate educational stream for the ultra-Orthodox, debate in recent years has focused on a relatively new and rapidly ascendant religious school system run by Shas, the Sephardic Haredi political party. The network, known as *Ha'ma'ayan Hahinuch Hatorani,* began to attract large numbers of not only ultra-Orthodox but many traditional Oriental Jews (also known as *Sephardim or Mizrahim*: Jews with roots in Muslim or Arab countries of the Middle East and North Africa) attracted by a longer day than that offered by the public schools as well as free transportation and free hot lunches. In the period of my field research, then-Prime Minister Barak's coalition government faced a constant threat of collapse due to a controversy stemming from the Ministry of Education's refusal to provide supplementary funding to the Shas schools.[24] Yossi Sarid, the Minister of Education from the center-left Labor party, cited the educational system's poor management and possible corruption as reasons for withholding funding. This issue infuriated not only Shas supporters but many Ashkenazi ultra-Orthodox Jews who interpreted it as a secular Jewish official telling the observant community how to teach their children. (Sarid had indeed proposed educational reforms making financial support for non-public schools conditional on basic instruction in secular subjects such as mathematics, science and Israeli history, but the reasons Sarid cited for not transferring the money in this case were unrelated to those proposals.)

Oren, another Haredi supporter of separation (who uses all three justifications for his position), describes the religious institutions as subservient to the state:

> The Chief Rabbinical establishment is the toy of the state. It's under the command of the state. Although it seems to be an independent body, it is *not* an independent body. They are subordinate to the state. Today the Chief Rabbi is chosen by political forces; he doesn't represent Judaism any more than he represents the state. Maybe he, like the president, is a symbol for those outside Israel but for the state as a state he isn't a rabbi who symbolizes Judaism.

Finally, Yeshayahu, the young rabbi, says "there must be a separation between religion and state, because when religion is found inside politics, it ruins it completely. Religion is completely decimated. Totally ruined. I think there should be more Jewish life in the state, but not through politics."

Arguments Against Separation Among Israeli Jews

Unlike the case for separation, which includes three potentially consistent lines of reasoning, the three main arguments against separation I found in my interviews come from widely divergent perspectives: (1) *Sanctity of the State:* The birth and first few decades of the State of Israel represent the dawn and early stages of the Jewish people's messianic redemption. Close integration of Judaism with the state is essential to move forward on that path. To denude Israel of its religious elements is to turn the clock back on redemption, undermine Judaism and subvert divine will. (2) *Jewish Continuity:* Separation of religion from state (a) will have little or no effect on the lives of Torah-observant Jews in Israel. However, (b) it will greatly exacerbate a trend of secularization and assimilation among the large non-Orthodox majority in Israel. Keeping religion and state together is necessary to prevent a rift in the Jewish nation from becoming an outright split. It ensures the survival of one Jewish people. (3) *Too Radical:* The call from many Israelis to separate religion and state rests on a faulty assumption: that protection of religious freedom and pluralism requires such a radical measure. Maintaining an integration of religion and state is possible while making partial reforms to Israel's religion-state arrangement that pave the way for less coercion and greater individual freedom.

It should be clear, up to this point, which subjects tend to make the first argument: Religious Zionists. Haredim use the second argument most frequently; Religious Zionists often argue (b) but without premise (a), given that the latter clearly contradicts the argument from the sanctity of the state. While both Haredim and Religious Zionists are concerned about assimilation of Israeli Jewry, the former see the state's laws and institutions that encourage greater observance as intrinsically valuable. In contrast, the Haredim tend to view the state as having merely instrumental value. The third argument, I argue below, is really not an argument against the *concept* of separation, as most Israelis understand it. It is, instead, a hesitation on the part of some Israeli liberal activists pushing for change to associate themselves with the *term* "separation of religion and state." The reluctance seems to stem from a fear—not necessarily justified, according to my findings—that such a tag is out of the mainstream and thus potentially damaging to their proposals' chances for acceptance.

Sanctity of the State

Religious Zionism, as I explained in chapter 2, finds holiness in the state of Israel, placing it on a par with the holiness of the land of Israel and the people of Israel. Observant Jews in this category are the least likely of Israel's Jews to advocate separation of religion and state. For them, as for some secular Zionists, Judaism *is* the state and the state *is* Judaism. But unlike secular Jews such as Shulamit and Yoram, Religious Zionists such as Avi, Zvi, Nahman and Yoel are devout and believing Jews for whom the Israeli state, with its religious character, is central to their faith. It not only represents the beginning of the glorious messianic end (as several of the subjects point out), but constitutes a political entity that fulfills and enables a rich Jewish life in the here and now. Avi explains why:

> Everything is built together. It's one container that includes everything. It's not as if there's religion, and there's state—as if there's a spiritual life and a practical life and they don't go together. To the contrary: the only way that religious life may be expressed is in practical life and in day-to-day life.

For Zvi, religion and state should "absolutely not" be parted; separation would be "a kind of catastrophe." Nahman's image is potent: "In my opinion it's impossible to separate between religion and state. It's like cutting the head off from the body. Because if you separate religion from the state, what is left of the state? What is left of the religion? It doesn't sound logical at all." This from the same subject who, as we saw in Part I above, thinks that Israel *isn't* really a Jewish state, since its people and laws aren't sufficiently Jewish. Yet Nahman regards the state and Judaism as so intertwined on another level that he cannot fathom the difference: he cannot see where one begins and the other ends. Yoel expands on the notion of Judaism as a totalistic faith, telling me his stance on separation before I even ask a question specifically on the subject. He brings up the issue early in the interview:

> Q: Do you think Israel is a Jewish state?

A: Yes. Very much so.

Q: How so? What makes it so?

A: [sighs] First of all the fact that it's in Israel. The background and reasons for which it was founded, and by whom it was founded. The purpose makes it Jewish. I believe the citizens of the state give it a Jewish aspect. The laws of the state give it a Jewish aspect. I do not believe in separation of church and state. I think they are very much together. You know, I said before that I don't believe that there are aspects of life that have nothing to do with religion. I think religion has everything to do with the state and politics, just like it has to do with keeping Shabbes. There are *halachic* views on these things. I believe that *halacha* applies to everything, and it has to be spread out. . .But you have a problem if you're a person who loves Jews and you want the state to be Jewish and respect Shabbat, with stopping the busses, and all that. It's a problem. It's something that has to be addressed, and as I mentioned before, I think that by creating mutual understanding and mutual respect, these things can be solved. And they can be breached.

After stating that Jewish law has universal application—and important ties to the state—Yoel addresses the concerns of those who disagree with the religious aspects of the state. Like other Religious Zionists, Yoel is not blind to secular Jews' opposition to a religious state. He understands that many Israeli Jews resent policies such as the requirement to marry and divorce via the Rabbinate and the prohibition on public transportation on Shabbat. But he believes that "mutual understanding" and "mutual respect" will allow the secular and religious publics to reach a compromise. The solution to which Religious Zionists consistently turn draws upon a distinction found in many forms of liberalism: a separation between public and private. The distinction basically runs this way: We do not seek to interfere in what you do in your private lives, but you should not object to the state's official observance of Judaism in public. We will tolerate your choice to desecrate Shabbat in private and to eat in non-kosher restaurants, but you must to tolerate restrictions on Shabbat buses. Zvi clearly expresses this common Religious Zionist approach:

> Every person can do what he wants. No one can come and tell me that today that if he wants to he can't go and eat at non-kosher restaurant. There are lots of non-kosher restaurants. There are twice as many discothèques, even here in Jerusalem, considered the capital city of Israel, the Holy City. Things are open on Shabbat, too. But it's not appropriate that there could be, for example, a state-owned bus company like Egged beginning to operate on Shabbat, because it belongs to everyone. Why doesn't El Al fly on-

Shabbat? Because El Al is an airline that's owned by the state of Israel, the people of Israel is composed of a host of different groups, and the state is supposed to represent everyone. Therefore it doesn't fly on Shabbat. It's not appropriate. An airline that flies on Yom Kippur would hurt me in a very personal way. If the airline flies, that shows that the state has no values and has no sentiment for Yom Kippur or for Shabbat. That would simply hurt me personally. What state am I living in? Is it cut off completely from Shabbat and Yom Kippur?

As I said, I don't want there to be a halachic state, but I want at least the political institutions and bodies, buses, big supermarkets [to observe Jewish tradition]. And don't start playing mind games, ranting and raving, because it doesn't hurt anyone. Do you think it really and truly bothers them so much not to take buses on Shabbat? Often people don't go anywhere for days at a time. Most people in Israel have vehicles. The state of Israel is the most car-congested state in the world! So it hurts that much?...

Come, let's say this: people have to compromise, just as I compromise on lots of things. An Israeli can compromise on three years of his life, the years that are supposed to be the best, when someone anywhere else studies in college and we need to be far from home, moving around, running around, dragging things around, doing guard duty, and doing things we don't want to do. It's tiring, it's exhausting, and it's difficult. So what? I think that an Israeli is obligated to do it. People compromise on things. So what? Compromise isn't a bad thing. Compromise is the basis of social understanding. Without compromise, it's impossible to live together. End of story. It's a fact that we see the explosions when everyone just gets fortified in his own position and can't see the other side at all. What does that lead to? That simply leads to a rifts and everyone hates the other, and why? We must compromise. It's like a married couple. A married couple that doesn't compromise will divorce after a year. It's very simple. It's a very simple calculation. It's the basis for understanding. One needs to understand the other.

Here we have what appears to be a pragmatic, fair-minded proposal, at least on the surface. It's clear what we do not have: a dogmatic demand that all Jews keep the religious commandments. Both sides, says Zvi, must compromise for the sake of political stability and social peace. The religious will live with the knowledge that their neighbors eat *treif* inside and outside the home; that restaurants, bars and discos are open on Shabbat, even in Jerusalem; that all but a few public roads and highways are open to traffic on Shabbat. But in exchange, the secular must sacrifice certain conveniences for the sake of the nature of the Jewish state. They must assent to what sounds like the inverse of the American non-establishment principle, according to which the state must avoid policies or actions that endorse or seem to endorse religion. Instead, Zvi, Yoel, Nahman and Avi propose an *establishment principle* for Israel, according to which individuals are free to do what they like but the state *qua* state *must* align itself with a particular religion—Judaism—and *may not* do anything that explicitly contravenes Jewish law. In Yoel's language, "I would be very, very upset if the prime minister drove somewhere on Shabbes. If would be very offensive, because he is the representative of my nation. I think things that are done on a public level have to be respectful of our tradition." On the other hand, "what people do on a private level should never be restricted. So if Egged belonged to Joe Schmo" rather than the state of Israel, Yoel concludes, "it could run on Shabbat. I have no problem with that."[25]

The insistence on compromise, however, rests on a central and highly contestable premise: that the request for secular Jews to make sacrifices for the sake of Israel's Jewish character is a legitimate one. The legitimacy of the request, in turn, depends on the nature of the specific sacrifice in question and the strength of the argument that Israel should be faithful to its Jewish roots.

Jewish Continuity

The second argument against separation offered by some Haredi and Religious Zionist respondents is based on a sociological-religious goal: the survival and unity of the Jewish people (where the former is held to be contingent on some kind of the latter). Representatives from both groups of observant Jews ascribe high importance to the goal of bringing all Jews into a common fold and find Israel's religion-state connection essential to that end.

From the Haredi perspective, Nosson starts by acknowledging the competing view according to which separation of religion and state would have no effect on the ultra-Orthodox but quickly open a gulf between two halves of the Jewish people:

> Q: There are some who think religion and state should be separated. Do you agree with such a proposal?
>
> A: There are those among us [Haredim] who say yes, and they claim that we aren't succeeding on this path of ours and we aren't succeeding in anything but causing secular Jews to hate us . . . and they are becoming separated from the People of Israel: "What does it matter to us? We need to take care of the religious public and those who want to join it." There are those among us who say this. But the majority do not and it's important to understand why. We live very well despite the declaration of the state and nothing will happen to us if religion and state are separated. Just as we deal with the situation now, we can deal with it then. Our children will

continue to marry in the same institutions and we will continue to marry with Jews and kosher Jews. It won't damage *our* Jewish continuity. But the reason we oppose separation of religion and state is that it will guarantee that the secular public, in the course of two generations, won't be Jewish. That's because separation of religion and state will authorize civil marriage and civil naturalization. ...

In a very short time, there will be a complete separation between two parts of the People. We love our secular brothers and we don't want to lose them. We want to save our secular brothers from themselves. I think that if we would present things correctly but the problem is that the media distorts things—but if we would present the things in this way and if you'd do a poll on it, a large percentage of the People—up to 90 percent—would be against [separation of religion and state]. Even seculars—of course traditional Jews—but even the seculars don't want to keep Torah or Mitzvot but they want to remain Jews. They want to be sure that their children and their grandchildren will be Jews. If they only knew that separation of religion and state . . . would give no security at all, no security—in several generations their children won't be Jews. And so it's important to explain. We have survived many years and we'll survive longer. We worry about *them*.

Nosson's concern is thus not the survival of Jews per se. He is confident that Israel's 400,000 or so Haredi Jews will maintain their practices and beliefs regardless of what happens on the Israeli political scene with regard to separation of religion and state. His worry, rather, is for the continuity and survival of the wider Jewish people and—linked to that—for the souls of individual Jews. Although Nehama, too, wavers on whether to separate religion and state ("I truly, truly don't know"), she finds it "terrible" that with a separation, "we can save ourselves...preserve our religion among ourselves" but lose control over those on the borderline:

But what about the others? What about others who are traditional Jews and don't know and don't want to know? Will they marry goyim? There won't be any more Jews? For us it would be wonderful. But what about the others who don't understand, who don't keep all the commandments, who don't yet know? What will be with them?

Expanding on the latter point, Nosson introduces an analogy and unexpectedly relies on democratic theory:

If I have a brother, who, God forbid, smokes drugs, he'll get mad at me if I try to stop him from smoking. I'm out for his good. He can refuse but can't get mad at me! I want his good. I will save you

> from yourself. If you don't want me to save you, it pains me. But
> it's my right to use democracy to try to save you from yourself.

Nosson and Nehama propose sincerely that Jewish survival is at stake in Israel's decision over whether to separate religion from state. It's an empirical question, of course, whether they're right or wrong that separation would lead the non-Orthodox further astray, threatening not only their individual souls but the unity and continuity of Jews as a whole. (I treat this question at greater length in chapter 6.) But in either case the liberal has an instinctive and compelling objection: "Yes, you have the right to save others from themselves in a democracy. But you may not rely upon the apparatus and power of the state to do that. Your evangelizing must rest on your ideas and on your own power of persuasion, not the state's power to coerce individual behavior. If you want to save secular souls, you're on your own." Indeed, if liberalism stands for anything, it stands for the principle, as Locke put it, that "the care of the Salvation of Mens Souls cannot belong to the Magistrate."[26] And it reaches that conclusion not, as Locke's argument reads in the context of the quotation, because it is irrational to tie a citizen's chances for salvation to his luck in living in a state that happens to enforce true religion. To return to the first argument in favor of separation discussed above, liberalism opposes this kind of thing because it infringes on fundamental human freedoms: liberty of conscience and religious exercise.

Taking this argument as a baseline of liberalism, however, does not give us an easy answer to whether separation is or is not justified. As I suggest above and develop below, evaluating the justice of Israel's partial integration of religion and state is a multifaceted task. We need to take each notable factor of Israel's connection to Judaism separately in order to ask when fundamental human freedoms really are at stake. The discussion in chapters to come will show that the consensus view among secular and traditional Jews, buffered by the opinions offered by non-party-line Haredim and Religious Zionists, goes a significant distance in yielding a subtle, compelling and philosophically defensible conclusion.

Too Radical/Unnecessary

Some argue against separation of religion and state on the grounds that it needlessly revolutionizes Israel's ethos for the sake of pursuing religious liberty. Less radical steps could secure the goal more effectively, on this view, with less of a shake-up to society. This argument, however, appears to be limited to a very narrow swath of Israelis: liberal activists pursuing reforms of Israel's religious-secular status quo. One person in my interview pool makes this claim: Rabbi Uri Regev, head of the political branch of Reform Judaism in Israel. As the only non-Orthodox subject active in Israel's political realm, Rabbi Regev has reason to watch his words carefully. As the following exchange illustrates, he fervently resists being associated with the concept of separation:

> Q: Do you think there ought to be a complete separation between the state and the religious courts and the rabbinate?
>
> A: No. No. No. I am also a member of the board of "A Constitution for Israel." And I support the introduction of a bill on religious freedom. And that goes back to the draft constitution that was done at Tel Aviv University, with Professor Uriel Reichman and Professor Ariel Rosen-Zvi, etc. And our idea is not separation of religion and state. Our idea is accommodation. Our idea is maintaining and upholding religious freedom but not necessarily separating religion from state. Doing away with religious coercion is not necessarily doing away with religion in the public sphere altogether. So, as far as I'm concerned there can be public funding of religious needs, except it has to be done from a universal and objective basis to all, Jews and non-Jews, and within Judaism to all Jewish groups. I have no problem with religious courts, provided that turning to them is on a voluntary basis and not at the expense of having a civil option.

The repeated denial (three "no's") and the third person plural pronoun ("our idea") suggests that those proposing "A Constitution for Israel" made an explicit decision not to couch its proposals within a notion of separation.[27] Instead, he names his position "accommodation" and describes it as a series of measures that alleviate religious coercion while preserving some role for public manifestations of Judaism. What specifically does Rabbi Regev's vision hold for Israel's religion-state arrangement? As the next chapter shows, his specific proposals mirror those of other traditional and secular Jews who *do* profess support for the concept of separation. In fact, some of his positions go even farther than those of most subjects calling for separation.[28] Why, then, does he resist the label? In the continuation of our interview one week later, I returned to the question. As the exchange below shows, he refuses to associate himself with those who favor separation, even though his position on the Israeli rabbinate perfectly describes one aspect of the separationist agenda:

> Q: The second idea [I wanted your reaction to] is that of those who want to separate religion and state. We talked about that a little bit last time. But I want to hear a little more clearly how you relate to that phrase. And specifically speaking about the rabbinate...
>
> A: What's the question? What's the phrase?

Q: The phrase is *hafradat dat u'medina* [separation of religion and state].

A: Oh. I see, yeah.

Q: Specifically about the rabbinate, is it preferable to eliminate state recognition of the rabbinate? Or is it preferable to pluralize the rabbinate?

A: First of all, I think the label of separation of religion and state is, for the most part, a red herring. What is separation of religion and state? There are different models. What are we talking about? Germany and England don't have separation of religion of state, and they have a very high level of religious freedom. America does have separation of religion and state but every Congressional session opens with a prayer, and the currency bears the writing, "In God We Trust." But at the same time, there is a wall of separation that prevents schools from teaching Bible. So clearly, to me, the American model does not apply. And the question is what are we talking about when we say separation. I don't subscribe to separation of religion and state. I think that what we need is constitutional protection of freedom of religion, rather than separation. I have no problem with state funding of religious institutions and religious services, provided it is based on equitable, equal, universal criteria, for Jews and non-Jews. And I have no problem with kashrut being maintained in public institutions. I think the idea of a chief rabbinate is an anathema. ...

Q: So of the proposals made by those who do want a separation of religion and state, one plank of that platform you would assent to: that the chief rabbinate should not get recognition.

A: I don't assent to that plank! I look at the thing, and I judge every aspect of it on its merits!

Q: Sure, sure, sure. I'm not saying that you look at theirs and say, I agree with that, but that's one place where you *overlap* with their ideas.

A: [Sigh of annoyance] Probably.

I pressed Rabbi Regev on this point not in order to determine *whether* he supports the basic principles behind separation of religion and state in Israel. I already knew, by comparing the first interview I conducted with him with my other interviews, that he does. (To be more precise: his views closely match those of other Jews who speak in favor of the concept of separation.) I wanted to find out, rather, how strongly he wishes to disassociate himself from the label of "separation of religion and state" and to explore why. As the above excerpt shows, his dislike of the term "separation" is strong and he has coherent and principled reasons for disavowing it. Separation, Rabbi Regev says, is a vague concept. More importantly, while its presence does not indicate absolute secularity in government, its absence does not say anything conclusive about whether religious freedom obtains in a particular society. (If all you knew about Iran and Germany was that both systems did *not* feature separation of religion and state, you would know nothing about the differences in those states' policies of religious freedom and toleration.) So rather than pin a button on his lapel bearing a political slogan—one that may not in fact have the further negative effect of jeopardizing his political goals—Rabbi Regev talks about the specific issues.

To recap, the main conclusions of this section have been the following: (1) A significant number of non-Orthodox Jewish Israelis, and a smaller number of Orthodox Jewish Israelis, favor what they call "separation of religion and state." (2) Jewish Israelis who support separation use three related arguments: Liberal Freedom (the importance of individuals' right of free choice); Jewish Flourishing (the attraction of a de-politicized Judaism to alienated Jews), and Religious Autonomy (the possibility of independent development of Orthodox Judaism without state regulation or oversight). (3) Most Jewish Israelis who reject separation rely on either the Sanctity of the State claim (regarding Israel's religiosity as fundamental to divine will and redemption), the Jewish Continuity claim (hinging the Jewish people's survival on religion-state integration) or some combination of those arguments. Others, from a very different perspective, regard the proposal as Too Radical.

One central puzzle has already been vaguely outlined: How is it that Jewish Israelis both strongly support separation of religion and state and overwhelmingly endorse Israel's continued existence as a Jewish state? The answer, I've suggested, depends on a clarification of both the general ways in which Israelis tend to regard Israel as a "Jewish state" and the details they see underlying that concept. Another puzzle is yet to be outlined: the dominant position among Israeli Arabs that Israel should preserve certain of its religion-state connections even as it removes major expressions of Judaism from public life.

Separating Judaism and State: "A State of all Its Citizens"

According to most accounts of liberalism, a clear separation of religion and state is necessary to safeguard citizens' individual freedom and equality. In this section, the nuanced views of Israeli citizens in my interview pool give us renewed reason to break open that idea into two distinct matters: First, what problems of justice are associated with a state that supports *multiple religions*? Second, what problems of justice are associated with a state that allies itself with *one particular religion*? The difference is between a state that aids religion *per se*—whether to accommodate minority religious groups for reasons of fairness or to tap into what are believed to be religion's positive political purposes—and a state that affiliates with one specific religion. In the Israeli context, as we will see below, the distinction is seen in the differences between "separating religion and state"—the preferred slogan of most Jewish Israeli leftists—and "separating Judaism from state," my spin on the notion of "a state for all its citizens" often heard from Israeli Arabs. There is, as we will see below, some overlap between these two ideas. But separating religion from state—as that concept is understood by Israelis—does not necessarily mean transforming Israel into a state of all its citizens, or, in other words, separating Judaism from state. And separating Judaism from state does not necessarily require the separation of religion and state.

Separation of Religion and State: Israeli Arab Views

Although the notion of a state of all its citizens forms the backbone of Israeli Arabs' political platform, my Arab respondents also generally express support for some notion of "separating religion and state" in Israel: Nadia, Omer and Majjed advocate separation, Muhammad opposes it and Youssef holds a mixed view. Of the supporters, one (Majjed) is a self-described atheist, one (Omer) is a devout Muslim and a third (Nadia) is a traditional Muslim whose jean jacket and uncovered hair point to her secular leanings. Each of the three rely heavily on the argument from Liberal Freedom described in the previous section. First consider Nadia's words:

> There should be a total separation. There should be religious freedom for people. . .I don't say there shouldn't be Judaism—there should be Judaism. But Judaism should be between the individual and himself and his religious group. If I'm Haredi, let's say, I want freedom of expression. I want to be Haredi without anyone bothering me. But it shouldn't be written into the law that I enjoy a privileged status because I'm Jewish.

Notable in this comment is not only Nadia's affinity with traditional liberal conceptions of religious freedom but her willingness to place herself in the shoes of a Jewish woman—an ultra-Orthodox Jewish woman, no less—and consider the appropriate limits of state toleration for her beliefs. Her conclusion takes an unassailably liberal tack: negative freedom and protection from discrimination, yes; legally recognized special privileges, no.

In his response, Majjed too draws upon imaginary Jews to illustrate his point. He questions the justification for restrictive religious legislation on Israel's non-religious Jews:

> Religion is a personal matter [*davar ishi*]. Or it's supposed to be personal. . . .There should be an absolute separation between religion and state. . . .No one tells them [religious Jews] that they can't go to synagogue. But why must they coerce Yossi, the secular guy from Dimona, to study Torah? He doesn't *want* to. Or Eli from Beit She'an or someone else who wants to go hang out and have fun [*lalachet l'bilui*] on Shabbat—why can't he go? If you don't want to go out, fine, stay at home!

Like Nadia and Majjed, Youssef, the secular Christian Arab, finds no room for state involvement in religion. "Religion," he says, "is between man and God."

> A person can be religious, believe in God, without [state] budgets supporting him, without all the fancy accoutrements [*kishutim*] that advance religion. If a person wants to believe, he can do it alone to know what God is, to know what the Christian religion is, what the Muslim religion is, *alone*. There's no need for all of the [state] influences. It's too much—it's superfluous. Don't get me wrong: I don't mean, God forbid [*has ve'halila*], anything against religion itself. The value of religion stays the same. In my eyes, there is very dear value to the Christian, Muslim and Jewish religions. I told you I myself am far from religion, but I respect a religious person who wants to be religious. But to link the religious issue to money for religion, I'm against it.

The message of these three young secular Arabs—one Muslim, one Christian, one Druze—is that the individual should be free to worship as he chooses; should be free to choose *not* to worship; and should be able to make these decisions without the oppressive and distorting influences of state interference. But there is something missing from this analysis: a recognition of the importance of religious and cultural autonomy for Arab citizens of Israel.[29] The other two Arab subjects raise these issues, leading them to different views on religion-state separation in Israel. Muhammad, the traditional Muslim and Hebrew teacher, observes that the Arab community not only approves of but relies upon certain linkages between religion and state:

> A: Separation would be impossible. There's what you want, and there's reality [*yesh ratzui va'yesh matzui*]. The desire is to separate, but reality is different. In the Arab sector it is impossible to separate between religion and state, because we have things that are unique to our community.

> Q: So it is good that there are [state-recognized] Muslim religious courts?
>
> A: Yes.
>
> Q: And it's good that they have a monopoly on marriage, divorce and burial?
>
> A: Yes. They have autonomy. For example, we have a Mufti who is in charge of things related to religious issues. Sometimes we need to get approval or an order from the Mufti. There are things we receive from them, but it's in cooperation with the authorities, because they work with the Ministry of Religious Affairs.

Recall that in addition to the Orthodox Rabbinate's control of personal status issues for Israel's Jews, the Muslim and Christian religious authorities enjoy similar control over their respective communities. (In fact, as I note in chapter 2, the Muslim Sharia courts wield somewhat wider authority over Muslims than do Jewish courts over Jews.) Does this conferral of cultural rights to Israel's religious minorities raise liberal individualist claims against unfair religious coercion?

> Q: There are some people in the Jewish sector who don't want the Chief Rabbinate to have a monopoly on marriage, because they might want to get married without a rabbi, outside of religious auspices. Is there a situation like that in the Muslim sector?
>
> A: No, in the Arab sector there's nothing like that. With us, there's nothing like that. In our village there's a man who writes the marriage contract [ketuba[30]], and a Sharia court must authorize you to marry. Without that it's forbidden to get married. It's true he *can* get married without that, but not in Israel—he has to go to another place such as Germany. My brother married a German woman, so he got married there in a church.

The fact that Muhammad's brother married a Christian woman abroad—just as many secular Jewish Israelis or immigrants from the former Soviet Union wed in Cyprus—might seem to belie Muhammad's claim that all Muslims approve of the Muslim courts' control over marriage between Muslims and accept the unavailability of intermarriage inside the country. As in the secular Jewish world, there are at least some Muslims who want to marry outside the strictures—or even the community—of Islam. Despite that fact, and aside from individual complaints, however—in sharp contrast to the situation among Israel's Jews—there is no social movement inside Israel's Muslim or Christian communities pressing to abolish the millet system or to systematically limit religious courts' power.[31] When asked if religion and state should be separated, Omer first says he is "in favor of separating between the Jewish religion and the state and between the Christian religion and the Muslim religion and the state, because there are three religions here and not one particular religion." Twenty minutes later in the interview, Omer clarifies his position:

> Q: If you could write the constitution of the State of Israel. . .what would the relationship be between religion and state? What would this state look like?
>
> A: I would do this: For the political issues I would make a separation between religion and state. But for the things connected to tradition, like marriage and things like that, I would give each religion its own sector, such as separate religious courts for the Muslims and courts for the Jews with each religion having its own religious laws. Almost a [complete] separation between religion and state. If I wanted the Muslim laws to reign over everyone, I'd do a disservice to other religions.
>
> Q: So you want to separate but give autonomy to each religion.
>
> A: Yes, religious autonomy. Every religion should have its own court.

In this passage Omer is calling for a two-part solution to the question of religion and the Israeli state. On the one hand, he favors retaining the status quo millet system under which religious communities control basic communal and personal status matters of their members. On the other, he opposes the Jewish basis of many of Israel's generally applicable laws, framing his objection in ecumenical terms: "the laws should include all religions." When he says he would like to live in an Israel in which there is "almost a complete separation" between religion and state, what he means (as we will see below) is that he would like to live in an Israel that is not a Jewish state, and not a state for, of or by the Jews, but a "state of all its citizens."

A State of all Its Citizens: Israeli Arab Views

Despite the rather strident claims of three of the Arab subjects on the question of religion-state separation, a different slogan serves as the basis of the Arab subjects' views as well as of the mainstream Israeli Arab platform: Israel should be a "state of all its citizens." These words have become a catch phrase since the early 1990s as Israeli Arabs have become more expressive of their political power. Cleverly tapping into a concept whose label suggests that it ought to be supported, in principle, by Jewish Left, "a state of all its citizens" turns Jewish Israelis to face the implications of their dominance over the Arab minority. It challenges the very nature of Israel as a Jewish state. Azmi Bishara, an Israeli Arab Knesset member and the leader of the Balad party[32] (an Arabic acronym for the National Democratic Assembly), claims he coined the expression.[33] In a 1998 article in *Tikkun* magazine, Bishara offers the following explanation:

> I came back into politics and was elected to the Knesset to address this issue: the cultural marginalization of Israeli Arabs from their own identity and their civil marginalization from full citizenship. I want Israel to become a society which officially recognizes itself as a state which contains two cultures, one a Jewish majority culture, the other, a Palestinian national minority living inside a Jewish majority, sharing citizenship. Israeli society must recognize Palestinian national identity as a legitimate nationality to be respected—this is my project, and the compass for my political activity. The state itself may have the cultural character of the majority, but its relationship to citizens should be regulated by citizenship and not by their religious identity—in short, I want Israel to become a state of its citizens.[34]

Several questions pop out of this initial take on the concept. First, if Bishara's goal is for the state to recognize two cultural groups in Israeli society—a Jewish majority culture and a Palestinian minority culture—why place the emphasis on the individualist notion of *citizenship* rather than, say, group rights or Palestinian-Israeli autonomy? Why not "a state of both its nations?" Second, what does it mean that the "state itself" may legitimately broadcast the "cultural character of the majority" culture? Does this apply to state symbols, institutions, leaders, holidays? Or does it merely pertain to certain non-governmental facets of Israeli society, a term he uses interchangeably with "state"? Third, how can a state whose relationship to its citizens is "regulated [only] by citizenship" and not by "religious identity" properly account for two (or more) national groups whose boundaries are constituted, in large part, by religion? The thoughts of my subjects on the meaning and justifiability of a "state of all its citizens" will help clarify some of the tensions in Bishara's formulation.

When asked what the term "state of all its citizens" implies, both advocates and opponents of the prescription for Israeli politics cite a handful of related, yet notoriously contested, ideas: democracy, multiculturalism, equality, rights and neutrality. Several of the respondents note that the phrase implies an Israel that looks very much like the model of pluralistic liberal democracy: the United States. One Jewish subject, Aaron, explains that "it is a pejorative term" when used by members of Jewish religious parties: " 'What do you guys want, a state of all its citizens?!' It is a euphemism when used by [Jewish] Israelis to object that what you're talking about is a binational state or a state that is not totally Jewish."

Each of the five Arab respondents expresses support for the notion of a state of all its citizens, including both subjects (Omer and Muhammad) who have reservations about "separation of religion and state." According to Muhammad, the Hebrew teacher and activist in Israel's Zionist Labor party, "Reality says that it's truly a Jewish state, because the majority of the inhabitants are Jews. But I think that it should be a state for all its inhabitants, for all of the inhabitants."[35] Skeptical about "word games," Nadia is not enthusiastic about the phrase itself, but she believes strongly in several of the principles that lie behind it:

> I don't know what all of these phrases mean that have been used for several years already: "a state for every citizen," "a democratic state." I don't understand them. I understand something else: I want the Jewish aspects to be revoked in the state. I want it to turn into a state that won't be a state for the Jews. The Jews came, and they're welcome—no, they're not welcome. But they are already here. There's nothing to do about it. It's a fact and there's no way to fix what they've done. So that's it: they're here. We simply need to work—it's not so simple!—to work on the character of the state. I'm not wise enough to find a solution for this state. It's not simple; it's very complicated. But I want to *belong* to this place, and I want people who want to come here to have the opportunity. As long as there is no right of return for the people who were expelled from here—even if it was out of fear, it's still expulsion [pause]—they should have the right to return if they want. And the constitution should change such that Arabs and Jews will become equal citizens.

Several other subjects mentioned the discrepancy between the Law of Return—which gives any Jew the right to immigrate to Israel—and the lack of a similar opportunity for Palestinian Arabs who fled Israel after the 1948 War of Independence (whether by choice or out of fear) and now want to return to the villages and homes of their ancestors. Others also focus on the point about equality. Drawing on his conception of democracy, Omer defines a state of all its citizens as one in which

> the law will rule and the law will rule over all citizens in an equal manner. It won't relate to a Jew in one way and to an Arab in another way. If we're talking about a state of all its citizens, that means that the state serves all its citizens, no matter what his religion is, no matter what his language is and no matter what his political situation is. Equality for all the citizens!

Does Youssef agree that Israel should be a state of all its citizens?

Of course I agree! It *must* be thus in my opinion, because there are citizens of this state who live in it, who belong to it and they aren't included among the Jews. I belong to this state, I live here and I have an Israeli identification card. But when people say "a state for the Jews," they don't include the entire population in the state. Israel must get rid of this racism and include all of its citizens of the state. . . .That means that the rights a Jew enjoys, an Arab enjoys also. There should be equality. Every aspect of life in this state should be equal between the Jews and the Arabs.

Exploring Youssef's vision of absolute equality, I present a contrary view often heard among religious Jews and ask for his reaction:

Q: How would you respond to a Zionist who says to you: "The state is prepared to give all its citizens equality to a certain degree, but this is still a Jewish state and we must preserve the Jewish character of the state in a democratic framework. There are many Arab states but only one state for the Jews."

A: [. . .] From 1948, we wanted two states for two peoples and we see that today it's the only solution. We want equality. And we want them to change "Hatikva" and the flag, but the point is how to get that done. We must take one step at a time. Just as it was difficult in the 1970s and 1980s to say to a Jew that a Palestinian state must be established and he wouldn't accept that, today he won't accept a proposal to change "Hatikva" and the flag. But now he accepts the principle of equality. The next step in my opinion is equality, and after there's equality, we'll talk about other things, these issues that are also important. In my opinion there needs to be a certain gradual process in order to arrive at the final goal of full equality—even in the national anthem, even with the flag.

Q: You think equality should first be reached in the sense of economic and budgetary equality?

A: No. We must arrive at full equality but in order to reach full equality, and there is only one way: full equality will be gradual. From my point of view, would that [*halevai*] I'd wake up tomorrow morning and there would be full equality, but I see that in order to arrive at this full equality, there must be a gradual process of change in order to reach it. You take the thing the closest to what the Jews understand. They understand that we must reach economic equality. They understand that now, but they won't fathom any changes to the national anthem and the flag of Israel. But I say that with time they will understand that they'll need to change "Hatikva" and the flag too. We'll talk about it after [economic equality has been reached].

Q: So it has to be step-by-step process?

A: There must be full equality, but the only way is step-by-step from what we have today.

According to this piecemeal approach, Israel won't become a state of all its citizens until it has become, in substantive ways, a state *for* all its citizens. "Full equality" in Youssef's eyes—a situation in which Arabs see themselves as equal partners in the shaping and realization of Israel's raison d'etre—is not a short-term possibility. But nor is it merely a hoped-for utopia. In Youssef's view, fundamental changes in the state symbols that mark Arabs' exclusion will become possible as Israeli Jews take small steps toward providing Arab towns and villages with more ample budgets for better roads, sewage, housing and education. After recognizing the importance of equalizing Arabs' lives in material terms, Israel's establishment will come around to see the importance of fostering Arabs' political identity as Israelis. Since this cannot be achieved by assimilating Arabs into Israel's dominant Jewish ethos, it must be pursued by leveling the Jews' political-ethical identity to a much lower common denominator. And in the process, Youssef believes, the state will free itself of all vestiges of its national and religious Jewish identity.

Azmi Bishara's vision seems similar, although somewhat less unfriendly to some trappings of the Jewish state. He mentions, in the passage quoted above, that "state itself may have the cultural character of the majority." And he says elsewhere that "my feelings regarding the flag and the anthem are negative. They don't represent me. They represent something that negates me. But if the content of our lives in this country changes, then I am willing to live with a few symbols that mean something to the majority, in the hope that over time these things will change as well."[36]

How do Israeli Arabs hope to spur progress toward an Israel that is closer to a state of all its citizens? A basic element of the strategy is one that both Bishara and several of my respondents stress repeatedly: forging a unified front among the various branches of Israel's Arab population. Omer, Majjed and Youssef all emphasize this point at various points in their interviews. When I ask Omer which political party he favors, he prefaces his answer this way: "For me, everyone is Arab. Everyone is the same. We all vote the same way. We all demand help." (Omer, a Muslim, votes for Balad; Balad is led by Azmi Bishara, a Christian.) Here is Majjed's appeal for Arab unity:

Q: Do you think the problems facing Israeli Arabs are primarily religious, or primarily national-ethnic?

A: They are national-ethnic problems. The religious problems are
causing a schism in Israel. Today Israeli Arabs live in their own little communities, instead of being consolidated as a minority together. Today, there are Muslims, Druze and Christians. The
Christians want this, the Muslims want that. . . .Why? We [Arabs]
live in a very community-based society, [and] Israel is a society
that causes splits between everybody. When [Arabs] will all get
together, their voice will be much stronger.

Finally, Youssef gives a startling reply when I ask him how he gets along
with other Arabs:

Q: I want to close by asking some questions about your relationships with other groups. Let's start with Muslims. How much of a
connection in everyday life do you have with Muslim Arabs?

A: I don't want to answer that question because for me, there is no
separation between a Muslim, a Christian and a Druze. We are all
Arabs, we all have one nationality, and it's forbidden even to mention the differences. There are no differences at all among us.

Putting to one side the truth of this assessment—there is evidence, as
Majjed laments, that the various Arab groups in Israeli society do not get
along as swimmingly as Omer suggests—it's worth comparing the sentiment
to a comment from Bishara:

There can be no localized nationalism without a nation. And if we
are not Arab Palestinians, then we are Muslims, Druze and Christians. We are an unorganized group of religious communities. This
denouement is one of my worst fears of what might happen to the
fabric of Arab society in Israel...This is a real danger, because Israel does not give us an Israeli option. Israel does not recognize an
Israeli nationality; it recognizes only a Jewish nationality. If, in response to this, we give up on or are confused about our national
identity, we will not move to a transnational or post-national identity. Nor, for sure, will we become Jews. We will become pre-
national. We will become the minorities Israel wants us to become—Druze, Muslims, Christians—but not a nationality. And we
must have a nationality. National identity is the only modern identity; it is the identity of culture, the market and liberal democracy.[37]

A State of all Its Citizens: Jewish Views

Among the Jewish Israeli subjects in my study, opinions on the idea of a
state of all its citizens fall rather neatly along the secular-religious spectrum.

Haredim and Religious Zionists nearly unanimously condemn the idea. Secular and traditional Jews tend to favor it, although in fewer numbers and with conspicuously less gusto than that with which they champion "separation of religion and state." When the Jewish subjects assent to the phrase "a state of all its citizens," to its underlying meaning, or both, in only one case (Ronit) do we see something like the picture of "full equality" Youssef outlines. And that is to be expected. As we saw earlier in this chapter, nearly all Israeli Jews in my study—and, as scientific surveys show, Israeli Jews in general—have a hard time fathoming an Israel divorced from Judaism. Although they disagree over questions of religion and state—construed narrowly as state-imposed religious observance (Shabbat regulations, marriage laws) or religious exemption from civic duty (Haredi youth deferring army service for yeshiva study)—they are fairly united in their unwillingness to give up living in (some kind of a) Jewish state.

First listen to a few of the Jewish subjects who support the notion of a state of all its citizens. Naomi, the young *kibbutznikit*, favors the idea and defines the concept this way:

> A: It's a state in which an Israeli Arab can live here exactly as I do, with all the rights and all the duties I have. Every citizen who wants to live in the state of Israel should live here and should have the same thing. There should be no separation between an Arab citizen and an Israeli citizen, and a citizen from any other country in the world. Everyone who wants to come live here can live here.
>
> Q: You said "duties" also?
>
> A: Duties. One duty is to serve in the army. I think that Arabs need to also. Arabs serving in the IDF creates something of a problem, because it's as if they're fighting against their brothers. So the Arabs should do national service I think.
>
> Q: Both Haredim and Arabs.
>
> A: Exactly. You can't live in a state and only enjoy its rights!

Although Naomi is among the most vocal subjects calling for separation of religion and state—and sees herself as liberal across the board—her support for "a state of all its citizens," as Israeli Arabs construe the phrase, is mostly in name. Note that while Naomi thinks Arab citizens deserve equal rights, she insists they fulfill the duties of citizenship as well.[38] Naomi links that to an unrealistically open immigration policy which would give instant citizenship not only to every Jew and every Arab who desires it but to anyone worldwide. This push toward liberal universalism, ironically, displaces the primary tenet of Bishara's—and the Arab subjects'—conception of a state of all its citizens. Rather than regard the Palestinian citizens of Israel as a minority culture deserving of special recognition and protection, it sees them as individuals who are no more or less deserving than anyone else (placing them on a par with, say, Israel's foreign workers). And finally, she commits a revealing rhetorical error. In arguing that there should be no separation between an "Arab citizen" and an "Israeli citizen," she conflates "Israeli" with "Jewish" and illustrates one of the central complaints of the Israeli Arabs: Under present conditions, there is no room for Arabs in the Israeli polity.[39]

Other secular and traditional subjects profess support for the idea of a state of all its citizens while showing only lukewarm acceptance. Chaim pauses, saying only, "Ah…it's a problem…everyone who's a citizen should get equal conditions, and be equal. But it's a problem." And Shulamit reveals something of her attitude toward Arabs in the following passage:

Q: Do you think Israel should be a state of all its citizens?

A: Of?

Q: Of all its citizens.

A: All its citizens? Well, it is, isn't it?

Q: Do you think it is?

A: Is Israel a state for all its citizens? The non-Jewish citizens are the Israeli Arabs. They are citizens, though they are second-degree citizens.

Q: What makes them second class, do you think?

A: They were always "satans." Not trustworthy. And they, sometimes, you know, sometimes it turns out to be true, but you can't really trust everyone at the same point. Even today, there are many Israelis who think that the Arabs are "*gayis hamishi.*" You know what is "*gayis hamishi*"?

Q: A fifth column.

A: Yes. And that, they don't serve in the army, so they don' t have the same rights as other young Israelis. And many of them are still taken to be enemies. This year I had a dispute with one of my Arab students. And he thinks the other way around, that we are all racists, you know…

Q: Did he say that to you?

A: Yes, he said that to me. Not about me, but he said that about another woman who kicked him out of the dormitory. And I said, "So why did she do that?" And the first thing he said, "Because she is racist!" And I said, "What do you mean, there are many Arabs in the dormitories. Why did she do it to you only? Because you have been awful to her! You have been abominable. That's why. Not because you are an Arab." But that's how they look at us. And many many Israelis think that. It's very hard for me, for the interrelationships between us.

Q: Do you think that the Arabs who think that many Israelis are racist, for example, are right?

A: Um, there are many Jewish Israeli racists, probably yes. No doubt about it.

Israeli Jews such as Naomi, Shulamit and Shmuel may or may not be "racists"—"racism" is used freely in Israeli discourse as a term for unjust treatment or discrimination, both when motivated by negative feelings for a certain "race" and when not so motivated—but their words show them to be less sensitive to the social, economic and political hardships Arabs face than they are angry about their fellow citizens' untrustworthiness and lack of civic commitment. Several secular leftist Jewish subjects, however, sound more genuine in their support for a state of all its citizens. Consider Tanya, who thinks that Arabic should be a "required second language" in the schools because "a large portion of the inhabitants of the state of Israel are Arab...it's like in California, where everybody learns Spanish." For Tanya, a state of all its citizens is one that

> takes into account non-Jewish people too. . . Druze, Bedouins, Arabs. They are Israelis. As time passes I think that we are emerging as a state that's very unkind and intolerant. In essence, very many things that others did to us in the course of history we are doing to others today.

And for Ronit, the woman with an Arab boyfriend, support for a state of all its citizens far surpasses her desire to see a separation of religion and state in Israel. In fact, Ronit introduces the phrase in our interview before I even raise the question:

Q: Do you think Israel should be a Jewish state?

A: I think it needs to be a state for all its citizens [*medina bishvil khol ha'ezrahim shela*], with no discrimination. But we should do it, as it's said, "all the way" [she says "all the way" in English] without any discrimination: for those who have served in the army and

those who haven't served in the army, etc. . . . .If you define the
state under the definition of a "Jewish state," you put the non-
Jewish citizens outside the norm. So it doesn't work. . . . .The state
must be made into one for all its citizens.

Expanding on her proposal, Ronit says "it's all a question of money,"
but adds that "Arabic should be a compulsory language in the schools. You
don't know how much it irritates me that I don't know Arabic. Really. I so
regret not knowing it. I feel like I'm losing out."

For every Israeli Jew in my study who entertains the notion of a state of
all its citizens—whether reluctantly or with enthusiasm—there is another
who rejects the idea as spelling the demise of the Jewish state. (Of the
twenty-six Jews in the study, twelve approve of a state of all its citizens and
fourteen disapprove.) Two connected arguments lead these subjects to their
conclusion: First, a state of all its citizens would mean the dismantling of all
signs of the Jewish character of the state, everything that makes it special.
Second, through changes to the Law of Return, a state of all its citizens
would invite a demographic nightmare in which Arab citizens would out-
number Jews within a generation or two and Zionism would expire.

According to Avi, the young Religious Zionist whose parents immigrated to Israel from Maryland when he was a toddler,

> A state of all its citizens ... [is] a state that Jews live in, just like in
> the United States, or any other state where Jews live. It's a very
> pluralistic state, a state where everyone can live according to his
> own ideas without any coloring [tzivyon] and without any content
> [tochen] or specific ideal [idial] that belongs to the state, as a state,
> as something that unites the state. It's just that everyone who lives
> there sets its character [m'affyen et ha'ofi] and there is no character
> [ofi] that is above and beyond those who live there. Do I think that
> it should be like that in Israel? No. I think that the State of Israel is
> a state that must have a Jewish tint [tzivyon], a shading [tzivyon]
> with the Jewish heritage, and if we say that this is a state of all its
> citizens, then essentially there is no tint [tzivyon] and nothing that
> stands above those who live here.

Yoel's interpretation is similar:

> What it means, I think, is that Israel should become the United
> States. I may be a little bit extreme in this. It means that each per-
> son has a right to vote, and each person has the same amount of
> rights and amount of debts toward society. There have to be equal
> rights to determine the course of the country. And there should be
> no Jewish affiliation to the state. It would just be a state of all its
> citizens, in other words, that the state should not have a Jewish
> symbol or Jewish anything and...nothing about the state should

hurt a Muslim. The symbols of the country, of the state, shouldn't contradict the Moslem belief or contradict the Christian belief, or contradict people who do not believe.

And when I ask Nehama her whether Israel should be a state of all its citizens, she gives an ironic (and vehement) reply:

> Absolutely it ought to be a state of all its citizens. The question is, which citizens? If you make goyim citizens, then what kind of state is this? What kind of citizens are those? If you make everyone who wants to be a citizen a citizen, what is a citizen? Is this a state like all other states?! So if this is a state like all other states, why should we call it "the state of the Jews?" What's the difference between the state of Israel and the United States? There is no difference at all. There is nothing special [*ein shum yihud*]. . . .Is this a state of the Jews? Not at all. Other than that, especially now, with the Leftist leadership in control, is this truly a state of all its citizens? Surely everyone sees that it's not. Everyone sees that the Right cannot say what they want to say. That Haredim cannot say what they want to say. In the state of Israel, others can say everything they like about Haredim. Anything they want: "leeches," "parasites," whatever they like. *That* is a state of all its citizens?

The Jewish *tzivyon* of which Yoel, Avi and Nehama speak—the color, the uniqueness, the special character that makes Israel *feel* like a Jewish state—is at risk, they say, in a state of all its citizens. A country already infiltrated by McDonald's, Home Depot and American conceptions of freedom, Israel would become indistinguishable from the United States if it were to renounce its Jewish nature in an attempt to make Arabs into equal partners in the polity. Zvi, the Religious Zionist, offers an historical and religious justification for rejecting the concept of a state of all its citizens:

> A: A "state of all its citizens" means to give absolute equality. . . beyond absolute equality. It means that the state of Israel will have no Jewish symbols. That it will not be defined as the state of the Jews, as it was established. When it was established, the Declaration of Establishment defined it as a state of the Jews. As long as it's defined thus it cannot be a state of all its citizens. We would need to actually remove the Jewish symbols. You can't define a state that has Jewish symbols and say that it's a state of all its citizens. There are Muslims here too. There are tons! So we'd need to remove Jewish symbols. Given this, it's obvious that it's relevant to not-necessarily-religious symbols like the flag and the national anthem. Our flag is built in the shape of a Star of David and a *tallit*. It cannot reflect someone who has no connection to the Star of David or *tallit*. Our national anthem speaks of the hope over two thousand years, of the longing Jewish soul. That's can't speak to an

Arab person. So we'd need to cancel those things too. That from
my perspective is what a state of all its citizens means. Do I agree?

Q: You surely don't agree.

A: Absolutely not, and I'll explain why. It's quite simple. The people of Israel have been through enough, and has been justified in
the course of all the past generations, starting with the Exodus
from Egypt, the Inquisition, the Pogroms, the Holocaust . . . that it
truly needs its own state. Jews deserve their own state. And they
even arrived at that conclusion. It's impossible to ignore it. The
main nationality that's found here is the Arab nationality across
from us. With all due respect to the Arab nationality, its people
have twenty-two states while the Jews have one state! One state!
So in my view it's totally unfair, it's not defensible [to advocate a
state of all its citizens]. At the end of the day, what will be? What
can be? At the end of the day a dictatorship could arise here. I
don't know what will come to be, but it won't be connected to Judaism, that's for sure. And again the wheel could turn back and
they'll coerce the Jews, force them into ghettos. I don't want it to
come to that. I as a Zionist nationalist religious person believe that
the State of Israel constitutes the beginning of the redemption.
Really the beginning of the redemption. I don't intend to give up
on something like that. It must be the national home for the Jews
and this national home has been, from the time of the Bible, in
Eretz Yisrael, not anywhere else. At the Zionist Congress when
Herzl suggested Uganda [as a possible site of the Jewish national
home] everyone cried out. Why did everyone cry out? Because
they know that the land of our fathers is Eretz Yisrael. It always
was and it always will be. When we say, "land of our fathers," we
don't mean "fathers of every citizen of the world," but the fathers
who led to the establishment of the Jewish nation. . . . So the state
of Israel must be, and I hope with God's help, will be forever forever a Jewish state and a state of the Jews. For at the end of the
day, why did we come here?

No one makes the messianic point as clearly or as fervently as Zvi, but
several other traditional and religious subjects (Yoel, Richard, Nahman, Rita
and Nosson) join him in using the history of the Jewish people, God's promise of the land to the Jews or the story of Zionism to justify Israel's existence.
Nahman, for example, asks: "What did we fight for? What did all the Jews
come to Eretz Yisrael for? My wife came from England—she is an English
citizen and has all the rights—so what did she come here for, for it to be the
same as everywhere else in the diaspora [ba'hul[40]]?" And a few subjects address the demographic impact of a fully realized state of all its citizens. Oren,
the liberal Haredi, finds the notion "problematic."

A: If the state is not a Jewish state, how will it decide who to let into the state, and who not to let in? Today there's the Law of Return: everyone in the world who is Jewish and wants to live in the state can enter without a problem. The moment we turn the state into a state of all its citizens, that means that we are Israeli citizens and it doesn't matter when we come from, and then there could be...a non-Jewish majority. . .The state is more dear to a Jewish Israeli than to a non-Jewish Israeli, because the Jewish Israeli is aware that he has been driven out of all of the states in the world. Fifty years ago he wasn't wanted anywhere; there was anti-Semitism. He is afraid of these things, and here he has a home [bayit], he has his place, his country that he cares about and that he will protect. A non-Jewish man, if there's a war here tomorrow, will abandon the country and find another one. He has no kinship [zikah] with this state. He has an affinity [zikah] for a good state, so if tomorrow America looks like a better state for him, he'll go to America or somewhere else. These things aren't important to him. If the state becomes a state of all its citizens, all kinds of people could begin coming here, no matter from where, even non-Jews. And their interests could conflict with the idea of the state as it was when we built it.

Q: If a state of all its citizens doesn't mean changes in immigration policy but means instead that Jews and Arabs who already reside here would become equal citizens, what do you think about that?

A: It's a problem. Even a leftist in favor of peace and returning territories—even he understands that Arabs want this country. It's not like, for example, the blacks [cushim] in the United States who wanted equal rights, freedom of choice or things like that. From the perspective of the blacks [schorim] in America, there is no fight about who will run the state. The conflict is over equal rights: they wanted to be able to vote, they wanted good schools and resources like everyone else. Here it's different. Here's a fight over the state, who will rule here, who will be the boss and who will decide. From the Arabs' perspective, Jerusalem is just as holy to them as it is to us. And not just Jerusalem, many other places too. They think we stole their state and they want to return. That means that if I give equal rights to Arabs, it puts the state in certain kind of danger, a danger like shooting yourself in the foot.

Oren then cites Israeli Arab riots that took place the week before our interview and mentions the brotherhood that Arab citizens of the country feel with Arabs "outside the Green Line" (i.e., in the West Bank and Gaza), concluding that "it is very complex and problematic for the state to give equal rights, especially to the Arabs." Yoel and Nehama prescribe more extreme

measures to guard against the internal Arab threat. Yoel believes that Arabs
should be disenfranchised on all questions of vital national interest:

> And I do not agree with it [a state of all its citizens] at all! I find it
> very disturbing. I think it's a Jewish state, and has to remain a Jew-
> ish state. And that even to request that the state should not be a
> Jewish state is downright chutzpah. I don't believe that Arabs de-
> serve to determine the course of our country. I don't think... I find
> it very painful that an Arab could end up deciding—as did hap-
> pen—if we are going to give back Hevron or not, for example. If
> we're going to give away Hevron, or if we're going to give up the
> Golan when we make peace with Syria. I would like to say that I
> don't think they have the same amount of rights that Jews do. It's
> hard for me to say it because I have an American background and
> have the general politically correct feeling that democracy is the
> best form of government until now, and so on and so forth. But I
> do not believe that they have the right to determine the course that
> our country is to take. I do believe it's a Jewish country and it is
> the Jews' only country.

What, specifically, is Yoel worried about?

> Imagine you're trying to pass a decision in government if you're
> going to go send the planes to Entebbe to save the plane. Now
> imagine half the government's Arab. As it happens—it could be—
> that in twenty, thirty, forty, fifty years the way things are going
> demographically, it's not an unimaginable scenario. Imagine you
> try to pass that decision in the government and the Arabs say,
> "No, I don't think you should go back for the prisoners [hos-
> tages]!" You know, it's absurd!!

So when it comes to major questions of national fate—territory, rescuing
hostages, peace agreements, immigration—Yoel believes that Arab citizens
should have no say. "You can't pick someone who's not objective or not on
your side," he explains. "This is a Jewish state and you [the Arabs] are on the
other side. Why are you deciding for me, if we are going to do this as a Jewish state?" Yoel is quick to introduce a caveat to his argument, though. Arabs
already here should keep their citizenship. And when the issue is not one of
national fate but rather an everyday economic or political matter affecting
their towns and their families, Arabs "*should* have a voice" and should be
represented in government decisions.

Nehama takes Yoel's idea one step further. In the following passage, I
ask Nehama about her dreams for Israel:

> Q: What about the non-Jews who are citizens of the state?

A: From the start they wouldn't be included as citizens according to the constitution.

Q: According to your [wished-for] constitution.

A: Of course.

Q: So what would you do with them?

A: They can live and stay in Israel. They will have no duties, so why should they have any rights? They will get the minimal basic rights but nothing beyond that. . . . Whoever wants to become a citizen must get the permission of the state and not say: "I like it here, I want to be a citizen, but you do what you want." I am your enemy but give me citizenship? It's ridiculous, no?

So in place of a state of all its citizens—and in place of a state of its first-class (Jewish) and second-class (Arab) citizens—Nehama believes that Arabs should never have been given citizenship in the first place. Yoel believes, somewhat less radically, that their political rights should be seriously curtailed.

Of the religious Jewish subjects, only three express any sympathy for the concept of "a state of all its citizens": the liberal Rabbi Rosen, the twice-born Haredi Yeshayahu and Ganit. Of the three, Ganit is the only subject who seems to endorse the idea—as she conceives it—whole-heartedly:

I think there are several aspects to [a state of all its citizens]. The state of Israel must give equal rights, both equal political rights and social rights, to all its citizens. If schools are needed in the Arab sector, then the state must provide schools to the Arab sector in proportion with their population and appropriate to their needs. That is clear to me... It is true that there must be a clear Jewish character. This is a Jewish state. But there are other citizens [Arabs] that must receive what they deserve. That is completely clear to me. It is true that this is a Jewish state whose norms are as they are, but it's a state of all its citizens in the sense that Arabs enjoy political rights. That's how I see it. Now I see that I am making a distinction, without announcing it, but it's a distinction that must be accepted. They can vote in elections; they must be provided with all the economic benefits according to the criteria of Israeli citizens; there should be no discrimination in areas such as education or any other right. But this is a Jewish state in a certain sense. There is importance to the symbols that represent the Jewish state.

In admitting that she is "making a distinction without announcing it," Ganit means that absolute equality between Jews and Arabs is not possible in Israel. The state's Jewish symbols and official recognition of Jewish holidays will always signify some division between Arabs and Jews. But she thinks that this level of equality is not necessary in order for Israel to be "a state of all its citizens." All that's required for Israel to realize this standard, she says, is to guarantee Arabs equal political rights (which it does now) and to provide them with a fair and proportionate share of state resources (which, she says in other passages, it currently fails to do). Because the state must be "first and foremost" a Jewish state, it must not attempt to fashion itself into a state that is entirely neutral. It should be, in her view, a Jewish state of all its citizens.

Conclusion

Is that concept tenable? Can a Jewish state featuring no clear separation of religion and state be a state of all its citizens? Can it be a true democratic state? This chapter has illustrated the great complexities involved in answering those questions: what is a democratic state? what is a Jewish state? what does "separation of religion and state" entail? what does "a state of all its citizens" amount to?

The position advanced by Ganit at the close of the previous section represents a good jumping-off point for considering the details of Israel's religion-state arrangement as they affect both its Jewish and Arab communities. We can't answer the questions that began the previous paragraph simply by analyzing the concepts or even by analyzing the ways in which Israelis regard those concepts. Only by looking more closely at the subjects' positions regarding the specific nodes at which religion and state interact in Israel—the manifestations of Israel's Jewish nature—will we be able to make progress on the central question for which Israel provides this book's major case study: In what ways and to what extent may religion play a part in constituting a liberal state? The answer to enduring questions about the proper role of religion in liberalism is not an easy one. It screams for nuance. For each of the myriad ways in which religion and state may come together, there are different concerns, different worries and different opportunities.

Before beginning this exploration, however, one point bears mention. The assessments of Israel as a state of all its citizens by some of the Arab and religious Jewish respondents represent a challenge to the very idea that chapters on the details of Israel's religion-state arrangement are necessary. For subjects such as Majjed and Youssef on one side, and Nehama and Nahman on the other, the idea that there could be a state of all its citizens that is also a Jewish state is absurd. On one point these very different Israelis are in surprising agreement: Judaism and liberalism are unable to coexist in the constitution of the State of Israel. Israel must choose. It can be a Jewish state, unified by an official version of Orthodox Judaism that impinges upon its non-Orthodox Jewish citizens and marginalizes Israeli Arabs, or it can be a liberal democratic state, stripping itself bare of its Jewish character and guaranteeing equality, rights and freedom to all citizens, Arab and Jewish alike. It can be one or the other; no compromise is available.

I reject this outlook and undertake the detailed analysis to follow not because I think that either the Arabs or the Orthodox Jews make incoherent points. To the contrary, both sides represent important reminders of the limits of reconciliation between liberalism and religion, and between liberal and religious individuals. As segments of a diverse society who represent substantial minorities of the population, these groups' views ought to be listened to and taken seriously. But the present-day state of Israel in fact features something other than either of the extremes these groups favor; it simply *is* Jewish in some ways and liberal-democratic in others. To simply throw up our hands now and declare the project over is to assume without delving into the issues that liberalism has nothing to learn from Israel and that Israel has nothing to learn from liberalism. If Ganit is right—if it's possible to have some form of Judaism coexist with some kind of liberal democracy in the Israeli state—then the question of religion and state in Israel is really dozens of questions, with several at the forefront.

Notes

1. I use the terms "Palestinian citizens of Israel," "Arab citizens of Israel," "Palestinian Israelis" and "Israeli Arabs" interchangeably. The views of Palestinians who live outside of Israel proper (e.g., those lacking Israeli citizenship and living in the West Bank and Gaza Strip) are not discussed here.

2. The Knesset project to draft a constitution for Israel is described at <http://www.cfisrael.org//home.html> (29 July 2005).

3. In posing this question I read aloud the purpose clause of the 1992 Basic Laws (Basic Law: Freedom of Occupation and Basic Law: Human Dignity and Freedom) that includes the phrase: "This Basic Law is designed to anchor in a Basic Law the values of the state of Israel as a Jewish and democratic state."

4. I thank Noga Morag-Levine for her suggestion.

5. The way in which an archetypal Religious Zionist regards the state of Israel as Jewish might be loosely compared to the way a Marxist (on some interpretations) views a pre-revolutionary capitalist state as just: Israel is vastly preferable to a completely secular state (as capitalism represents marked progress over feudalism); it is a stage that must be passed on the way to theocracy (as capitalism is the penultimate step before the revolution); but a sea change in Israeli society is necessary before the end could ever be reached (as a proletarian revolution and an indefinite period of socialism are required before the state eventually withers away). Small groups of extremist Religious Zionists—much more radical and marginal than any of the Religious Zionists I interview here—seek to hasten the end by igniting apocalyptic confrontations. Some of these groups have attempted to bomb the mosques atop Jerusa-

lem's Temple Mount in this effort. See Gershom Gorenberg, *The End of Days: Fundamentalism and the Struggle for the Temple Mount* (Free Press, 2000). But the disengagement from Gaza in 2005 led many Religious Zionists to an ideological impasse: the secular state no longer appears to be a vehicle for conquering and possessing Greater Israel.

6. Extending the social contract argument, it might be argued that the state "inherits" its religiosity from its citizens (those who constitute the state). But this stretches the metaphor too far. We can imagine states acting in ways that endorse or appear to endorse a particular religion: state actors can declare that "America is a Christian country" or enact a bill requiring Bible study in public schools, or utter a prayer at a presidential inauguration. But the state doing these things via a state actor is fundamentally different from an individual doing those things herself. If we conceive religious action as individual or communal behavior that is based on each participant believing some kind of religious truth, official state action cannot itself be religious. A state, as a collection of institutions governing a certain territory, does not possess the power of belief. By doing the things of the kind listed above, the state affiliates itself with or expresses approval for Christianity. It does not, however, *become* a Christian or act as a Christian believer. All states can do in this regard is to facilitate or require individual or communal action through coercive laws, a strategy which, as Locke shows, might be (religiously) fruitless absent sincere belief on the part of the individual. See Locke, *Letter Concerning Toleration*, 27.

7. Seventy-eight percent of all Israeli Jews believe that Israel should have a Jewish character; when the ultra-orthodox are excluded, the figure approaches 90 percent. See Shlomit Levy, Hanna Levinsohn and Elihu Katz, *Beliefs, Observances and Values Among Israeli Jews 2000* (Jerusalem: Israel Democracy Institute and AVI CHAI Foundation, 2002), 14.

8. While Herzl is generally thought to have advocated something closer to a secular state of the Jews rather than a religiously Jewish state, his views are a matter of some debate. See Yoram Hazony, "Did Herzl Want a 'Jewish' State?" *Azure* no. 2 (Spring 2000): 37-73.

9. This reasoning may have led the Knesset to adopt the phrase "Jewish and democratic state" rather than "a democratic state of the Jews" in the 1992 Basic Laws: the drafters did not want the legislation to be seen as excluding Arabs.

10. See chapter 2, where I discuss the stance of the ultra-Orthodox Agudat Yisrael at the dawn of statehood.

11. An expression frequently used to refer to God.

12. Moshe, the Haredi man who refused my interview request, is associated with Neturei Karta. See "Haredim" in chapter 3.

13. But to be clear: Nosson thanks God, not the State of Israel, for the good fortune ultra-Orthodox Jewry has enjoyed since 1948.

14. A prayer expressing thanks and joy to God for divine redemption.

15. Arabs were formally allowed on the Labor Knesset list in 1973. See Deborah Sontag, "Israel's Next Palestinian Problem," *New York Times Magazine*, 10 September 2000, 50.

16. For an argument for and an attempt to explain this transformation of Israeli society see Yaron Ezrahi, *Rubber Bullets: Power and Conscience in Israeli Statehood* (Berkeley: University of California Press, 1998).

17. I erased references to "liberalism" or the adjective "liberal" in my questions after including them in early versions of my interview instrument. Although prevalent in the writings of Israeli scholars, the term is seldom used in everyday political conversations among Israelis. Instead, as I write above, "democracy" is often taken to imply many of the elements many liberals normally ascribe to liberalism (individual rights, toleration, rule of law, secularism, sometimes neutrality).

18. This is a general right to individual privacy, something like what Justice Brandeis termed "the right to be let alone" dissenting in Olmstead v. U.S., 277 U.S. 438, 478 (1928).

19. This idea has stirred a mini-debate under the "Jewish and democratic state" controversy in recent years. See Sammy Smooha, "Ethnic Democracy: Israel as an Archetype," *Israel Studies* 2, no. 2 (1997): 198-241, where he identifies other ethnic democracies as Northern Ireland from 1921-1972, Canada from 1867-1960, Poland between 1918-1935, and contemporary Malaysia. (Germany, he says, is close.) See also As'ad Ghanem, Nadim Rouhana and Oren Yiftachel, "Questioning 'Ethnic Democracy': A Response to Sammy Smooha," *Israel Studies* 3, no. 2 (1998): 253-67; Ruth Gavison, "Jewish and Democratic? A Rejoinder to the Ethnic Democracy Debate," *Israel Studies* 4, no. 1 (1999): 44-72; and Alan Dowty, "Is Israel Democratic? Substance and Semantics in the 'Ethnic Democracy' Debate," *Israel Studies* 4, no. 2 (1999): 1-15.

20. See *Encyclopaedia Judaica*, s.v. "Tithe" and s.v. "Terumot and Ma'aserot."

21. Though as stated earlier my sample is not representative of Israeli society as a whole, it does reveal trends in how various religious sub-groups relate to these questions. As I explained in chapter 3, my subject pool includes two (of six) Haredim and two (of seven) Religious Zionists whose views differ from the mainstream perspectives of their particular religious groupings. These outliers are Ganit and Richard among the Religious Zionists and Oren and Yeshayahu among the Haredim. In each of the four cases, the "outlier" subject supports separation of religion and state. It is reasonable to assume that the positions described by the eight observant non-outliers are closer to the dominant strands of thought in each sub-group.

22. The strength of Oren's point is diminished when we look at what most secular and traditional Israelis *mean* by separation. None of the subjects wants to strip Israel of all of its Jewish trappings. If Jewish symbols and religious education—not to mention a large Jewish majority—remain, it is not at all clear that secular Jews will be spiritually lost in a state featuring "separation" of religion and state.

23. Even more extreme are those for whom *any* political involvement—whether linked to the Zionist movement or not—is antithetical to Judaism. Recall Moshe, the Haredi man who refused my interview request yet proceeded to speak to me for forty-five minutes. His position that "politic is equivalent to Amalek" suggests a broader and deeper mistrust of the political world than that I am attributing to the Haredi rejectionists.

24. See, for example, Yoel Marcus, "Who is Teaching Whom a Lesson?" *Ha'aretz English Edition*, 13 June 2000; and Yossi Verter and Shahar Ilan, "Countdown Starts as Shas Ministers Quit," *Ha'aretz English Edition*, 21 June 2000.

25. Yoel describes the arrangement in his hometown as ideal: "I find Ra'anana a very perfect example. The way Ra'anana is built is like a very typical American town. There is a central avenue, a main street and everything comes out of it. None of the restaurants on that street are not kosher. Nothing is open on Shabbes on that street. And the reason why, is that there are a lot of religious people, so if people don't buy

it's not worth it. They *are* allowed. Every so often a store opens that is not kosher, and after five months it becomes kosher. But on the outskirts of town, or in the industrial area, there are movies and restaurants that are open on Shabbes, and there are disco-thèques open. And to me, that's the ultimate heaven. Why? Because I can live my life very comfortably within the city, and not have to deal with things open on Friday nights, and all that. And on the other hand, for them, it's right outside the city, twenty minutes walking or five minutes by car, it's right there. I don't think they should be deprived of their Shabbat—they decide how they define it. And good for them, if they want to go to the beach, or they want to go to the movies, I don't have a problem with that in any way. It hurts me in a way. I would like not to see or to hear of such a *hilul shabbes* [Shabbat desecration]. But if that's what people want to do, then that's their right."

26. John Locke, *A Letter Concerning Toleration* (Indianapolis, In.: Hackett Publishing Co., 1983), 27.

27. This group and its activities are comprehensively described in Guy Bechor, *Huka le-yisrael: sipur shel ma'avak* (A constitution for Israel: A story of conflict) (Jerusalem: Keter Press Enterprises, 1996) [Hebrew].

28. Rabbi Regev opposes Shabbat restrictions on public transportation, for example, while a number of secular and traditional subjects welcome or are unbothered by them.

29. This oversight cannot be accounted for by claiming that cultural autonomy is unimportant to Nadia, Majjed or Youssef. All three make at least passing reference to the importance of the millet system, with Nadia stating her position most clearly in defining the concept of democracy: "freedom for different groups to live according to their own ways."

30. Interestingly, Muhammad here uses the Hebrew word for the *Jewish* marriage contract to describe marriage contracts in general.

31. The Association for Civil Rights in Israel, an advocacy group that pursues education and litigation concerning a wide range of civil rights issues, is tracking a recent change in Muslim wedding contracts according to which any financial disputes between the spouses will be regulated by Islamic law rather than relevant Israeli civil law. ACRI is a primarily Jewish organization; no groups are active in these causes among Israel's Arab community.

32. The Sixteenth Knesset (2003-2006) included nine Arab members. (This number is down from eleven Arab MKs elected to the Fifteenth Knesset seated on June 7, 1999.) One of the nine Arab MKs is a member of the Labor Party. The remaining eight are distributed among Balad (three MKs), Hadash (a communist, Arab-Jewish party; two Arab MKs and one Jewish MK) and the United Arab List (also known as Ra'am, combining the Arab Democratic Party, the National Unity Front and moderate wing of the Islamic Movement; two MKs). Of the two Arab Labor MKs who served in the Fifteenth Knesset, Nawaf Massalha was Deputy Foreign Minister in Ehud Barak's government and Sallah Tarif was the first Arab MK to serve as a full government minister (in Prime Minister Ariel Sharon's government). He later left the government in the wake of a corruption scandal; see Gil Hoffman, "Tarif Elected First Non-Jewish Minister," *Jerusalem Post*, 4 March 2001.

33. See Sontag, "Israel's Next Palestinian Problem," 53.

34. Azmi Bishara, "Arab Citizens of Israel: Little to Celebrate," *Tikkun* 13, no. 4 (July/August 1998), 14-15.

35. The Hebrew word Muhammad uses here is "toshavim," which means "residents" or "inhabitants." The phrase "*medina l'chol toshaveiha*" (a state for all its inhabitants) is a variant of "*medina shel kol ezracheiha*" (a state of all its citizens). The former phrase technically refers to all who *reside* in Israel (including its many thousands of non-citizen foreign workers from countries such as Romania, the Philippines and Thailand), while the second encompasses only individuals possessing Israeli citizenship. In Israeli parlance, however, no such distinction rides on the difference in language. (This parallels the apparently interchangeable use of the terms in the Israel's Declaration of Establishment: "The State of Israel...will promote the development of the country for the benefit of all its inhabitants [*toshaveiha*] [and] will uphold the full social and political equality of all its citizens [*ezraheiha*], without distinction of religion, race or sex...") There is another subtle difference worth noting between the prepositions used with either term: the "*le-*" of Muhammad's formulation indicates that the state is "for" all its inhabitants while "*shel*" (of, belonging to) connotes ownership. Thinking of the difference along the lines of Lincoln's famous phrase, "for the people" implies that the state functions with the best interests of the people in mind, while "of the people" and "by the people" imply that the state comprises and is directed by the people-as-popular sovereign. The more frequently heard "state of all its citizens" stresses that Arabs deserve to feel a sense of belonging to, or partnership with, the state, not merely formal equal treatment *from* the state.

36. Ari Shavit, "Citizen Azmi," *Ha'aretz*, 29 May 1998, weekend magazine, 8-11.

37. Quoted in Graham Usher, "Exhausting the Dream," *Al-Ahram Weekly Online*, no. 375, 30 April—6 May 1998 <http://weekly.ahram.org.eg/1998/375/reg0.htm> (29 July 2005).

38. She also thinks that while it would be "idiotic" to require an Arab to sing the national anthem (which refers to the two-millennium Jewish longing for Zion), "he should stand up to respect those around him." Shmuel makes a similar point more passionately in commenting on Arab student demonstrations that had taken place in Haifa and Jerusalem the week before the interview in April 2000. "I was very angry, even though everybody has the right to say what he thinks. But it is very insulting to hear from an Arab student, that 'my state is a Palestinian state.' Every student—every student in the university—is subsidized by the state. And when he pays he pays much less than he has to pay in order to be in the university. And therefore the state subsidizes every student who attends the university. Now this student comes to the university, the Israeli state subsidizes her studies, and she dares to say, 'my state is a Palestinian state.' If it is a Palestinian state, go learn in Bir Zeit [a Palestinian university on the West Bank]! Why do you come to learn here? This is something that is not fair. Because you don't spit in the well that you drink from, right? And this is what she does. OK! I don't enforce you to be in a state that you don't want. OK, so go to the Palestinian [university], go to learn in Gaza. Why do you learn in an Israeli university? This is something that is not right. Now you can claim—I can tell you that in the relationship between Jews and Arabs not everything is right. There are many things that they are—they don't have equal opportunity. But on the other hand, they don't have equal obligations. So if you want equal rights, you have to contribute. So if you do service for the community, -- OK, you can't go to the army, right. But go for three years and work in a hospital and contribute your efforts to the state by doing this. This is right. I would respect this. But you can't at the age of 18 not go to the army and

not only *that*—without making the obligation to the state you have the audacity to come and say this is not your state. OK, so I am very angry about it!"

39. Later in the interview, Naomi makes the same mistake: "There's a settlement near Jerusalem called Neve Shalom where Arabs and Israelis live." (By "Israelis" she means "Jews.")

40. "*Hul*" is an acronym for "*hutz la'aretz*," or "outside of the Land [of Israel]". The term shares its spelling with the Hebrew word for sand, which also means "secular" and "everyday"; it is frequently used in both modern and liturgical Hebrew as an antonym for "holy" [*kodesh*]. "Outside the Land of Israel" thus imparts a sense of lowliness or even profanity, a meaning Nahman suggests in this passage.

Part II
Controversies Among Israeli Jews

Chapter 5
Kashrut, Shabbat and Religious Education

How is it that the vast majority of Israeli Jews (with the exception of Haredim in the rejectionist camp and some "post-Zionist" leftists) support the continued existence of Israel as a Jewish state, while at least half of them, and perhaps two-thirds, favor what they regard as separation of religion and state? In this chapter and the following two, we will trace the contours of this seemingly counterintuitive position. The analysis will show that while religious Jews often find deep theological significance in Israel's Jewish characteristics, secular and traditional Jews support the Jewish state mainly, though not exclusively, on national-cultural grounds. This leads them to affirm those religious aspects of the state that are more amenable to public, non-religious interpretations while they tend to reject those whose justifications stem exclusively from properly theological considerations. The issues in this chapter divide into two categories: those over which Israeli Jews are in wide agreement, and those which spur moderate disagreement.

Matters of Widespread Agreement

Four elements of Israel's religion-state arrangement meet with wide support among all sub-groups of Israeli Jews: (1) observance of Jewish dietary laws in state and army kitchens; (2) funding for religious education; (3) Jewish state symbolism; and—although to a somewhat lesser extent in recent years—(4) the Law of Return. I will discuss the third aspect in chapter 8, where my attention turns to matters of dispute between Israeli Arabs and Israeli Jews. The former two elements—kosher kitchens and state-funded religious schools—were originally part of the "status quo" agreement reached before hthe dawn of statehood.[1] These religious aspects of the state are primarily *accommodationist*: Kosher kitchens make it possible for religious youth to serve in the army and for religious and secular Knesset members to have lunch together; funding for religious schools facilitates the provision of culturally specific education for Israel's religious Jews and religious non-Jews alike. But the two elements are also, secondarily, *symbolic*. They express the state's affiliation with traditional Jewish ritual and its belief in the importance of religious schooling (or at least in parents' interest in directing their children's education). Both arrangements garner support, or at least untroubled acceptance, among Jews and Arabs alike.

Kosher State Kitchens

Twenty-six of the thirty-one subjects give their blessing to the fact that all of Israel's government kitchens—in the Knesset, in government buildings, in the prime minister's house, in the army, in all state catering institutions—strictly observe the Jewish dietary laws of *kashrut*. Among other stipulations, this means that cafeterias are often designated as *"basri"* (meat-only) or *"halavi"* (milk-only) to facilitate observance of a central tenet of *kashrut*: meat products and milk products must be certified kosher and scrupulously separated, with different pots, pans, dishes and utensils used to store, prepare and serve each. The Kosher Food for Soldiers Ordinance (1948) provides for kosher meals for all Jewish soldiers in the IDF, while the requirement for other government kitchens to serve kosher food remains an unwritten rule stemming from the unofficial but entrenched status quo agreement.[2]

Of the large majority of subjects who support the maintenance of kosher kitchens, some are effusive while others are better characterized as neutral on the question.[3] Still, neutrality constitutes tacit affirmation of the continuation of the practice. Among Religious Zionists, Richard says, *kashrut* in these kitchens "must be the case." Yoel agrees and says that when it comes to army kitchens, it's "definitely" important to maintain *kashrut*. Haredim concur. Oren finds the provision "unavoidable" because "the army enlists people who are religious...and those who keep the tradition [traditional Jews]...and keep kosher too. There are many people who are non-religious yet do not eat meat and milk together, pork or things like that. It's a matter of being considerate." Yehuda says the kitchens must "of course" be kosher. Two of the Haredi subjects fault the state for not guaranteeing adequate standards of *kashrut* in the army, however. Nehama speaks of a soldier "who was religious and was sure that everything is kosher in the army. Suddenly," she says, "he discovered that he was eating meat and milk together!" And when she was in the army, in the era before she became more religious, "I remember the chef cooking fish and chicken together!"[4] Jonathan Rosenblum, too, refers to the misled soldier: "A recent example was when a career religious army officer found out that the army kitchens were not kosher, and he made a big to-do about it. He found out that the army is not interested in maintaining any standards of *kashrut*. So, of course, no Haredi soldier would ever eat anything in the army kitchens. . . .That's one reason you don't want to send your eighteen-year-old kid to the army, because he may not have the courage to stand up in front of an officer and say, 'I am entitled to kosher food.' "

Despite being less strict about *kashrut* in their own lives, the traditional subjects tend to agree that state kitchens ought to be kosher. Rotem argues, "all the kitchens should observe *kashrut*, because the army right now is one of the only places in Israeli society where all different religious factions meet." Aaron agrees: "Army kitchens are critical in this country, and we must make it possible for everyone to come. The army isn't going to serve gourmet food anyway, so. . .I think that the state needs to take care of the religious population." Finally, despite the anti-religious tone of some of the secular subjects, none call for an outright reversal of the current policy. Naomi and Mina both suggest that "alternatives" should be available so that, in Mina's words, the state "does not force anyone to keep kosher." But they are not opposed to the state operating a kosher kitchen as long as a non-kosher alternative is available. And other dyed-in-wool seculars such as Shulamit don't mind the arrangement: "It doesn't bother me. Of course, if you have religious and non-religious eating together you should be considerate about the religious. It would be much more expensive to have two kitchens." Ronit, too: "I don't keep kosher, but I don't think it's bad that they keep kosher in the state and army kitchens. I don't know if it's ideal, but it's not terrible."

Two Arab subjects offer mild objections to Israel's kosher kitchens. Nadia objects that this arrangement "stems from the fact that the state is Jewish" and sacrifices people's freedom. "People should do what they want to do. Why compel them?" Still, she allows that "it's the Jews' conflict, not mine. From my point of view, I don't care. I think it's the Jews' problem that they need to eat kosher food. If it bothers them, they need to fight it." Interpreting the question as one about the prevalence of kosher restaurants generally, rather than state-run kitchens, Majjed thinks it is a "big problem. . .when you go to a restaurant and want to order white meat, pork." The other Arabs have little to say either way on the question. But Muhammad, showing again his inclination to highlight commonalities between Jews and Muslims (even has he passes over the differences between the Jewish and Muslim dietary laws), claims, "I keep *kashrut* in my house too. Everyone is free. It is a hallowed custom [*minhag mevorach*]."

Government Funding for Religious Education

Perhaps the central locus of conflicts over interpretations of the Establishment Clause in the United States has been the schoolhouse. May the state subsidize parochial students' rides to school? May it supply them with textbooks, computers, remedial teaching? May the public schools sponsor teacher-led prayer, moments of silence, Bible reading? Is there a constitutional problem with student-led prayers at graduations or football games? What about government vouchers parents may use to reduce tuition to private, including parochial, schools? All of these questions, among others, have been vigorously debated since Justice Hugo Black (citing Thomas Jefferson) raised a "wall of separation between church and state" in the *Everson v. Board of Education* decision of 1947.[5] That very year, in Israel, Zionist leaders sent a letter to the Haredi leadership pledging at least grudging approval for something quite different in the emerging "status quo": ultra-Orthodox autonomy over a separate, government-funded religious educational system.

With no wall of separation, and no Establishment Clause, Israelis have no firm ground for a constitutional argument against government funding of religious education. Yet we might still expect to hear objections, given the number of Israelis who favor separation of religion and state. Surprisingly, very little opposition exists to the fundamentals of Israel's funding scheme for education. Of the twenty-two respondents who express at least some support for separation, nineteen also advocate using state monies for religious instruction. Even die-hard Israeli liberals affirm, in principle, direct state funding for religious education.

Israel's complex education program is specified in its State Education Law of 1953 (last amended in 2000). According to this law, there will be two "official" streams: (1) "state education" ("education administered by the state according to a curriculum unlinked to any political party, communal body or other extra-governmental organization, to be monitored by the Minister of Education or a person authorized to do so by him"); and (2) "state-religious education" ("state education whose institutions are religious in their way of life, educational plan, teachers and supervisors, and which educate students for a life of Torah and Mitzvot in accordance with religious tradition and in the spirit of Religious Zionism"). In addition, primarily for the non-Zionist Haredim who were promised autonomy over their own educational system in Ben-Gurion's letter, the eleventh clause of the State Education Law stipulates that the Minister of Education may specify

> arrangements and conditions for recognizing unofficial institutions as recognized educational institutions, guiding their basic mission, administering them, supervising them and supporting them with state budgets; the Minister will decide on this support and its amount.[6]

Many religious and non-religious schools outside of the official state streams are today "recognized educational institutions" that receive varying amounts of financial support from the state's coffers. By far the largest of these are two Haredi school networks: the Independent (*Atzma'i*) stream of the Ashkenazi ultra-Orthodox party Agudat Yisrael, and the *Ma'ayan Hahinuch Hatorani* stream run by Shas, the Sephardi ultra-Orthodox party.

While a number of respondents in my study would like to see certain changes in the *ways* in which Israel distributes funds to secular and religious schools, only two subjects (Majjed, the communist Druze and Yeshayahu, the eccentric Haredi) profess disappointment with the essentials of Israel's policy of supporting both state-run and independent religious schools. In contrast to the zeal with which he expresses most of his answers, Majjed offers this view with a mild "I would prefer":

> The Catholics have sources for raising their own money. Muslims can solicit donations very beautifully. And Jews, if they want, have places

to look too. Moskowitz[7] will be very happy to donate money to Haredi Jewish education. I would prefer that the money go to people in need [*b'metzuka*]. The majority will go to Arabs, to new immigrants and to Jews in the South.

Moving beyond Majjed's welfarist justification for diverting Israel's expenditures on religious education to other sources, Yeshayahu says,

> In my opinion they need to stop that. Because if we do a separation of religion and state...usually religious institutions in most of the world don't receive [government funds] and if they do, they receive them only according to certain criteria. We should copy the same arrangement present in the United States....All state-religious, Haredi, nationalist [schools]—everything that's not state-based—must be independent.

Yeshayahu, notably, is the only subject to mention the separation of religion and state in the United States in this context. Aside from Majjed and Yeshayahu, none of the other twenty subjects who support "separation of religion and state" believe that this concept precludes government funding of religious education.

Opposition to government programs that aid or advance religion in the schools is vehement among Americans who strongly support separation. How could Israeli "separationists" differ so markedly from American "separationists" on this question? What considerations lead Israelis to this surprising view? The secular and traditional Jews in my study, along with several of the Arabs, tend to see the provision of state funds to multiple streams of education as a requirement, not an impediment, of liberal democracy. At the same time, however, they insist that funds be distributed fairly and equitably, and that schools receiving financing satisfy certain conditions. Shmuel's statement illustrates both branches of this view:

> Q: ... how do you feel about the fact that the state gives financial support to religious education?

> A: Basically I am in favor of a justified division of the budget to all students. One of the rules of democracy is that you give people the ability to live their own way. And if there are people who want to be religious that's fine and they are entitled to have their own budget, provided—*provided*—that they also learn concepts and educational fields on non-religious elements. The problem with the religious is that they don't teach secular subjects and the result is that their children are not exposed to basic concepts that are needed, that are required, for being a good citizen, a good person. Most of the Orthodox people are not educated people from my point of view. And this is something that I believe is done intentionally from their rabbis because I think that they understand that education entails a risk of losing their control and their group. ...And the way of the leaders to control these groups, the way it works, is to limit the knowledge of the people in order to have a better hold on them. And this is something that is very typical to the

extremists, not to the *Mizrachi* [Religious Zionists] but to *Neturei Karta* [rejectionist Haredim], people in Mea She'arim [a Haredi enclave in Jerusalem]. And they will come from Mea She'arim, what we call *hozrim be'sheila* [Haredim who abandon their Orthodoxy; lit.: "those who return with questions"]. And if you ask these people what they know, they didn't know basic algebra! They didn't know English, nothing! They didn't know history, except what his rabbi, and his family, and his...But if you say what was the French Revolution or the Industrial Revolution, they don't know. What were recent technological inventions? They don't know. They come to a secular world, and have a cultural breakdown. They couldn't manage to help themselves independently because they didn't have the tools to do it. This is something that I think is a crime! A crime!

Q: So you think money should be given to religious education, but that it should be conditional upon also teaching secular subjects?

A: Of course, of course. Because the children have their rights to live their own way of life. But the basis of democracy is that you have to let them choose. How can they choose? They know only one way! So from this point of view...It's good to teach them from the Bible and to show them the basics of religion. And I would respect it if they chose it when they grow up, OK. But they were exposed to all of the alternatives, right? And this is something that should be done when they are getting the budget. Right now, this is not the way it is, however. They are pushing for autonomy. They want their own autonomy to do what they want and I think that it is a crime.

Other secular subjects—including those who vehemently object to Haredim— share Shmuel's view. They want the state to fund religious education, based on a principle of equality, but they want it to get no more than it deserves. Here is Shulamit's view:

Well, to give money for religious education exactly the same as the secular education is OK. Only there is no proportion, there is no proportion. They should get what they deserve, not more than that. And they get much more than they deserve. They don't earn their living. There should be a certain kind of relationship between the state and its citizens. It is a give-and-take kind. You give to the state, and the state gives you back. But when it's a one-way relationship, like it is with the Orthodox, it's wrong! They don't give anything to the state. They are not productive. They don't contribute anything to the working sector. They don't serve in the army. They don't contribute anything to the defense of the country. Many of them don't pay taxes. All they do is take, like parasites! And this falls on me and on other Israelis because it is on my account. They take from me and we give them what doesn't belong to them. And they blackmail the government day and night for something they don't deserve. They cheat. They have twenty children; they count them twice. They abuse the state. And this is what is so annoying about them. I have nothing against Orthodox. They have the

right to live and let live. But they live and do not let live. They should
live their own life, and I should be able to live my own life.

This might read as only a tepid endorsement of state funding of religious
education. Shulamit is, after all, reserving most of her temper for complaints
about perceived Haredi abuses rather than crafting a justification for government
funding of religious schools. But this raucous passage is revealing: as emphatic
as Shulamit is in her critique of Israel's Haredi sector, she nevertheless begins her
response by saying that giving state money for religious education is "OK" and
that "they should get what they deserve," which amounts to financial support
that is "exactly the same as for secular education." Although she has serious objections to what she regards as disproportionate funding for religion, she has no
objection to fairer allocations. Shulamit's stand in favor of state-supported parochial schooling is thus made all the more significant by her palpable disdain of
Haredim: her principles overcome her personal feelings. She thinks Haredim are
"parasites"—but she *still* wants her taxes to support their schools.

Shulamit is not the only secular subject who affirms the state's responsibility
to fund religious schools despite a visceral dislike of the recipients of the aid. For
Naomi, "we give it to them not because we want [rotzim] to give it to them but
we are duty-bound [hayavim] to give to them." For Tanya, who sends her daughter to an art school that receives partial state funding, "the state also gives financial support for special secular education, so as long as it gives to special education generally, it must give to the religious. It's a kind of special education.
Everyone should be free to choose how he wants [to educate his children]."
Ronit, too, thinks that "the state must respect every [educational] stream and
give it funding." And Rotem, the traditional Jewish graduate student, "if the
state funds opera and supports football then there is no reason why it shouldn't
support religious education. But it must be in proportion to their numbers in
society, proportional to how many people are interested in it."

Less surprisingly, the Religious Zionist and Haredi subjects support funding
for the various streams of religious education.[8] And where secular and traditional subjects call for more secular studies in religious schools, Zvi (schooled in
the state-religious stream) thinks there is room for improvement in both directions: "Of course the state should fund religious education. I think that religious
studies need to be brought into secular schools, and that secular studies, mathematics and English, need to be introduced to Haredi schools." Ganit agrees that
funding is important ("I don't see any other way to do it") but holds that "there
must be equality between the different religious streams. Not only Jews, Arabs
too, and to others according to their numbers, and for Jews according to their
numbers." Ganit sends one of her children to *Horev*, a private religious school
near her Jerusalem home that is recognized, and funded, by the state. But, as
with other families who opt for a school outside of the official two streams, she
must pay a small supplementary tuition bill. (Yoel, who went to a private, state-
recognized yeshiva for high school, owed about one hundred dollars per month
in extra tuition.) Ganit thinks it is appropriate to pay for extras like longer school
days, more Torah-study hours per week, or hot lunches; she doesn't think the

state should write a blank check to any school that signs up. And when it comes to an independent school that bears no relation to the state's goals for the education of its youth—one "dedicated to the values of vegetarianism," for example—"I don't think the state needs to fund it at all."

A Matter of Moderate Controversy: Shabbat and Jewish Holiday Observance

Despite differences on the details, then, Israelis of all stripes favor two provisions of the status quo agreement. Both kosher state kitchens and state-funded religious schools are seen as accommodations of religious citizens—religious Jews, in particular—whose dietary restrictions or educational traditions require recognition and sensitivity in the Jewish state. More controversy between the religious and secular poles arise, however, when we look at the other two branches of the status quo (Orthodox control of family status issues and public Shabbat observance), and provisions such as draft deferments for yeshiva students. The questions of marriage and Haredi army service, the most serious of those disputes, occupy me in the next two chapters. Here I discuss a somewhat less contentious debate: the state's observance of the Jewish Sabbath and holidays.

Section 6A ("Days of Rest") of the Law and Administration Ordinance of 1948[9] proclaims "Shabbat and the Festivals of Israel"—every Sabbath (from sundown Friday to sundown Saturday) plus the two days of Rosh Hashana, Yom Kippur, the first and eighth days of Sukkot, the first and seventh days of both Passover and Shavuot—as "official days of rest in the state of Israel." Religious minorities may make other arrangements: "Those who are not Jewish have the right to establish days of rest on their Sabbaths and holidays. These holidays will be determined by each community according to the decision of the government that appears in the *Reshumot* [official gazette]."

In addition to establishing regulations regarding maximum daily and weekly work hours, rest time, work breaks and overtime, the Hours of Work and Rest Law of 1951,[10] as amended in 1969 and 1981, both limits and protects religious freedom. First—the matter under scrutiny in this section—it prohibits most businesses from opening on the official days of rest (as defined in the 1948 law), with a fine for lawbreakers. (Work deemed "necessary for [a] farm"—such as the daily milking of cows—is allowed, as is any work by a non-Jew "situated in the area of a local authority whose non-Jewish inhabitants, according to the determination of that authority, are at least 25 percent of its total population.") Second, the law's anti-discrimination provisions forbid all employment decisions based on an employee's religious observance of his or her days of rest.[11]

This law's work prohibitions on Jewish holidays and Sabbaths apply only to industry, business and agriculture (with some exceptions); they do not apply to places of entertainment such as bars, restaurants, theaters and cinemas. Likewise, the ban on public buses both within and between most Israeli cities on the days of rest admits of exceptions: the buses run in Israel's Jewish-Arab city of Haifa, for instance, and often begin their intercity routes to Jerusalem well before the end of the Sabbath on Saturday nights.[12] When the subjects in my study discuss their views on Israel's public observance of the Sabbath and Jewish holidays, their responses are far from black-and-white. Israelis are of two minds on this question. On one hand, many complain that the Sabbath laws constitute a form of religious coercion; on the other hand, even many secular Jews tend to find value in a day of rest and support some public recognition thereof. Jewish Israelis struggle among themselves much more strenuously over marriage laws and army exemptions for ultra-Orthodox yeshiva students than they do over official observance of Shabbat.

The case in favor of regulations designed to realize a national day of rest is made most robustly by Israel's Religious Zionist, and to a somewhat lesser extent, Haredi, Jews. Speaking of challenges to the Shabbat regulations, Avi warns of a slippery slope:

> If this is to be a Jewish state, it must be that way....In my opinion, if the shops will be open, if they show movies on Shabbat, if there will be public transportation somewhere, I do not agree with this. Someone who doesn't think as I do, someone who has other opinions, a Jew, includes himself as a Jew, and he says: "I am a Jew, I don't keep Shabbat, so why do I have to do this?" Yes. If you think of it that way, it's true: why *do* you need to do it? why *should* I force my view on you? But on the other hand, where will it end? Why Shabbat and not marriage, and why not circumcision [*brit milah*] and why not "Jewish" on the [national] identification cards?

If Shabbat becomes just another work day in Israel, Avi fears, the logic holding together the Jewish state will crack, leading to a flood of reforms that will, eventually, denude the state completely of its Jewish character. Yoel explains further why public Shabbat observance—particularly in terms of official acts of state—is so important:

> My argument would be that that is a sacrifice I would request for a Jewish state to have Jewish aspects. And one of the Jewish aspects is that we don't work on Shabbes. The Jewish tradition says that Saturday is not a work day....The Rabin government in 1977 fell because he flew over American F-15s on Shabbat. Rabin was Prime Minister from 1974-77 and his government fell for two reasons: one was that his wife held a bank account in America, which is illegal, and two was the religious parties left the government because he flew over F-15s on Shabbes! Despite the fact that they were for the protection of the country, he could have waited ten hours until the end of Shabbes! But he didn't. And the religious parties at the time had the strength to do that, and I think that's very important....Because on a national level, Shabbat observance is very important. When you start to lose sight of what is religious and what is not, how do we respect our tradition?...We should have respect for it and keep it in mind for everything that we put forward.

In citing Prime Minister Yitzhak Rabin's coalition woes in 1977—stemming largely from the religious parties' indignation that Rabin would ignore that Shabbat proscription on all forms of work and allow planes to fly over Israel— Yoel gives additional support to the *establishment principle* for Israel introduced in chapter 4. Whereas the nonestablishment principle in the United States means, on most readings, that the state may not align itself with (any) religion, the establishment principle for Israel (affirmed by most Religious Zionists) holds that the state must commit itself to respecting Jewish tradition in its laws and official acts. It must instill a Jewish character in the public ethos. But Yoel and other Religious Zionists do not call for enforcement of religious behavior in the private sphere. For Nahman, disrespect for Shabbat on a national level "hurts the society. A religious person wants to preserve his Judaism with freedom of choice, but people need to know that that's life, it's forbidden here, on Shabbat shops must be closed and that's important." He clarifies, however, that "when I say that people need to close their shops, it's not because I want to prevent them [from personally] desecrating Shabbat. If they want to desecrate Shabbat, that's their problem. I can't tell them not to." Nahman wants the shops closed not in order to prevent a secular shop-owner from breaking Shabbat—he knows that the very shop-owner will be watching TV at home, or driving to the beach—but in order to preserve a public sphere that matches the holiness, and the restfulness, of the day. Here is a glimpse of Nahman's reverence for the quietude of Shabbat, and his view of the value that even secular Jews attach to it:

> I don't see Judaism in an extreme way. I, as a religious Jew, say that. If others don't drive on Shabbat, it's better for me: fewer accidents, fewer headaches. I don't want to drive. I would like to take my kids to the beach, but I can't, so I take them on Friday. The only joy I have on Shabbat is to open the Torah, to read a little of the Jewish tradition [*musar*]…It's the only day I have a clear head to read…Other people read different things. They read A. B. Yehoshua [a prominent secular Israeli author], a great book, and enjoy it. There are some secular Jews on Shabbat who unplug themselves [*mitnatkim*] from the world. They want to hear no car, no theater, no anything. They want a quiet day, and to undo everything that has piled up over the week, it's really difficult. A lot of noise, a lot of screaming, running after time all the time. Never managing to do it all [*lo maspikim*]. During the course of a week, I never manage [*lo maspik*]. I arrive home to tell the kids "good night," play with them for half an hour, and they go to sleep….But on Friday and on Shabbat, it's the only day I feel I'm with the family. I don't want to go anywhere; I just want to be at home and enjoy what I have at home. I think many people lack something like that.

> Judaism is not coercion. Whoever says Judaism is coercion is wrong. But there are general, foundational things that people can't do. It's like you can't turn right onto a given street. Why not? But it's a democratic state! I'm sorry, but that's people being provocative—it's not dignified. We can find lots of solutions. Why not? There's no need to make provocations. I think that if there's a Haredi neighborhood that wants to close its street, it's not terrible. If they'll build a new road, so there's

a different road [to drive on during Shabbat]. It depends on how you look at it. I tell people, in the end we'll all die, there's no reason to hurry it up. To worry too much and to enter into all kinds of pressure isn't good—it'll give us gray hairs. So we need to get along with a measured eye [b'shikul da'at], without panicking.

Like Nahman, Nehama's Shabbat experience is enhanced by the state's role in shaping its public observance, but she doesn't mind that others desecrate the day elsewhere. The following is her response to a question about how the Jewish elements of the state affect her personally:

It's very comforting for me, having no public transportation in my neighborhood. What goes on in Tel Aviv doesn't matter to me. It does matter to me when other religious people are bothered, but I suppose that in religious neighborhoods [even outside of Jerusalem] there are no buses. [The atmosphere in Jerusalem] makes me very happy. It's very comfortable for me. For me, it contributes to a feeling of much greater holiness and Shabbat. But religious elements like the siren indicating the entrance of Shabbat [on Friday evenings] are found only in Jerusalem. That doesn't happen in other places. What other religious elements are there? It could be that I'm so used to it, I don't even see it.

Then, speaking about lax enforcement of the Hours of Work and Rest Law, Nehama notes that "often they let people work on Shabbat...closing their eyes to it: 'we didn't hear and we didn't see.' When they want to, they see; when they don't, they don't see. Now there's a religious Minister of Labor and Welfare, and he's very strict about it. But before that they weren't strict. It is true that they moved the turbine on Shabbat,[13] so they do what they like. I don't believe in that."

Nehama's relative indifference to what happens outside of religious neighborhoods stands in sharp contrast to the perspectives of some of her fellow Haredim. This exchange with Yehuda captures the difference:

Q: Let's think about Shabbat now. What do you think about the fact that most public transportation doesn't operate? Is that good, in your eyes, or not good?

A: Of course it's good. Every car that drives on Shabbat pains me. But they give permission [heiterim] for certain industrial plants to work on Shabbat, and these allowances [heiterim] are questionable.

Q: In what way does it pain you?

A: Very strongly.

Q: Because it changes the atmosphere [of Shabbat]?

A: Not because it changes the atmosphere. In our neighborhood, Shabbat is the height [shpitz] of Judaism, it's the climax [climax said in English]. And whoever desecrates [*m'hallel*] the Sabbath gives a good indication of his nature. If someone desecrates the Sabbath it's as if it touches the bird of my soul [*nogea ba'tsipor nafshi*], because Shabbat is the height of belief. He who keeps Shabbat announces and says that the Creator created the world and he rules the world. He who desecrates Shabbat destroys the roots of Judaism.

Shabbat violations occurring out of sight, across town, pain Nosson less than they pain Yehuda, but Nosson believes that Israel's Shabbat regulations are useful in providing minimum of *yiddishkeit* (Jewish knowledge) for disaffected Jews:

We don't care if there are stores open on King George Street [a main thoroughfare in Jerusalem]. That doesn't bother me. My neighborhood is sealed off. The problem is that they want to drive in my neighborhood. For the sake of the People of Israel, for the sake of the other part of the People of Israel [secular Jews], it's very important that at least there will be a minimum of Jewish character in public. It's for the good of the People of Israel that there will be at least this little bit. Again, we're clearly a minority. If the majority decides that it doesn't want to preserve the status quo, we can't force them. But it's our right to use our power . . . from a political perspective . . . so that we do preserve the status quo. . . . I think it's good for the People of Israel that it doesn't drive on Shabbat and it doesn't open stores on Shabbat. If people are angry with that, they can be angry with their representatives who make these agreements with us, but they can't be angry with us. That's very unfair. From one side, the secular man's representative comes to the Knesset, and he says to me: "I want to give the territories back to murderers. You want to keep Shabbat. If you'll help me return territories to murderers, I'll help you preserve Shabbat." If we've made a deal, we've made a deal. Or the other way around. He'll say: "I don't want to return territories. If you want to preserve Shabbat, help me not return territories." We made a deal. We made a deal. We made a deal. And now the person who sent the representative to the Knesset says: "You're doing religious coercion on me." But we made a deal democratically—what do you want? Somebody forced you? You chose the representative who made the deal. We made a deal. Why are you angry at me? I did the most legitimate and the most correct thing from my perspective, because it's best for the People of Israel. I did it because I love you.

The subjects' comments suggest three different reasons a religious Jew might favor Shabbat regulations: to preserve the official Jewish character of the state; to enhance private religious observance; and to help steer secular Jewish souls toward religion. Religious Zionists press the first and second points, as we have seen, while Haredim argue primarily the second and third. The cessation of buses, the closing of businesses and the wailing of the two Friday evening sirens in Jerusalem—one to indicate candle-lighting time, the other announcing the actual entrance of Shabbat—help create a special, even transcendent, atmosphere for religious Jews. They help mark off the day as one that is collectively recognized as a day of rest, with the quiet and peace that Shabbat brings. In addition, for Religious Zionists, the sanctity of the state is served each time it acts in the spirit of Judaism through such official acts. And for Haredim, who attribute no spiritual value to the state itself, the Shabbat atmosphere is potentially conducive to greater Jewish interest and observance among Israel's secular Jewry.[14]

What do Arabs think of the Shabbat laws? They are, by and large, indifferent. On one hand they see Shabbat in the same way they see the kosher laws: an expression of an official state association with Judaism that makes little difference in their lives. On the other hand, because the Shabbat laws are not binding on Israel's religious minorities, and because these communities are free to set their own days of rest, there is also a strong connection to Israel's policy of funding religious education and supporting separate Jewish, Muslim and Christian schools. The Arab subjects' comments include no complaints and even, in two cases, indicate a certain respect for the Jews' decision to observe their own Sabbath in public. Nadia illustrates this perspective:

> I live in Beit Hanina, and I can drive freely. In Nazareth, too, there are no Jews so you can drive wherever you want to go. It bothers secular Jews a lot, I think, but as soon as you have a car, it isn't an issue....I think that the Jews are very wise to keep Friday night and Saturday free of buses, from a religious point of view. I think it's smart. But it doesn't affect me.

Muhammad says the lack of buses "doesn't bother me."

> We rest on our Shabbat too. And who uses public transportation today? There are a lot of cabs in the village. Pick up the phone, and a taxi will come and take you. And today, everyone has his own vehicle. Maybe in the 60s and 70s [it was a burden not to have public transportation, but not today]. But Shabbat is our day of freedom. Two days: Friday [the Muslim Sabbath] and Saturday. On Friday we don't teach and [most people don't work].

And as for shopping?

> We have autonomy. We have a store here that's open on Saturday. Actually, Jews come to shop in our villages on Shabbat all the time! Everyone comes and goes shopping in Tira [a nearby Arab town].

For Omer, the issues of Shabbat legislation are simply irrelevant:

> I cannot begin to speak about these things, because it has to do with the Jewish religion. I respect it. But it's for another religion. They preserve their religion, and I respect that.

Little opposition to the state's Shabbat policies, then, is voiced by Israeli Arabs. When we turn to secular Jews, the story gets more complicated. Many secular Jews express dissatisfaction with some elements of the Shabbat regulations. The complaints they raise, however, are relatively mild, and a substantial portion crumble under scrutiny. Despite what might be expected, some Israeli secular Jews—as Nahman's excerpt above suggests—in fact derive profound benefits from the state-abetted Shabbat peace. The benefits may not be properly religious or spiritual, but they are benefits nonetheless.

Starting with the case against the Shabbat laws, we find that the argument from liberal freedom figures prominently. Mina bases her preference for the buses operating on Shabbat on a Lockean tenet: the state simply cannot enforce religious belief: "Those who want to keep Shabbat—they should keep it. But to try to convince someone to keep Shabbat without explaining the reason—he simply must—it's not out of free will. There's something phony about it." Naomi calls the ban on Shabbat transportation "terrible and tragic. It's chutzpah. There are soldiers who need to get to their bases on Shabbat. My brother is a soldier and I need to take him every Saturday[15] to bring him to the base, because he has no bus. It's the height of chutzpah." Tanya, too, provides a cogent critique based on the impracticality of shutting the country down for one day a week:

> I think it's wrong. I think it's wrong. In every normal country, the day on which you can most do things is on your day off from work. The only day in which I can get around and do my shopping and enjoy a trip to the stores is on Saturday. In the middle of the week I'm working, and I have no time on Friday since they close everything at 1:00 pm. It's not OK. It's really not democratic. What they should do is go to all the religions and give us three days off weekly—Friday for the Muslims, Saturday for the Jews and Sunday for the Christians—then we'll have enough time.
>
> Q: There's not enough time for rest?
>
> A: There is enough rest. No one here dies from too much work. But it's rest according to our Jewish definition. You must sit at home, eat, and at best watch TV, if you have a TV. And you can go for an outing if you have a car. If not, you're stuck at home. You sit at home and rest. Under the definition of a "day of rest" you rest. You sleep, you eat, but you have no culture of leisure. You have rest that is forced on you from above.

As appealing as the traditional Jewish notion of rest may be to religious Jews, Tanya holds, there is no justification for imposing that conception on others who might enjoy a more active form of rest on their only full day off from work each week. Rivka emphasizes the discrepancy between the haves and the have-nots that the lack of public buses exacerbates. "It's a scandal!" she says. "It injures people who have no car, who don't have enough money. I am socialistic! It's very bad." For those with cars and less empathy with the car-less, however, the restrictions aren't so limiting. Or at least the restrictions are worth the minor inconveniences they create.

Shulamit, who insists upon a separation of religion and state and taps into a seemingly endless reserve of insulting words when discussing Haredim, slowly lets her true view sneak out in this exchange:

Q: Buses on Shabbat?

A: Well, I have a car, so...

Q: If you didn't have a car, how would you feel?

A: I think if people if they want to travel on Shabbat or if they need to get somewhere, to make them use cabs [is unfair]—because it costs a lot more—[they should] be able to use public transportation!

Q: Of course, that would change the atmosphere of Shabbat that you talked about earlier.

A: Nachon. Nachon. [Right, right.] Well, I'm thinking more about intercity buses. [Pause.] If I...I think they should be able, yeah... I told you that I was ambivalent about Shabbat. But if it's a problem, you drive around [the blocked-off roads]. Where I live, if you don't have a car, you can't go out of the neighborhood. It's far.

[...]

Q: Speaking again about Shabbat, how do you feel about the rule that most businesses can't be open on Shabbat? Some places of entertainment like movies, cinemas and restaurants can, but businesses in general cannot. Should that situation remain?

A: Well that's the law of the state that you have to be closed at least one day! So you have to change the law, not only perhaps the law of no separation between country and religion, between state and religion. But look, it is the law. You have to close down one day.

Q: My question is, do you approve of that law or do you think it should be changed to allow businesses to open?

A: The same...But some people can't really do anything if you don't keep things open. They work six days a week, and not five days a week. And when are they going to shop? Friday is only half a day. And it's difficult for many people. It is difficult. But if there are going to be buses, they might as well open the shops, you know. But then [gloomily], goodbye to Shabbat *allll-tooo-geth-er.*

Q: It sounds like you're ambivalent about that too.

A: Well, *hanuyot* [shops]? I...It doesn't bother me that they are closed on Shabbat. They open on *motzei Shabbat* [Saturday nights, after Shabbat ends] now. Most of the *hanuyot* are open on *motzei Shabbat.* So, you can shop in the morning, or in the evening, you know?

Shulamit, despite her adamant secularism and her instinct against religious legislation, does not want to say goodbye to Shabbat altogether. She savors the peace and quiet it brings on her Saturdays. She appreciates the rest. And although she discusses and in some measure sympathizes with those who don't have cars, or who want to go shopping on Shabbat, ultimately she finds greater value in keeping the buses off the roads and the stores closed for one day a week. The inconvenience, she notes at the close of the passage, is minimal: shopping is available until Friday afternoon, and it starts up again right away after Shabbat ends on Saturday evening. Shulamit would scream at a Haredi politician who asked her to make a sacrifice for the sake of religion, but she in effect is asking the same thing of secular Jews like Tanya whose "culture of leisure" clashes with the state-specified culture of rest every weekend.

Shulamit's stance on this issue captures the ambivalence of the Israeli public debate about Shabbat and shows why, despite sharp moments, it is one of only moderate controversy. Certain aspects of the state's regulation of activity on Shabbat are inconvenient to certain people. But there is no restriction on what individuals may do in their homes—or on where they can travel on Israel's roads (in private cars, in taxis, or, in some parts of the country, in buses owned by private companies)—and there are plenty of opportunities for Jews who want to go to a restaurant or a movie on Shabbat. On top of that, it is not only Religious Zionist and Haredi Jews who find value in the Shabbat rules governing Israel's public square. A significant portion of Israel's traditional and secular publics, too, ascribes at least some value to the atmosphere of Shabbat that the rules facilitate. These conflicting values—a concern for liberal freedom alongside a desire for a nationally recognized day of rest—help to soften secular protests against the general idea that the state should promote Shabbat, but they heighten conflicts over issues perceived as Haredi demands to impose Orthodox will on others or on the state. That is why, when religious parties tried to halt the Shabbat turbine transport in 1999[16], a leftist group, One Israel Youth, was on site to cheer in support as the truck passed through Bnei Brak (the exclusively Haredi town near Tel Aviv) on Friday night and why representatives from the anti-religious Shinui party showed support by escorting the convoy along its route. The comical nature of these demonstrations—young Israelis hailing a huge turbine, rumbling down the highway at glacial speed, as an icon of religious freedom—shows that conflicts like these do not strike at the heart of Israel's designation of Shabbat as a day of rest. They concern, rather, symbols of power politics between religious and secular forces. Disputes about the basics, about the substance of Israel's long-standing Shabbat regulations concerning public transportation and store opening hours, provoke less division.

Still, Shabbat is an endless topic of discussion, and events such as the turbine crisis are not rare occurrences. The issue, by all measures, is more contentious in Israel than is the debate over the "blue laws" in much of the United States. Prohibiting the sale of alcohol or the opening of businesses on Sundays, these laws are rarely challenged as violations of the Establishment Clause. They are rightly seen, instead, as laws which, though religious in origin (with often explicit pro-Sabbatarian justifications) now serve secular purposes. In *McGowan v. Maryland* (1961), the Supreme Court upheld Maryland's laws proscribing most labor, business and commercial activities on Sunday. The Court held that despite the law's clearly stated purpose and language (to prohibit "Sabbath Breaking" and "pro-fan[ing] the Lord's Day"), amendments to the law, especially in light of changes in the political culture, "seem clearly to be fashioned for the purpose of provid-ing a Sunday atmosphere of recreation, cheerfulness, repose and enjoy-ment...[T]he air of the day," Chief Justice Earl Warren concluded, "is one of re-laxation rather than one of religion."[17]

The principle expressed in *McGowan* still holds forty-five years later: what may have been an illicitly religious law in its inception becomes constitutionally unproblematic when its social meaning can be tenably described as secular. This doesn't mean, of course, that all citizens must regard blue laws as primarily secu-lar: religious Christians are free to see them as promoting church-going or as proscribing sinful activities. The point is that the religious interpretation is not the only or the dominant reading of the law. In Israel, the case is similar in that a significant minority (Haredim and Religious Zionists) give the Hours of Work and Rest Law a purely religious spin while many secular and traditional Jews find non-religious meaning in the state-mandated cessation of work and public transportation on Saturday and holidays. The difference is that Israel's religious parties continually attempt to steer the state in the direction of greater Shabbat observance and urge it to pursue or refrain from certain activities on grounds that are hard to characterize as legitimately *public* reasons. Whatever the enjoy-ment a secular Jew extracts from her Shabbat rest, for example, it is not increased by the knowledge that the state is not transporting a turbine on Saturday.

So an important contextual distinction between the American and Israeli cases is one of religious doctrine: whereas the requirements Christianity posits for a holy Sabbath overlap nicely with those necessary to pursue secular public goods such as "recreation, cheerfulness, repose and enjoyment," Judaism's many rigorous and esoteric rules concerning proper Shabbat observance go well be-yond, and may contradict, secular Jews' vision of a day of rest. Christianity calls for abstaining from shopping and from sinful activities such as gambling and drinking; Judaism prohibits all activity the rabbis connect to the thirty-nine cate-gories of work (*melacha*), including innumerable deeds (such as driving a car, turning on lights, cooking, even tearing toilet paper or squeezing a sponge)[18] that are hard to describe as morally depraved or as threats to the public health.[19] These intricate strictures thus leave plenty of room for Orthodox Jews in the Knesset to press for changes in state policy that stretch well beyond what less observant Jews are likely to support. They also push the boundaries of what a liberal political order ought to accommodate.

Notes

1. I discuss the status quo in chapter 2. The other two elements of the agreement—state observance of the Sabbath and delegation of Jewish marriage, divorce and burial to rabbinical authorities—are more controversial than kosher kitchens and religious educa-

tion. I deal with Shabbat laws in this chapter and with marriage laws, one the most contentious issues among Israeli Jewry, in chapter 6.

2. The status quo is "entrenched" in concept, but, as we have seen, not in all of its details. Certain aspects of the status quo, especially with regard to public Shabbat observance, have drifted in the direction of greater secularism in recent decades.

3. Regulation of the private import and sale of non-kosher products, not surprisingly, is more controversial than observance of *kashrut* in public institutions. In 1994, the Knesset passed the Kosher Meat Import Law; in 1998, it extended the ban indefinitely. Though it prohibits the importation of non-kosher meat under most circumstances, this law does not ban the sale of non-kosher meat or place limits on its consumption. The law is designed, rather, to avert the market effects of wide-scale import of non-kosher meat: lower prices. See Liat Collins, "Meat Law Passes Final Reading," *Jerusalem Post*, 19 March 1998. Although there is no national legislation concerning the sale of non-kosher meat, some municipalities enforce additional kashrut regulations. In 1999, the Be'er Sheva District Criminal Appeals Court unanimously rejected an appeal from several shop-owners who were fined for violating a local ordinance prohibiting the sale of "pork or pork products intended for consumption." See Yuri Shmuckler et al. v. the Municipality of Ashkelon and the State of Israel 7182/98, 566 (3)99, (1999) [Hebrew]. Referring to those who reject these restrictions—the 1994 law was unanimously upheld by the Supreme Court in 1996—Zvi says, "I personally don't understand why there must be an obsessive desire on the part of the state to import pork, because, from my point of view, over the generations, many Jews *died* for this cause, died to avoid eating it! So why must some people be so adamant about bringing it into Israel?"

4. Although not a strict rule of kashrut, dietary norms prohibit the casual mixing of fish (a *parve* food, classified as neither milk nor meat) and meat products.

5. Although he sketched a very rigorous standard for separation in the dicta of his 5-4 majority opinion, Justice Black held that a New Jersey statute reimbursing parents for their children's bus fares to private religious schools did not violate the Establishment Clause. See Everson v. Board of Education of Ewing Township, New Jersey, 330 U.S. 1 (1947).

6. This is my translation from the Hebrew text.

7. The reference is to Irving Moskowitz, a wealthy Canadian Jew who has donated millions of dollars to ultra-Orthodox institutions in Israel.

8. There are three exceptions: Yeshayahu, as described above, opposes funding. Richard, the Religious Zionist, criticizes the current system's stream-based approach as propagating a fractured Jewish society; he'd prefer a unified state-provided Jewish education common to all Jewish citizens. And in line with his rejectionist anti-Zionism, the Haredi Yehuda would prefer ultra-Orthodox education to be completely free of state oversight and funding: "If they didn't give us money, they wouldn't be able to tell us what to study and what not to study." Since Haredim are forced to pay taxes, however, Yehuda thinks it makes sense to get some of their expenditure back in the form of education grants. (In practice, the state requires very little of funded religious schools in the way of secular education. That is what subjects like Shulamit and Shmuel complain about.)

9. *Pekudat Sidrei Ha'shilton Ve'ha'mishpat* (Law and Administration Ordinance) (1948). Israel Ministry of Justice, *Laws of the State of Israel*, vol. 1 (1948), 18.

10. *Hok Sha'ot Avodah U'menuha* (Hours of Work and Rest Law) 1951. Israel Ministry of Justice, *Laws of the State of Israel*, vol. 5 (1950-51), 125-33; vol. 23 (1968-69), 60-61; vol. 35 (1980-81), 133-35. For a record of amendments to this law, see Zvi H. Preisler, ed, *Legislation in the State of Israel: Arranged by Subjects with Six Indexes*, vol. 2 (Jerusalem: Ketuvim Publishers, 1997—updated to April 1, 2000) [Hebrew], 989.

11. Jews are limited to the Jewish days of rest, while non-Jews may choose to rest on the days designated by their particular religious community *or* on the Jewish days of rest.

But merely claiming to observe a particular religion is not sufficient; subsection (b) of section 9C allows employers to verify the veracity of employees' or potential employees' claims: "A person in need of an employee may request a person who has stated as specified in subsection (a) to deliver to him, not later than seven days from the date of the request, a written affidavit under section 15 of the Evidence Ordinance (New Version), 5731–1971, containing particulars substantiating his statement, including particulars attesting to his religious convictions and his observance of the commandment of his religion, and if he is a Jew, to his observance of the dietary laws, both in and outside his home, and to his abstention from traveling on the Sabbath." *Hours of Work and Rest (Amendment) Law*–1981, Ministry of Justice, *Laws of the State of Israel*, vol. 35, 133.

12. In the summer, when the sun sets after 8:00 pm, the Sabbath extends into the late evening, making a return trip to Jerusalem inconvenient for many relying on public transportation. Debates concerning the Shabbat observance of Egged, the nationally subsidized bus company, and of El Al, Israel's national airline, come up occasionally in the Knesset. On February 16, 1993, one Knesset member submitted a question to the Minister of Transportation noting that Egged's time schedule is not always updated seasonally, resulting in bus trips beginning before the end of Shabbat on long summer days. Another MK, on March 7, 1993, inquired about a letter he had received reporting that some of El Al's Saturday night flights took off before Shabbat ended. In both cases the Minister of Transportation denied the claims and gave assurances that El Al and Egged were in full compliance with Shabbat and holiday regulations. *Divrei HaKnesset* (Knesset records), Second Session of the 13th Knesset [Hebrew], 6431-32, 6434.

13. Nehama refers here to a coalition crisis in August 1999 over the transportation of massive turbines on Shabbat. Several months into his administration, Prime Minister Ehud Barak nearly lost two Haredi coalition parties, United Torah Judaism and Shas, who objected to the Shabbat violations involved in hiring Jewish employees for this purpose. (The transport of the 250-ton turbines from their place of manufacture in Ramat Hasharon to a new power station in Ashkelon was planned for Friday night and Saturday in order to prevent midweek traffic snarls stemming from the road-wide trucks rolling down Route 4 at five kilometers an hour.) Finally a compromise was reached according to which the Shabbat violations would be minimized—the turbine would not be loaded or unloaded on Shabbat, and as many workers as possible, including the drivers, would be non-Jews—and the religious parties would stay in the coalition. Yair Sheleg and Anat Cygielman, "Turbine, Government Arrive Safely," *Ha'aretz English Edition*, 29 August 1999. Member of Knesset Avraham Ravitz of UTJ said during the crisis, "The problem is not the turbine itself. It is the whole situation which has turned in into a symbol of the state's contempt for the million citizens who observe Shabbat and for the Shabbat itself." Yair Sheleg and Avirama Golan, "UTJ to Bolt if Turbine is Moved on Shabbat," *Ha'aretz English Edition*, 26 August 1999. This case is an example of Israeli religious parties' general strategy of crying foul over a relatively minor incident—similar transports were made many times during previous administrations, including in that of Barak's predecessor, Benjamin Netanyahu—in order to show their strength or attempt to exact concessions on other issues such as draft deferment or increased educational funding.

14. While they find no inherent value in the Jewish state, Haredim sometimes take offense at state actions that contravene Judaism. Nosson, for example: "With the issue of public transportation it's even more [critical], because public transportation is subsidized by the state and its taxes. I'm a partner in that, and so it's of course my right to say that I don't want to be an accomplice in the desecration of Shabbat." The argument is structurally identical, in the inverse, to an American atheist's objection to government funding of religious institutions on the grounds that such a policy makes him an unwilling partner in propagating religious belief.

15. The word "Shabbat" in Hebrew is the weekly holiday as well as the name for the day on which it falls: Saturday.

16. See footnote 13 above.

17. McGowan v. Maryland, 366 U.S. 420, 445-448 (1961).

18. See Hayim Halevy Donin, *To Be a Jew: A Guide to Jewish Observance in Contemporary Life* (New York: Basic Books, 1972), 90-96.

19. The "standard of review" that Jewish law applies to these rules might be called ultra-strict scrutiny: there is to be no tradeoff between observance of the law and any competing goals, no matter how compelling the interest. According to the principle of *pikuah nefesh* (saving a soul), there is only one exception: when human life is at stake, Jews have a duty to break Shabbat. Driving to the hospital, then, is not only allowed but required in cases of emergency.

Chapter 6
Marriage Law

Debates in Israel over religious education and even Shabbat transportation sound like family skirmishes compared to those over Israel's marriage laws and the military draft exemptions enjoyed by ultra-Orthodox yeshiva students. In contrast to the issues covered in the previous chapter, marriage and draft deferments strike at the heart of fundamental questions of civil liberty and civic duty. They are central to an assessment of Israel's status as a liberal democratic state. From a religious perspective, these issues are crucial as well: the monopoly on Jewish marriage and exemption from IDF enlistment are often thought to be essential to Jewish continuity and to internal Haredi unity, respectively. For both sides, the stakes are high. In this chapter and the next I sketch the rival arguments through the voices of my subjects and try to sort out their relative merit.

One might wonder at this point what happened to all of the subjects who claimed they wanted to separate religion and state. Do they really want separation? Or do they misunderstand the concept? Finally, in this chapter, we see what the twenty-two subjects mean when they call for "separation of religion and state." Supporters of that motto, and opponents too, focus squarely on one issue: the Orthodox monopoly on matters of Jews' personal status. Since its birth Israel has offered no civil marriage option. Adopting the British Mandate standard inherited from the Ottoman rulers of Palestine, Israel formalized its personal status laws in the early years of statehood. The Religious Courts Law (Marriage and Divorce Law) of 1953 delegates the task to Israel's various religious communities, which means that Israel's Chief Rabbinate and its attendant religious courts hold exclusive jurisdiction over the marriage of Jews. Those wanting to marry outside the Rabbinate, those who want to marry someone of another religion, and those whose Jewish credentials are not accepted by the Rabbinate nevertheless have an exit option: a civil wedding ceremony abroad.

We have seen that there is very little correlation between the subjects' responses to the question of religion-state separation and their responses to the questions on many specific Jewish aspects of the state. Support for separation, for example, does not automatically entail either opposition to or support of Shabbat restrictions on public transportation; nor does it indicate resistance to kosher kitchens or to state funding for religious education. Although opposition to separation generally carries a *more* predictable set of beliefs on specific matters, it too prescribes no particular political platform. (Those Arabs, Religious Zionists and Haredim who oppose separation often do so on very different grounds.)

When we come to the question of civil marriage, however, we see most subjects responding as we would predict given their positions on separation of religion and state. In all, twenty-five of the thirty-one subjects' views answer these two questions in the same way. Among the Jewish subjects, the figure is twenty-two of twenty-six. That is, Jews supporting separation of religion and state are apt to support civil marriage (with two exceptions among the respondents) and those opposing separation tend to oppose civil marriage (with another two exceptions). Among these four exceptions, three are easily accounted for.[1] This strongly suggests that when Israeli Jews talk about separation of religion and state, they're talking chiefly about the sole area of Israeli law in which the state hands exclusive jurisdiction to the religious authorities and, in effect, subjects citizens to religious law.[2]

Given the correspondence between attitudes on the concept of separation and attitudes on civil marriage, it is not surprising that the arguments deployed by each side of this issue draw heavily on the arguments concerning separation described in chapter 4. In the debate between Jewish Israelis over civil marriage, the issue comes down to individual freedom and/or Jewish flourishing, on the one hand, and Jewish continuity and/or the sanctity of state, on the other. Among Arabs, for whom Jewish flourishing and Jewish continuity are of no concern, civil marriage is debated on different terms. As I describe below, the relevant factors for Arabs are individual freedom and Muslim or Christian autonomy under the millet system.

Arguments for Civil Marriage

Let's begin with the argument in favor of civil marriage.[3] The argument from liberal freedom is paramount among the secular and traditional Jewish respondents, nearly all of whom oppose the Orthodox monopoly. Shmuel, the professor in Haifa who traces his line back to Rashi, thinks that

> people should have the ability to choose. If someone wants to be married in a religious way, fine. But if he doesn't, the state should

give him the opportunity [not] to do so. I believe that it will change.

Rivka, too, thinks "there should be equal jurisdiction for everybody," not only for religious courts, to dictate the terms of marriage. Religious marriage, she says, "should have nothing to do with the state." Both of her two married children apparently agree, choosing to bypass the religious courts entirely by having their weddings abroad:

> A: My son and his wife were married in Gibraltar. In Gibraltar, yes. Just imagine. [Laughs.]
>
> Q: Cyprus is a very popular place to go, isn't it?
>
> A: Yes. My daughter was married in Cyprus, my eldest daughter. She was married in Cyprus and she didn't have any other ceremony. No, she didn't want [another one]. And my son, they were married officially in Gibraltar and some months later we had this big wedding with the rabbi in our community [at the Conservative congregation]. It was a very nice wedding, and they made their own *ketuba*. Her sister, my daughter, wrote the *ketuba*. It was very, very nice. It was very important to them. And they came to Shabbat *hatan-kalah* [service in honor of the engaged couple] in the *beit ha'knesset* [synagogue]. It was very nice. And all the family was very happy about the way it took place. And it was their choice, the couple's choice and I was very happy about it, it had a lot of meaning for me.

Among secular Israelis, a trip to Cyprus, Gibraltar or elsewhere is increasingly popular as a way to escape the requirement to wed via the Rabbinate. All three of Naomi's mother's siblings, for example, married abroad: two in Cyprus, one in Las Vegas. Citing examples such as those of Rivka's son, some traditional Jews respond to those who suppose that civil marriage would lead to rampant assimilation and divide the Jewish nation. Here the argument from Jewish continuity overlaps with the argument of liberal freedom. Consider this exchange with Aaron:

> Q: What about the jurisdiction that the state gives to religious courts in determining questions of marriage?
>
> A: I would eliminate it. I would eliminate it. I would allow people to go to religious courts if they chose. I don't think they should have an exclusive right to determine it, because there too they represent one form of the Jewish code of law. And there are a lot of people who don't abide by it. I think they would be surprised to see how many people would consult religious courts if it wasn't

imposed on them. Some would avoid them. But a lot of people would take them into consideration. They would certainly go to them for marriage. They would want a *Jewish* ceremony. I think the Reform movement has proven that without a shadow of a doubt. A rabbi I know tells me he's got 450 weddings scheduled for June, July and August of this year. And he could schedule more if he could find the rabbis to officiate.

Q: So people who have Reform weddings in this country have to also go abroad...

A: They have to go abroad or work out another arrangement. Right. But the fact these people want a *huppa* [Jewish wedding canopy]...they want something that resembles traditional Jewish wedding...they don't want the kind of extreme reformism that you once saw in the United States, and still see, without a *huppa*. They want all the trimmings of what they have come to know as a Jewish wedding. They want to break the glass, the want the Hebrew, they even want contracts! They have a right to contracts. But they conceptualize it differently. If you put x's and y's, you get a contract. But the content of the contract is up to you. And they want the wine and all sorts of things...and I think they deserve it.

Q: You think there should be an option for civil marriage, but you think that if there were, more people would choose a Jewish marriage.

A: Absolutely. Oh, absolutely. They would opt for another form of religious marriage that the current establishment does not permit...I bet the percentage of people who don't have some kind of Jewish wedding, aside from going abroad, is probably very small. It would be an interesting study to take a look at that.

Q: Do you think that if there were such a free market of Judaism in the state, that Reform and Conservative branches would rise?

A: My hunch is that they would rise, and that they would adapt and change. They would not be like American movements. There would probably be some, hopefully, some bloc known as Liberal Judaism. And I think they would really have an impact. I'd love to see it; we'll find out.

Aaron contends that a civil marriage provision would lead many Jews not to justice-of-the-peace ceremonies that are stripped of Jewish content but to a number of alternative Jewish ceremonies. He bases this on anecdotal evidence that increasing numbers of Israeli Jews are presently opting for a non-Orthodox but Jewish wedding in Israel—purely ceremonial, with no legal validity—after getting legally married abroad. Rotem, whose wedding was planned for several weeks after our interview,[4] agrees that civil marriage would not spell the end of non-Orthodox Jews getting married Jewishly in Israel. She also describes an element of the process that she finds particularly problematic from the perspective of liberal freedom:

> Q: ...starting with marriage, I know this is something that is affecting you personally. How do you feel about the state giving religious courts jurisdiction over marriage?
>
> A: Jurisdiction yes, monopoly no. It is very, very wrong. This all evolves from the principle of separating state from religion. I think most Israelis will *still* choose to go to the Rabbinate and that's fine. But there are ridiculous things, like every woman who gets married has to go to the *rebbitsyn* [a rabbi's wife]. Did you know that? Did you know?
>
> Q: No. Please tell me!
>
> A: Yeah! Every woman has to get a little *petek*, a little note, from the rebbitsyn saying she has been to one or two meetings, and in these meetings the rebbitsyn gets to lecture to seculars because they see secular women ... it's unbelievable! They tell them how important it is to keep *nidda* [Jewish law requiring married couples to abstain from sex during and seven days following menstruation] and how important it is, whatever, with respect to *chazal* [an acronym for *chachamim zichronam livracha*—the Jewish sages]. I don't know what nonsense they tell them. And they try to explain to them how it is more healthy, a whole lot of bullshit. And they have the state's authority to do this for every single woman who gets married in Israel!!
>
> Q: So you go to the rebbitsyn of the rabbi who's in charge of the community? Is that how it works?
>
> A: Yeah, the wife of the rabbi. It doesn't have to be the one of the rabbi doing the marriage; it can be another one. This is a *clear instance* of something undemocratic. They're forcing their views on people who are not interested in hearing it. And this is very, very wrong. So I think it should be allowed to have civil marriages.

Rotem points out how Israel's delegation of authority to the rabbinical courts involves not only having an Orthodox rabbi at one's wedding, and being required to sign a *ketuba* [marriage contract] that satisfies Jewish law, but mandatory one-on-one religious instruction on sexual morality prior to the wedding. Picking up on that point, Yoel, the Religious Zionist who strongly supports a rabbinical monopoly on Jewish marriage (for reasons I discuss below), nevertheless finds much fault with the ways in which the

Haredi religious courts relate to their clients. His complaint begins with his and his wife's experience with the rabbinate, but it extends to the negative impression Yoel feels the Haredim in charge transmit to secular Jews:

A: I find marriage very problematic. Very important and very problematic. I say very problematic only after getting married because I had to deal with them. And I found it extremely, extremely un-user-friendly...

Q: Tell me what the problems are with the way marriage happens now. Why is it not user friendly?

A: The law says that you have to get married through the rabbinate. The rabbinate people...were really not nice and extremely arrogant. And a very big turnoff to religion. I walked in there, I walk around with my *tsitsit* [fringes of a four-cornered garment worn under the clothing by Orthodox men] out and I have a yarmulke, and my fiancée at the time was dressed modestly, and they just weren't nice. You'd think that this is the time that each person in Israel has to meet religion. This is the point—everyone gets married, more or less—you have to meet up with it. You would think that they would make it something that, when you finally need a rabbi, they would make it welcoming and happy. They could be more understanding. When we were getting married, we were waiting in the waiting room, and a girl walked in wearing a long skirt to her ankles but with short sleeves. I don't know, but she looked like she tried. She didn't look like she was trying to be...you know the way that girls are walking around today. She thought she was wearing a nice long skirt, and wasn't in any way dressed in tight or revealing clothes. It looked like she put in some thought.

Q: She was trying to dress modestly for the rabbi.

A: Yes, which is I think important and it's a nice thing. But, they said, "how could you walk into a rabbi's house with no sleeves?!" And they went and got her something you wouldn't use as a rag and told her to put it on so she could go in and see the rabbi. And I'm thinking, why in the world would anyone in their right mind *want* to do this? Why? Why must they make it so miserable for them to do this? And there were a lot of people who walked in and...the law requires that the women have *tahara* [family purity] classes, the women learn the marital laws. Now, how do they enforce it? They have one of the teachers, and she signs the form. There are very personal things in these lessons. So my wife did the classes through her rebbitsyn of her community in New York. Now, we brought a letter from her. She wrote a letter, "My name is this, I grew up in this area, I went to this school, I went to this high

school, and I learned here, and I have the authority of the Orthodox Union, and yada yada yada, and my husband is..." Her whole
life was there. Everything. Her whole resume was there... So we
have the letter, and we took it to the rabbi, and he looked at the letter, and said to me, "I don't care. You have to learn with someone
who I trust. I don't care who you learned with. Not good enough.
You have to learn with someone who I trust."

What are they going to do? Are they going to come into the bed-
room? There's no way this can possibly be enforced, the keeping of
family purity. The purpose of learning is so people can understand. Now if he is saying this to me, and we look like a nice religious couple, what is he saying to guys who don't know our
world? God knows how they...I have a friend, an Israeli who got
married here, and they told him that unless they followed the
laws, their kid will be retarded, will be born without legs, you'll
have a kid who is blind, or deaf. If you're running a company or
you're selling a product, and you want people to buy your product—or you don't want people to hate your product. Forget you
want them to buy it. You don't want them to *hate* it! A little
bit of...you know what I mean? And I found it so offensive! It bothered me so much. And I said you know what? Before that I was
very much against it. "How could you say, you don't have to have
Jewish marriages, and it's very important. And people will end up
not getting married by the rabbinate, we'll have a split people, because how will my grandchild know that your grandchild is Jewish...." I was very much convinced of that. But after I got married,
I shut up. I can't say that anymore, because I can't blame anyone
not wanting to go through that process! Personally I would have
enjoyed jumping on a flight and getting married, getting a license,
and then coming back here and having a wedding with my rabbi
and doing everything I want to do.

I think that if religious Jews—Haredi, non-Haredi, whatever—
don't do anything to change this, it's going to end up blowing up.
There's no way that can continue.

Despite all this, though, Yoel does *not* think that the religious monopoly
on matters of personal status should be lifted:

Q: So you think there should be an option for civil marriage?

A: No! No, again, see this is my problem. I do not believe there
should be civil weddings or an option for civil marriage. I feel very
strongly about it. I believe that things have to be changed.

Q: So your criticism is of the rabbinate, that the *rabbinate* should
change.

A: They have to *realize*. When we walked in to see the rabbi, and gave him a form, and he said, "Why isn't this signed here?! How come your father's signature isn't here?" You know, he didn't say anything about the father's signature before. Obviously, this is the first time I'm going through this process. I didn't know! I just didn't know! It would be really helpful if they would make a list, "Hello, welcome to the rabbinate. We're happy to see that you have decided to get married. A hearty *mazel tov* [congratulations]. To start the initial processing, please bring in this form and two passport pictures and mazel tov to you and good luck." Some kind of a list, telling them, "you're going to have to be taking *tahara* classes." If you had to do that, so you would do it. I don't think anything has to change religiously. Instead the process should reflect the beauty of the religion and the marital laws. And I think it's something that has to happen, the rebbitsyn can show some understanding and talk to them on another level, and not by turning it into a Dark Age mysticism.

In contrast to Yoel, Ganit, the sole Religious Zionist who advocates civil marriage, finds no value in requiring non-believing Jews to marry according to Orthodox practice. Ganit believes that Israel "must institute parallel systems to enable people the possibility of choice in marriage and divorce." She is clear, however, that the state has a responsibility to protect not only the negative liberty of citizens who want to marry in a non-religious manner, but also the positive liberty of religious citizens who want to be sure their marriage partners meet requirements of Jewish law. "Whoever wants to marry in a civil manner should be able to do so," Ganit says, but the state has an important role to play in keeping close track of its citizens' choices and the circumstances of their weddings:

> There must be a clear registration and it must be accessible to people so that there won't be a situation in which a religious person wants to marry and he doesn't know whom he's marrying because there's something in the system that can cause him to perhaps marry someone who's forbidden to him.

In other words, a comprehensive list must be kept to help concerned parties find out whether a potential marriage partner is suitable according to Jewish law. To be complete, it would include more information than Israel's Population Registry provides. The document would detail each spouse's lineage, as well as prior marriages and divorces, and list the wedding ceremony as civil or religious. (The latter may also involve listing where the wedding took place, whether the traditional Jewish marriage formula was uttered, who officiated, who the witnesses were and whether they were religious, etc.) Ganit is not alone in making this point. Of the four Haredi subjects who express at least partial support for civil marriage, three note that careful record keeping is essential. Most of them cited *yuhasin*, the Jewish laws requiring clear determination of an individual's personal status. If the Jewish state is going to allow civil marriage, the argument holds, it must give the Orthodox communities this information to help its members avoid forbidden marriages.

Oren says "authority but not exclusive authority" should be given to the religious courts. "Whoever wants an Orthodox conversion will go to the Orthodox. The Orthodox will keep their own genealogical scroll [*megilat yuhasin*]. Whoever wants to marry in the Orthodox way will also divorce in the Orthodox way." Nehama, perhaps the most conflicted subject on this question, sees two sides to the issue. On one hand, she thinks that separation of religion and state would be "terrible." Speaking as a member of the Haredi community, Nehama says "we would save ourselves, make *sifrei yuhasin* [genealogical books] and keep our religion within ourselves," but it would lead the secular and traditional Jewish populations astray. Despite that worry, she does not find any justification for withholding the option of civil marriage:

> A: I cannot oppose civil marriage, because everyone does what he wants to do. If he doesn't do it here, he'll go to Cyprus. Who can prevent it? Of course I'm against it: everyone will be able to marry any way he likes?! But people can't force their opinions on other people. So if they don't do it here, they'll go to Cyprus and do it there.

Arguments Against Civil Marriage

The arguments against civil marriage and in favor of retaining Orthodox control on matters of personal status stem from the same considerations that inform those subjects' rejection of separation of religion and state that we looked at in chapter 4: Jewish continuity and the sanctity of the state. Respondents using these arguments are committed to preserving the unity of the Jewish people above all; Religious Zionists also point to the holiness of the state as a reason to keep marriage in the hands of the rabbis. While both Haredim and Religious Zionists generally favor maintaining the status quo on marriage, their emphases differ, and the uncertainty we find in some of the responses—particularly those of the Haredim—reflect an internal dilemma.[5]

The dilemma for Haredim proceeds from two conflicting values, one internal to their sub-community and one applicable to Jews at large. On the first score, Haredim are preoccupied with preserving their way of life and ensuring that their children receive a strong upbringing in Jewish law and custom. Shrinking from what they regard as the extremely pernicious effects of secular culture, many Haredim keep to their own neighborhoods as much as possible, eschew television and mainstream newspapers, and generally seek to avoid interactions with the non-Haredi world. This sector of Israeli Jewry seeks unmitigated autonomy over its religious affairs and its religious educational system. In conferring jurisdiction to rabbinic courts in matters of Jews' personal status, the state nevertheless maintains a dose of influence over how the rabbis exercise their authority. The Israeli Supreme Court, for instance, regularly reviews religious courts' decisions to determine whether they fall under the limits of their power. Haredim resent state encroachments on their autonomy—particularly when they come in the form of decisions penned by Chief Justice Aharon Barak, the judge many ultra-Orthodox decry as an "enemy of religion."

On the other hand, the Haredim relish their position of relative autonomy and seek to preserve the influence they have on the lives of all Jewish Israelis. Their external goals are met by ensuring that most Jewish Israelis observe the proper Jewish rituals at major life events, thus maintaining something that can be called a "Jewish people" even if most of the Jewish people choose to defy traditional Jewish law in their homes. The most crucial rituals, from the Orthodox point of view, relate to defining the boundaries of the Jewish family. Only by maintaining control over the rules of entry (marriage law) and rules of exit (divorce law) can the wider Jewish family—*klal Yisrael*, the Jewish community worldwide—be preserved as one people. There are two related worries: intermarriage and illegitimacy. According to the first, a provision for civil marriage will enable Jews to marry non-Jews in Israel and thus pull away from the faith. An intermarrying Jew will often be led away from Judaism, and it is even more likely that the offspring of an intermarried Jewish woman—who is considered fully Jewish according to *halacha* (Jewish law)—will fail to identify with his religion. (*Halacha* does not consider offspring of a Jewish father and a non-Jewish mother to be Jewish.) According to the second problem, viewed as more problematic, the lack of mandated religious marriage will cause a crisis of *mamzerut*, or illegitimacy. Children of marriages forbidden by *halacha* (these include unions between a *Cohen*[6] and a divorcee, between close relatives, or between a man and a previously married woman who did not undergo a *halachic* divorce) are considered *mamzerim*. They and their offspring, stigmatized with an irrevocable brand of illegitimacy, may marry only other *mamzerim*. This is root of the concern about civil marriage "creating a split in the nation": not only will *mamzerim* grow in numbers, it will be difficult to track them and ensure they do not marry Jews who themselves are not *mamzerim*.

Though terse, Yehuda's comments on this issue capture the Haredi tradeoff. Recall his reticence to address to my earlier question about whether Israel should separate religion and state, as well as his eventual answer: "I think that it is necessary to separate the religion from the state and for them not to meddle with religion." When it comes to the question of civil marriage, though, Yehuda has other ideas: "Q: Do you think that the Haredim must have the monopoly on matters of marriage, divorce and burial, or should people have other options? A: No. It *must* be in the hands of the Haredim, because otherwise there will be mixed marriages, Jews marrying goyim." So Yehuda supports separation of religion and state—on the basis of the religious autonomy argument—but rejects civil marriage on the basis of the Jewish continuity argument. He wants to have his babka and eat it too: full autonomy for Haredim from the state in matters of *halacha* and education (the internal aim), and continued control—delegated by the state—over other Jewish citizens' marriages, divorces, and burials (the external aim).

Nosson's position is more internally consistent: no to separation and no to civil marriage. He takes the time to explain carefully why civil marriage would be a dangerous proposition, even given the existing alternative of going abroad for a civil ceremony:

> Q: The situation today is that if a Jew wants to marry he must do it via the Rabbinate. He has the option of traveling to Cyprus or to the U.S., to go outside of Israel, to marry there and to return. The marriage will be registered by the state, not by the Rabbinate, but by the state. What's the difference between that situation and the situation in which there's the option for civil marriage inside the state of Israel?

> A: The difference is very simple. From the perspective of Torah there's no difference. We are against the state allowing non-Jewish marriages performed outside the state. They didn't ask us about this, and that's a pity. And that is a big problem for the People of Israel. But it must be understood that it's not similar, because still the option isn't attractive to very many people and only a small minority here choose it. And it's possible to keep track of this minority and to know who's OK and who's not OK. The moment there's separation of religion and state, there will be no way to track it. If people don't *marry* in the Jewish manner the problem isn't as grave. But the problem is that when someone marries he's happy, holds a grand event, he wants to invite his parents and his grandfather and his grandmother, and when they separate religion from state they'll continue to get married in Jewish weddings, but when they come to get divorced and there are laws and there is pressure and tension, they will do it the easiest way: they'll go to court and request a divorce. And when they want to marry again, it doesn't matter where he got married—he won't be able to marry in a religious ceremony. Even without marrying, if they bear children, they'll be *mamzerim* [illegitimate children].

Whoever does it [marries civilly] truly endangers himself, but he
also endangers the whole Nation. The moment religion and state
are separated, the majority of the Nation—other than those who
come and register with our community—will disappear. We won't
be able to track them. It may be just a matter of numbers, but the
quantitative difference is a significant difference. As it is we can
still keep track of things, but that way we won't. The moment you
lose control there will be two Peoples here.

Here we have a religious-communal argument piggybacking on an empirical claim: The value of a single, unified, recognizable Jewish people is
basic to Judaism, but Jewish unity and continuity would be endangered if
the state of Israel made civil marriage available to its Jewish citizens. That's
not because most Jewish Israelis don't care about Judaism—to the contrary,
Nosson claims that around 90 percent care deeply, and would want to keep
religion and state together to maintain Judaism—but because they "aren't
strong enough to make it happen."

What will happen? A woman marries according to Jewish religion
and law. After that when she wants to get divorced—the Rabbinate isn't so simple—her husband has to give her a *get* [a divorce
document]. But she will do the easy thing. If she wants to marry
someone else and her husband is impeding her, she'll go to [civil]
court and get divorced. She'll want to use the Rabbinate but she
won't be strong enough. But when the existing order is burst open,
God forbid, the people with the best intentions won't be able to
follow through on their will.

Whereas Haredim know exactly how to follow Jewish law, Nosson argues, less observant and less knowledgeable Jews will fall into a trap, unwit-
tingly separating themselves and their offspring from other Jews and con-
tributing to a split in the nation. They need the Orthodox rabbis to lead them
around those traps. And this problem is not limited to the inability to marry
religiously without going through a *halachically* proper divorce:

There was a case a few years ago in Tiberias, when people came to
register their marriage with the Rabbinate and they discovered
that they were brother and sister, from the same father, not the
same mother. How did this happen? Because the Rabbinate checks
who your father is, who your mother is, who knows that you're
single. They build backwards and so they find these things out.
With civil marriage there's nothing like that. In five minutes you're
married. And that's just one example. The moment you start up
something like that, in which there's civil marriage, that's saying
we don't know what's happening with them. We don't know what
is going on with them—we can't marry with them.

Nosson's argument here is disingenuous in two ways. First, it assumes that marriage laws either operate according to *halacha* or lack standards entirely, permitting citizens to marry anyone in any way they like. In fact, liberal democracies typically impose many restrictions on marriage, including prohibitions on incest and polygamy as well as rules setting who counts as a valid wedding officiant. Legislation providing for a civil marriage option in Israel might include similar provisions. Second, the upshot of the argument ("we won't be able to marry with them if they start marrying civilly now") is a red herring. Even today, Haredim very rarely marry Jews outside their sub-community, no matter how impeccable the non-Haredi Jew's lineage. The attempt to turn this into an argument appealing to the marriage prospects of the Haredi community itself is weak.[7] The real aim is external. As Nosson put it more candidly earlier in the interview, "We love our secular brothers and we don't want to lose them. We want to save our secular brothers from themselves."

Jonathan Rosenblum, the head of a Haredi public relations organization, is torn on the question of civil marriage less because of the internal vs. external dilemma that haunts Yehuda than due to conflicting strands of the external goal alone. While it is in the interests of Haredim to maintain the nominal Jewishness of all Israeli Jews through common religious marriage laws, it is also important to attract secular Jews to Orthodoxy. Both of these goals are worth pursuing vis-à-vis the wider Israeli Jewry community. There may be a difference in tactics, Jonathan suggests, depending on whether the goal is ensuring that Jews remain *Jews* or whether it's encouraging Jews to become more *religious*. The Orthodox monopoly on marriage may buy the former at the expense of the latter, by alienating those who flinch at the requirement to marry and divorce according to *halacha*:

> Q: How important is it that the rabbinate retains exclusive control of Jews marrying Jews in this country?
>
> A: [sighs] Here my views are…I go back and forth on this issue. …There is the real practical issue of attracting *ba'alei teshuva* [newly religious Jews]. As a *ba'al teshuva*, my greatest interest is that people should become religious. And I recognize that the degree to which the state is involved in [religion], people feel religion is an outside encroachment on their lives rather than something positively chosen. It is very negative for your ability to speak as one Jew to another. So there is a part of me—the part of me with a very religious world view—which is all for separation of church and…state and religion. I don't mean separation in the same sense as the First Amendment in America where there would be no governmental support for religious schools. But my view doesn't happen to be the view of the leaders of my community.

Despite his worries that secular Jews will drift further and further away as they feel more and more imposed upon by the Orthodox establishment, Jonathan ultimately sides with Avraham Ravitz, one of the leaders of the Haredi United Torah Judaism party:

> Q: Some people insist it's very important to maintain the Orthodox monopoly on marriage because it's the only way to keep the people together, to keep the *am* [people] together.
>
> A: I absolutely see that. I see both sides of the issue. Because, I think, as Rabbi Ravitz said to me, there is 20 percent of the country that has no connection to anything in the Jewish tradition. They can do what they want. They can bury themselves. If they want to cremate themselves, they can. Let them do what they want. We can't stop them. It's not that we're indifferent to what they do, but we can't stop them, so we would let them do what they want. The way Israeli society is often portrayed is, a large Orthodox group, and a completely secular group...but the so-called "secular" here is far more observant than the so-called Conservative or Reform person in the States. Of course, there are exceptions. But in general that's the case.

What does Jonathan take from this? If 20 percent of the Jews in Israel are hopelessly lost to the secular world, and around 20 percent are already Orthodox, it makes sense to court the middle group. Jonathan seems to agree with the strategy of writing off the extreme seculars—let them cremate themselves, he says, despite Judaism's prohibition on cremation—and maintaining the Orthodox monopoly in order to keep the large group of traditionally minded Jews in the fold. The 20 percent on the extreme will yell and scream, but they will yell and scream in *any* case, and they will exercise the Cyprus option rather than submit to Orthodox marriage. But those in the middle—people like Rita, my Moroccan subject in Ra'anana, and, more pointedly, her kids—are at some risk of teetering toward secularism if given the chance. The Orthodox control of marriage is an insurance policy for maintaining (most of) the People of Israel as one united nation, and, it is hoped, for encouraging the traditional to come closer to Orthodoxy.

Religious Zionist subjects share the Haredi goal of maintaining the unity of the Jewish nation. Nahman, for example, complains that Israeli Jews who go abroad to marry "only cause problems" and states his primary reason for retaining the rabbinate's control of Jewish marriage:

> We want to be a Jewish people. You see outside of Israel how much assimilation there is in the United States and England and in Europe. A guy marries a goy because he loves her, and in the course of two generations there are no more Jews. I'm not trying to

tell people how to marry or with whom to marry. It's a symbolic act. Do it.

Explaining this position, Nahman notes that "I do lots of things *only* because I know that it will preserve the nation. For example, if they tell me I have to evacuate a Jewish settlement, even though I'm a religious person, I'll evacuate it. If not, everyone will do whatever he wants, and there is no more army. There are a few things it is very important to preserve, institutions like the army, like the rabbinate. They are our foundations. If we lose them, we're finished." So according to Nahman, the rabbinate's control over marriage is as important to the security and continuity of the state of Israel as its military strength. Just as he is willing to compromise on his principle that Jews have every right to live on the West Bank, secular Jews should be willing to compromise a few minutes of their time (and perhaps their conscience) for a traditional Jewish wedding. In both cases, the value of the unity of the Jewish people is most important. Just as the Israeli Defense Forces would collapse if every soldier acted in line with his own preferences rather than according to superiors' orders, "the state will begin to crumble," Nahman predicts, if civil marriage is instituted.

Yoel echoes Nahman's argument: Jewish marriage is key to Jewish survival, and demanding it of all Jews—as a "symbolic act" for those who reject its premises—is hardly an onerous request:

Q: What do you say to a secular Israeli Jew who says, "You know what? I'm secular. I don't want to go through a religious marriage. I also don't want to go to Cyprus to get married. I want to do it in Israel. I want to have a civil marriage. There's an option for those who are religious, there should be an option for those who are secular to have a secular ceremony." What's your argument to that person?

A: My argument is, that he belongs to a nation. And our nation, our people, have been through a lot, in two thousand years in *galus* [exile] and before that. And the sacrifice has to be made today in order to guarantee the continuation of our people as one people. And I would ask him to try to understand that to make the sacrifice of having a rabbi marry you, you don't have to have a *huppa*, and all the things that religious people do, walking around each other. You can have the *huppa* outside or before the wedding, or the day before the wedding. You know what, have the *huppa* the day before if you don't care about it. I would ask him to make that sacrifice for the continuation of our people as one people. Because if it is not done that way—and I would explain this—two, three, four generations down the road, his kind who would choose to marry civilly and the other kind who will marry by the rabbinate, will not be able to intermarry. And that will create two different peoples. Now if you look at our history, as I understand it, his claim would disappear. As has happened over the centuries. And I would ask him to make that sacrifice for the benefit of our people. And as my brother, as someone who is part of my people, I think that's that. After seeing what we've been through and seeing where we're going and what we're doing, I think that's a legitimate thing to request... And if you want to [marry civilly], I would like to make it inconvenient for people to do it.

It is clear from Nahman and Yoel's comments that the interest in secular Jews marrying religiously isn't tied to an expectation that the secular Jews will become religious, or even that they will have any positive feeling toward religious rituals associated with marriage. Yoel's comment suggests that the groom and bride can chew gum or chat on their *pelephones* (cell phones) while the rabbis do their thing: it is emphatically the act that matters, not the intention. The interest is much less one of proselytization than it is a communitarian claim: "whatever you believe personally, you *owe* this to your nation. Your nation depends on your individual decision to act according to Jewish law when marrying."

Linked to and beyond that point, however, is another: Most of the Religious Zionist subjects see the political linkage of religion and state on this question as a theological necessity. Their support for the Orthodox monopoly, then, is tied to but not contingent on the need to protect the Jewish nation. Subjects such as Avi would advocate the status quo arrangement even if the vast majority of Israeli Jews were observant and could be counted upon to *choose* the Orthodox way in marriage and divorce on their own:

> If we say that we are a Jewish state, then there are certain things that are associated with that expression. It's not enough to just say, "I'm Jewish." If I'm a Jew, that means that I must marry in the Jewish way.

For Avi, duties are ascribable to Jews as Jews by the state. What if a nonreligious Jew, one who "doesn't believe in religion at all," refuses a religious wedding? "I would try to explain to him the importance and, beyond that, explain what marriage is according to Judaism—and he would agree with me." Why the need to compel a religious ceremony, then? Because not all Jews will be convinced, and—the point I want to stress here—because without religious marriage, Israel will abandon its *raison d'etre.*

> Q: Is it important that religious marriage remains part of the state, and not part of the non-political civil society?
>
> A: Yes, because if it weren't that way, what would the difference be between me and others who live in Israel? Just some other

group that lives in the state? Don't dare call that the "state of Israel." It would be a state in which different groups live, each according to its own customs, with everyone who wants to separate from his group going off and establishing another group of his own.

Here Avi's statement may be read as a renewed objection to a multicultural "state of the Jews" in which individuals decide for themselves how to practice Judaism while the state remains neutral among competing conceptions of Jewish (and other) life. In such a vision, he claims, nothing is left of the substance of the Jewish state, and nothing elevates Jews to a special place within it. Zvi seconds Avi's call and draws a sharp distinction between civil marriage in Israel and outside Israel:

> Q: What do you say to someone who wants to marry or divorce or be buried in a non-religious manner? Do you think there should be a civil body that would handle this?
>
> A: Not within the state. Outside of Israel they do this. But in our state there must be a Jewish character. A person goes through a religious ceremony and it takes about an hour, but this ceremony *matters*. It matters a great deal. Even if someone is secular, it doesn't mean he needs to get all stirred up about this. There are certain points at which people need to see the beautiful things in Judaism. And it's times like these: the *huppa* [marriage ceremony].
>
> Q: If you don't want to get married religiously you can go...
>
> A: Do it outside Israel. This state must be identified with Jewish markers, and the moment you open this up [to alternatives], you say that this way is not necessarily the correct way from the point of view of the state. It says that the state doesn't necessarily have to be that way, doesn't have to have Jewish markers. It's something that could inflict damage on all the religious institutions of the state. What will be left of the religious institutions? What will be left of the Jewish flavor of the state? It would be sad.

Even the relatively liberal Rabbi Rosen believes there is "a majority of the Israeli population who wants religious marriage because they see that as the big prerequisite to the continuity of the Jewish people." Including himself in that majority, he says that while "religious legislation should be reduced to a minimum...there might be very often certain basic principles that everybody would agree with." He is thinking of fundamentals such as marriage. In a moment of reflective insight, Rabbi Rosen submitted the basic underlying principle of exclusively Orthodox marriage—the continuity of the Jewish people—to scrutiny:

Now, maybe someone would come along and say, "There is no Jewish people anyway." [Laughs.] I'm not sure that's a myth that Israeli society is willing to acknowledge. And you can discuss the value of living with myths, even if they're not true. But assuming that you have this myth, that there is one people, and that's what the Israeli street feels, it might very well be the street doesn't want secular marriage.

Conclusion

What would liberalism say about Israel's present marriage arrangement with regard to Jews? It seems clear that John Rawls or any liberal theorist would regard the unavailability of civil marriage as a violation of basic liberty of conscience: it makes citizens subject to a religious authority whether or not they accept its legitimacy or believe the religious truths it represents. Israel's delegation of authority to Jewish religious courts requires a large group of citizens (secular and other non-Orthodox Jews) to adhere to the comprehensive religious doctrine of a minority (ultra-Orthodox Jews) when participating in major life events such as marriage and divorce. Worse, it excludes hundreds of thousands of Israeli citizens from marriage entirely: those who are not recognized as Jews by the rabbinate (a problem for many immigrants from the former Soviet Union) or those Jews who wish to marry non-Jews. It sounds like an easy case: imposing a particular interpretation of Judaism's marriage laws on all Jews constitutes a clear violation of a basic civil liberty, so any arguments in favor of the monopoly fall outside of public reason. That said, such a quick assessment fails to take note of the salient differences between the political society that Rawls's theory openly presupposes—the United States—and Israel, a polity that was founded as a Jewish state and that conceives of itself in its Basic Laws as "as Jewish and democratic state." As such it misses an important feature of the debate over marriage in Israel.

Putting aside the clear difficulties liberalism would have with Israel's marriage laws, it is significant that all of the main arguments on this issue— those in support of civil marriage as well as those *against* civil marriage— function in Israel as public reasons. The political values of individual freedom and religious pluralism put forward by opponents of the current system are clearly in line with Rawlsian public reason. But the values on the other side of the debate, although inspired by religious commitments, are hard to characterize as nonpublic values when we keep in mind the following two considerations: First, the vast majority of Israeli Jews regard Jewish unity as an extremely important value. From the lesson that the Jews' divisiveness in ancient times was the impetus for the destruction of Solomon's

Temple in 70 C.E. and ensuing dispersion; to the copious graffiti on Jerusalem's streets in which both sides accuse the other of "dividing the Nation"[8]; to the strongly held expressions of Israelis across the religious and political spectrum—unity is a predominant aspiration. Second, as we saw in chapter 4, Israel is, according to the overwhelming majority of its Jewish citizens, a Jewish state. The continual and heated debate over exactly where Israel's Jewishness is or ought to be located, and over how Israel's Jewish values and its democratic values conflict or cohere, is nevertheless built on significant agreement on the broad outlines. Nearly every Jew both believes his state to be Jewish and wants his state to be Jewish.

When Jews debate the question of civil marriage, then, the considerations put forward by the Orthodox Jews are not only *not* sectarian, they are public political values accessible to all Jewish Israelis. And these are not simply Jewish concerns but the concerns of any political society that seeks its own preservation over generations. Rawls mentions that the state has a legitimate interest in some aspects of family life, notably "the institutions needed to reproduce political society over time."[9] If the reproduction of an Israeli political society with a Jewish majority is necessary to maintain Israel as a Jewish state, it may well be a legitimate interest of the state to regulate marriage in ways that conduce to that goal.

This is not to say, however, that there is anything approaching a consensus over the best way to realize those values in public law or to determine the proper legal arrangement for Israeli marriage. In the *Kulturkampf* between Israel's religious and secular publics, the various sides draw diametrically opposing conclusions about particular constitutional and policy questions. While secular Jews are interested in Jewish unity and continuity of the Jewish people, they generally do not believe that such a goal requires an Orthodox monopoly on marriage. Some hold that breaking the monopoly will lead secular Jews to freely choose a religious wedding—whether Orthodox, Conservative or Reform—where they currently run from religion. Others point to the existing loophole that brings thousands of Israelis to Cyprus each year for civil marriage, as well as to countries outside Israel where Jews seem to survive as one people despite their diverse marriage options. Finally, although a Jewish state is very popular among Israeli Jews, the various sub-sectors of the Jewish public regard the concept of the Jewish state in incongruous ways, with Religious Zionists favoring a state that incorporates at least some aspects of religious law and secular Jews preferring something closer to a "state of the Jews" with Jewish symbolism and a Jewish majority but little or no officially imposed religion.[10]

Engaging the Orthodox on their own terms, it is possible to show that the vagaries of Jewish law actually advise against requiring secular Jews to marry religiously, if the goal is preventing a rift in the people. Making the argument from Jewish continuity, Orthodox Jews in Israel often say that civil marriage will create a split in the nation by producing large numbers of *mamzerim* (illegitimate children) who cannot be tracked. (Under Jewish law, a *mamzer* may marry only another *mamzer* and a Jew who mistakenly marries a *mamzer* enters into a forbidden union from which any offspring are also *mamzerim*.) But, as some civil marriage advocates point out, the offspring of an unmarried Jewish couple are *not mamzerim* according to *halacha*. Since civil marriage is not considered a valid marriage according to Jewish law, the child of a couple married civilly *is* legitimate. The problem of *mamzerut* (illegitimacy) arises only when a woman marries according to Jewish law, separates from her husband *without* securing a valid Jewish divorce and re-marries. According to *halacha*, the woman is still married to her first husband because a *halachic* divorce never occurred; this makes offspring from the second marriage illegitimate.

Mandating religious marriage for secular Jews, then, might amount to "putting a stumbling block before the blind." It may exacerbate rather than solve the problem of Jews becoming "two peoples" who are unable (from the perspective of the religious side) to intermarry.[11] For a Haredi response to this argument, consider Nosson's sociological claim raised earlier: Many Jews will continue to marry religiously even with a civil option, but will be "too weak" to pursue a religious divorce and will revert to the civil courts to dissolve their marriages—resulting in potential *mamzerut* upon re-(civil) marriage.[12]

Assume for a moment that Nosson is right: Israel gives its Jewish citizens the option to marry civilly, hordes of seculars take advantage of the opportunity, and a significant upsurge in *mamzerut* follows within two generations. Is the harm to Israel's Jewish sector grave? Haredim and Religious Zionists may say yes, because the nation has been "split into two" and because Israel has taken a large step away from being a Jewish state. But is the present Orthodox monopoly the right way to achieve meaningful Jewish unity? Reason and experience[13] dictate that state attempts to compel the unity of citizens will fail. Forcing citizens to undergo procedures or religious rituals they reject, in fact, is more likely to lead to resentment and disunity. And that is what we see in the Israeli case.[14] After nearly sixty years of state-hood, the rift between Israel's religious and secular publics has never been more intense. The policy of giving the Orthodox control over non-Orthodox Jews' marriages, divorces and burials may have had some success in main-taining ethno-racial unity (limited by married immigrants entering Israel, as well as the Cyprus option), but this success pales in comparison to the pol-icy's utter failure to consolidate the Israeli Jewish nation into a people that sees itself as a unified whole. Racial unity is a tenuous glue for religious groups. It purchases nominal unity—the ability of a particular group of peo-ple to be considered "Jewish" in the eyes of Orthodox Jewish law—at the cost of embitterment, antipathy and, even, the risk of civil war.

The fact that these debates take place on the level of public reason, then, does not mean that liberalism has nothing to say about the conclusions reached in such debates. It does not mean that liberalism should be neutral on the question of civil marriage. In Rawls's terms, the *ideal* of public reason—the terms on which fundamental questions are debated in a polity—is tempered by the *content* of public reason, which includes a list of basic rights and liberties, an assignment of priority to those rights and liberties and adequate means for taking advantage of them. Rawls notes, properly, that the content as well as the ideal of public reason are pliable: different polities will specify a different list of fundamental rights and liberties depending on their political cultures and predominant comprehensive doctrines. Still, the right to marry and the right of freedom of conscience would seem to be fundamental to any liberal democratic society. So although the concerns of Orthodox Jews about the continuity of the Jewish people and the Jewish character of the state are relevant concerns for the Israeli polity, the position that rejects any change in the status quo is clearly unacceptable.

Israeli Jews should be able to marry outside the Rabbinate without leaving Israel. This seems clear. It also seems clear, however, that the state may properly take some role in accommodating some of the concerns of those on the other side of this debate. Although their anti-civil marriage public reasons rest on contestable empirical judgments, they are far from groundless. It would not be contrary to public reason or antithetical to liberalism, for example, if the state chose to aid in the Orthodox effort to keep careful records of all marriages performed in order to track intermarriages and other unions forbidden by Jewish law. The problem of *mamzerut* has significant implications for some of the Jewish communities in Israel. It might be possible to facilitate all Jews' freedom to marry by both allowing civil marriage *and* keeping documents that could inform those religious Jews considering a marriage partner of certain facts that would be helpful in determining his or her suitability. Although this would clearly mark a linkage between religion and state, it would pose no danger to the liberties of citizens—a danger that the current Orthodox monopoly clearly entails.

Notes

1. The four nominal outliers are: Yehuda and Nehama (Haredi), Richard (Religious Zionist) and Rabbi Regev (Traditional). I consider them "nominal" and not necessarily meaningful outliers because for all but one of these subjects, the question of marriage is still central to the question of separation, and vice versa. The two Haredim in this category—Yehuda supports separation but not civil marriage while Nehama rejects separation and accepts civil marriage—seem to be caught in a paradox: The stronger the state's role in ensuring the survival of "one people," the more likely it is to encroach upon Haredi beliefs and practices; but the more hands-off the

state is toward religion, the less power Haredim will have to save Israel's wider Jewish community and solidify their own ultra-Orthodox adherents. The concerns about Jewish continuity and religious autonomy, then, pull Haredim in different directions on both separation and civil marriage, making it less puzzling why they would advocate apparently disparate views. Rabbi Regev, as discussed above, favors civil marriage but not what he regards as a radical program of separation. Still, civil marriage is his highest priority issue. These three views, then, pose no conceptual challenge to the tie between separation and marriage in the Israeli context. Richard is the only meaningful outlier: His is the only concept of separation of religion and state that seems untethered to a position on the marriage laws.

2. Two of four Arab respondents who support separation do not support civil marriage. Youssef is unfamiliar with the issues involved with civil marriage and expresses no opinion; Omer, like Muhammad (who opposes separation), sees it as incompatible with the autonomy of Muslim Shari'a courts.

3. The debate over reform of Israel's marriage laws is complex, with a range of ideas presented as alternatives to the current system. Rather than enter into the policy details of specific proposals here, I treat the issue more generally and ask what reasons may be given for retaining or significantly changing the status quo. For a discussion of several possibilities for adjusting the current system, see Pinhas Shifman, *Mi mefahed mi-nisuin ezrahim?* (Who's afraid of civil marriage? The case for reform) (Jerusalem: Jerusalem Institute for Israel Studies, 1995) [Hebrew], ch. 5. Shifman suggests four competing models: civil marriage only for individuals who are unfit for marriage according to religious law (those who are *not* unfit must still marry halachically); civil marriage and divorce as an *alternative arrangement* to the religious system of marriage and divorce; civil law as the *exclusive arrangement* for marriage and divorce, with a choice of civil or religious ceremony; and an *integration of religious and civil law* which might entail coupling civil marriage with religious divorce *or* allowing civil marriage only under the watch of a rabbi.

4. Though her wedding was to take place inside Israel, through the Rabbinate, Rotem was working with the officiating rabbi to add certain elements to the ceremony not normally found in Orthodox weddings.

5. Surveys show that Haredim in Israel are overwhelmingly in favor of the current monopoly on Jewish marriage. A *Jerusalem Post* poll from September 2000 showed that over 90 percent oppose civil marriage. In wavering on this question, my subjects are clearly not representative of the wider Haredi community. But their views are windows into the diversity of ways Haredim may view these issues, and the conflicting principles at stake from the Haredi viewpoint. My six Haredi subjects thus demonstrate the dilemmas more readily than a representative selection of Haredim likely would have. Five of the six Haredim in my pool had undergone significant religious transformations. In their former lives, one was basically secular (Jonathan Rosenblum), one Religious Zionist (Oren), one traditional (Nehama) and one (Yeshayahu) moved away from his Haredi roots and then, turning back, brought new knowledge and new attitudes to his faith. And a fifth, Nosson, turned from modern Orthodox to Haredi when he immigrated to Israel in his teens. Only Yehuda is exactly as religious today as he has always been. Although all six subjects share a fervent dedication to Jewish belief and teaching, and a strict observance of Jewish law, many of them bring insights and perspectives from their earlier lives that shape their political views in sometimes subtle, sometimes less subtle, ways.

6. Based on their paternal lineage, Jews belong to one of three classes—the Cohen priestly class, Levite or Israelite—a hierarchy that played a more significant role in ancient times.

7. There is one way to spin it as an internal aim, and this could be what Nosson is thinking: Secular Jews who one day *hozer be'teshuva* (become Orthodox) may in fact be, according to *halacha*, either non-Jewish or *mamzerim* owing to the decisions of their parents or grandparents. (A non-Jew can convert to Judaism, but a *mamzer* is a *mamzer* for life and may marry only another *mamzer*.) So this matter becomes one of direct concern for the Haredi community insofar as they expect to attract those now on the outside into their circle.

8. In the spring and summer of 2000, ubiquitous graffiti in Jerusalem variously identified the ultra-Orthodox Shas party and the Leftist Meretz party as the culprits in bringing disunity to *Am Yisrael*: the People of Israel. "Shas is dividing the Nation!" sometimes appeared across the street from "Meretz is dividing the Nation!"

9. Rawls, *Collected Papers*, 587.

10. It may be objected that in identifying anti-civil marriage arguments as public reasons, I have forgotten Israel's non-Jewish citizens—the one million Israeli Arabs for whom Jewish continuity and the Jewish character of the state are hardly pressing concerns. The views of this fifth of Israeli society are indeed an essential aspect of a wider assessment of the justice of Israel's religion-state arrangement. However, for the specific inquiry at hand, the religious (yet public) reasons discussed above are not hopelessly sectarian arguments that liberalism should condemn as narrow expressions of one sector's sectarian views. Here's why: Given the millet system in Israel, the directly relevant "public" at issue here (thinking only of whether civil marriage should be available for Jews) is the Jewish public. The values at issue here are indeed inaccessible to Arabs, but the question those values are cited to address is irrelevant to them as well. Very little opposition to the millet system is heard among Israel's Muslims and Christians. Ironically, then, the anti-civil marriage position favored by Israel's Orthodox Jews would be much more compatible with the interests of Israel's Arabs than would the pro-civil marriage stance of secular Jewry, which would effectively deny the cultural rights Israel's non-Jewish minorities have come to rely upon to maintain their communities' religious autonomy. See Shifman, *Who's Afraid of Civil Marriage?*, 5.

11. See Shifman, *Who's Afraid of Civil Marriage?*, 7.

12. Detailed discussion of various policy proposals is beyond the scope of this book, but it should be noted that one alternative has been raised that would address Nosson's concern by requiring couples to divorce in the same way they married: a civil divorce for a civil marriage, a religious divorce for a religious marriage.

13. Don Herzog discusses three strategies for forging Christian unity in sixteenth- and seventeenth-century England: latitudinarianism (agreeing on a core belief that "Jesus is the Christ who died for our sins" while defining the rest of religion as "indifferent things," trappings not essential to salvation); passive obedience (outwardly complying with the state religion while inwardly whispering disagreement); and outright repression. The state balked at the first, the dissenters at the second, leaving repression of religious pluralism as the tool of choice. Don Herzog, *Happy Slaves* (Chicago: University of Chicago Press, 1989), 158-62. Israel's marriage law harnesses a rare mix of all three strategies: It prohibits non-Orthodox weddings between Jews (repression) but leaves an exit option (Cyprus) and justifies the policy by appealing to a lati-

tudinarian baseline for Israeli Jews ("you at least want a Jewish wedding and legitimate Jewish children, don't you?") and allowing secular Jews to only passively comply with the Orthodox strictures (smirking through the blessings, if necessary). The
Israeli case differs from the English one in that the repression is directed toward Jews,
not religious minorities. (This also makes it less oppressive: going through a religious
wedding typically doesn't require a secular Jew to disobey a *rival* faith.) Also, the state
objectives differ: the English, as Herzog sees it, were desperate to secure a pre-
modern vision of social order by enforcing (profession of) a common belief. Israel, by
contrast, is accommodating a religious minority (as part of the status quo agreement),
which in turn is attempting to preserve the boundaries of an ethno-religious group;
belief is beside the point.

14. Pointing to the "hundreds of thousands of religious Jews in Western lands,
who conduct their family life according to Torah in states which recognize civil marriage and divorce (as in England) or even require them (as in Imperial or Weimar
Germany)," Yeshayahu Leibowitz agrees that worries of a "split nation" are misplaced: "Civil marriage will not annul the institution of religious marriage. . . . [T]he
fear of dividing the nation as a result of rescinding the Law of Marriage and Divorce
is ridiculous and perhaps insincere." Yeshayahu Leibowitz, *Judaism, Human Values
and the Jewish State* (Cambridge, Mass.: Harvard University Press, 1992), 180-81.

Chapter 7
Military Service

Israel's first Minister of Defense, David Ben-Gurion, agreed in 1948 to grant military service deferments to 400 of Israel's most promising ultra-Orthodox yeshiva students. This quota, intended to help revitalize centers of Jewish learning after their decimation in the Holocaust, doubled to eight hundred in the late 1960s. Then, as part of the coalition agreement between the right-center Likud party and religious parties, the limit on deferments was lifted in 1977 and broadened to include not only yeshiva students "for whom Torah is their calling" [she'toratam omnutam] but also newly religious individuals, teachers in the Haredi Independent educational system and graduates of religious professional and secondary schools. The number of exemptions reached 17,017 (5.4 percent of eligible draftees) in 1987, 28,772 (nearly 8 percent of draftees) in 1997 and soared to 41,450 in 2005.[1]

On December 8, 1998, the Israeli Supreme Court issued a landmark ruling[2] declaring illegal the arrangement for yeshiva students' exemptions from army service. According to the Court, sitting as a rare panel of eleven justices, section 36 of the Defense Service Law (Consolidated Version) of 1986—which gives the Minister of Defense the power to order exemptions and deferrals "for reasons related to the size of the regular forces or reserve forces of the Israel Defense Forces or for reasons related to the requirements of education, security, settlement or the national economy or for family or other reasons"—is too open-ended and gives the Minister too much administrative discretion. Although the Court held in its unanimous opinion (written by Chief Justice Aharon Barak) that the present arrangement is illegal, it did not rule on substantive matters. Instead, the Court sent the issue to the Knesset, giving the legislators twelve months to craft a more precise law concerning the standards and arrangements for yeshiva students' draft deferrals.[3]

Rather than miss its December 9, 1999 deadline—which would have brought all deferments to an immediate halt, per the Court's ruling—the

Knesset requested and received an extension from the Court. After being granted two more extensions, giving it a total of an additional year to act on the 1998 ruling, another Supreme Court ruling on December 20, 2000 denied the government additional time. Then, after the Knesset gave itself a four-month extension in January 2001 and passed a bill on March 7, 2001 to extend the status quo arrangement for another two years, two MKs and a Tel Aviv attorney petitioned the Supreme Court to cancel the extension on the grounds that it contradicted the 1998 *Rubinstein* ruling and the principle of equality as found in the two 1992 Basic Laws. The Court, again sitting as a panel of eleven, rejected these appeals and approved the Knesset's two-year extension of the status quo arrangement.[4]

Behind these two and a half years of tumultuous intra-Knesset and inter-branch wrangling is a polarized public debate concerning whether and in what manner Haredi youth ought to be conscripted. On August 23, 1999, then-Prime Minister Ehud Barak appointed a ten-person commission, headed by retired Justice Zvi Tal as well as six religious members, to propose legislation on the issue of yeshiva draft deferments.[5] In March 2000, the Tal Commission issued its report to the consternation of activists on both sides of the issue. According to the commission's proposed law, deferments for yeshiva students would continue, with no limit on their numbers. However, the proposal introduced a new concept—a so-called "decision year" [*shana hachra'ah*]—giving yeshiva students reaching the age of twenty-three a free year in which they may pursue work, further study or vocational training without being subject to the military draft. After the decision year ends, the student has several options: he may return to yeshiva and continue to enjoy deferments from IDF service; he may enlist for a shortened, four-month period of military service; or he may commit to one year of civil national service within the Haredi community. The proposal was designed to maintain the status quo but to add an option for Haredi youth that would increase their opportunities to enter the labor market and ameliorate the rampant poverty among Israel's ultra-Orthodox Jews.

Among the subjects in my study, few knew much (if anything) about the details of the Tal Commission proposal. (The interviews were conducted in the months following its release, before the Knesset took up the matter in earnest.) And despite—or, perhaps, due to—the moderate and conciliatory nature of the Tal recommendations, both sides' political representatives found little to embrace in the report. In the Knesset, the result initially was deadlock. On the streets, the result was, on the one hand, anti-Tal Commission graffiti peppering the streets of Mea She'arim, a Haredi enclave of Jerusalem, and Bnei Brak, an all-Haredi town near Tel Aviv; and on the other, hunger strikes by secular students and demobilized IDF soldiers protesting the commission's recommendations.[6] The past few years have borne out the secular opponents' worries. Since the Tal Law was enacted in 2002, only

1,115 Haredi students have opted to take the "decision year" and of those only 31 have enlisted to perform military service.[7]

What are the arguments Israelis use to support or oppose the mass exemptions given to yeshiva students? The debate in Israeli civil society is multifaceted; many different kinds of considerations come into play. The arguments in favor of the exemptions fall into three rough categories: religious/communitarian, practical, and liberal. According to those who rely upon religious/communitarian reasoning, the yeshiva students engaged in full-time study are engaged in an inherently valuable practice that brings divine benefits to every Jew living in Israel. According to the practical position, Haredim are not needed in the army, and their enlistment may even have a negative effect on the state's national defense. And according to the liberal argument, Haredim are entitled to deferrals under their right to freedom of religious practice or, as a community, under a right to cultural preservation.

On the other side, among those who have reservations about the exemptions of Haredi youth, arguments range from social contract reasoning concerning civil duties to a rejection of the "religious freedom" argument to worries about the negative impact on Haredim who do not serve. First, the social contract argument points out that citizenship entails certain duties as well as certain rights, and that the Haredi exemptions constitute an unjust inequality that benefits a particular segment of the population at the expense of everyone else. Second, the argument that the exemptions are not necessary for religious liberty observes that because there is nothing inherent in military service that ultra-Orthodox Judaism prohibits, the excuse is a false one. And third, Haredim deprive themselves of a valuable education by staying out of the army, and miss out on an important opportunity to heal rifts between themselves and Israel's secular Jews.

There is a notable feature of the debate to watch for in the pages to come: the arguments in favor of the exemptions and the arguments against the exemptions are mixed and matched in many of the subjects' positions. For all but the most hard-line secular or fervent Haredi subject, there is a clear recognition of conflicting values at play in the debate. That is, while a religious subject may find inherent value in intensive Torah study, he usually also appreciates the pull of the social contract argument and sees the need to address it. And while a secular Jew may strenuously object to the unfairness and inequality of the deferrals, she might also consider the practical point—that the IDF may not need Haredi soldiers—or the liberal values of religious liberty or cultural preservation; she will seldom call for immediate, forcible conscription of all Haredi youth. So despite the vehemence and sometimes incommensurable ideas found in the passages excerpted below, there is, among most subjects, at least minimal appreciation of the strength of the other side's argument.

Arguments in Favor of Deferments

Aside from most of the Arab subjects, who approve of the IDF exemptions for mainly self-interested reasons—they don't want to serve, either[8]—the clearest defenses of the current system of Haredi army service deferrals come from Haredim themselves. Nosson and Yehuda are the most vigorous spokesmen for this position. Let's start with my exchange with Yehuda, who attempts to undercut the social contract argument often heard from the other side.

Q: I have a question about the deferrals from army service that yeshiva students receive. Is this an important issue?

A: Today it is an important issue.

Q: Do you think the Knesset should pass a law allowing the deferrals?

A: Yes. I think that they should do that. If they do not, we here [around Mea She'arim] won't go. They won't take us, even by force. We will not go to the army. We were here before the state and they cannot compel [l'hayev] us to go to the army. We lived here hundreds of years before the state; we didn't join the army. Then they arrive and declare a state and force us and coerce us to go to the army. We do not recognize the state or the army and they cannot compel us to go to the army.

Q: So you think the number of deferrals should not be limited?

A: It's better for them if they don't make problems for us—because in any case, we won't go. There are other problems. They don't want us in the army. You know? They don't need all the Haredim going to the army! One [Haredi soldier] will say that he wants the kitchen this way, and that, and here he has Shabbat, and here he says his daily prayers. . .they don't need it. The whole thing is demagoguery [demagogia]. This whole mess with the army is demagoguery. You can be sure. They don't want us. The whole thing is just cheap demagoguery.

Q: What would you say to someone who says: "Citizens must take and give, give and take, and the Haredim who don't serve in the army are taking from the state and not giving"?

A: I told you earlier that we pay taxes just like everyone else. We have families blessed with many children, more than the seculars, and we must buy apartments for our children [a common practice among non-Haredi Israelis as well]. We have to pay a lot of taxes. For lots of things. It's not what you call, give and take. We receive in return what we paid in taxes. They aren't doing us any favor. They can go back where they came from!

Q: But they bring security to the entire country.

A: Before the state was founded, was there any problem here? My grandmother told me that when she went to a wedding, who was the babysitter? An Arab neighbor who lived here in the Old City [of Jerusalem], and when I went to a wedding, who was the baby sitter for the infant? An Arab neighbor. All the hate between the Arabs and the Jews started only with the Zionists. They are responsible for it, so they should take care of it. Now they should reap what they sowed, big time [sh'ye'achlu et zeh b'gadol].

Q: It's the state's problem and they should. . .

A: Take care of it.

By drawing on the point that Haredim are not needed—or wanted—in the military, Yehuda argues that the call for universal conscription is disingenuous. And by summoning the history of the ultra-Orthodox rejection of Zionism—"we were here first, when all was peaceful"—he argues that one essential element is missing from the social contract reasoning according to which Israelis all owe equal duties to their state: the element of consent. The Haredim, Yehuda insists, not only withheld express consent to the Zionist project but also offered unequivocal rejection of the secular Israeli state. The latter, he might argue, cannot be mistaken for a kind of Lockean tacit consent that obligates the quiet citizen who enjoys the state's protection and public services. By refusing to recognize the state, the rejectionist Haredim place themselves outside the social contract, free of both the rights and the duties of citizenship. There would be no need for an army, he claims, had the Zionists not taken over and transformed peace-loving Arab neighbors you'd trust your child with into hate-filled terrorists. So the Zionists should populate their own army, not call innocent Haredim into battle to defend Israel against conflicts they had no role in creating. The only relationship Yehuda maintains with the state is one of financial give and take: he pays taxes, they provide services.

But this argument fails to convey why Haredim should be exempt from all state duties. Only a small minority of Haredim are true rejectionists and even they enjoy significant benefits from their citizenship—despite their denunciation of Zionism. Many Haredim are active politically and nearly all take advantage of public transportation (including several special bus lines which segregate men and women in sensitivity to Haredi scruples), national

health insurance, child allowances and subsidy for yeshiva study. All enjoy
police and fire protection, as well as the state's infrastructure and other basic
services. Beyond the consent argument, Yehuda makes another point that
dominates the debate among Haredim who are more accommodating of the
Israeli state. It is a more serious proposal:

> A: The [Religious Zionsts] used to have a lot of representatives in
> the Knesset. Today they have only six. And that's because they
> don't educate their children for extremism [kitzoniut]. Their chil-
> dren go to the army, and there they take off their kippot. Mizrahi
> [Religious Zionism] has no future. They know it. Because educa-
> tion must be for extremism. If education is toward compromise,
> the child is tempted to stray. They have no future.

> Q: And that's a reason why they shouldn't serve in the army?

> A: Of course. That is one of the reasons. They go to the army and
> they live a life of indulgence [hayei matiranut]. Where will they be-
> come God-fearing [yirat shamayim]? From life there? There's an-
> other thing: there are televisions there, there is Internet. We are in-
> oculated [mehusenet] from that. We don't have all of those things,
> so we are able to educate our children for extremism. Our envi-
> ronment is more protected [mehusenet].

For the Haredim, a tightly knit, intensely religious community for whom
Judaism "is like life itself" (Yehuda), proper rearing and education of the
children is fundamental. Exposure to the secular world beckoning across the
street from their neighborhoods—movies, secular bookstores, rock music,
immodestly dressed men and women, discotheques, non-kosher restaurants—is to be kept to a minimum. When riding on public buses, eyes are
averted. When encountering non-Haredi visitors to their neighborhoods—
those who are not kept away by signs beseeching outsiders, in bold red Hebrew and English letters, to dress and behave modestly[9]—alternate routes
are taken. Televisions and Internet connections are rarely found, for they
bring "all the world's filth" (Yehuda) into the sanctity of the Jewish home.
And joining the army at the age of eighteen is the ultimate risk for a young
Haredi. There, mixing with all types of Israelis, including secular Jews, traditional Jews and those who call themselves "religious" Zionists, the young
Haredi will hear perspectives on the world and on Judaism he has never
heard before and meet temptations he hasn't dreamt of. The risk of assimilation is one of the Haredi sector's greatest fears. Here is Nosson discussing
the problem:

> The worst thing that could be for the People of Israel is for us to
> send our youth at the age of eighteen, at the age of "stupid teens"
> [tipeshesray][10], and you can't understand this, because aren't capa-

ble of understanding how we educate our children. We raise them in a kind of spiritual greenhouse. I cannot describe it to you because you aren't capable of understanding it. You have to get to know it from up-close. And to take the youth when he's growing up in a greenhouse and expose him to the atmosphere of the army is, quite simply, certain to damage his spiritual health. And so to send this youth at that age to this army—it's not just that it won't contribute anything to the People of Israel, but that it will damage it, God forbid. Some people say that there is no kosher food in the army, but there is not kosher *atmosphere* in the army!

Nosson then turns on the sarcasm, explicitly tying this argument to a conception of religious freedom that the Israeli Left ought to respect, if it is to apply its own principles consistently:

We can't send our kids there. You don't have to agree with that. It doesn't matter to us if the Lefties, if Shinui and also Meretz and all of them would say to their voters: "Gentlemen, there is a community of Haredi people who think that the good of the People of Israel is served by them not serving in the army. I said that although we do strive to enable freedom of conscience, in this instance, being that the burden on us is too heavy—we have to serve three years in the army, and if they would serve we'd have to serve only two and three-quarters years, or two and a half years—therefore in this case we aren't prepared to give them freedom of conscience and we want to conscript them by force."

Nosson's mordant tone obscures the import of his argument: Israel's Haredim are entitled to freedom of conscience and to freedom of religious practice. If serving in the army makes it impossible for Haredim to fulfill their religious mission—if it calls on them to violate their conscience in fundamental ways—it may indeed be unfair and hypocritical of secular Israel to forcibly enlist them. But Nosson's argument raises, not settles, the question. Haredim, after all, are not Quakers. They are not pacifists. As Nosson says, somewhat exuberantly, one day it will be *only* Haredim in the army, with the secular minority sitting on the sidelines.[11] So the present-day exemptions for yeshiva students are not given on the basis of a religiously based conscientious objection. Nothing in Jewish law prevents religious, even ultra-religious, Jews from serving as a soldier in a military.[12] The exemptions are based, rather, on the secondary effects that military service might inflict on individual Haredim and, more to the point, on Haredi life generally. The worry is sociological: Haredim will stray from ultra-Orthodoxy if they are brought into the army, and the "inoculated" environment Yehuda mentions will be breached by the virus of secularism. But because Judaism is all encompassing for Haredi Jews, the sociological worry is a religious worry.

Aside from the motivation of protecting Haredi children—and Haredi life in general—from secular culture, Religious Zionist and Haredi subjects alike frequently turn to a justification of a very different sort for yeshiva students' exemptions. Rather than assert the religious or cultural autonomy rights of the Haredi sector, this argument is meant for *klal Yisrael*—all of Israel's Jews. It is a communitarian argument with a religious basis. As such, it should be considered a contribution to Israeli public reason (whether or not it is a good reason). According to Yoel, the Religious Zionist,

> The fact that Torah is being learned helps the soldiers sitting on the border in Lebanon. More or less. I think the Haredim believe in that also. I don't think the Haredim in any way—although individuals do abuse the system—I don't think the rabbis try to do it just to get their guys out of the army. I think they believe in what they are saying, that learning Torah is a very important value in our lives.

Nosson expands on this conception of yeshiva students as Israel's soldiers on high:

> Why don't we serve in the army? If you ask the secular person influenced by the media . . . he'll say we don't feel like part of the people, we don't care about the people, we are parasites, we shirk our duty. You must understand—and I don't say that they must agree with us—but I do think that most of them will agree with us if they would hear us correctly, but even without agreeing with us . . . many people say that we don't serve in the army because we say that we don't need an army. If they had heard the voices of the great men of Israel [the ultra-Orthodox rabbis who opposed the Zionist project], they wouldn't need an army today. But there is no doubt that today, with the situation as it is, we need an army, because all around us are hundreds of millions of Arabs who want to give us a very large territory: the Mediterranean Sea. So we need an army today. When we become a majority here, With the Help of God, *only* we will serve in the army. Everyone who's not religious will get an exemption from the army. We don't say that we don't need an army. But it must be understood that the army isn't the main thing. What brings victory isn't the tanks. What brings victory is help from the heavens [*siyata dishamaya*]. Help from the heavens is achieved by keeping Torah and Mitzvot. And so the tanks and the helicopters are important as an endeavor; and people must make these efforts, but it's not what determines the outcome. What determines the outcome is the Jews keeping Torah and Mitzvot, and so the best thing for the people of Israel is for us to sit and learn, because, thank God [*baruch hashem*], there are enough tanks and helicopters. Students of Torah and keepers of Mitzvot are very much lacking.

Nosson has an anecdote to back up his claim:

> Even the secular public knows very well what miracles have been
> accomplished in the IDF battalions. I heard that a group of officers
> from Israel came to the West Point Military Academy and there
> they analyzed the battles of all kinds of armies—all kinds of fa-
> mous battles—learning tactics and strategy. Then they saw that
> they didn't analyze the battles of the IDF. Why don't they analyze
> our battles, the battles in Sinai, the Golan? Because it is impossible
> to analyze the battles of the IDF—they are not natural at all. It's
> possible to learn from them because it is not natural. All the mira-
> cles in all the wars: why do we merit them? Believe me, it is for the
> merit [bizchut] of the Torah.

Other Religious Zionists, in addition to Yoel, do believe Nosson. Zvi, for
instance:

> The study of Torah is what makes the People of Israel special. It is
> what held us together for thousands of years in the Diaspora. It is
> what guarded over us. And it succeeded in strengthening us in the
> course of everything we went through. It is the basis of our exis-
> tence. Whoever wants to study Torah with all of his heart should
> study Torah with all of his heart—and should do it the way it
> should be done.

> I believe that there should be a group whose role is to study Torah
> twenty-four hours a day. They should study it all day long—not
> work, not do anything else, just study Torah all day long. It's what
> is called "Torah is their calling" [torato omnuto]. And why? Because
> just as there are soldiers down below [hayalim shel mata] there are
> soliders up above [hayalim shel ma'alah]. [An army and prayer] for
> me, is the winning combination [ha'shiluv ha'menatzeah]. So there
> are those who study Torah and there are soldiers. . .[the students]
> don't necessarily need to be geniuses. Those who truly want to
> learn Torah and who love it and do it with all their heart should sit
> and study Torah—it's their role.

Three primary defenses are thus available to Israelis who speak in favor
the exemption of yeshiva students from military service. First, as Yehuda
avers, rejectionist Haredim have no political obligation to the state of Israel
since they predated the Zionists and opposed the project of building the
State of Israel from the beginning. They are thus not party to the social contract that confers duties—especially military obligations—upon citizens.
Second, as Nosson develops most persuasively, Israel has an obligation to
protect the religious free exercise rights—and perhaps cultural autonomy

rights—of its Haredi citizens. It would violate those rights by requiring impressionable Haredi youth to leave their "spiritual greenhouse" for the secular wilds of army life. And third—another argument that tries to appeal to the wider Jewish community—Torah study is responsible for the miraculous military victories that Israel has won against it enemies.

Arguments Against Deferments

But many Israelis do not accept the idea that black-hatted yeshiva students are Israel's spiritual guardians against Arab military attack. And even those who do, such as Yoel and Zvi, do not reach the same sweeping conclusions that many Haredim hold with regard to their military service exemptions. Many secular, traditional and Religious Zionist subjects take umbrage at the unequal burdens they assume vis-à-vis their Haredi neighbors when it comes to three years of service at age eighteen, the several weeks per year of reserve duty they must serve well into their fifties, and more generally, the very real hazards of putting their lives on the line to defend the country. The two most frequently heard arguments against Haredi draft deferrals are the social contract/equality of duties objection and the complaint that, with many "students" lollygagging in the streets or holding jobs in contravention of the terms of the deferrals, the system is rife with exploitation.

Let's begin, though, with the subjects who share at least a portion of the Haredi world view: the Religious Zionists. These subjects, all of whom find great value in Torah study, and some of whom see great value in (at least a portion of) Haredi youth learning full-time to help protect the state of Israel from on high, dismiss the widespread and unlimited deferrals as unfair and unnecessary. Zvi explains his position with reference to the Haredi Nahal program.

> Q: Do you think it is a problem that many yeshiva students do not serve in the army?
>
> A: It depends. I say that the situation today in which there are many, many people doing it—in my opinion they can choose to serve in the army and study, such as those in the Haredi Nahal unit that was established. But, and I say this again, it hurts people who do want to study Torah. The rabbis need to know how to filter, to know who can go study in the army—who can go to the army and do Torah studies in parallel—and who should instead stay to study Torah exclusively, someone who can contribute much in Torah scholarship.

Zvi's view is that while the Knesset should not limit the number of deferrals for true Torah scholars, it must improve its level of oversight so that cheaters are not given a free ride. Avi, who served in a secretive, elite combat unit during his four-and-a-half year stint in the army, has even less patience for the Haredim who avoid the draft. He isn't sure, however, that Israel needs them as soliders:

> I too studied [in a yeshiva] for one year before I went to the army, and I returned afterwards happy with that. I have no problem if someone thinks he must study during his entire life—he should study all his life!—but there is something practical he has to deal with too. He has to go to the army. As for important practical questions such as, do we truly need all the Haredim in the army today—because I have no idea what we'd do with all of them—would they just be guards? It could be we really need all of them, and everyone is obligated to come, march forward and enlist.

Nahman is more emphatic on this point:

> There are Yehiva boys who truly want to live all their lives in the yeshiva. That's how scholars are produced. I agree with that. I am ready to fund them too, for the state to fund them as much as they need. But there are many yeshiva students who study at the beginning and after that want to stop, but if they want to stop they don't want to go to the army. So they catch a ride [tofsim tremp] [on the state's bill]. These we must get out of the yeshivas to the army and out to work. A yeshiva isn't a bomb shelter [miklat]. And if necessary, I say that we need to get them out by force. The problem they create is that the institution of the yeshivas becomes a commercial enterprise, an institution that's unclean. That starts when the rabbis worry: "Ah, he'll have to go to the army, it'll be a big mess [balagan] for him." On the contrary, when they don't go to the army or to yeshiva, they fall apart. Today many of them exploit the system to escape going to the army.

Ganit agrees and makes the social contract argument more explicit:

> My husband does tons of reserve duty—and it's a very heavy burden on us—we feel a deep sense of injustice. It is clear to me that there needs to be absolute equality in this matter. This was always clear to me. I mean, whoever wants rights must also have duties. That's clear. There are frameworks that allow them to serve without compromising their religious lifestyle, first, and second, it's clear that many kids at enlistment age who don't join the army don't really study. Even if I do recognize the importance of Torah study, there is a sense that the boys are exploiting the situation— they don't study, they bum around or they work.

And the most adamant Religious Zionist subject is Richard, who cites a litany of reasons to oppose draft exemptions for Haredim:

> (A), it's important that all citizens identify with the state. (B), one
> of the real and possibly most powerful educational experiences for
> Israelis to encounter one another. (C), if not everyone is called out
> to service, it is discriminatory. (D), perhaps the greatest cost is the
> antagonism between the religious and the non-religious sectors.
> You can't have one sector that doesn't put its lives on the line
> when the rest of the country does.

Jewish subjects across the spectrum frequently draw upon the reasoning Richard cites in (C), a version of what I have been referring to as the social contract argument. Secular subjects Shulamit, Naomi, Tanya and Yoram, and traditional subjects Rivka, Shmuel, Chaim, Rotem, Aaron and Rabbi Regev all make this point.[13] But the reasoning common to (A), (B) and (D) plays a significant part, too: many subjects note that in addition to being unfair to all Israelis who serve in the army—in relieving Haredim of a heavy duty that virtually everyone else performs—the exemptions are bad for Haredim and exacerbate the already tense relationship between Israel's secular and religious sectors. Respondents who quarrel with the Haredi draft deferments thus often mix expressions of injustice or unfairness with comments that speak to the special needs of the Haredi community or the health of the wider Israeli polity.

Rotem, for example, thinks it is "terrible" that tens of thousands of yeshiva students receive deferrals from army service ("I'm quite active in the fight for getting yeshiva students to serve"), but she stresses that "we should be aware that they are a very unusual faction in society" with "their own unique life." As part of her sensitivity to this fact, Rotem argues that sharply limited exemptions should be granted:

> I think a very small percentage of extremely, extremely brilliant
> Talmud scholars should be exempt, just like in the secular world
> there are exemptions for brilliant musicians, for brilliant
> [atheletes]. . .and for very, very successful models. And it's very
> important, I have to add. I have some friends who were exempt for
> the musician reason. If they couldn't, it would be the end of their
> musical career, and Israel would never have any outstanding mu-
> sicians. It's that clear. Exactly the same for football [soccer]. And in
> the same way, the Haredim should have their hundred-a-year bril-
> liant scholars who should be allowed to be exempt. But no more
> than that.

For the vast remainder, Rotem concludes that "they should be forced to do volunteer work for exactly the same number of years as anyone else, with a very clear option of being able to serve in the army." Many other subjects opposed to exemptions share this position. For Chaim, "volunteering would be excellent: volunteering in the community, for the disabled, for the needy, for new immigrants." And Rivka, the secular-cum-Conservative museum curator, who ordinarily has little patience for the Haredim, urges "caution" in the matter of the draft. Her view reflects less a sense of indignation at the Haredi position in the social contract than a worry about what the exemptions threaten to do to the ultra-Orthodox and to the secular world's relations with them.

> Q: What do you think about the fact that many Hareidi yeshiva students don't serve in the army?
>
> A: [Big sigh, pause.] I think this is not good for them. It makes a bad feeling of inequality that disturbs people very, very much. On the other hand,. . .they should serve, they should serve, but it is not very practical today. I don't know if they want to keep out of the army. So I think this is a very complicated question and I also respect the Haredim who have a very, very special way of life and I don't want to force them to do things against their beliefs. So there is a problem here. There is a problem. And I think we need to be very. . .to *zahir* [to be cautious]. . .
>
> Q: Be cautious.
>
> A: . . .cautious, cautious about it. It's a very populistic question here. I think we. . .in this case we should be very, very cautious from many aspects because this is very complicated.

Among Rivka's concerns is the prospect of greater numbers of separate army regiments, such as the Haredi Nahal units, comprised entirely of religious soldiers:

> I don't know if I want to see Haredi regiments in the army. I'm afraid they are too chauvinist. I'm afraid how it's going to affect. . .The problem is: the army is supposed to be democratic, like it should have nothing to do with the political views of the soldiers. Now if there are going to be special regiments for Haredim, it's like the *yeshivot ha'hesder* [Religious Zionist yeshivas that mix Torah study with army service] , I am very concerned about *yeshivot ha'hesder*. These people have a very, very definite and special political point of view. And I think it's not good for an army in a democratic state when there are regiments that are politically committed.

Another traditional subject, Rabbi Uri Regev, is highly critical of the current arrangement but wary of a wholesale reversal of the deferral policy.

> I think there is probably no more frustrating issue in this saga than the shameful mass exemption of yeshiva students from military service. The abuse is so obvious that I think that makes it all even more unpalatable. One could understand the initial request for Ben Gurion for the exemption of the remnants of the Shoah, which encompassed a group of approximately four hundred yeshiva students. Its growth into a core of thirty thousand that are provided with the expenses of their studies and their living expenses—albeit modest, but nevertheless living expenses—coupled with the exemption from military service, creates an extremely unhealthy environment which is both discriminatory in terms of the assurance of equal civil and political rights, the equal share in undertaking the defense of the country and the people, which is a cherished notion in the Bible! It is clearly antithetical to the Bible! . . .It's a fiction. It's a political deal used to strengthen the hold the leadership of the Haredi community has over its members. And therefore it's an impossible deal.
>
> Having said all of that, I'm not sure that mandatory draft for all is a realistic expectation. And I think creative ways should be developed whereby the army would be able to make its decisions in terms of how many that it wants to draft, needs to draft. . . .And making that population accessible to draft may provide for a whole rethinking of military and national service altogether. But how can people best utilize their talents or abilities for the benefit of the society as a whole and the defense needs of the state? And having stated the morally and religiously unacceptable nature of these mass exemptions, I'm not sure that the answer therefore is drafting all of them. So I'm open to all kinds of solutions that may entail partial exemption, provided that it be done on grounds of reasonable criteria meeting the needs of the army and of the national service.

Conclusion

In one sense the civil marriage and yeshiva draft debates are alike: they both address matters of privilege enjoyed by Israeli Orthodox Jews at the expense of non-Orthodox Jews. But there is an important difference: Whereas the former concerns basic human rights to freedom of conscience and to marry that are presently denied to Israeli Jews seeking a non-Orthodox wedding, the latter entails no specific rights violations. It entails, rather, a privilege for

Haredim to bypass a duty to which all others are obligated and a concomitant incapacity of secular Jews to do the same, at least on such a large scale. Is this arrangement unequal? Yes. Is it unfair? Quite possibly. But is it a violation of secular Jews' rights? No, or at least not in the same sense or to the same degree as is Israel's delegation of marriage law to rabbinical authorities.[14] The harms stemming from the mass deferrals are best described in other terms.[15]

Several factors make the debate over yeshiva students' military service exemptions particularly troublesome. First is the conflict internal to the views of many secular, traditional and Religious Zionist subjects who believe, with varying degrees of indignation, that mass exemptions represent injustice, unfairness and inequality, but who cannot fathom, or do not see the need for, a mass transfer of the Haredi boys from the yeshiva hall to the battlefield. As Ronit puts it, "There are two levels. From the point of view of the public, it isn't fair and it isn't democratic . . .and they need to serve; but from the practical point of view, I think the army doesn't need them." Second is the conflict of interest inside the Haredi sector. Haredim seek protection of their religious lifestyle from secular influence but suffer from two ills that the deferrals exacerbate: economic dependence and poverty, on the one hand, and a worsening *Kulturkampf* with non-Haredi Israeli Jews on the other. The third tension brings to the fore a prominent debate within contemporary liberal theory over the proper way to deal with illiberal, insular groups who seek certain forms of detachment from the wider political culture.[16] Should the state promote the liberal norm of equal citizenship— requiring all Israeli citizens to perform the same military service—or should it defer to the liberal norm of toleration and accommodation of difference?

The interviews do not point to a single solution to this question, of course, but they do suggest that the debate ought to move away from a strict equality view and toward a version of liberalism that stresses the political virtues of accommodation and compromise. Even the most militantly anti-Haredi respondents—Naomi, Shulamit, Shmuel—offer proposals for alternative arrangements for Haredim that stop short of insisting that Haredi youth serve in exactly the same manner as non-Haredi youth for equal periods of time. These and other subjects might hold Haredim in seething contempt, yet they curb their policy demands, commonly suggesting a period of national service in place of military service. They thus explicitly or implicitly acknowledge the injustice, political impossibility (or both) of immediately conscripting all Haredim reaching the age of eighteen. Despite the rhetoric of rights and duties, then, despite the cries against Haredi "draft-dodging" and demands for "one nation-one draft," the Israeli political culture seems committed to carving out special arrangements for Haredim. Liberalism, as it operates on this matter in the Israeli climate, speaks the language of abstract rights but tempers that talk with a recognition of the importance or necessity of making room for Haredi autonomy within mainstream Israeli society. Shulamit, who calls the Haredim "violent. . .parasites. . .who suck the country's money," suggests nevertheless that yeshiva students could, in lieu of military service, "do national service for the people, work in hospitals, work in development towns or settlements, do some special activities for the good of their own communities." She is ready, despite her ire, to absolve all Haredim of the duty of defending the state with their lives as long as they do some kind of national service. Tolerance for Haredim is sometimes offered grudgingly, or even resentfully, but it is offered nonetheless.

But the *Kulturkampf* rages on, largely because the Haredim demand much more than Israeli liberals are willing to give. And that is the real problem: not an inability of either side to compromise, but the seemingly impossible task of finding a compromise that all sides could agree to. Although liberalism is, as are Israelis in general, committed to letting individuals within groups maintain cultural particularity, it does not sanction such group autonomy at all costs or in all ways. The recommendations of the Tal Commission constituted an earnest attempt to bridge a gap between protecting the Haredi culture's autonomy from secular Israel, providing opportunities for young Haredim to enter the workforce and maintaining the rule of law. But while some Haredim accepted the Tal Law when it was passed by the Knesset in the summer of 2002, many others condemned the "decision year" provision giving yeshiva students a bye from army service and freeing them to pursue other educational or job opportunities outside the yeshiva. This option, Rabbi Uri Regev predicted in 2000, would result in the departure of a large number of Haredi youth from Torah study.

> A: The idea is, that as soon as you provide them with an option to choose whether to remain in the yeshiva or go out in the world and work for your living, and continue to be exempted, then you remove the threat of "once you step out you'll be drafted," many people will choose to leave the yeshiva. Many on the Tal Committee, realizing that they may not be able to prevent them, still opt for the lesser evil: "All right, if we can't draft them, let's at least give them the option of integrating into the marketplace." So that's the idea of bringing down the age and giving them a year of sorting out for themselves.
>
> Q: So that's why so many Haredim disapprove of it.
>
> A: No question about it.
>
> Q: So that's why you see graffiti on Strauss St. saying, "The Tal Commission are Murderers."

A: I haven't seen the graffiti, but I can see that it is not only the militant secular element that rejects the Tal recommendations but also the Haredim are not happy. Because the little change that it provides, is too much in terms of what they currently enjoy. Again, not the yeshiva students. Nobody cares about the yeshiva students! Because it's clear that the intellectual elite that are generally immersed in the study of Torah are not going to be affected. One way or another, they are not going to be affected. But the masses out there who don't belong in the yeshivas, who in Europe never went to the yeshivas. . .There was no need for twenty yeshivas! You didn't have a whole community, you know, give up life and exempt themselves from the responsibility of making a living for their families!!

Contrary to Rabbi Regev's prediction, fewer than one percent of Haredi men haven taken advantage of the decision year and very few have decided to leave the yeshiva.[17] But his comments about the community's economic challenges are still salient. By all accounts, the draft deferments contribute to an increasingly dire economic situation for the Haredi sector in Israel.[18] Sixty percent of adult males—out of heads of families that average 7.6 children—choose yeshiva over paid employment. How do they make ends meet, and, as is custom, purchase apartments for their children upon marriage? Families with fathers in yeshiva, on average, gather at least 70 percent of their income from the state: about half of this comes from the stipends the government provides yeshiva students (in 1997, about $200/month)[19], and about half from child allowances (which are substantially higher for families with five or more children)[20]. The rest usually comes from the wife's earnings. But all of this together still leaves over half of Israel's Haredi population under the poverty line. In 1995, families with fathers spending their days in yeshiva (with 4.5 children, on average) earned an average of $1,150 a month as compared to $2,750 for the average two-parent Israeli family (with 2.1 children).[21] And with the sector doubling in size every seventeen years, the strain on the state's coffers is likely to become much more burdensome. All of this worries Rabbi Regev and other subjects, who are concerned that Haredim will become more and more dependent and less and less economically viable if full-time yeshiva study continues to be the life-long path for so many Haredi youth.

This presses the question of how large a role the state ought to have in ensuring the survival of its constituent cultures. Assuming that the state may justifiably exempt at least some Haredim from the military draft on cultural rights grounds, may (or must) it link this policy to one that has the effect of keeping nearly all Haredi youth enrolled in full-time religious study? Is it correct to create incentives that help Haredim keep their children in line?

Israeli liberals like Uri Regev—those who deplore the draft deferments but sanction some compromise on the question—implicitly grant the

Haredim some leeway in keeping their best students in yeshiva and protecting their communities from the potential distortions of secular culture. They are willing, and rightly so, to grant Haredim limited autonomy from the duties of Israeli citizenship. As we've seen, the theoretical basis for the position is not that of ultra-Orthodox religious conscientious objection, speaking precisely, but sensitivity to the sector's insular religious-cultural community practices. And this active toleration is all the more important in light of Israel's status as a Jewish state: the state's connection with Judaism lends independent weight to securing conditions for all pockets of Jewry to live a meaningful life. So Israelis have both liberal-democratic reasons and Jewish reasons to maintain a military draft under which Haredim are subject to different rules. The tricky question is what precisely those rules should be. A difficult balance must be achieved. On one hand, the system should allow the Haredi community to preserve some its insularity from the rest of Israeli society. On the other hand, the arrangement must be seen as just by other sectors of Israeli society and must remove perverse incentives that exacerbate Haredi impoverishment.

The tensions between orthodox and secular Jews in Israel—and the sometimes fiercer battles among various branches of orthodoxy—make it very difficult to maintain both Jewish and liberal commitments simultaneously. But this is, at best, half of the problem facing Israel's constitution. As we will see in Part III, controversies between Jews and Arabs represent at least as challenging a set of queries as the intra-Jewish disputes.

Notes

1. Shahar Ilan, "Dehiat ha-gius shel bahurei yeshivot" (Draft deferment for yeshiva students: a policy proposal), Publication #4/10 (Jerusalem: Floersheimer Institute for Policy Studies, December 1999) [Hebrew], 7-9.

2. Rubinstein v. Minister of Defense, H.C. 3267/97, 715/98 (1998).

3. I use the terms "deferral" [dehiah] and "exemption" [p'tor] interchangeably below. Under the present system, deferrals are renewed annually or bi-annually for students who sign an affidavit stating that they are engaged in full-time study in a yeshiva and not employed. Penalties are in place for students who sign false affidavits, but enforcement is rare due to yeshiva heads' financial interest in receiving state funds (the more students, the larger their budget) and halachic norms against turning in another Jew. See Shahar Ilan, "The Yeshiva Students' Not-So-Secret Lie," Ha'aretz, 9 December 1998. This de facto exemption from army service becomes official when the student reaches the age of forty-one; married men with four or five children are exempted earlier (at age thirty-five or twenty-nine, respectively). Divrei Knesset [Knesset Proceedings], Response of the Deputy Minister of Defense to Question No. 352, 14 March 2000 [Hebrew], 417.

4. Gideon Alon and Moshe Reinfeld, "Knesset in Mad Scramble to Save Yeshiva Draft Deferrals," *Ha'aretz*, 21 December 2000; Moshe Reinfeld, "Yeshiva Draft Bill Challenge at High Court," *Ha'aretz*, 12 March 2001; Moshe Reinfeld, "11 Justices to Decide on Yeshiva Draft," *Ha'aretz*, 10 May 2001. See also Yehuda Ressler v. Knesset of Israel, S Ct 24/01 (2002).

5. The commission was charged with three tasks: (1) to develop recommendations for a law enabling a continuation of military deferments for those for whom Torah is their calling; (2) to create frameworks and arrangements to enable army service for yeshiva drop-outs and "street Haredim" ne'er-do-wells; and (3) to set conditions for Haredi youth no longer interested in yeshiva studies to enter the labor market. See Ilan, "A Policy Proposal," 7.

6. I often saw the Mea She'arim graffiti while riding the bus from central Jerusalem to the Hebrew University. "The Tal Commission are Murders" [*va'adat tal rotzhim*] and "Karelitz is a Murderer" [*karlitz rotzeah*] were the most ubiquitous scrawlings. The opposition was even more pronounced in B'nei Brak, the town that in 2000 claimed Tal Commission member Mordechai Karelitz as its Haredi mayor. See Avirama Golan, "B'nei Brak: Slowly Coming to Terms," *Ha'aretz*, 4 July 2000. The protest group, Tekuma [Awakening], held its hunger strike in a tent outside the Prime Minister's office. See Itim, "Tal Committee Hunger Strikers Receive Support, Promises from MKs," *Jerusalem Post*, 2 July 2000.

7. Yoaz, "Tal Law Proving Difficult to Implement."

8. Muhammad: "That's their issue. Just as I have my opinion and my justified reason not to serve, they have their reasons too, their perspectives. We are one on this issue." And Majjed: "I'm not in favor of Haredim serving in the army. If I would be for them serving in the army, then others would say that I too need to serve in the army. But I don't want to serve in the army." Nadia is the only Arab subject who expresses a contrary view. "As an Arab," she says, "I don't know." But "if I were Jewish, [I'd think] that it isn't fair. Simply not fair."

9. One large yellow poster on Mea She'arim St., signed by "Residents of the Neighborhood," reads, in Hebrew and English: "DO NOT ENTER OUR NEIGHBORHOOD IN GROUPS….The residents of our neighborhood are committed to preserving—for themselves and their children—high religious standards in matters of dress and modest behavior. The fact is that visits by **groups** of any kind, even if they were to conform to our standards and even if they were to be made up exclusively of people from our neighborhood, would be difficult for us to tolerate." Another sign, at the eastern entrance to the neighborhood, bellows in large Hebrew letters: "You are entering a Haredi neighborhood. PASSAGE FOR WOMEN **IN MODEST CLOTHING ONLY!** Long sleeves * Long skirts * No bare skin."

10. This slang term, a playful combination of the Hebrew words for "stupid" (*tipesh*) and "teenager" (*esrei*), connotes a frivolous, impressionable adolescent.

11. He is referring, apparently, to the eventual Torah state to be established in Israel at the end of days.

12. Naomi and Rita both argue for the compatibility of Orthodox religious practice with army service. According to Rita, the Yemenite mother of four,

> There is no reason why my son should serve in the army and a Haredi boy shouldn't. Why shouldn't he serve in the army? Every traditional [*masortit*] and religious [*datit*] family [sends its children

to the army]. Why [don't Haredim]? What happened? What's the problem? If it's for health reasons, I accept it. For someone who wants to be religious in the army, believe me, he can be religious. There are many soldiers in the army with knit kippot [*kippot serugot*] who are religious and they never have a problem, so why should others have a problem?

Going beyond this argument—which takes no account of the Haredi objections to IDF service—Naomi points to a program started in 1999, the Haredi Nahal, that recruits ultra-Orthodox young men for three years of army service and study in special IDF units: "Let's start with the fact that there are already yeshiva boys who serve in the army. *That* is what's so funny. They are so anti-army, but on the other hand there is already a complete battalion in the army that belongs to the yeshiva boys." See Mazel Mualem, "Haredi Nahal Would Be the Model for Yeshiva Draft," *Haaretz*, 12 December 2000.

13. Naomi leans heavily on social contract reasoning, extending her critique to non-Haredim who duck their duties and suffer for it in the future:

> We weren't born to die, just as they weren't born to die. But if it's a duty, one of the duties we have for living in the Land of Israel, there's another possibility. They don't have to serve in the army. They could also do national service—something that the state needs. . . . Not to do any service is unacceptable to me. It's not acceptable on the backs of secular Jews either. At my kibbutz, two friends didn't go to the army. Pacifism was their excuse. But that's nonsense. They simply didn't want to go to the army! Today they can't find work anywhere the minute they say they didn't serve in the army. That is a problem in the State of Israel. [Where I work] we don't accept [as emissaries abroad] anyone who didn't do the army, because as an emissary you need to be someone who has gone through what happens here in Israel.

14. It is sometimes said that giving deferrals to Haredim may violate a secular Jew's right to equal treatment. A claim right, however—a right to do x, e.g., a right to marry in accordance with your religious or non-religious beliefs—is more fundamental than a right to enjoy a privilege that other citizens enjoy. Liberalism would not assert a basic right *not* to serve in the Israeli army, for example; non-Haredi youngsters thus suffer no claim right infringement when they are called up to the army (regardless of whether Haredim are drafted or not).

15. In the Rubinstein case, the Minister of Defense claimed that the non-enlistment of the yeshiva students posed no significant harm to the security needs of the state. Another official noted, however, that conscripting the Haredim would result in shorter compulsory service periods and significantly lighter reserve duty obligations for men. Gidon Sapir, "Drafting Yeshiva Students in Israel: A Proposed Framework of the Relevant Normative Considerations," *Plilim* 9 (2000) [Hebrew]: 250-51n95.

16. See Steven Mazie, "Consenting Adults? Amish 'Rumspringa' and the Quandary of Exit in Liberalism," *Perspectives on Politics* 3, no. 4 (Decmeber 2005): 745-59.

17. Yuval Yoaz, "IDF to Tell Court: 30% Increase in Tal Law Deferments Since '98" *Ha'aretz*, 10 July 2005.

18. Eli Berman, "Sect, Subsidy and Sacrifice: An Economist's View of Ultra-Orthodox Jews," Discussion Paper No. 98.08 (Jerusalem: Maurice Falk Institute for Economic Research in Israel & Jerusalem Institute for Israel Studies, 1998).

19. Varda Schiffer, "The Haredi Education System: Allocation, Regulation and Control" (Jerusalem: The Floersheimer Institute for Policy Studies, 1998), 22.

20. The Large Families Law, passed in November 2000, leaves child allowances for families with three children at $170 per month. It increases allowances for families with five children to approximately $560 (up from $490), six children, $772 (up from $650), eight children, $1200 (up from $950). Nina Gilbert, "Finance Minister Slams Family Aid Bill as 'Born in Sin,'" *Jerusalem Post*, 2 November 2000.

21. Berman, "Sect, Subsidy and Sacrifice," 13.

Part III
Controversies Between Israeli Arabs and Jews

Chapter 8
Symbols

In the intra-Jewish debate over several major connections between Judaism and state in Israel, the Arab voice is largely absent. Arab citizens of Israel are quiet on the questions raised in Part II—and their views play a minor role in the public debate—either because an issue lacks salience for them or because they are generally in favor of a particular religion-state linkage. Kosher government kitchens and Shabbat regulations don't tend to bother (or affect) Arab citizens, and government-financed education for all streams and all religions typically garners strong Arab support. Palestinian citizens of Israel, whether Muslim, Christian or Druze, tend to appreciate the autonomy their religious authorities enjoy vis-à-vis matters of family law and personal status. And, since they do not serve in the army,[1] Arabs have little problem with Haredim enjoying exemptions as well.

But another set of linkages between Judaism and the state does elicit significant Israeli Arab resentment and opposition. These aspects of the state are not those condemned as "religious coercion" by secular Jews but those interpreted by Arabs as manifestations of Israel's exclusionary, Jews-first (or Jews-only) Zionist character. These are, then, substantially different and often at odds with the elements Israeli Jews have in mind when they call for "a separation of religion and state." The elements to which Arabs draw our attention, rather, press toward "a state of all its citizens" in which Arabs enjoy equal treatment in terms of social and political rights, economic opportunities and state symbols. Their aim, as we saw in chapter 4, is to separate not *religion* per se but rather *Judaism* from the Israeli state. Most fundamentally, many Israeli Arabs (including four of the five subjects in my study) call for alteration of the Law of Return which, in Majjed's words, gives instant citizenship to a Jew from Brooklyn but denies the same to an Arab whose family lived in Palestine for generations and fled during the 1948 war. This legislation, indeed, marks the state's clear preference for Jewish immigrants. I forego a detailed consideration of the issue, however, owing to the special considerations involved in questions of immigration, naturalization and citizenship rights. Such an exploration of the justice of political membership rules would take me too far afield. Instead, I adopt, but cannot fully justify here, the view that states ought to have relatively free reign in setting conditions of membership[2] and turn to several issues concerning how citizens are treated once they are admitted to citizenship. These, in my view, are the more pressing questions for liberalism. In this chapter, I look at three elements expressing Israel's preference for one sector of its citizens over another.

The Golan Heights Referendum

The first dimension to consider concerns the political status of Palestinian citizens of Israel. Although the Declaration of Establishment guarantees Arab citizens equal political liberties, including the right to associate, vote and be voted into office, Arab parties have never been included in a ruling government coalition and only one Arab Knesset member (from the Zionist Labor party) has ever served in the government as a cabinet minister. (Ironically, this first Arab minister served in Prime Minister Ariel Sharon's right-wing Likud government that took office in 2001—but his tenure ended in disgrace.[3]) Not even a leftist government such as that of Prime Minister Ehud Barak from 1998-2001 invited Arab parties into its coalition, although it did depend on their support to advance its controversial peace agenda. The Israeli political climate, from right to left, hesitates to bring Arab parties into the national consensus. And as the example of debate over the Golan Heights referendum in 2000 shows, a large portion of mainstream Jewish Israeli society is unwilling to allow its fate to be determined by its Arab minority. Instead, Jewish Israelis often call for the need to secure a "Jewish majority"—one that relies on no Arab votes—when significant matters of national interest are at stake.

Background

Since the fall of 2000, when a resurgence of violence between Israel and the Palestinians suspended the peace process, once-heated discussions about prospects for peace with Syria have dwindled to silence. But in the early, more optimistic days of then-Prime Minister Ehud Barak's tenure, Syria was near the top of the national agenda. When campaigning for office, Barak pledged to make any Israeli withdrawal from the Golan Heights conditional upon a national referendum. A lush territory in the country's northeast corner that Israel captured from Syria in the 1967 Six Day War, the Golan Heights is populated by 17,000 Jews and several thousand Druze. It is beloved by Israelis for views over Lake Kinneret and the Galilee, abundant natural beauty, hiking trails winding through riverbeds, ski slopes on Mount Hermon and soil that nestles the grapes used in Israel's best wines. Although polls showed that around half of Israelis were willing to trade the Golan for a peace agreement with Syria when such an agreement seemed imminent in the middle of 2000, no one was anxious to give it up.

The Knesset first approved the Golan Heights Law on January 26, 1999, requiring both a special majority vote of Knesset members (61 of 120), and a majority in a national referendum prior to any territorial concessions on the Golan Heights as part of a peace agreement with Syria.[4] As negotiations with Syria picked up in November 1999 and produced signs that Barak was willing to hand back all or part of the Golan Heights, the right wing began pushing for more stringent obstacles to such a deal. In December, Likud MK Uzi Landau advocated excluding all Israeli Arabs from the referendum on the grounds that it would be unfair for Arabs to tip the scales toward returning Jewish land to Arab neighbors.[5] In a column appearing in *Ha'aretz*, Israel Harel (a leader of the Golan settlement effort) cited a Gallup poll finding that 72 percent of all Israelis believed the destiny of the Golan Heights should be decided by a "Jewish majority." "The majority of the Israeli Jewish public," he wrote, "deeply resents the idea that the country's Arab citizens will be given the opportunity to determine the fate of the Jewish people in the Land of Israel."[6]

Several proposals were floated as alternatives to Landau's transparently anti-democratic solution (which opponents labeled "racist"), including one that would require a 60 percent majority in a referendum. On March 1, 2000, the Knesset gave preliminary approval to a bill sponsored by Silvan Shalom of Likud to require a referendum majority of 50 percent of all eligible voters (rather than 50 percent of votes cast) to ratify territorial concessions.[7] With this approach, even assuming Israel's typically high voter turnout of around 80 percent, 60 to 65 percent of votes cast would be necessary to approve a transfer of territory. Such widespread approval was highly unlikely.

Policies and attitudes of discrimination often perform their nefarious work under the cover of ostensible neutrality. What is remarkable about the question of a referendum in Israel is that most of those seeking to negate the influence of the Israeli Arab vote on the future of the Golan Heights did so openly, billing the special majority requirement as necessary to "ensure that Israel's future is decided in Jewish votes and NOT Arab Palestinian votes!!"[8] There are exceptions to this heated rhetoric, and some reasonable voices discussed national referenda on the merits. Moshe Arens, for example, pointed to the super-majorities required for constitutional amendments in the United States, the Canadian Supreme Court's ruling that a "clear majority" would be required for future referenda concerning Quebec secession and the risks involved when major decisions on controversial issues flow from tiny majorities. "When viewed through such a lens," he writes, "the requirement that extremely important issues be approved by substantial majorities is not such a bad idea after all."[9] From the other perspective, Ze'ev Segal noted that a referendum would pose risks to Israeli democracy in aggravating the society's many cleavages, undermining opportunities for political consensus and inviting cynical use of referendum results by politicians. Israel, Segal wrote, "is based on the Knesset as the source of popular sovereignty" and has resisted referenda in the past in favor of "processes of compromise, which are crucial to polarized societies."[10]

Respondents' Views: Racism and *Pikuah Nefesh*

This debate was a sideshow, however. The main motivation behind the demand for a special majority was clear to all: to strip Israel's Arab citizens of the ability to sway the referendum results, but to do so without technically disenfranchising them. Of the subjects in my study, eight (three Religious Zionists, three Haredim and one traditional Jew) advocate leaving Arabs out of the vote entirely; another two (one Religious Zionist, one traditional Jew) believe that although all citizens should be included, the referendum should be stacked against the Arabs with the requirement of a special majority. Most of these ten subjects provide similar reasoning for leaving Arabs out, whether blatantly or by design.

According to Zvi, his position against including Israeli Arabs "is not an issue of racism." The Arabs, he says, "don't have a side" in the conflict between Israel and Syria:

> Arabs of Israel can enter into Syria...and they'll be accepted. The same for Israeli Arabs in the Knesset....But I today cannot enter Syria. If I were to take just one step into Syria, I wouldn't last long. What does this mean? That the conflict is not between Israeli Arabs and Syria...The conflict is between a Jewish Israeli and Syria...and so we need a Jewish majority. Without a Jewish majority, it means that there's no majority agreement for withdrawing from the Golan.

Several subjects go further than Zvi, claiming not that Arabs are neutral in the conflict but actually in allegiance with the enemy. Oren, despite his self-described "pretty liberal" views, thinks it is "unwise" to include the Arabs:

A: Their interests are diametrically opposed to those of the state. The majority of the Arabs are on the side of the Syrians, so it doesn't make sense to give them power on such a significant issue. It wouldn't be fair from the point of view of the interests of the state. It would be like including the Syrians in the referendum! It's exactly the same thing!

Q: But the Syrians are not citizens of the state of Israel.

A: Yes, but these citizens come with a "limited warranty": they don't have any fewer rights when it comes to everyday issues, but for something like this—which is essential to the interests of the state as a state that protects its own security—I think it's important not to include them. Let's say this: if Syria attacks Israel tomorrow after we make a peace agreement, I am certain that the Syrians will not attack Bethlehem or Gaza—they'll attack Jerusalem and Tel Aviv and Haifa. That's where they'll attack. They won't harm any Arab neighborhoods because their brothers live there!

Oren forgets here that the Arabs living in Bethlehem and Gaza are Palestinians, not Israeli citizens with voting rights, and that Jerusalem and Haifa are home to significant numbers of Arab residents. But his basic point is echoed by Nosson:

Q: Is it important to include Arabs in a referendum?

A: Of course not. This question is a question of fate for Jews. It is a question of pikuah nefesh [a Talmudic principle according to which "saving a soul" trumps most other religious obligations]. For Arabs, it is not a question of pikuah nefesh. Who will they drive into the sea? They won't drive the Arabs into the sea. For them it's not a life-threatening issue. So why should we let Arabs decide on a question that's pikuah nefesh for us and not pikuah nefesh for them, knowing that their loyalties are first and foremost to their Arab brothers? They are not objective!

Yehuda agrees that Arabs hold subjective interests contrary to those of the state and "will say that we have to give it [the Golan] back." For Nehama, Arabs should "absolutely not" have a say in the referendum "because they will decide according to their interests and not according to my interests and those of the People that resides here."

The decision of whether to support Arab participation in the referendum for some subjects turns on the strength of their commitment to democracy. Both Richard and Nahman, for example, observe that leaving Arabs out would be an affront to democracy. For Richard, this "is non-democratic but it cannot be helped"—sacrificing political principle is necessary in order to protect the integrity of the Jewish state. For Nahman, the question is "very difficult, a stumper."

> I know from the start that they [Arabs] will vote in favor of return-
> ing the Golan to Syria. But I don't know how it's possible to pre-
> vent them from voting, because if we try they'll say: "What kind of
> a state is this? This is no state." And you know how the settlers are
> going to vote, too: they'll all vote against it. So there is no choice
> but to let the Arabs vote. We call ourselves a democratic state,
> even though we know they aren't loyal to us. If there were some
> legal way to stop them from voting, I would do it. But I can't pre-
> vent them and, to my dismay, they'll have to be included in voting
> in a referendum.

Two other Religious Zionist subjects are less grudging in their support for Arab participation. Ganit describes any attempt to neutralize their votes as "discrimination" and "very dangerous. They vote in the Knesset, and in the Knesset very fateful decisions are reached [as well]." Rabbi Rosen warns of "going down the road of cultural apartheid and making Arabs into second-class citizens...The democratic process has to be favored, because if not, then I think it's the beginning of a slippery slope." And all of the secular Jewish subjects, as well as all traditional subjects but Rita (who would leave them out) and Shmuel (who favors a special majority), support full inclusion of the Arabs on grounds of equal citizenship. For Rotem, even the proposal for a special majority is "absolutely wrong, it's bigotry. Arab votes are equal to the Jewish votes. I'm really opposed to the idea that Jewish votes should count for more than Arab votes. Extremely, extremely wrong. Of course they should have the same weight as ours do."

Not surprisingly, all of the Arab subjects take umbrage at the Likud's attempts to exclude, or defuse, their votes. Even Muhammad, who claims to be a "proud Israeli" and waxes patriotic about Israeli democracy, finds this strategy unfair.

> That is anti-democratic and I am against it. It's an extreme anti-
> democratic step. Their theory, their perspective is to keep all of the
> Land of Israel—from the [Mediterranean] sea to the [Jordan] river.
> They want to neutralize the Arab vote and that is not democratic.
> It is unacceptable to me.

Omer and Youssef call the proposal "extreme" as well. Youssef says "there is no better proof than this of the discrimination and the racism" that prevails in Israel's political climate. And Majjed, as usual, is the most biting:

> Maybe they want me to polish the Likud's shoes, too? I'm a hu-
> man being who relates to others as human beings, but listening to

> Arik Sharon and [then mayor of Jerusalem Ehud] Olmert speak I
> have discovered that I am half a man and all the Arabs are half
> persons, and for every Jew there are two Arabs, because a half-
> person and another half-person makes a whole person. That's
> what it implies. That is the *pinnacle* of racism.

It is clear that neither liberalism nor any conception of democracy could fathom the exclusion of any group of citizens from political participation. The equal basic political liberties, including the right to vote and run for office and the freedoms of speech and assembly, are fundamental. They are prerequisites of liberal politics. That Israelis would even consider a proposal designed to limit the voting power of a particular sector of the population—let alone forge a coalition to pass such a bill on its first reading—bespeaks a strongly illiberal streak in the political climate.

The charges of racism that predominate in debates over the treatment of Arabs in Israel, however, are worth clarifying. The term "racism," as most commonly used in the United States, refers to attitudes and actions that stem from ascribing negative characteristics to a person based on her perceived "race." On this conception of racism, racist comments include hurling insults ("Jews are greedy," "Blacks are lazy") while racist actions include violent or discriminatory treatment of individuals (refusing to rent an apartment to a black person, physically attacking someone because he's Asian). But in Israel, where Arabs condemn the Golan referendum bill as "racist," another conception of racism comes into play. This is a notion of unequal treatment that is not necessarily linked to beliefs in the inferiority of another group.[11] It is, in other words, unjustified nationalism, or unjust exclusion of an ethnic or national group. This kind of proposal *may* stem from racist thinking of the first type: a Jewish racist might want to keep Arabs out of the voting booth because they are *genetically* untrustworthy. But the desire to exclude does not stem from a supposition that Arabs are "half-persons" (in Majjed's words). It does not suppose that Arabs are inferior in mind or morality or intellect. They are not being excluded as children or animals. The main reason for exclusion, rather, is because Arabs are believed to be a non-objective (as if objectivity is a requirement for other Israelis' political participation), anti-Zionist (although no one claims that Haredi anti-Zionists should be disenfranchised) fifth column who do not have the public interest in mind. The problem is overblown nationalism: a pervasive attitude among Israel's right wing, and parts of the left wing, that the public interest includes *only* the interests of Jews and the Jewish character of the state. Too often Arabs are simply not given consideration as citizens who matter. Using Rousseau's categories, since Arabs are seen as unable to participate in the general will of the state, they are seen as a "corporate will" separate from that of the general society that is not only different from but perhaps directly at odds with the national interest (and possibly in cahoots with the general will of another country, or another people).

This attitude leads right-wing politicians like Michael Kleiner, the sole Knesset member representing the Herut party at the time, to propose legislation encouraging Arab citizens of Israel to emigrate to Arab countries. The proposal, which then-Knesset speaker Avraham Burg called "racist" and refused to bring to the floor for discussion, would have provided exiting Arab citizens with an "emigration basket" in exchange for ceding their Israeli citizenship. (They'd have thirty days to change their mind, as long as they hadn't already moved to an enemy state.)[12] This may be somewhat kinder and gentler than the late Rabbi Meir Kahane's proposal to forcibly "transfer" Israeli Arabs to Arab countries, but its mechanism of bribery—here's your cash, give me your citizenship—marks another insult to Israel's one million Arab citizens and shows the extent to which some conceptions of Israel as a Jewish state compete tragically with democratic values.

Language, Anthem and Flag

Political, social and economic discrimination are not the only factors that embitter the Arab citizens of Israel. In addition to attempts to minimize Arabs' voting strength or limit its access to state lands, many of the state's institutions and symbols, to Arabs, represent exclusion and intolerance. In depicting the state's official connection to Judaism and the Jewish people, the national anthem, the state flag, the state's official symbol and the dominance of the Hebrew language mark Jewish supremacy in the state of Israel. They are clear signs of Israel's non-neutrality with respect to religio-nationality, or what we might think of as the state's "conception of the good." The good of the state, as codified in the Declaration of Establishment and basic legislation, is linked to Judaism, to Jews and Zionism. In terms of procedural matters the state is committed to certain aspects of liberal democracy—including the rule of law, individual rights and popular government—but its substance, its color, its history and its ethos are decidedly Jewish. How do Israeli citizens relate to these symbols?

Jewish Views

The Jewish subjects in my study—both those in favor and those opposed to "separation of religion and state"—almost universally approve of each of the main elements of Israel's Jewish symbolism. The state flag has a Star of David (strongly associated with Zionism, but of relatively recent origin and not of significant religious value) as its central motif, bordered by two blue horizontal stripes symbolizing the blue fringes of the *tallit* (prayer shawl).[13] The official state symbol is the seven-branched *menorah* (candelabra) that was used as a central ritual object in the Second Temple in Jerusalem; it represents the history of Jewish sovereignty in the Land of Israel as well as Jewish life in the Diaspora. Hebrew, the language of the Jewish people, has its roots in the Bible and the ancient Israelites and its renaissance in the efforts of Eliezer Ben-Yehuda, who updated the language for modern use in the late nineteenth century. Although Hebrew and Arabic are both official languages, Hebrew clearly has preference: Supreme Court decisions are issued in Hebrew only; traffic signs in most parts of the country are in Hebrew and English, but not Arabic; and while the vast majority of Israeli Arabs speak fluent Hebrew, very few Israeli Jews can utter more than a few words of Arabic. Finally, the national anthem, "Hatikva," sets these lyrics to a slow, sorrowful score, building to an emotional climax in the repetition of the final two lines:

> Still within our hearts
> The Jewish soul yearns
> Eastward, forward,
> An eye looks toward Zion
>
> Our hope is not yet lost
> The hope of two thousand years
> To be a free people in our land
> The land of Zion and Jerusalem[14]

Of the Jewish subjects, only three harbor hostility for the national anthem. Interestingly, they sit on opposite ends of the religious spectrum. Ronit, the secular Jew who dates an Arab man, says,

> A: I can't *stand* it [said in English]! What is this stuff about "to be a free people in our land"? Aren't we? We subjugate others now. That's it, it's enough already: we need something happy. Were you here during Independence Day?
>
> Q: Yes.
>
> A: There was a ceremony broadcast on television from Mount Herzl. Every year I watch this ceremony on television. This year there was a sort of happy atmosphere: not intense and heavy, just happy. And it put me in a good mood. Enough with carrying the burden of our troubles, as if we're such pathetic wretches [*miskanim*]. We aren't!
>
> Q: Which song would you prefer instead of Hatikva?

A: I can't think of one at this moment, but there are twenty thousand songs that might work.

Meanwhile, Yehuda, the Haredi father of twelve, declares that "no one believes in that [the Jewish people's pinings for the land of Israel] anymore. No one today cares about the state. Everyone today looks out for himself, for his own pocketbook....There are no true Zionists." Nehama, the Haredi *ba'alat teshuva*, thinks the anthem "needs to be changed." "We've already arrived at the year 2000," she jokes, referring to a line in the song. "What's next?" Then she says, "It doesn't bother me, because it doesn't mean anything to me."

Hatikva does mean something to each of the remaining twenty-two Jewish subjects, all of whom support keeping the national anthem intact. This deeply and broadly diverse group of respondents is not of one voice, however, on the reason for doing so. There are three kinds of answers. Some subjects cite an emotional, nationalist connection to the song; others see religious meaning in its words; and others, feeling little spiritual or personal bond with the anthem, nevertheless think that it's something that simply shouldn't be changed.

The Haredi Yeshayahu, idiosyncratically Zionist, gives an example of the first type:

> I very much love that song. I value it very much. It's a very, very beautiful song, a song that in my opinion expresses the incredible longing of the Jewish people to come to freedom from its Diasporas, a song that really expresses the suffering of the Jewish people. It greatly pains me that young people today abandon their Zionist heritage; abandon the beautiful songs, songs of the Land of Israel...

Aside from Chaim, who says he "loves" the national anthem, secular and traditional subjects are less effusive in expressing a personal connection to the song. (Many simply say that they "approve" or "have no problem" with it.) To find rhetoric matching that of Yeshayahu, we have to turn to the Religious Zionist subjects, for whom Hatikva expresses an ongoing hope for religious salvation. Avi explains:

> Hatikva has an element we can call religious. "The Land of Zion and Jerusalem"—these words say so much. Before they settled on "Hatikva," some wanted to use "Shir Ha'ma'alot" ["A Song of Ascents"] [15] in its place. In the end, they chose "Hatikva." I think that these two songs say, more or less, the same thing. The hope hasn't ended: that is to say, as long as we live here in this world and there are Jews in the Diaspora and there is danger to the Jewish people, the hope remains the hope. There truly is hope, wherever it is, a

hope for something better—maybe you'd call it the coming of the Messiah, that in essence all of the Jews live here as one people.

Asked whether he'd prefer a more clearly religious alternative to "Hatikva," Avi responds that "it is very religious, although it isn't spelled out" in the song. "There are many, many concepts that the nation simply doesn't know are religious! In my opinion, 'Hatikva' is part of religion—it's not something secular, not at all." Zvi agrees:

> I very, very much love the national anthem. I truly think that it's one of the most beautiful and most emotional songs there is. When I hear a woman with a good voice sing it, I shed tears....The "yearning Jewish soul" comes from very eminent poets during the Jewish Middle Ages such as Ibn Gavriol and Yehuda Halevi who said, "my heart is in the East and I am in the West." He was living in Spain and he said, "my heart is in the Land of Israel." That's what it reflects. The song reflects that, even though a secular Jew wrote it.

Several of the Jewish subjects, though emotionally and religiously un-swayed, think it is wrong to change things like the national anthem after they have been set. Shmuel represents this view: "There are certainly songs whose words and rhythms are better than Hatikva. But it's a matter of tradi-tion. It's something you fear to touch. So this is something that we don't touch." Tanya personally feels "nothing for or against the national anthem"; she believes, however, that "you don't change the national anthem mid-stream, unless there's a revolution." Ganit provides similar reasoning, but mentions that the topic is open for discussion if Israeli Arabs truly feel ag-grieved:

> I don't know. I wouldn't change these things. I haven't thought enough about the issue of the anthem, but I don't think we need to change it. There are things you shouldn't touch—out of some sort of tradition and out of a feeling that today there's an inclination to destroy all the sacred cows, that you can get rid of everything. There is no need [to destroy all sacred cows]. It's important to leave a certain quantity of them as they were just because that's the way they were. This may be a kind of conservatism....I don't see a reason today to harm them [national symbols]—especially today, especially in light of their [Palestinians'] political awaken-ing. But I say again that it's an issue that should be raised and de-bated if possible—I'm not sure how—but if it should be, then a debate about it should be started. I wouldn't want to [change "Hatikva"], but I say that if it comes to a point where people feel that the basis of their rights is being harmed, we should try to see

how it's possible to make some sort of balance, integration [*izun, shiluv*].

Rotem describes her moral quandary over the anthem and other Jewish symbols of the state:

> These are things I have only started thinking about pretty recently. Because emotionally Hatikva for me brings tears to my eyes almost every time I sing it. But I also feel that if I had to I'd…I'd give my life for Israel. From that sense, I am a hundred percent Zionist. But I can't help but think how the Arabs feel when they sing this anthem, and…they probably don't feel too good about it. Maybe we could add another verse that talked about the Arabs in this country. I don't know if I would really want to change it because it is such a very, very meaningful song. I like that it doesn't involve God…too much. I think it manages nicely to connect different factions within Judaism, which is not a small thing to do. If someone could come up with a nice anthem that was suitable for [both Jews and Arabs], then I would give in on that one [laughs].

When it comes to the state flag, the pattern of views among the Jewish subjects is similar: several lavish communal-religious significance upon it,[16] the vast middle approves of it with relatively laconic support, and a handful disdain it.[17] On the question of whether Hebrew ought to remain the favored official language of the state, the Jewish subjects are nearly unanimous in their approval. The only points of contention in the interviews concern the 20 percent of the country whose first language is Arabic, and the approximately seven percent (Haredim) who speak Yiddish at home and in school. Some (Ganit, Tanya, Ronit and Rotem) think the state educational system should do more to teach Arabic to Israeli Jews, and Haredim and Religious Zionists debate whether modern Hebrew, as laid down by Eliezer Ben-Yehuda, still counts as the *lashon hakodesh*—the "holy tongue."[18]

Arab Views

But how do Arabs feel when they speak Hebrew, hear "Hatikva" or see the blue-and-white of the Israeli flag? The subjects in my study generally divide four to one on these questions, with Muhammad being the only respondent who seems relatively unfazed by the Jewish symbolism of the state. Each of the four younger subjects disapproves of the state's national anthem and the Star of David on the flag.

Speaking about the national anthem, Majjed spares the ambiguity: "'Hatikva' should be abolished and taken away to a thousand hells [*l'elef azalzel sh'yikhu oto*]." What does he feel when he hears the song?

Repulsion [*go'al nefesh*]. There's a line in "Hatikva" that says: "The
Jewish soul longs for..." I'm not a Jewish soul. The anthem is a
sign of the racism of the state. The Star of David that's on the flag
is another. The Star of David doesn't mean anything to me. We
have nothing in common. Why should I identify with that?

But when I ask if his feeling when encountering these symbols is closer
to sadness or to anger, Majjed chooses apathy: "It does nothing for me."
When Omer hears "Hatikva," he says, "I feel as if it is not my state. It's as if
it's the Jews' state, because in the song "the hope" refers to the Jewish state,
the Land of Zion, and those ideas don't relate to Arabs." Nadia uses a word
that comes up time and again in the Arab subjects' comments on Israel's
symbolism: belonging [*histaychut*]:

I don't hear "Hatikva." I have no place to hear it. I wouldn't be
willing, for example, to stand and have them sing "Hatikva" for
me. If I were an athlete, let's say, I wouldn't be willing to stand
and have them sing me "Hatikva" under an Israeli flag. Those
[symbols] do not belong to me. I have nothing to do with them. I
do not belong [*lo shayechet*] to them.

Youssef echoes this sense of alienation:

First of all, I do all I can [*mishtadel*] *not* to hear "Hatikva," because
it speaks more of Zionism and not of Judaism. I am against Zionism, that's clear. But I am not against Jews. When I hear "Hatikva,"
I feel as if I do not belong [*lo shayach*] to this state. That is how I
understand "Hatikva," because Arabs aren't mentioned there, only
Zionism.

Later in the interview, Nadia expands her critique to link her alienation to a
sense of powerlessness that keeps her out of politics and away from the voting booth:

[Hatikva] belongs to *them*. In the state of today, I cannot change
anything in this state. I can work on changing the character and I
can request things to change, but as long as the state defines itself
as first and foremost a Jewish state, as a Zionist state, as a state of
the Jews, *we are guests here*. So I cannot change it. I don't like it, but
I can't change it as long as the state is Jewish. It's their right. I can't
get involved in it.

Some of the other Arab subjects are more willing to get involved; their
alienation spurs them to action rather than acquiescence. Omer, Youssef and
Majjed all imagine alternatives to the current flag or national anthem that

would help them feel a closer allegiance to the state. Omer proposes the following sample lyric for his dejudaized anthem: *"Let us be friends, as time goes by we are becoming better friends, becoming like brothers."* He suggests "one Israeli symbol and one symbol for the citizens belonging to each of the other religions in the state: Islam and Christianity." Majjed weighs in with own ideas for the flag: "What do you think about a dove with an olive branch? Or we could use [the image of] Che Guevara, which is a little Socialist—a Communist wouldn't be appropriate." Several of the Jewish subjects are willing to consider new models for the flag, too. Ronit doesn't want to erase the Magen David from the flag, but allows that "maybe we could add something else next to the Star of David" for the Arab minority. Tanya expands on this idea:

> There may be room to add other symbols to the flag in order to create a feeling of partnership [*shotafut*], as when they added stars to the American flag. I'm not against that. I know people will have problems with that, because symbols aren't meant to be changed, but I'm not at all against it because there's a not-insignificant group within the State of Israel that feels it doesn't belong [*lo shayechet*]. So I wouldn't mind if there'd be a Star of David alongside a crescent and a cross. We have Muslims and Christians, too. But what would we do with symbols for the Bedouin and the Druze? Everyone has symbols. Maybe we need to place stars on the side so that everyone will have a name, and it will belong to everyone.

Judging from the comments of the four Arab subjects who complain about their feeling of alienation, Tanya is certainly tapping into a major sentiment among Arab citizens of Israel when she says this group "feels it doesn't belong." Before moving to an assessment of the Jewish symbolism in the state, however, we should listen to the words of Muhammad, the only Arab subject who professes much less frustration with the flag, the anthem and the dominance of Hebrew. He prefaces his comment on "Hatikva" by telling me that during the national siren on Yom HaShoah (Holocaust Remembrance Day), he stands silent in memory of the six million slain Jews:

> First of all, I stand and observe the minute of silence on Holocaust Remembrance Day. I studied history and on every Holocaust Remembrance Day of the people, and especially the Jewish people, I stand during the one-minute siren. It's my duty.

> The anthem, "Hatikva," represents me, because I am a citizen of the state and I agree that I am an Israeli. I am proud to be an Israeli. Why? I'll tell it to you straight: When I was a student, I didn't feel discrimination. I was like any other student. In Tel Aviv, I lived in an apartment without any discrimination. I traveled to

Washington, D.C. I have a good financial situation and live with an Israeli identification card. I am an Israeli citizen, so it's my duty [to approve of "Hatikva"]. I know the words, too. I give it the respect it deserves.

Muhammad does not make a habit of *singing* the national anthem; he shows it "the respect it deserves" by standing as it is sung and not calling for its abolition. As for the other Jewish symbols of the state, Muhammad makes frequent use of a revealing phrase: "I live with it" [*ani hai im zeh*] or "I'm reconciled to that" [*ani mashlim im zeh*]. In all, he uses expressions such as these six times in the course of the interview. And he relentlessly stresses the positive:

Q: What do you think about the national anthem, the flag and the official emblem of the state, a *menorah*?

A: Those are things that the state determined. The character of the state is Jewish, that's understood from the beginning. It doesn't bother me. I live with it. The things I want, that are special to me, I enjoy. I told you that we have autonomy from a religious perspective. We have integrated schools. We study here because we are citizens and that represents us because we live with it, because we're citizens of the country. We even have Arab players in the soccer team!

Discussing the dominance of the Hebrew language—a subject he teaches to Arab youth—Muhammad emphasizes the commonalities with Arabic:

Q: Hebrew is the favored national language. Should that change?

A: First of all, in Arabic and Hebrew, 60 or 70 percent of the time the roots of the words are the same. I can show you many examples of words that come from the same root...It's easy for me, because the Arabic teacher teaches Hebrew to the Arab students. For me, and for my children, we have no problem with Hebrew, because we master the language by grade eight or nine. Reading, definitely, and pronunciation, more or less, too, speaking. [These skills] enable contact with the Jewish population. So there's no problem with that. Just as you speak English and Hebrew, it's the same thing.

On a question filled with not only symbolic but substantive preference for Jews—the Law of Return—Muhammad is a bit less pleased. But he casts his resistance in benign terms (the size of the country) rather than those used by each of the other Arab subjects (discrimination against Arab citizens).

And he refrains from calling for a similar right of return for Palestinian Arab refugees from the War of Independence:

> Q: What do you think about the Law of Return, which gives preference to Jews? Should that remain or be changed?
>
> A: That's understood from the beginning and it's natural. I don't agree with that clause a hundred percent, and I don't protest it. I'm reconciled to it [mashlim im zeh]. I don't agree a hundred percent because I worry that this is a small country and it's not big enough for everyone. But I agree with it and don't protest it. Live with it.
>
> Q: If you had the power, do you think it should be changed or that Arabs should be added [to the category of individuals who are entitled to instant citizenship]?
>
> A: No. Maybe on the West Bank there's room. But here inside Israel there isn't room; it isn't realistic. And whoever left Israel [in 1947-49], left of his own accord [mirtzono]. No one forced him out [giresh oto]. Some left because they were afraid—that's their problem. Some fled in order to live elsewhere, like my brother who lives in Germany now. It was his own free will. He wants it. Why should I worry about him being able to return? He's doing it [living outside Israel] of his own accord!

What are we to make of Muhammad's responses, which waver between pride in Israeli citizenship and resignation to Israel's exclusive Jewish characteristics? How should we view his stance in light of those of other Arab subjects, who complain that the current Jewish Zionist symbols represent inequality and alienation from the state? When I tell Majjed about Muhammad, here is his reaction:

> In my opinion, he errs. If he is proud [to be an Israeli], this person, he should come and explain to me what he is proud of. That he salutes the flag of King David from the Bible? What is he proud of? That Qualansuwa [Muhammad's village] every winter is flooded with water because there's no money for it in the state budget? What is this person proud of? What exactly is he proud of? Maybe his father cooperates [with the state]. I don't know exactly what this guy is proud of. If he would only explain to me what he is proud of to be a citizen of the state of Israel. Because in Syria he wouldn't be able to open his mouth? So what if in Syria he couldn't open his mouth?...I don't understand what he's proud of. I would be happy if you would introduce me to this man so he could explain to me what he is proud of.

Majjed then characterizes the divisions of Israel's Arab population this way: first is the group he, Nadia, Omer and Youssef seem to fit into, a politically aware cadre who battle against "cooperation" with the state and demand equal rights for Arabs; second is a politically unaware sector that simply "runs after the food"; and third are the "cooperators," those like Muhammad and other Labor-party Arabs, who "live with" the state as it is and give implicit, if not explicit, legitimacy to Israel's Jewish character. Each group, Majjed thinks, represents about a third of Israeli Arabs.

Conclusion

No liberal state ought to treat its citizens unequally in terms of their political rights or social or economic opportunities. Rigging a national referendum in order to nullify the vote of Israeli Arabs, for example, is an illiberal and intolerable manifestation of Israel's alliance with Judaism. But what about the symbols? Can liberalism accept a state flag or a national anthem with religious motifs that speak only to the favored religio-national majority? Jacob Levy thinks that the legitimacy of state symbols is not, properly speaking, a matter of political justice. Referring to disputes over the Confederate flag in South Carolina, South African holidays recalling Afrikaners' racism-tainted history and motifs appearing on new Bosnian license plates, among others, Levy notes that "in none of these cases are any rights or resources, any property or powers, directly at stake. The state actions do not limit any person's liberty or seize any person's goods. As such they seem to fall outside the scope of theories of justice, as those are usually understood."[19] He argues, however, that "liberalism, and a liberal state, ought to come to grips with the moral importance of symbolism" owing to the "tremendous importance symbolic disputes can have to their participants."[20]

Although Levy is mistaken that contemporary theories of justice lack the resources for analyzing disputes over symbols—Rawls, after all, lists "the social bases of self-respect" as a primary good all citizens require in order to pursue their life plans[21]—the interviews with Arab citizens of Israel suggest his admonition is appropriate. If liberalism is committed to a rich notion of equality, it should be worried about not only gross violations such as disenfranchisement and unequal access to state lands but also symbols that communicate a message of disempowerment, alienation or exclusion. If political loyalty is reinforced by symbols that tug at the heartstrings—referring to a shared history, a collective fate or common aspirations—it may be both immoral and politically inexpedient for a state to introduce symbols that leave twenty percent of the population cold (think Muhammad) or irate (think Majjed).

But to say that symbols matter to liberalism is not to say that all particularistic symbols are unjustified, or that they pose harms of the same type or
same degree as those that more concrete forms of discrimination entail. Although Youssef demands equality across the board—no Star of David, no
"Hatikva," no *menorah*—he plots a strategy for achieving equality that puts
first things first:

> A: We want equality. And we want them to change "Hatikva" and
> the flag, but the point is how to get that done. We must take one
> step at a time. Just as it was difficult in the 1970s and 1980s to say
> to a Jew that a Palestinian state must be established and he
> wouldn't accept that, today he won't accept a proposal to change
> "Hatikva" and the flag. But now he accepts the principle of equal-
> ity. The next step in my opinion is equality, and after there's equal-
> ity, we'll talk about other things, these issues that are also impor-
> tant. In my opinion there needs to be a certain gradual process in
> order to arrive at the final goal of full equality—even in the na-
> tional anthem, even with the flag.

> Q: You think equality should first be reached in the sense of eco-
> nomic and budgetary equality?

> A: No. We must arrive at full equality but in order to reach full
> equality, and there is only one way: full equality will be gradual.
> From my point of view, would that [*halevai*] I'd wake up tomorrow
> morning and there would be full equality, but I see that in order to
> arrive at this full equality, there must be a gradual process of
> change in order to reach it. You take the thing the closest to what
> the Jews understand. They understand that we must reach eco-
> nomic equality. They understand that now, but they won't fathom
> any changes to the national anthem and the flag of Israel. But I say
> that with time they will understand that they'll need to change
> "Hatikva" and the flag too. We'll talk about it after [economic
> equality has been reached].

> Q: So it has to be step-by-step process?

> A: There must be full equality, but the only way is step-by-step
> from what we have today.

Youssef does not explicitly say that substantive equality is more important than symbolic equality in this passage, but his plan should be read as
more than just a strategy for progressively winning the Jewish majority over
to the Arab vision of a "state of all its citizens." The plan also represents an
implicit assessment of which are the most salient issues for Israeli Arabs today. The most pressing matters are political equality and socio-economic
equality: adequate roads, schools, land and sewers, as well as a willingness

to include Arab parties in governing coalitions. The state's symbols might be unwelcome, distasteful, even offensive, but they are not at the top of the Israeli Arab agenda; proportionate provisions in state budgets, most notably, are. Still, this hardly resolves the issue. Part IV will tackle the problem more comprehensively by analyzing the harms symbols pose and by exploring several ways to alleviate them.

Notes

1. Druze Israeli citizens do typically serve in the IDF, owing to their tradition of loyalty to the government of the state in which they reside. Not all young Druze fit this mold, however; Majjed found a way out of his army duty (ostensibly because he failed the physical examination).

2. I generally follow Michael Walzer's argument for a "(limited) right of closure" in chapter two of his *Spheres of Justice* (New York: Basic Books, 1983), 63. Without some authority to restrict immigration, he writes, we would live in a "world of radically deracinated men and women...The distinctiveness of cultures and groups depends upon closure, and without it, cannot be conceived as a stable feature of human life" (39). Still, matters such as the status of guest workers and refugees pose challenges and prescribe limits to a state's ability to write its own rules of membership. Yael Tamir suggests that the Law of Return "would only be justified if the largest minority in the state, namely, the Palestinians, would also have a national entity in which they could enact a similar law." This proposal sees national self-determination as a primary good to which each individual, and each nation, is entitled. But it untenably makes a state's right to control its own destiny in matters of immigration contingent on international processes over which the state has, at best, only limited control. Perhaps the world would be more just if a Palestinian state existed which gave a right of return to Palestinian nationals, but Israel has direct control only over its own laws, not over whether a Palestinian state will come to be or what its laws will be. (Indeed, this is a complexity facing any theory positing rights for individuals *qua* human beings and not *qua* members of political societies: there is no feasible distribution mechanism for these primary goods across states.) See Yael Tamir, *Liberal Nationalism* (Princeton: Princeton University Press, 1993), 160-61.

3. Salah Tarif, of the Labor party, resigned as minister without portfolio on 29 January 2002 while under criminal investigation by the attorney general. Shortly thereafter, MK Tarif's parliamentary immunity was lifted, and on 19 February 2002, he was charged with bribing a public official and breaching the public trust. According to the charge, Tarif surreptitiously met with Rafael Cohen, then head of the Population Registry (charged with bribery and breach of public trust as well) and offered him two thousand dollars to arrange citizenship for Huseini Yunis Badran, a resident of Baka a-Sharkiya. Allison Kaplan Sommer, "Tarif Charged with Bribery, Breaching Public Trust," *Jerusalem Post*, 20 February 2002.

4. Nina Gilbert, "Golan Law Passes; Special Majority, Referendum Needed for Withdrawal," *Jerusalem Post*, 27 January 1999.

5. Hirsch Goodman, "Barak's Real Test," *Jerusalem Post*, 24 December 1999.

6. Israel Harel, "What the Golan Demonstration Means," *Ha'aretz*, 13 January 2000.

7. Gideon Alon, "Government Goes Down to Defeat on Syria Referendum Bill," *Ha'aretz* , 2 March 2000.

8. This language appears in a mass email message sent by Amir Wilker, chairman of the B'tey Movement (Golan Citizen Action Network) urging recipients to lobby Shas Knesset members to support the bill. It should be noted that the email misconstrues (or misrepresents) the purpose of the bill. It is not meant to nullify "Arab Palestinian" votes (Palestinians living on the West Bank and in the Gaza Strip are not Israeli citizens and do not have a vote). It is meant, rather, to nullify the votes of Arab citizens of Israel who enjoy, theoretically at least, complete political equality with Jewish Israelis.

9. Moshe Arens, "The Wisdom of a Big Majority," *Jerusalem Post*, 7 March 2000.

10. Ze'ev Segal, "Withdraw from the Golan Referendum," *Ha'aretz*, 20 December 1999.

11. My point is that instances of political racism stem largely from the second type of racism. Racism of the first type, however, is also rampant in Israel, and surely feeds into the second type. The term "Arab work" describes a job shoddily done, and insults referring to Arabs as smelly, as dogs, or as terrorists are common. During my field research trip a flyer arrived in my Jerusalem mailbox advertising a house painting service that listed among its features quick service, professional painting, reasonable prices and the promise of "Jewish work"—implying a higher standard than the average "Arab work."

12. Ariel Kahane, ed., "Proposal to Encourage Emigration," *Arutz Sheva News Service*, 26 July 2001.

13. Alec Mishory, "The Flag and the Emblem" Israel Ministry of Foreign Affairs website, <http://www.israel-mfa.gov.il/mfa/go.asp?MFAH0cph0> (25 August 2005).

14. My translation from the Hebrew.

15. "Hatikva" became the Zionist anthem in 1905. "Shir Ha'ma'lot" was indeed one of the contenders: it is Psalm 126, typically sung before grace after meals on Sabbaths and holidays. The first lines of the psalm read:

When God returns the fortunes of Zion
It will be like a dream fulfilled
Our mouths will be filled with laughter
And our tongues with songs of joy.

16. Avi: "The religious significance is that we, as Jews, have something in common, something common to all of us—it doesn't matter what—that will stay that way forever." Zvi: "Secular Jews created the flag, but what is it made up of? It's built on the *tallit* and the Star of David, utterly Jewish symbols. The Star of David and the tallit are not just for religious Jews. The flag is for every Jew, no matter who he is: religious or secular."

17. Ronit worries that "non-Jewish citizens will have a problem with it," while for Yehuda, the Zionist flag makes illicit use of Jewish symbols and is meaningless: "Who said that the flag is a rag? Some professor said that the flag is a rag, ten years ago.... I don't see in it anything at all. This flag does not speak to me."

18. Nosson, who speaks only Yiddish at home, claims that Ben-Yehuda "perverted and corrupted the holy tongue" by introducing words from other languages and choosing the Sephardic pronunciation over the Ashkenazic pronunciation. Yehuda complains that Ben-Yehuda "wrote the language on Shabbat with a cigarette in his mouth" and relishes the story of his death: "According to the Torah it is forbidden to write on Shabbat and it is forbidden to smoke on Shabbat. He died in the middle of writing one Shabbat day. Whoever desecrates the Sabbath, it is written in the Torah, 'he who desecrates, in the course of his desecration he will die [*m'hollel mavet yamut*].' Write down that it's not the holy tongue, it's just the national language of Ben-Yehuda." Zvi, speaking as a Religious Zionist, counters that "there is no doubt" that Hebrew is "the holy tongue."

19. Jacob T. Levy, "State Symbols and Multiculturalism," *Report from the Institute for Philosophy and Public Policy* 20, no. 4 (Fall 2000): 16-22.

20. Levy, "State Symbols," 17-18.

21. Rawls defines the social bases of self-respect as "those aspects of basic institutions normally essential if citizens are to have a lively sense of their worth as persons and to be able to advance their ends with self-confidence." Rawls, *Justice as Fairness: A Restatement* (Cambridge: Belknap Press of the Harvard University Press, 2001), 59. In a 1968 paper, Rawls writes, "a sense of our worth is perhaps the most important primary good." He explains: "For our self-respect, which mirrors our sense of our own worth, depends in part upon the respect shown to us by others; no one can long possess an assurance of his own value in the face of the enduring contempt or even the indifference of others." Rawls, "Distributive Justice: Some Addenda," in *Collected Papers*, ed. Samuel Freeman, (Cambridge: Harvard University Press, 1999), 171.

Chapter 9
Land

On March 8, 2000, the Israeli Supreme Court issued a decision hailed at the time as Israel's *Brown v. Board of Education*. Israeli Arabs, the ruling proclaimed, could no longer be discriminated against in the provision of state lands. Commentators in Israel and abroad praised the decision as a watershed for Israeli liberal democracy. After fifty-two years of discrimination, the headlines read, Israel had finally recognized the moral and legal necessity of treating its Arab citizens—a sector that makes up just under 20 percent of the state's nearly seven million people—as equals.

The story behind the landmark Israeli Supreme Court case, *Ka'adan v. Israel Lands Administration*[1], begins in April 1995. Adel and Iman Ka'adan wanted to move from Baqa al-Gharbiya, their impoverished village with poor schools and inadequate services in the Lower Galilee of northern Israel, to green, prosperous Katzir with prettier streets and better educational opportunities for their children two kilometers up the hill. When the Ka'adans walked into the offices of the Katzir Cooperative Association—created in 1982 by the Jewish Agency, which had received the land from the Israel Lands Administration—they were refused an application to build a home. Katzir, the Ka'adans were told, does not admit Arabs; according to the Jewish Agency's mission, the land is for Jews only. A few months later, the Ka'adans turned to the Association for Civil Rights in Israel (ACRI), which petitioned the Supreme Court to compel Katzir to accept the couple's request. In February 1998, when the Court finally spoke, Chief Justice Aharon Barak noted that "this is one of the most difficult and complex judicial decisions that I have ever come across."[2] Rather than issue a decision, he recommended that the parties "do everything possible to find a practical solution to the petitioner's problem" by themselves.[3]

Exactly ten months later, the parties informed the Court that their efforts had failed, forcing the judiciary to act. In the majority opinion authored by Chief Justice Barak, the Court held by a four-to-one margin that the principle of equality—"one of the fundamental values of the State of Israel" as evinced in the Declaration of Establishment and prior court rulings—barred discrimination against citizens of Israel based on considerations of religion or nationality. It concluded that the Israel Lands Administration "was not permitted, by law, to allocate State land to the Jewish Agency for the purpose of establishing the communal settlement of Katzir on the basis of discrimination between Jews and non-Jews."[4]

In reaching its main conclusion that the Jewish Agency's action violated equality, the Court cited several international human rights conventions, a few traditional Jewish sources and—most notably—the holding in *Brown v. Board of Education:* " 'separate but equal' is inherently unequal." Chief Justice Barak argued that the reasoning in *Brown* which spoke against segregation in American schools condemned the Jews-only admittance policy in Israeli towns as well: "...separation sends an insulting message to the minority group, makes it stand out from the general [public], emphasizes the difference between the minority and the others, and exacerbates feelings of social inferiority."[5] Barak could have drawn from a less famous but more directly relevant American precedent: *Buchanan v. Warley* (1917), a decision that prohibited residential segregation by race, even if the purpose is to keep racial peace. In *Buchanan*, the court ruled that the state may not seek to ameliorate racial hostility "by depriving citizens of their constitutional rights and privileges," even if its motives are free of racial animus.[6]

Barak noted that in the half-century since the United States Supreme Court decided *Brown* in 1954, debates have sprouted suggesting that in certain cases policies of separation may actually serve equality, or produce benefits exceeding the harms of inequality. He mentioned one local example: a policy of leasing Israel Lands Administration lands exclusively to a Bedouin population being resettled by the government into permanent homes. Such a policy is justified, he wrote, because it secured Bedouin interests and protected Bedouins as a discrete cultural group. But Barak offered two reasons why no similar benefits stem from the segregation in Katzir. First, he wrote, the effect of the policy is not beneficent but discriminatory; it is, considering the disparity in living conditions between Baqa al-Gharbiya and Katzir, separate and *un*equal. Second, because Katzir is open to all kinds of Jews, its residents do not constitute a "special group" with distinguishing characteristics. There is thus no legitimate purpose to be found in maintaining exclusivity only with regard to Arabs.[7]

The court explicitly held back from a decision questioning the legality of other Jewish Agency projects, including *kibbutzim* and *moshavim* (two kinds of communal settlements dotting Israel), and specified that the ruling applies only to future allocations of state land. And the remedy the Court initially provided was toothless. Rather than order the Katzir Cooperative Association to immediately sell a plot of land to the Ka'adans, it required it only "to consider the petitioners' request" to buy the land, and to do so—lifting another line from *Brown v. Board of Education*—"with all appropriate speed [*bimhirut ha'reuyah*]."[8] An ACRI petition to find the settlement of Katzir in contempt of court and require it to accept the family into the community was rejected by the Supreme Court on April 2, 2001. Applying the notion of equality on which it had originally ruled, the Court held that Katzir had the right to consider the Ka'adans' application and interview them before deciding if they should be admitted. It added, however, that Katzir must provide a list of criteria for admittance and, if they refuse the application, reasons for rejection.[9]

In September 2003, Ka'adan and ACRI again petitioned the court in light of two developments. First, an internal Jewish Agency document from July 2000 was uncovered stating that since the *Ka'adan* decision seemed to close all legal loopholes allowing discrimination, the agency would attempt "not to make any noise in the system, and continue to do what we have been doing." The strategy was not to try to circumvent the decision, or to fight it politically, but to quietly disrupt the verdict's implementation by ignoring it and sticking to its pre-*Ka'adan* policy.[10] Second, the Ka'adans received a formal rejection from the Katzir admissions committee with a vaguely worded explanation indicating they had been turned down because it would be difficult for them to socially integrate into the community.[11] Based on these new facts, the September 2003 ACRI petition asked the Supreme Court to force the Israel Lands Administration to offer a plot of land to the Ka'adans in the area of Katzir they had originally requested, in a spot on the western hill with a view of the surrounding valley, at 1995 prices. Before the Court could rule on the issue, however, the Israel Lands Administration came through with an offer on October 1, 2003. It was less than the couple wanted: a plot of land in a new neighborhood in Katzir, without a guaranteed view, and at current market prices (which were much higher than rates that prevailed in the mid-1990s when the Ka'adans first wanted to buy).[12] Finally, in May 2004 the Israel Lands Administration decided to sell the Ka'adans a plot of land at 1995 prices, and in April 2005 the family received the contract. After ten years, the Ka'adans and their four daughters had won their legal battle.[13]

Israeli Arab Views on *Ka'adan*: "A Pointless Fight"

When I conducted my interviews in the Spring of 2000, the Katzir case was fresh news. It was not, however, fresh in the minds of all of my otherwise politically aware and educated subjects. In fact, to my surprise, I had to describe the circumstances of the case to fully half of my respondents: they hadn't heard of it. And most shocking of all, four of the five Arab subjects—

each of whom displayed high levels of political interest and knowledge on other issues—shrugged their shoulders or furrowed their brows when I mentioned the Ka'adan family's court battle. Only one of my Arab respondents, Muhammad, knew about the case; he hadn't heard the decision, though. If *Ka'adan v. Israel Land Administration* is the *Brown v. Board* of Israel, someone forgot to tell the Israelis. Despite the three-page paean to liberal equality in the text of Chief Justice Barak's opinion—"the state must respect and defend the right of every individual in the state to equality," "equality is the fundamental value of every democratic society"—the decision has done little to improve the status of the Arab citizen of Israel. Still, it has spurred several legal challenges to discriminatory land policies.[14] And it set the stage for Attorney General Menahem Mazuz, in early 2005, to order the Jewish National Fund to sell lands to Jews and Arabs on an equal basis.[15]

Many of the subjects needed a quick lesson on the facts of the case, but few needed prodding to express an opinion on the outcome. Since the subjects were unfamiliar with the details, their comments moved beyond *Ka'adan* to address a sociological issue of great salience to average Israelis that was largely passed over in the text of the Court's opinion: models of Jewish-Arab coexistence in Israel. Every subject has something to say on this question, with the vast majority expressing doubts about the prospect or desirability of Jews and Arabs living together in the same neighborhoods, towns or apartment buildings. Even those respondents who speak out in favor of the Supreme Court's decision in the Katzir case note the limited reach of the verdict and the unshakable practical reality of Israeli life which neither sector seeks to change: separation of Jew and Arab.

The theme is most clearly found among the five Arab respondents' comments. Unlike black Americans in the 1950s—many of whom sought integration into white public schools and into American society in general—these Arabs and their neighbors are hardly banging on the doors of Jewish towns across Israel hoping to be welcomed in. Adel and Iman Ka'adan are the exception to the rule. In the view of my subjects, the Ka'adans deserve to buy a home wherever they like, but they're a little weird for wanting to live in a Jewish town. Muhammad, who built his own house in Qualansuwa, begins by saying that "first of all, I think that everyone has the right" to buy a home anywhere in Israel. "I'm for the ruling."

> But let's be realistic. That's life. That's custom. To tell you the truth, in my opinion the person doing this is demagogic. It's a provocation. It's only for the media. Why? Because an Arab can't live in a Jewish settlement, and a Jew can't come live in an Arab settlement because it's not realistic and doesn't happen! Why? First of all from the point of view of his children. The way of life, the holidays. It creates conflicts. It's not realistic. That's the issue. I think he deserves it, but it's not realistic and I'm not for it, because

every society has its customs, its agreements, its understandings, its prejudices, its opinions. And they're different; it's a fact that they're different. It's impossible. It's a fact that Jews don't come to live with us in Tira or in Taibe [two Arab villages], because they know that they can't live with us, because their ways of life are different from ours....I think they must give—any Arab should get permission to buy. But after a month or two he'll say: 'This isn't for me. See you later [*shalom shalom*]." And that's it. Or he'll have to become like everyone else, follow the customs, the tradition. If all that isn't for him, it's all just a big show [*hatzagah g'dolah*]."

Other Arab subjects cite the problems with Jews and Arabs living next door to one another but take a more positive view of the ruling. Youssef regards the ruling as "progress" toward the goal of "full equality for all citizens." For Nadia, the decision is "great [*ahlah*]."

But I wouldn't want to join that battle. I wouldn't want to live with neighbors who don't want to accept me. It's a pointless fight [*ma'avak davka*], let's say it that way. It's pointless [*davka*]: I don't want to live with neighbors who don't want us. It's a pointless fight. In principle, the guy won. I respect him [*khol ha'cavod lo*] for being willing to invest so much effort, and I respect the Supreme Court. But it's meaningless [*stam*]. It's television, it's the media, it's a one-time issue. It could happen again if other people want [*to move to a Jewish town*]. But in the end, it doesn't do anything for me.

Majjed, too, approves of the principle but takes little pleasure in the thought of moving to a place like Katzir:

The Supreme Court permitted them to buy there? Unlike these guys who sought to buy a house in the village of Katzir, I wouldn't want to buy a house there. If it was just for the purpose of sending a message, it's totally fine. I agree with the message. Just as there are homes here in the Silwan that Jewish settlers took over [in East Jerusalem], so in Katzir Arabs can do likewise. Jewish houses in the Silwan in the middle of the Arab quarter that belongs to East Jerusalem! But if he intends to actually live quietly in the village of Katzir? That sounds a little strange to me.

When asked if he would ever consider leaving Umm al-Fahm, his hometown, for a Jewish village, Omer expands on the oddity of the Ka'adans' decision:

No, I wouldn't want to move from my city, because all of my friends and my entire heritage are in the city. I am connected to my tradition and to my society and I cannot get up and leave. I

would be like a stranger [*adam zar*]. I don't believe that Jewish society would accept me, but I myself wouldn't be happy to leave
my land and my society.

On the Katzir verdict, all five Arab subjects—the one who knew something about it and the four who did not—speak in one voice. It is a good ruling in that it recognizes Israeli Arabs' rights to equality of opportunity in
land buying, they say. It is praiseworthy as a step on the way to less discrimination and greater equality for Palestinian citizens of Israel. But practi-
cally, the case means very little to the vast majority of these citizens. In reality, very few would ever consider moving to a town in which they would be
surrounded by Jews, their lives directed by the Jewish holidays, their children taught in Jewish state schools. Only a handful of Arabs—Muslim or
Christian, religious or secular—would be willing to give up the rich communal traditions of their villages or towns, not to mention the land of their
birth, for the promise of a greener garden or a nicer house. And this is not
only because such a move entails leaving a town full of Arabs for one full of
Jews. None of the Arab subjects would countenance moving one day to a
Palestinian state, either—the establishment of which they all nevertheless
strongly support. According to Muhammad, the majority of Arabs—"and
I'm one hundred percent sure of this"—won't move to Palestine, should it
become a full-fledged state.

> First of all, it's hard for a person who was born here to leave the
> place. Here is where you were born and raised and raised your
> family. It's very difficult to leave your village and move to another
> village. When you move to another village, you become a foreign
> seedling [*neta zar*]. It's hard to get acclimated. They look at you
> like we look at those who come to us from the West Bank. In our
> village no one even leaves to live in other Arab villages! You live
> in the village, and you stay in the village. For example, I know a
> lot of people [Jews] who...the father is in Tel Aviv, one son is in
> Carmiel, another is in Be'er Sheva. With us [Arabs] it isn't like
> that....It goes against tradition and custom. That's one thing. The
> second thing: it's good for us here. We aren't segregated here. To
> the contrary: we have rights. We have everything. A good eco-
> nomic status. The reality is we live in a good situation from an
> economic point of view. Therefore we decide to stay here. I think
> everyone is like that. Surely in another five or six years a Palestin-
> ian state will arise. Only a few from our area will move there, be-
> cause, for example, there the standard of living will be lower.
> Aside from standard of living, you will feel like a foreign seedling
> and it's hard to acclimate. It's better here.

As for the other four Arab subjects, none of whom yet enjoys the economic security of Muhammad (being university students or recent gradu-

ates), the first reason for staying put—hesitating to leave one's home—is plenty. Majjed won't move to Palestine "because I am a resident of M'rar. My land is there and I will stay there." Nadia thinks that if she is to be a "true Palestinian," she should stay where she is, in Jerusalem. Omer says: "I won't leave my city [Umm al-Fahm], because if I leave my city it's as if I'm leaving my land behind." And Youssef concurs: "This is my land and I will stay here. I want the Palestinians to establish their state…but I won't live in a Palestinian state because I will continue to live where I was born."

These subjects' strong resistance to transplanting their lives to another locale is a consideration wholly absent from Chief Justice Barak's transplantation of *Brown* into the *Ka'adan* decision. In leaning on the concept of "separate but equal is inherently unequal," he ignores the prevalent Arab preference for state recognition and improved state funding of Arab towns rather than integration rights into Jewish towns. And he fails to address the parallel attitude among many Israeli Jews. As the comments of the subjects illustrate, even Jews who support the result in *Ka'adan* dispute the notion that equality requires Arabs and Jews to live in mixed localities.

Jewish Israeli Views on *Ka'adan*: "Oil and Water"

Jewish opponents of the ruling condemn the decision on a number of levels. The right-wing and religious parties decry it as "heralding the end of the State of Israel as the Jewish state" (a statement of the center-right Likud party); or marking "a black day for the Jewish people, Zionism and the State of Israel" (a Member of Knesset for the National Religious Party, representing Religious Zionists); or "destroying the state" by violating a *halacha* (dictate of Jewish law) that "prohibits selling land to non-Jews in the Land of Israel" (MKs from United Torah Judaism, an amalgam of Haredi parties).[16] Among the subjects in my study who oppose the ruling, three main arguments arise. The decision (1) erodes Israel's character as a Jewish state; (2) threatens the security of the Jewish state; or, a point supporters of the verdict cite as well, (3) presupposes an unrealistic and undesirable model of Jewish-Arab co-existence.

Zvi, the passionate Religious Zionist, voices the first objection, based on a full-bodied conception of the Jewish state:

> A: The Supreme Court ruled against the will of the state. The state religion determined that there is preference for dedicating the lands to Jews because this is a Jewish state. The Supreme Court ruled that this constitutes [illegal] discrimination. What does this say to me? It says to me that now there can be no preference given to a Jew to really perform Jewish redemption of Jewish land in the

Land of Israel. That is, from its point of view, there are no religious considerations here. ...

Q: Jews have special rights to the land that Arabs lack?

A: They are supposed to. For the same reason that this is the state of Israel, that this is the Land of Israel, the Land of Israel to which the Jewish People came to establish a national home. ... Preference means preference concerning Jewish land—that it must be for Jews. We define the Land of Israel as the Land of our Fathers, the Land of the Jews. Just as we define it as the Land of the Jews, that means that preference must be given to Jews to settle in it. It's very simple.

This argument challenges the idea of equality as a guiding value. Consistent with the leading Religious Zionist vision of the Jewish state, Zvi's claim points to the choice Israel must make when it faces a disconnect between democracy and Judaism: according to Zvi, the Jewish element must prevail. Equality for Arabs takes a back seat to the Jewish claim to ownership of all of the Land of Israel. Zvi also resents Chief Justice Barak's willingness, in rendering his decision, to contravene a state decision—that of the Israel Lands Administration, operating via the Jewish Agency—and to ignore all religious considerations. He thus sees the Katzir decision as an ominous sign of the wearing away of the "Jewish" side of the Jewish and democratic state.

While this first objection identifies a threat to Israel's religious essence, the second comes from Religious Zionists and Haredim, as well as some secular and traditional Jews, who worry about a threat to national security. Yoel, another Religious Zionist subject, explains the reason Israel supported the establishment of towns like Katzir in the Lower Galilee:

They specifically built Jewish towns in the middle to ensure that there would not be a big concentration of Arabs with no little Jewish towns in the middle. Now that's something that's in the national interest....Sometimes you find it's in your national interest to discriminate, so you discriminate! The Arabs should feel free to do whatever they want. But if you have a matter of national interest that it's important to build a Jewish settlement somewhere—and it's of national importance—we basically have a stable life here with the Arabs but sometimes you have to separate....When you try to build a Jewish town in the Galil where there's a big Arab concentration, that's in the national interest! So if you're going to build a town in an area of Arab concentration and it will be all Arab you are putting yourself in jeopardy!! And putting yourself in jeopardy is not smart.

In making this appeal to national security, Yoel, like many Jewish subjects, professes no personal bias against Arab citizens of Israel. But his embrace is tepid:

> I would like to see a society in which Arabs are not discriminated against. Everyone to my knowledge where I work is Jewish. I would have no problem if there were Arabs there. Again, as long as no one is threatening me or killing me, assuming that it's all nice and dandy, I have no problem with an Arab in any way. I would find it very refreshing even, I think…I would welcome him with both arms. I would have no problem if a neighbor in my building would be an Arab.

So Yoel would receive an Arab into his workplace or apartment building happily, as long as the Arab in question isn't threatening his life. (He admits he'd be uncomfortable if more than a few Arabs moved in next door.) When we look at some of the subjects' views, latent assumptions about Arabs become explicit. Nosson, a Haredi from Givat Ze'ev (a Jerusalem suburb, just across the 1967 border in the Samarian desert on the West Bank), thinks that "for Arabs to enter a Jewish settlement is a terrible threat [nora ve'ium]." Rita, a traditional Jewish woman of Moroccan origin who lives in Ra'anana, near Tel Aviv, says she feels that "an Arab isn't trustworthy: he'll meet you and sink a knife into your back. It's scary." Nehama, a traditional-turned-Haredi Jerusalemite, when asked about the Katzir case, lets loose:

> This isn't the state of the Jews. We have fought for so many years for this state to be a Zionist state and to be a Jewish state and suddenly we're giving them everything back. What did you fight for? What are you giving away? What "discrimination"? Should we bring Arabs into the [government's] security council, tell them all kinds of security secrets about the Nation of Israel? They are our enemy! We need a little logic, we need to keep our head on our shoulders. So what will be? So tomorrow someone will say: "Give [the Arab] your home" and they'll give away their home? That's discrimination? Where is the limit? They are clearly our enemy! I believe with a full heart that they are our enemy. It's sad we're giving them the state, to give them all the security of the People of Israel. Truly.

The third objection to the Katzir decision stretches across all sub-groups of Jews and is put forward even by subjects who praise the decision. It is premised on the same contention that led Majjed to call the Ka'adans "weird" and led Nadia to see the case as a "pointless struggle": Arabs, by and large, do not want to live with Jews, and Jews, by and large, do not want to live with Arabs.

Shmuel, an engineering professor at Haifa University, expands on this idea with particular passion. He becomes increasingly animated as he describes his view on the decision; it is the first time in the interview that his voice rises above an uninspired whisper:

A: *This* is something that I don't understand. From a judicial point of view, the Supreme Court is right. Because you have the freedom to live wherever you want. So you do have the choice. But this is not the natural choice. This is a matter of reason. Now what I mean by reason is that, you prefer to live in a neighborhood or an area where you can contribute or be enriched by the environment. Now if for example I take my family and go to [an Arab village] to live there, they don't want me. And I wouldn't want to live there because I don't have the same mentality, I don't have the same culture, I don't have the same language. There are so many differences, that actually there is a good reason *not* to be there. So for me I think that [the Ka'adans' court case] was more of something to do than to really want to live there. Because if you live in a neighborhood in which there are so many differences, then I think it would be better for you and for the environment or the neighborhood not to move there. And you can see this in Haifa. Haifa is a mixed city which has large Jewish and Druze populations and also Christians and this is something that is going on. You can see here and there odd Arabs in Jewish neighborhoods. But they are not accepted. Not accepted, I mean, culturally. They are not regarded very well. You don't see many Arabs learning in Israeli schools....The beauty of the scene is that everybody knows his place. So I know that I live in, I belong to a neighborhood where people behave like me. If my neighbor has other holidays and different mentalities, it doesn't go along. So I think [the Ka'adans' case] was more of a ploy to show that "I can enforce the law" [than an attempt to move to Katzir]...And I'm sure after the decision, when the family goes and lives in the neighborhood, they will be disturbed...how do you say...

Q: Discriminated against?

A: Not discriminated but not accepted. Disregarded. So I think that they are right but they are not smart: this is what I have to say. It's like a Jew would come and live in New York in a black neighborhood. Would you understand that? Or a black comes and lives in a Jewish neighborhood, how would you accept it? This is the same way. Judicially, it's OK. Mentally, culturally, you would feel horrible, right?! The same way!

Q: So you wouldn't pick up your family and move to an Arab village or an Arab town.

A: Of course not! Of course not!

Q: How would you feel if an Arab moved in next door?

A: There are some Arabs around here. But they are not accepted. They don't have friends...I speak with them. I have Arab students. I have people who I am engaged with. But I think that when you have cultures and mentalities that are different it is better for them to be separated than to be enforced to be mixed. Because they don't mix. And I think the best way to live in peace and harmony is if everybody is doing and has his own way of living. And the Jews live in Jewish neighborhoods. To live together is much more fundamental, because then you have the culture and holidays and ways of life and so forth, and they are different! And they don't mix....Now this is not racism! You need to understand, it is not racism. It is something I would say is a natural event, natural behavior. You can't take big fish and mix them with the small fish and say [bangs on table]: "Well, live together. You are all fish, right?" Of course they are all fish, but they have different mentalities, different behaviors. And they don't mix! If I could give you an example, there are materials that mix together and form solutions, and other materials that do not mix together.

Q: Oil and water.

A: Yes, oil and water. And if you take the oil and water and force it, it won't work.

I provide this lengthy excerpt because despite Shmuel's mildly racist undertones and the excesses of his analogy to the relationship of blacks and Jews in New York[17], many of the Jewish subjects—and all five Arab subjects—share the essence of his view. Tanya, a secular leftist, notes that although there is "a lot of mixing" in certain neighborhoods in the city of Haifa (where she grew up), "overall, there is little mixing...and there will be no synthesis. That's a fact. I think we'll have to go through another two hundred years or so at least before people will be open enough to learn to overcome" the differences that keep them in separate communities. Nevertheless, she approves of the ruling on liberal egalitarian grounds, as does liberal Shulamit: "Well, the [Supreme Court] was right! I don't think, if I were they, that I would want to live in a Jewish, an altogether Jewish, neighborhood. Just like I wouldn't want to live in an altogether Arab neighborhood. I don't mind living in a mixed neighborhood. So I don't know why they want it! But as far as the law is concerned, they have the same rights to buy the land as I do."

Importing *Brown v. Board*

In the U.S. Supreme Court's unanimous decision in *Brown v. Board of Education*, Chief Justice Earl Warren implicitly raises two important questions that help distinguish and direct the debate over Israel's Katzir case. The questions arise in light of a pair of passages near the end of the opinion. The first:

> To separate them [black children in grade and high schools] from others of similar age and qualifications solely because of their race generates a feeling of inferiority as to their status in the community that may affect their hearts and minds in a way unlikely ever to be undone.

After citing several sources attesting to the detrimental effect of segregation on black children, Warren writes,

> We conclude that in the field of public education the doctrine of "separate but equal" has no place. Separate educational facilities are inherently unequal.[18]

Emerging from these two sentences are puzzles as to the ruling's reach, on one hand, and its ultimate justification, on the other. The first puzzle—whether the doctrine of "separate but equal" might indeed have a place in fields other than public education—was resolved by the court in later rulings that extended the holding in *Brown* to transportation and other public accommodations. But the second puzzle remains. In the first sentence above, and with the much-discussed footnote eleven listing seven social science studies, Warren disputes the claim (made by Justice Brown in *Plessy v. Ferguson* in 1896) that segregation creates no "badge of inferiority" other than one that "the colored race chooses to. . .put upon it."[19] In the second sentence, however, he finds that separate is "inherently" unequal. Is separate in fact *inherently* unequal (in public education and elsewhere), or is it only contingently so? Does Warren need the social science evidence to establish his point? If so, does the adequacy of the ruling turn on the quality of the social science? Could segregated schools be justified, on Warren's reasoning, if it could be shown that they contribute to a richer educational experience and better self-confidence for blacks and whites alike? Many constitutional experts dismiss footnote eleven, finding the real rationale in *Brown* to lie in the contention—presented most eloquently by Justice Harlan in his *Plessy* dissent—that segregation is *inherently* unequal.

But because the social context of race in 1950's America differs so significantly from Jewish-Arab national-religious disputes in the Israel of today,

Chief Justice Barak's citation of "separate but equal is inherently unequal" in *Ka'adan* amplifies the ostensible confusion in *Brown*. Majjed, Muhammad, Nadia, Youssef and Omer all grew up in all-Arab towns, but they do not view that experience as one of stigmatization or oppression. They do not feel that living in separate towns is "insulting" or makes them into "social inferiors"—the negative effects of separation Barak identifies in his ruling. Far from it. These Arab respondents object to their villages and cities receiving "unequal" state care and investment, but not to their being "separate" from Jewish areas. As their comments indicate, their self-confidence, their cultural and national sense of belonging, their very notions of themselves, are bound up in their communities. They don't want to leave their homes—not for a Jewish town, not for a Palestinian state, and not for another Arab village inside Israel. Even those few Arabs who do desire entrance into Jewish towns—the Ka'adans, for instance—do so because they hope for a better material life, not because they feel a badge of inferiority in their current environs. If anything, moving to Katzir may win the Ka'adans a more pleasant neighborhood and better schools at the cost of a distinctively Arab life and a sense of cultural belonging: they risk uprooting themselves and becoming, in Muhammad's words, "foreign seedlings."

This dip into the minds of thirty-one diverse Israelis provides a crucial backdrop to understanding the Katzir decision and its aftermath. The primary lesson: Despite Barak's footnotes, the reasoning in *Brown v. Board of Education* is largely inapposite to the Israeli case. *Ka'adan* imports a principle into Israeli law that enjoys little support in any sector of the Israeli population. It represents a misguided, if well-intentioned, effort to protect Israeli Arabs' interests and elevate their status. As one commentator has pointed out, Barak "refrains from challenging the objectives of the state's policy regarding the main issues on the agenda of the Palestinian-Arab population in Israel...namely their collective rights as a national minority."[20] And as another observer claims, "American-style integration is almost inconceivable" in Israel because no demand for a Jewish-Arab melting pot, and no true civil rights movement, "can be observed in the Israeli context."[21] There is very little interest among Jews *or* Arabs for integration of this sort; both sectors believe equality is best pursued without it.

But what does this mean for the justifiability of the ruling in *Ka'adan*? On any account of liberal equality, a policy that puts the basic interests of citizens belonging to one national-religious group ahead of those belonging to another is to be regarded with high suspicion. The *Ka'adan* court seems to agree with this perspective, but it leaves the crucial socio-economic issues far in the background. It makes no mention of the gross disparities of Ministry of Housing funding for Jewish and Arab towns and villages, or of the controversy over state expropriation of Arab lands.[22] It thus makes little headway toward correcting the state's inadequate regard for the interests of its

Arab citizens. What does liberal equality require? Is integration, à la *Brown*, the answer? Liberalism should demand proportionate state support for Arab towns. It should insist upon material equality: Jewish towns shouldn't be green and lush and safe while Arab villages are dirty and unkempt with poor schools. But this is (so far) only to say that there should be equality in state funding and attention for Jewish and Arab towns, not that there must necessarily be a turn away from the idea of separate Jewish and Arab towns as the dominant paradigm. The subjects' views provide some important context here: there is a real interest, among both Arabs and Jews, in separate localities for their respective sectors. Joint Jewish-Arab towns like Neve Shalom/Wahat al-Salam[23] and Jaffa—while intriguing options for some—need not serve as models for wholesale integration of the two sectors.

Although the court decision may not have been the place for a sociological assessment of Arab and Jewish living patterns or for a full critique of Israel's land policy—a judge's main task, of course, is to address the legal question before him—Barak's use of *Brown* seems oblivious to ideas prevalent in Israel's political culture and to the stark differences between the Israeli and American cases. It is radically decontextualized. It thus rings hollow—and has produced little substantive change—despite the force of the liberal rhetoric found in the text of the opinion. As John Rawls emphasized in his later writings, a receptive political culture is crucial to liberalism's success. To foist an idea on people who think very differently, whose history and traditions reflect a different reality, is not only to show insufficient regard for the diversity of democratic political cultures (as Rawls claims in *The Law of Peoples*[24]), it is to risk political failure. "In the long run," Rawls writes, "the leading interpretations of constitutional essentials are settled politically. A persistent majority, or an enduring alliance of strong enough interests, can make of the Constitution what it wants."[25]

It is difficult to say exactly what Israelis will make of their emerging constitution, but it seems unlikely that significant portions of either the Arab or Jewish sectors will champion joint living arrangements in the foreseeable future. A state policy that allows and even facilitates many of its citizens' choices to live in separate localities is justified, as long as conditions in the towns are truly and meaningfully equal. Disparities in housing budget allocations that unfairly advantage Jews should be eliminated. At least until such equality is reached, however—and there is reason to doubt this is possible—there should be an entry option for Arabs into Jewish towns, and vice versa. No plausible national security risk is involved in this arrangement (despite dubious claims to the contrary),[26] no damage to a legitimate conception of a Jewish state is threatened (by legitimate I mean one that also takes into account Israel's democratic character), and those citizens who prefer to live in self-contained villages have little cause to worry. Why shouldn't they worry? Because, as the interviews suggest, very few Arabs are likely to take advantage of the opportunity to move into Jewish localities, and perhaps even fewer Jews are likely to want to move to Arab towns. *De facto* segregation will continue even as integration becomes more of a possibility for those few who seek it.

Ka'adan properly provides all Israelis with a right to enjoy free and equal access to live where they choose on state lands. On a more symbolic level, it ameliorates Israel's poor record of unequal treatment for Arab citizens. If the court had provided a more direct remedy than the grossly ineffectual one contained in the original decision, therefore, the holding in *Ka'adan* would have been correct. But the reasoning was aloof to context, and thus flawed. Discriminatory admissions policies like Katzir's are *not* wrong because they brand Israel's Arab minority with a badge of inferiority or impose a social stigma on them; as we've heard, from Israel's Arabs themselves, they do nothing of the kind. These policies are wrong, rather, because they lock individual Arab citizens out of opportunities to pursue better lives for themselves and their children and communicate a message of state disregard for a fifth of its citizens. They attempt to enforce a separation in an inappropriate context—a context within which conditions on the Arab side are undeniably and egregiously unequal to those on the Jewish side.

If this, and not stigmatization, is indeed the problem with Katzir's exclusion of Arabs, should the right articulated in *Ka'adan* continue to be protected if and when Israel improves its land policies and achieves real equality between Arab and Jewish towns? Or will the justification for *Ka'adan* (as I have reformulated it) then run out, as the rationale in *Brown* might be argued to disappear with the publication of new studies showing positive effects of, say, all-black schools? Should Katzir be able to keep the Ka'adans out, in other words, if Baqa al-Gharbiya were to become the shining village down the hill? I fear this question won't soon arise, given that the disparities between Arab and Jewish living conditions in Israel are only worsening. If true equality is someday reached, however, the state will need to undertake a comprehensive reassessment of its land policy. On one hand, it seems wrong to ignore the desires of many Arabs and Jews who may still want to live separately. On the other hand, policing such a separation, except in certain kinds of communities such as *kibbutzim* and *moshavim*, is a serious limitation on property rights and a roadblock to potential social change that neither sector might envision today.

Notes

1. Ka'adan v. Israel Lands Administration, H.C. 6698/95 (2000). Translations from the Hebrew court decision below are mine. For an excerpted English version of the decision, see *The Jewish Political Tradition, Volume Two: Membership,* ed. Michael

Walzer, Menachem Lorberbaum and Noam J. Zohar (New Haven: Yale University Press, 2003), 545-54.

2. Quoted in Serge Schmemann, "Israeli Learns Some Are More Israeli Than Others," *New York Times*, 1 March 1998, 1, 10. See also Moshe Reinfeld, "Land-Hunting Arab Couple Puts High Court in a Quandary," *Ha'aretz*, 18 February 1998.

3. Ka'adan v. Israel Lands Administration, § 5.

4. Ka'adan v. Israel Lands Administration, § 40.

5. Ka'adan v. Israel Lands Administration, § 30.

6. Buchanan v. Warley, 245 U.S. 60 (1917).

7. Ka'adan v. Israel Lands Administration, § 30. Chief Justice Barak's claim is technically accurate but naïve of the sociological reality in Katzir (pop. 2000): the town is home to no Haredi Jews and almost one thousand immigrants from the former Soviet Union. According to one resident, "That the Ka'adans are Arabs is irrelevant. We wouldn't accept a Hasid from B'nei Brak either. It's a matter of integration into the life of the community." Quoted in David Ratner, "No Arabs nor Haredim Need Apply Here," *Ha'aretz*, 9 March 2000.

8. Ka'adan v. Israel Lands Administration, § 40. In contrast to the *Brown* ruling, which applied to all segregated public schools in the country, the Katzir case involved one applicant who wanted to build a home in a single settlement. In light of the gaping difference in scope between *Brown* and *Ka'adan*, Ruth Gavison is thus correct that "it is not at all clear why there's a need in this case for such an extended timeframe." See Ruth Gavison, "Ha-omnam yehudit ve-demokratit? Mashmauto shel din Katzir" (Truly Jewish and democratic? The significance of the Katzir decision), *Kivunim Hadashim: Journal of Zionism and Judaism* no. 2 (April 2000) [Hebrew]: 28n1.

9. Justice Heshin told the ACRI attorney: "Your petition was based on the principle of equality. So let the Ka'adans undergo the same process as anyone else wishing to join the society." Quoted in Dan Izenberg, "Katzir Wins Right to Interview Arab Applicants," *Jerusalem Post*, 2 April 2001.

10. Aryeh Dayan, "Reasons to Discriminate, Part Three," *Ha'aretz*, 17 September 2003.

11. See Dayan, "Reasons to Discriminate." In August of 2003, a leader of the Jewish settlement of Eshchar in the Upper Galilee told a group of visiting American Jews (of whom I was one) that there is a single "hard criterion" for determining whom the hilltop town accepts into its community: "you must be Jewish." (Beyond that, there are a number of soft criteria, largely social factors, according to which the council chooses new members.) When I asked the leader how this policy could possibly be squared with standing Israeli law after the Ka'adan decision, he suggested with a wink that turning down an Arab applicant would be easy to justify—even according to the recent ruling. The council could simply cite reasons other than the applicant's Arab nationality in explaining the negative response. But in Eshchar, unlike in Katzir, the question has never come up: in the nearly twenty years of the settlement's existence, no Arab has approached Eshchar's town council hoping to build a home.

12. Ziv Maor, "Arab Family Finally To Get an ILA Offer for a Katzir Plot," *Ha'aretz*, 1 October 2003 and Dan Izenberg, "ILA Allocates Land in Katzir to Arab Family," *Jerusalem Post*, 1 October 2003.

13. Yuval Yoaz and David Ratner, "ILA to Allow Israeli Arab Family to Build in Jewish Town," *Ha'aretz*, 10 May 2004; "Adel Ka'adan—The Freedom to Live in Coexistence," NIF News, <http://www.nif.org/content.cfm?id=2180&currbody=2 News>

(3 August 2005). For another account of the couple's struggle, see Eetta Prince-Gibson, "Letter from Katzir: Won't You Be My Neighbor?" *Hadassah Magazine*, May 2001, 47-49.

14. Two Israeli Arabs seeking to buy an apartment in Ramle, a city of 53,000 Jews and 13,000 Arabs, were turned away, they say, because of their nationality. The 221-unit complex in question is designated for demobilized soldiers—which is to say, almost exclusively Jews—under the age of 35. The men petitioned the Court in April 2001. Ha'aretz Staff, "Ramle Arabs Go to Court Over 'Vets-Only' Housing," *Ha'aretz*, 23 April 2001.

15. The decision sparked a backlash from Israel's right wing. Yuval Yoaz, "AG Mazuz Rules JNF Land Can Now Be Sold to Arabs," *Ha'aretz*, 27 January 2005; Yuval Yoaz and Amiram Barkat, "Rightist MK: Fire AG for Letting Non-Jews Buy JNF Land," *Ha'aretz*, 28 January 2005.

16. Quoted in Gideon Alon, "Court Ruling Outrages Right," *Ha'aretz*, 9 March 2000.

17. The 2000 census shows that New York City is, indeed, very segregated by race. The segregation does not, however, approach the scale of that between Arabs and Jews in Israel. Jews and blacks live together (though, since the riots of the 1990s, not always peacefully) in Crown Heights, Brooklyn, and elsewhere in the city. The factors of land, religion and nationality are much less pronounced (to put it mildly) in New York than they are in the Israel. And there are no legal restrictions, of course, on neighborhoods in which members of various races or nationalities may rent or purchase homes.

18. Brown v. Board of Education of Topeka, 347 U.S. 483 (1954). Excerpted in *Brown v. Board of Education: A Brief History with Documents*, ed. Waldo E. Martin, (New York: Bedford/St. Martin's, 1998), 173-74.

19. Plessy v. Ferguson, 163 U.S. 538 (1896). Excerpted in *Brown v. Board of Education: A Brief History with Documents*, ed. Martin, 80.

20. Tikva Parnass-Honig, "The High Court Decision on Katzir: Nemystification [sic] of Its Claims for Equality," *News From Within* 14, no. 4, April 2000, 3.

21. Nomi Maya Stolzenberg, "The Phantom of Integration" (commentary on the *Ka'adan* case) in *The Jewish Political Tradition*, ed. Walzer et al., 554-61. Stolzenberg overstates the case a bit here. There is certainly more of a concern for advancing civil rights in Israel than there is in, say, Saudi Arabia. The Association for Civil Rights in Israel, for example, has been influential in defending gender equality, religious freedom, freedom of expression, gay and lesbian rights and Israeli Arab equality, among other human rights concerns. Still, despite some successes in court, there is hardly overwhelming domestic popular support for these causes. Only five percent of ACRI's annual budget stems from Israeli contributions, with the balance coming largely from American and European sources.

22. One legal advocacy group for Israeli Arabs points out that the state owns 93 percent of the land of Israel and allocates only two percent of its housing funds to Israeli Arabs—a rate one-tenth of that which would be proportionate to their 20 percent share of the population. Adallah (The Legal Center for the Rights of the Arab Minority in Israel), *Legal Violations of Arab Minority Rights in Israel: A Report on Israel's Implementation of the International Convention on the Elimination of all Forms of Racial Discrimination* (Shfaram, Israel: Adalah, March 1998), 49.

23. A 45-family Arab-Jewish village in central Israel founded by a Dominican monk in 1972. Its name means "Oasis of Peace." See www.nswas.com for details.

24. "If all societies were required to be liberal, then the idea of political liberalism would fail to express due toleration for other acceptable ways (if such there are, as I assume) of ordering society." John Rawls, *The Law of Peoples* (Cambridge: Harvard University Press, 1999), 59.

25. John Rawls, "The Domain of the Political and Overlapping Consensus," in *Collected Papers*, ed. Samuel Freeman (Cambridge: Harvard University Press, 2000), 496.

26. Several right-of-center Israelis I have spoken with say that the Saudis or other Arab governments plan to take advantage of the *Ka'adan* ruling by paying Israeli Arab families handsome sums to move to Jewish settlements in the Galilee, thereby changing the demographic balance and dismantling the Jewish state from the inside. I have encountered no evidence of such a plot, however, and it seems farfetched—especially in light of the dearth of Arab requests for admittance into Jewish towns in the six years since *Ka'adan* was decided.

Part IV
Conclusions

Chapter 10
Lessons From Israel

Two disconnects haunt religion and liberal democracy in Israel: the gulf between Israeli and American understandings of "separation of religion and state" and the rift between Jews' and Arabs' visions for reconstituting Israel's religion-state arrangement. The former poses a theoretical problem for liberalism; the latter presents a political and social challenge to Israeli lawmakers attempting to forge a constitution that represents the interests of all Israeli citizens.

We had a strong hint, in chapter 4, that Israelis' conceptions of separation of religion and state are different from those governing understandings of First Amendment law in the United States and quite different from the neutrality principle some see as the heart of liberalism. Many of the Jewish subjects, we saw there, claim to support both the concept of separation *and* the idea of Israel as a Jewish state. In chapters 5, 6 and 7, we added some flesh to that conundrum, seeing which aspects of the Jewish state Israelis think are compatible with separation of religion and state and which are incompatible. The theoretical challenge is heightened, however, by the arguments Israelis make in defense of separation. Their reasoning often flows from analysis that liberalism would endorse, if not explicitly rely upon. One of the most frequently raised arguments in this regard goes back to Locke's argument for religious toleration: the state may not legitimately coerce individual compliance with the dictates of religion, because religion is a private matter. Another is based on equality of duties: the state may not grant benefits to one group of citizens at the expense of another.

If liberalism's strongest reasons for separating religion and state are the same reasons Israelis tend to cite when advocating a separation, why do the details of Israelis' favored religion-state arrangement differ so markedly from the requirements liberal theorists suggest? In other words, liberals and many Israelis agree that religion is best kept out of politics in order to protect the individual's right to worship, or not worship, as she chooses. How, then, can many Jewish Israelis support separation while at the same time endorsing Israel's Jewish symbols, kosher government kitchens and state-funded religious education? Why are these liberal Israelis tentative and divided in their assessment of laws governing public Shabbat observance, rather than strongly against them? How can the notions of separation of religion and state that prevail in Israel's political culture be analyzed in connection to the more familiar liberal and American versions thereof?

The key to understanding this puzzle rests in part on a second disconnect, less easily resolved: the conflict between Jewish and Arab assessments of Israel's religious establishment. Stated conceptually, I argued in chapter 4, the difference is between separating *religion* and state (Jewish Israelis' platform) and separating *Judaism*, or the Jewish nation, from the state (Israeli Arabs' platform). Looking at the details, we find that the issues of the highest salience to Jews—marriage law and draft deferments for yeshiva students, and to a lesser extent, issues like Shabbat restrictions—are nowhere to be found on Arabs' agenda. And while many liberal Jews appreciate the need for substantive equality for the Arab minority, these issues are generally not the ones that stir their political zeal, and Israeli Jews almost universally reject the Arab demands to dejudaize Israel's public ethos. The Israeli Arab position, no less than the liberal Israeli Jewish position, differs from a classic notion of religion-state separation: in their "state of all its citizens," Israel will continue to dole out control of personal status issues to Muslim and Christian (and Jewish) religious courts, and will continue to fund religious education for each community.

Israeli Jews who favor separation of religion and state yet advocate a Jewish state do not view kosher state kitchens, the menorah, the Star of David, the national anthem or even limited Sabbath observance or funding for religious education as *religion*-state linkages. They see these as part of a secular Israeli nationalism, or as reflections of Zionism, or as a merely civil religion. This lens results in a somewhat distorted view: these and other features of the state, contrary to Israelis' claims, do in fact connote affiliations between religion and state. But this secular Jewish Israeli outlook is telling, even in its partiality. It calls into question the knee-jerk separationism characterizing much of contemporary liberal thought according to which *any* type of religion-state connection is inherently suspect.

The source of the sweeping liberal resistance to religion in politics, however, is not difficult to identify. The various connections between religion and state examined in part II and part III illustrate many of the worries that liberals have about religion infiltrating the political world: religious freedom jeopardized (Israel's marriage laws), religious privileges overblown (draft deferments), religious minorities excluded (the Golan Heights referendum debate). But looking at these quite different examples should push us to analyze each religion-state linkage separately, and we should not be too quick to dismiss every such association as out of bounds. Neither Arabs nor secular Jews are troubled by a broad array of connections between religion and state—from kosher state kitchens, to funding for religious education, to limited Shabbat observance in the public sphere. To the contrary: many of the subjects, though not religious (or not Jewish), express compelling justifications for some of these policies. The fact that there are many ways in which religion is apt to produce or result in injustice when associated with the state should not obscure the fact that not all linkages are equally problematic in their essence—and that some may be benign or even rich additions to a liberal democratic regime. The question that closed chapter 4—is a Jewish and democratic state possible?—thus has a complex and nuanced reply.

After delving into the ways in which Israelis regard their state and relate to its Jewish and democratic aspects, we see that there is no easy response to the question of whether religion is compatible with liberalism. The only answer to such an undifferentiated query is: yes, no and maybe. As we draw conclusions about the question of religion in a liberal state, the watchword is caution. As Wittgenstein writes, "one thinks that one is tracing the outline of the thing's nature over and over again, [but] one is merely tracing round the frame through which we look at it."[1] For the same reason that riveting on the American experience obscures some aspects of what liberalism requires, reasoning from the Israeli case to the universal is dangerous. We should resist assuming that the conventional American liberal ideal of separation is the single worthwhile interpretation of how to respect religious liberty, *and* we should be wary of accepting my Israeli subjects' ideas at face value. Still, the views of the respondents are instructive in their contrasts and puzzlements. A certain wisdom about questions of religion and state lies in their (often dueling) comments.

Applying the general conclusion from chapter 1, where I argued that religion-state questions should be debated on their merits rather than discarded out of hand, below I evaluate different kinds of religion-state connections by asking what liberal purposes they may serve and what risks to liberal values they may pose. Three different types of religion-state interactions may be distinguished according to the degree of suspicion with which we ought to regard them: symbolic interactions (religion represented in a state's flag, national anthem, holidays and public ethos), financial interactions (religion supported in state budgets for educational and other services), and theological interactions (religion directly identified with the state apparatus for the purposes of developing, applying and enforcing religious law).

Because the issues are complex and vary significantly from polity to polity—and because, as we have seen, the variations in political culture and social context make a difference in justification—abstract principles are not especially helpful in guiding normative judgments about religion-state interactions. As Oliver Wendell Holmes wrote in his famous dissent in *Lochner v. New York*, "general propositions do not decide concrete cases." The claims, for instance, that a state must "protect religious liberty" or "remain neutral with regard to religion," or "tolerate minority cultures" raise more questions than they resolve, and untenably float above relevant differences in political context. In suggesting guidelines on religious issues, then, I supplement the language of political philosophy with a general, but less rigid, evaluative tool from jurisprudence: standards of judicial review. These standards are often presented as the "level of suspicion" with which a particular policy ought to be regarded: low, intermediate or high. Each corresponding standard (respectively: rational-basis scrutiny, intermediate scrutiny and strict scrutiny) guides deliberation by asking how worrisome certain kinds of government pursuits are as potential violations of individual rights. A more rigorous standard is applied to policies that fit in a more worrisome category. So a judge, and a liberal interpreter, should look more carefully at certain kinds of policies than others, and demand more in the way of a justification—that is, a more compelling state interest and a tighter means-end link between the policy and the state interest in question.

By turning from my transcripts to this heuristic strategy, I am not leaving the Israeli subjects' views behind. I am, rather, stepping back to consider the arguments from the interviews in a more critical light and to use this critical engagement to draw general conclusions about the opportunities and risks of public religion in a liberal democracy. The judicial analogy is not meant to imply a cold, detached form of reason but one that is engaged, attentive and sympathetic. I see myself not wrapped in a judicial robe but open to the ideas of a very diverse subset of the Israeli polity, attempting to conscientiously consider and evaluate those ideas. It is impossible to draw conclusions with which all of my interview subjects would agree. Instead, I would expect everyone in the interview pool will find something with which to disagree in what follows, and I have no doubt that several subjects will find themselves in vehement disagreement. I will be satisfied if I address their worthiest arguments seriously and fairly.

One basic point was revealed in the interviews: simply calling for "separation of religion and state" is insufficient. Such a position is not only indeterminate; it forecloses some connections between religion and state that are compatible with liberalism while failing to clarify exactly why others are worrisome or dangerous. In the three sections below, I make a case for the following:

1. *Symbols*: Symbolic religious elements in the state, and noncoercive public observance of certain values and holidays, while at times illegitimate, are generally the least suspicious and the least problematic from the perspective of liberalism. The question of symbols divides, though, into less and more

problematic elements. What I call "plural" religious affiliations need satisfy only low-level scrutiny, while "exclusivist"
affiliations should be regarded with somewhat heightened
suspicion.

2. *Funding Religion:* All questions involving religion and the expenditure of government funds or the distribution of civic duties, while in many cases compatible with liberal ideals, ought
to be regarded with heightened (intermediate) scrutiny. Although there are compelling liberal justifications for providing financial backing for religious services and religious education, or for exempting some citizens from the duties others
must perform, the potential for abuse, divisiveness and discrimination is high. Whether a liberal state appropriately un-
dertakes these kinds of policies will reflect the state's overall
character—its political culture, history and founding principles—and whether it identifies with a particular religion. It
should, in all cases, beware the risks.

3. *Imposing Religion:* The highest scrutiny should be reserved for
government policies that take sides not only on religious
questions but on theological questions—i.e., not only affiliate
with Judaism but take on the mantle of defining what is and
what is not proper in Judaism—or that subject individuals'
rights to the control of extra-governmental religious authorities. The standard I suggest here is one of strict scrutiny, the
level of judicial review deemed nearly impossible to survive.
So nearly every religion-state interaction in this category
should be ruled out in a liberal democratic state.

Symbols, Holidays and the Public Ethos:
Low to Intermediate Scrutiny

Does liberalism demand that symbols marking the boundaries of a state's
public ethos welcome all citizens equally? Does it entail the removal of any
religious vestiges from state holidays? Does it require a state to speak to all
its citizens in an impartial way? Two contrasting responses to these questions might be sketched that draw upon different views about the nature and
moral status of "expressive harms" committed by democratic nation-states[2]:

1. Liberal states must choose national symbols and holidays
that are neutral or broad enough in meaning that all citizens
can freely identify with them without compromising their
core beliefs or values; *or*

2. Liberal states need not worry about the effect of their symbolic speech on its citizens at all; those who identify with the
symbols will do so, those who don't, won't; state expression
can do no harm.

Some liberals sensitive to the expressive harms states are capable of inflicting might be inclined to choose the first option. In urging official state neutrality, this position extends Ronald Dworkin's notion of equality as "equal concern and respect"[3] from its application in matters of distributive justice to symbolic questions of how a state represents itself to its citizens and to the world. A liberal state, on this view, has no business expressing an official connection with a single religion, nation or people through symbols such as its flag or national anthem. The state, respecting the fact of pluralism, should choose unifying holidays (such as Thanksgiving in the United States) and neutral symbols (such as stripes) whose motifs cannot reasonably be rejected by any citizen.

Although this rubric for evaluating Israel's state symbols has initial appeal, it falters when we realize that expressive harms come in a range of intensities, not all of which can, or should, be avoided. More specifically, it fails to draw an important distinction between two quite different types of religion-state connections that fall under this category: what we might call *plural state affiliations* in which the state endorses one way but makes room for others (national holidays, languages and calendars, for example) and *exclusivist state affiliations* in which the state, in Hobbesian mode, consolidates all competing claims into a single product (e.g., national symbols such as flags, anthems and emblems). In both cases the state is expressly siding with a particular religion and abandons any semblance of official neutrality.[4] But there is a significant difference between the two: Minority groups may, with appropriate legislative provisions, "opt out" of the *plural* state affiliations with religion and enjoy a parallel religious affiliation of their own. For example, although Saturday is the official day of rest in Israel, Muslims and Christians are not forced to partake in this weekly holiday or to abide by the restrictions on the opening of businesses that apply to Jews. According to the law, non-Jews may celebrate their own Sabbaths on Friday or Sunday, as is their custom.

As the name implies, though, *exclusivist* state affiliations are univocal and ask citizens to make a starker choice: to participate or not to participate. When it comes to a flag or an anthem, citizens can "take it or leave it": they can fly the flag or not, sing the national anthem or not, see themselves as represented in the symbols or not.[5] On these matters and with these media, the state does not permit alternate voices a say. There are no separate flags that non-Jewish Israelis may choose to fly, no alternative anthems (neither lyrics nor melody) that non-Jewish Israelis may choose to sing, no multiple official state emblems that non-Jewish Israelis may choose to design.[6] In these areas, the state not only *links itself* with a religious image, it claims a *monopoly* over that linkage. It not only endorses Judaism, we might say, it makes that endorsement exclusive and implicitly prohibits alternatives. Of course, individuals are free to sing or fly or think anything they like (although it was a crime until recently to display a Palestinian flag in Israel); but in doing so citizens cannot be said to be representing the State or reconstituting or pluralizing its symbols. Attempts to do any of these things, depending on the laws in force, will be subversive at worst, irrelevant at best.

The distinction between exclusivist and plural religious affiliations, as patterns of the subjects' responses suggest in chapter 8, entails a difference in their moral status as well. Recall that Arab and Jewish Israelis disagree sharply about the Jewish symbols associated with the state. Jews (with the exception of most Haredim) broadly support the Star of David on the flag and the Zionist references in the national anthem, even if they sometimes do so with tepid voices, while many Arabs see these and other manifestations of the Jewish state as symbols of exclusion, discrimination and alienation. There is much less disagreement, however, concerning what I have called *plural* public expressions of Judaism, such as kosher state kitchens and Sabbath and Jewish holiday celebrations: Jews and Arabs alike express varying levels of support (ranging from indifference to enthusiasm) for these elements of the public ethos. This variance in the quality of Jewish-Arab disputes—agreement on the acceptability of certain Jewish elements of the public ethos alongside sharp disagreement over others—marks a substantive difference between the liberal suitability of the two sub-types of religion-state linkages on the symbolic level. In short, plural religious symbols are only mildly suspicious in a liberal state, while exclusivist symbols are somewhat more suspicious.

Religious symbols of the plural type may constitute expressive harms in a liberal state, but these harms are seldom serious. When considered in light of their benefits, as my study's subjects (both Jewish and Arab) apparently did, non-coercive plural religious affiliations should not be seen as especially problematic from a liberal perspective. Kosher state kitchens do not restrict private eating habits; do not violate religious scruples of those who do not keep kosher; allow individuals of widely different religious backgrounds to eat together, perhaps stimulating greater social cohesion; and affirm the society's broadly defined Jewish ethos. Exclusivist affiliations, however, should be more suspicious from the perspective of liberalism. These affiliations—if not only exclusivist but also exclusionary—may provide no means for some citizens to view themselves as represented or as full and equal partners in a regime. As several of my Arab subjects passionately argued, the Star of David and Hatikva don't just leave them cold. These exclusivist religious symbols, for Majjed and Youssef, Nadia and Omer, are "alienating" and "racist": they draw Arab citizens, nearly one of every five Israelis, out of the circle.

How should we regard these charges? We should begin by addressing whether, despite their more illiberal potential, religiously rooted exclusivist symbols are ever compatible with a liberal state. The answer to that question, as a quick survey of world regimes shows, must be yes. That is to say: few if any liberal democracies would pass the muster of the Dworkinian neutralist standard. The United Kingdom's flag, recognized but never legally adopted as the national flag, features the intersection of three crosses: the red St. George's flag of England, the white St. Andrews's cross of Scotland and the red (diagonal) St. Patrick's cross of Ireland. Although the design of the Union Jack may aim to satisfy both Englishmen and Scots, it may be read to exclude the Welsh, not to mention all Britons who are not Protestant. By placing St. George's flag in the foreground, atop the others, the flag also communicates a political history of English domination over the other two kingdoms and implies a continuing symbolic claim to Ireland, notwithstanding the fact that only Northern Ireland has been part of the U.K. since 1921.[7]

Even in some states with constitutionally mandated separation of church and state—France and Ukraine, to pick two—the seemingly neutral stripes of color carry religious meaning, or at least stem from religious sources.[8] Interestingly, one of the few states whose flag would arguably pass the most rigorous test of expressive harm is Costa Rica, a state that is officially (if benignly) linked to Catholicism.[9] And it doesn't take religious symbols to cause harm. At various points in the history of the United States, blacks saw slavery when they looked at the American flag; Native Americans saw conquest and colonization. That they may not feel these negative reactions today, or not feel them as strongly (although many certainly still do), is due not to a change in the symbols but to progress in the status of indigenous and minority groups. On the neutralist interpretation, the very existence of Israel as a self-described Jewish state may constitute an impermissible expressive harm against its non-Jewish citizens. But this *reductio* equates, as the United Nations once did, Zionism with racism. [10]

Given the inescapability of non-neutrality, there is no reason to regard all exclusivist religious symbols—simply because they are religious—as proscribed by liberalism. To do so would transform liberalism into a doctrine denying independent states the right to even the most rudimentary form of political culture. It would thus give liberalism little grip in addressing solutions to problems in the real world. As Yael Tamir writes,

> every state must operate within a cultural-historical context; it must have an official language(s), a flag, an anthem, public holidays and public celebrations. It must build monuments, print money and stamps, adopt a historical narrative and a vision of the future. As feminists and members of national and racial minorities discovered long ago, the idea that a state can be void of any cultural, historical, or linguistic affiliation is a misleading illusion—which is not only naïve but also oppressive.[11]

Yet the comments of the Arab subjects echo in our ears: every Arab interviewee but Muhammad expresses profound disagreement with Israel's state symbolism. The other four become palpably upset when discussing the Star of David, the menorah, or the national anthem. Do their claims have any grounding within a theory of political liberalism? Yes, in a sense. But the claims of the Jewish subjects who approve of their flag and anthem—some of whom express feelings of deep attachment to these symbols—have a home within liberal theory as well. The challenge is how Israel might achieve what Rawls terms a "proper patriotism" reflecting its majority's religio-national culture while also providing the outlines of a society to which all of its citizens may stake a claim.

Despite its several unfulfilled—or as-yet-unrealized—promises, Israel's Declaration of Establishment addresses that very challenge. Israel was established, as the Declaration makes clear, as a Jewish state. Its orientation, its history, its leaders, its organizations, its mission and its people were (and are) predominantly Jewish. But there is really only a single concrete element in the Declaration that qualifies as "Jewish": that the new state will be "open to the immigration of Jews from all countries of their dispersion." In contrast, although the word "democracy" is never used, the Declaration proposes a number of liberal-democratic principles:

> The State of Israel...will promote the development of the country for the benefit of all its inhabitants; will be based on the precepts of liberty, justice and peace taught by the Hebrew Prophets; will uphold the full social and political equality of all its citizens, without distinction of race, creed or sex; will guarantee full freedom of conscience, worship, education and culture; will safeguard the sanctity and inviolability of the shrines and Holy Places of all religions; and will dedicate itself to the principles of the Charter of the United Nations.[12]

Of course, many background features that made the state Jewish go unmentioned in the Declaration. But the adoption of Hatikva as the national anthem and the choice of the Star of David for the flag's central symbol is not a story about sticking it to the Arabs.[13] It is a story of Zionism, a nationalist movement that arose in the late nineteenth century, seeking to develop national symbolism representing its people's history and to bring together a large and diverse coalition of Jews from Europe—riven though they were about the proper character, if any, that ought to define a Jewish state. A fair assessment of the situation, I think, would conclude that the Zionist movement, and then the State of Israel, were not "acting on an improper attitude" (Anderson and Pildes's phrase) when it decided on these symbols. Israel did not undertake its plans with the express or hidden purpose of communicating a message of disdain or exclusion for its Arab minority. However, as

Anderson and Pildes argue, the inappropriateness of an action is a product not only of a state's "conscious purposes and intentions," but also of the social or public meaning of the action itself. This means that expressive harms can be committed inadvertently: a state might act "negligently or thoughtlessly"; it may operate "in ignorance of social conventions or norms"; or it may act on latent but unconscious "attitudes or assumptions."[14]

We should, then, adopt neither of the two principles with which we began this section. Contrary to the first, strict neutrality of symbols and culture is an unnecessary and futile aspiration a liberal state. But contrary to the second principle, expressive harms do hurt; some hurt a lot; and liberal states must be mindful of the very real damage they can cause. Rejecting these extremes should lead us to a middle way:

> Liberal states need not be neutral and need not limit themselves to universally applicable symbols and holidays; they may, instead, specify symbols and festivals that refer to the history and aspirations of its majority even if minority groups find it difficult or impossible to relate to them, *provided that* (a) the symbols do not connote a negative message about the minority group and (b) minority groups may celebrate their own holidays freely.

If states should be seen as justified in using at least some particularistic motifs in their symbols, how do we determine what is acceptable and what is not? How do we navigate the tenuous boundary between unobjectionable expressions of national solidarity and intolerable attacks on an out-group?

There may be no principle that will always yield a clear-cut distinction. But part of the answer involves the reasons and purposes that lie behind the choice of symbols. If Israel, for example, is responsible for inflicting illiberal expressive harms on its non-Jewish population, it seems guilty not of purposive action but of negligence: its leaders may have lacked the foresight to predict that Arab citizens of Israel would become so dissatisfied with their lack of representation on Israel's flag and in its national anthem. Perhaps the founders of Israeli should have known that in addition to stirring patriotic fervor in Israeli Jews who wave their flags on Israeli Independence Day, the images of the Star of David and *tallit* would express a message to non-Jews that they are unequal participants in the national ethos. With regard to holidays, on the other hand, Israel was far from negligent. It made explicit legal provision for Muslims and Christians to celebrate their own Sabbaths and holidays; as Muhammad comments, "we have autonomy."

Two additional considerations suggest why the middle-way rubric is justified and how it should be applied: one about the way a message is communicated, and another about how it is heard. On the speaker's end, there is a moral distinction between an intended and an inadvertent expression of harm (one that Anderson and Pildes do not discuss). Returning to the distinction between plural and exclusivist religious affiliations, imagine if Israel had refused to make Arabic an official language at all, or if it required Muslim shopkeepers to close down on the Jewish Sabbath (Saturday) rather than on the Muslim Sabbath (Friday), or if "Hatikva" had spoken not of the "Hope for Zion" but of, say, the "Hope to drive out the Arab barbarians." A state that *aims* to oppress or alienate a portion of its citizenry, and does so in explicit terms, commits a more severe expressive harm than one that does so unintentionally or by omission. Likewise, the severity of an expressive harm is also, in part, a product of political and social context and the way in which marginalized groups interpret the expression. I agree, with Anderson and Pildes, that an expressive harm may exist whether or not it is perceived as offensive by the targeted group.[15] But the harm is more hurtful, and thus more morally serious, under certain conditions. The flag of Switzerland, a Swiss cross on a red background, contains unmistakable ties to the Holy Roman Empire, and thus to Christianity. It thus constitutes something of an expressive harm to Switzerland's non-Christian citizens. But the harm is effectively nil; the flag symbolizes not xenophobia but compassion, neutrality and peace, and despite a related controversy surrounding the International Red Cross,[16] no one calls for its replacement.[17]

In contrast to the Swiss example, Israel's flag appears to Arab citizens in a context of pervasive inequality. The substantive harms that Israel inflicts upon its Arab minority make the expressive ones much more poignant and problematic. Calls to change the symbols might be quieter if Israel provided its Arab sector with better schools, land access, health care and infrastructure; included Arab parties in governing coalitions; instituted a policy of affirmative action for Arab citizens in state jobs; and appointed more Arabs as ministers in the government or justices on the Supreme Court. But as Arabs become less and less happy with their lot, and more and more aggrieved at unabated discrimination, the Star of David looks to them more and more like a symbol of oppression. Not all Israeli Arabs take this view; recall the tight connection Muhammad draws between his ability to "live with" the Jewish symbols of the state and his "good financial situation" and life without discrimination. For him, the expressive harm is minimal. For the other Arab subjects, it is significant. This is not to say that objections to an exclusivist symbol will necessarily begin to fade as resource equality is improved: today's continuing debate over the Confederate flag in the American South shows that. But the extent to which minorities recoil from a symbol like the Star of David—developed, again, to express the Jewish people's desire for a state and not to express hate or violence toward any other group—has a lot to do with how fairly the state treats its minorities.

What is to be done? How are we to know if the public interest in patriotism and unity is sufficiently compelling, and if the means used are sufficiently well suited to justify exclusivist religious symbols? Those in charge of selecting symbols for a new polity, or revising them as a polity evolves, should attend to the perspectives of outlying groups—citizens who might take serious offense at expressions of the majority's religious culture. But they should not ignore the right of a majority to a "proper patriotism" fostered by the limited but essential and unifying power of national symbols.[18]

Apart from their connection with other forms of discrimination and inequality, state symbols favoring the majority population are seldom so virulent that they should be immediately replaced. Some symbols—certainly the swastika, probably the stars and bars of the Confederate Flag—carry a history of institutionalized violence and aggressive disdain for a minority and represent significant expressive harms unto themselves. Others, like the Star of David on Israel's flag, or even the stars and stripes on the American flag, have come to be seen by some as symbols of exclusion or even racism despite their largely innocent roots. So under certain circumstances, liberals might have reason to consider (as did several of my subjects, both Arab and Jewish) how a minority might be made to feel more connected to an exclusivist national symbol without making it unattractive to the majority.

Of the two possible strategies—finding entirely new symbols, or keeping the current motifs and supplementing them with others—the latter is more plausible for a case like that of Israel. Several subjects suggest, for example, adding a crescent and a cross to flank the Star of David (Tanya) on the flag, or appending a stanza to "Hatikva" that contains language and ideas inclusive of Arab citizens (Rotem). These and other compromise possibilities are worth considering to make a religiously affiliated state more welcoming to its minorities. In a remarkable Knesset discussion about a new constitution held in 2005, right-wing Likud MK Michael Eitan proposed changing a reference to "the Jewish soul" in Hatikva to "the Israeli soul"; a Shinui MK suggested adding a stanza in Arabic. Even if these changes seem unlikely, given fierce opposition and the fact that the anthem was written into law in November 2004, this conversation of the Constitution, Law and Justice Committee was a promising sign of openness to reconciliation with the Arab population.[19] Still, a liberal state should not be held to an impossible standard: assent will never be unanimous. Someone will always feel left out. In light of this, liberals should devote more of their energies to fighting the substantive inequalities that pique minorities to condemn symbols rather than to attacking the symbols themselves.

Funding Religion: Intermediate Scrutiny

If a complete separation of religious symbols and state is not a requirement of liberal justice, what should we make of funding for religious institutions and education? Should the state limit its affiliations with religion to certain non-problematic symbolic matters of national ethos, and maintain a hands-off stance with regard to religion in its budgets and expenditures? The United States, it might be said, takes this position. It has certain non-oppressive symbolic links with religion in general and with Christianity in particular—"In God We Trust," presidential prayer breakfasts, "God Save the United States and this Honorable Court," Christmas as a national holiday—but draws the line at government funding of religion. Occasional markers of affiliation, yes; dollars of support, no.

This oversimplifies the matter: in the United States, religious organizations enjoy fire and police protection, not to mention tax-exempt status; they also receive government funds for a number of purposes, including charitable work. A number of recent Supreme Court decisions have upheld various types of funding for religious institutions.[20] These benefits are typically understood, however, not as aids to religion *per se* but as secular goods provided on a neutral basis. Some decry these developments as violations of the Establishment Clause; others claim that the true beneficiaries of the proposed legislation are not churches and other religious institutions but the individuals who are served by the charitable work or educational programs. There is, however, a common assumption at work on both sides of this public debate: the government has no role in funding religion *for religion's sake*.

In the Jewish state, of course, the story is very different. Israel takes an active role in providing direct funds for religious education—full funding of state-religious public schools and generous partial funding of "recognized" religious private schools; for synagogues and ritual baths; for a Chief Rabbinate; for religious courts and local religious councils; for stipends that support ultra-Orthodox students who spend their days studying Torah rather than working or serving in the military. Religion is massively subsidized in Israel. Judaism is the primary beneficiary, but other religions enjoy support as well.

Should liberalism tolerate such widespread government funding for religious services and institutions? Or ought it to insist on financial independence for religion—an unfettered market where religions rise or fall on the basis of the expressed intentions of individuals to join in and contribute? Does government funding of religious services create the spiritual equivalent of market distortions which lead some sects to enjoy more success than they would by going it alone? Does it push some people further from religion than they might be if a more rigorous separation were imposed?

In answering these questions, contemporary liberals tend to take their cue from Establishment Clause jurisprudence in the United States. If something is prohibited by the Establishment Clause—or, in the event of an uncooperative Supreme Court majority, if something *ought to be read as* prohibited by the Establishment Clause—the reasoning goes, it must be illiberal. The

Establishment Clause is read as standing for government neutrality with regard to religion.[21] It implies that the state has no role in aiding or suppressing religion. It means, even more urgently, that the state must avoid playing favorites in religious matters. It demands, on retired Justice Sandra Day O'Connor's reading, that the state not present itself in a way that may be interpreted as endorsing one religion, or religion in general. American academic liberals, using these ideas as a lodestar for what liberalism commands about religion, arrive at similar conclusions. No liberal state should inject itself in the battle for dollars surrounding religious groups and religious doctrines.

But why, exactly, is this the case? (It can't be true just because the Establishment Clause says it's so.) What might liberalism look like bereft of the Establishment Clause guise? Is there, indeed, an argument that could drive a wedge between what the First Amendment requires and what liberalism requires? There are important considerations that should lead us to be wary of government funding of religion. But liberal claims on the other side of the question may be made as well. And the Israeli case—fleshed out nicely by the comments of my diverse subjects—shows that while both sides of the debate have their merits, the case for funding is worth a closer look than is often supposed.

Recall the surprising finding from the discussion of state funding of religious educational streams in chapter 5: Although many subjects quarrel with the extent of government funding of religious schools, and often express opposition to the lack of secular studies in these schools, very few of them reject the fundamentals of Israel's funding scheme for education. Nineteen of the twenty-two subjects avowing at least limited support for the concept of separation of religion and state nevertheless advocate using state monies for religious instruction. Israelis of all stripes from my study—Haredi, Religious Zionist, secular, traditional and Arab—believe in direct state funding for religious schools and other religious institutions.

I will discuss the case in favor of such funding below. First, though, it would be helpful to get a handle on the risks associated with drawing on state monies for religious causes that give many justified cause for concern. Determining whether liberalism can permit—or even ought to require—such funding will depend on the balance of the risks with the benefits, and the likelihood that, with scrupulous oversight, the risks may be managed effectively. I approach this issue by comparing the relatively mild Israeli complaints about state funding with one of the classic liberal condemnations thereof in early American history: James Madison's "Memorial and Remonstrance."

Three very different objections to Israel's funding of religious education arise in the interviews. First is the worry from a Haredi subject, Yehuda, that despite the name of the Ashkenazi ultra-Orthodox educational system

(*Atzma'i*, meaning "Independent"), its semi-official status and receipt of government funds makes it subject to an unwelcome degree of control by the state secular authorities: "They teach children for heresy!" Second is the opposite worry voiced by many secular, traditional and Religious Zionist Jews: the state ought not fund these schools without demanding that they teach appropriate doses of math, science, history, English and Israeli citizenship. As it is, some schools leave their children ill prepared to live in the modern world, should they choose to. And third, liberal subjects complain that the Haredi politicians corrupt the system, "looting the public coffers" (Rabbi Uri Regev) and receiving much more than their fair share of educational funds.

In his frequently cited "Memorial and Remonstrance" (1785), James Madison raises fifteen points in opposition to a bill that would have established a tax to support teachers of Christianity—and, implicitly, propped up the Anglican church—in the Commonwealth of Virginia.[22] Of the fifteen arguments, five concern primarily religious matters. An ecclesiastical establishment, Madison writes, is contrary to the idea that faith emerges from "reason and conviction, not by force or violence"; is unnecessary to Christianity, a religion that does not depend "on the powers of this world" for its vitality; turns Christian virtues "into animosities and jealousies"; hinders the spread of Christianity by making non-believers less likely to join the fold; and promotes "pride and indolence in the clergy, ignorance and servility in the laity, in both, superstition, bigotry and persecution." These have merit, but they speak mainly to Christian believers; they have limited direct relevance for a liberal argument against state-funded religious services. The final point concerning the sullying effects of politicized religion, however, raises one of the most important problems with state funding of religion that the Israeli subjects raise as well: the risk of corruption to both religion and polity when a particular faith community is on the state's dole.

Of Madison's remaining ten points, three are of particular note. First is his Lockean claim about limited government and the separation of political and religious spheres that it entails. The people become "slaves" when the legislature oversteps its bounds and deigns to regulate matters concerning religion (para. 2) to which no one gives up her rights upon vacating the state of nature for civil society (para. 4). Historically, when a church has been linked with the state, it has given comfort to "throne of political tyranny: in no instance have they been seen the guardians of the liberties of the people" (para. 8).

Second, we have the first of two arguments (stretching over paragraphs 3, 9 and 15) that employ slippery slope reasoning to warn that the Virginia assessment—while seemingly innocuous in itself—has dire logical consequences, including, ultimately, not only infringements on the cherished right of religious free exercise but the loss of *all* fundamental liberties. "It is proper to take alarm at the first experiment on our liberties," Madison admonishes.

"We hold this prudent jealousy to be the first duty of Citizens, and one of the noblest characteristics of the late Revolution" (para. 3). While some may not think it necessary to rebel at a small tax supporting religious teachers, they ought to think again:

> Who does not see that the same authority which can establish Christianity, in exclusion of all other Religions, may establish with the same ease any particular sect of Christians, in exclusion of all other Sects? That the same authority which can force a citizen to contribute three pence of his property for the support of any one establishment may force him to conform to any other establishment in all cases whatsoever? (para. 3)

Three pence might be a pittance, but it foretells doom for the republic. Once the principle that citizens may be taxed to support religion gains legitimacy, there is no logical stopping point short of full ecclesiastical establishment. And there is no principle which would prevent a particularly odious sect from occupying this role in the future. If you don't want to be subject to a church that is not your own, you'd better not agree to provide state support for even a church you think is the true one. Tomorrow, *you* might be on the sidelines paying to support a religious establishment you reject, and submitting yourself to further forms of exploitation.

The message becomes even more urgent in the second slippery slope argument Madison raises in paragraph 15, the final passage of the "Memorial and Remonstrance." Having argued that a church tax leads to establishment, and that establishment threatens religious free exercise, he now warns that the loss of the right to free exercise entails the loss of every fundamental right guaranteed by the nascent constitution:

> Either we must say, that they may controul the freedom of the press, may abolish the Trial by Jury, may swallow up the Executive and Judiciary Powers of the State; nay that they may despoil us of our very right of suffrage, and erect themselves into an independent and hereditary Assembly, or we must say, that they have no authority to enact into the law the Bill under consideration.

There are no third ways: Either this bill to fund Virginia religious teachers' salaries through taxation is defeated, or the Bill of Rights and the structure of the U.S. government crumble. Religious liberty, as one of the rights most highly prized by the colonists, is the keystone to legitimate government.

What are we to make of these arguments? Is Madison's "Remonstrance" a convincing tract against even minor state funding of religion? Many of the points raised in the piece ring true, or at least ring familiar. But not even the most ardent activist for church-state separation today makes the case that spending three pennies of tax money on religion would bring us to the end of liberal democracy as we know it. None of the major U.S. advocacy groups policing separation, for example, raised a finger at the national prayer service held in the aftermath of the September 2001 terrorist attacks on the World Trade Center and Pentagon. None blink an eye at the tradition of taxpayer-funded clergy offering prayers before every session of the U.S. Congress. None wave "Separation Now" placards at presidential inaugurations, where ministers routinely invoke the name of God, and even Jesus, in praying for the nation's new leader.

Madison's slippery slope arguments, though still cited today in debates and Supreme Court opinions, are less effective than they were when they were first articulated. A tenable slippery slope argument must establish, first, that a *slope* exists: that a common principle is at work in both the immediate case (i.e., a small tax) and the nightmare scenario (i.e., a denial of free exercise and the destruction of the Bill of Rights), that the two eventualities are logically of a piece or might be so construed by real actors. Second, even if such a principle is found, a slippery slope argument must tell us why the slope is *slippery*, and why there is no logical stopping point that would prevent the slide from the (in itself, unproblematic) first step to the (horrible) last. Madison has something of a common principle linking the tax to the nightmare —"government ought to aid religion"—but its generality dilutes its persuasiveness. We can imagine many sub-principles under this category that would be mutually exclusive: "aid all religions impartially" and "aid Christianity," say; or "provide religions only financial support" and "make Quakerism the state religion." We could, in other words, easily redescribe the principles such that the first and last points do not fit on the same slope. But the weaker link here—emphatically so in our day, much less so in Madison's—is the lack of a case for the slope's slipperiness. The checks and balances of existing legislation and the legislative system, the judicial check of the federal court system, public opinion, lobbying groups, the constitutional text—any of these could serve as potential stopping points on the free-fall from innocuous taxes to an oppressive Christian state. Together, they constitute a fairly secure bulwark against the fundamental transformation of the United States from liberal democracy to theocracy.

In the era in which Madison was writing, however, the American republic wasn't even ten years old. It was a fragile, developing political system with untested institutions, leaders, laws and traditions. Worries about unjust religious taxes were prominent in many of the founders' minds.[23] While today we would find little risk in slippery slopes of the kind Madison warned about in the "Remonstrance," we'd be remiss to criticize his arguments at the time for the same reason.

The slippery slope arguments are never heard in Israel, for an obvious and for a somewhat less obvious reason. First, it is silly to speak of the risks of a tax turning into an establishment in Israel, because there already *is* an

establishment of sorts: Israel already is a Jewish state. Second, this establishment is, in itself, hardly an oppressive one for most Israelis. They have
been in the belly of the beast, one might say, and it's not so bad. They have
slid to the bottom of the slippery slope, and found no nightmare. They don't
worry about religious education funds leading to an odious outcome, despite the fact that they strongly disagree with some of the religious elements
of their state as they know it. They denounce the religious monopoly on
marriage and divorce, for example, but they do not see this as in any way
entailed by state funding for religious institutions. When they complain that
Haredim take more than they deserve—that the ultra-Orthodox Shas schools
raid the public coffers to provide a longer school day, hot lunches and free
bus rides—Israelis remove the argument from the slippery slope, transferring it to the welfarist liberal plane of distributive justice: who ought to get
how much, and why. Their argument is not with the principle of state-
funded religious education, but with specific policies and actual allocations
the Knesset and government ministries provide.

I mentioned above that U.S. advocacy groups such as Americans United
for Separation of Church and State no longer stake their position on Madison's slippery slope arguments, although they sometimes use similar rhetoric. They appropriate his "three pence" line not to warn of a theocratic
apocalypse but to urge a quite different, much tamer, and conceptually problematic argument: the injustice of being forced to pay for something you
don't agree with. Perhaps because of the change in circumstances between
1785 and today, and the implausibility that funding faith-based charities
would herald the collapse of freedom of religion and all constitutional guarantees, the point from the advocates now is strident but banal: "Forcing taxpayers to subsidize religious institutions they may or may not believe in is
no different from forcing them to put money in the collection plates of
churches, synagogues and mosques."[24] Arguments of this structure have
been used often in recent years in the United States to oppose state funding
for various projects, both religious and non-religious. Former New York
Mayor Rudolph Giuliani used it repeatedly in his battle with the Brooklyn
Museum of Art in the fall of 1999 over a controversial exhibit featuring a
painting of the Virgin Mary decorated with elephant dung: "[T]o have the
government subsidize something like that," he said, "is outrageous."[25] He
repeatedly questioned the justice of forcing taxpayers to pay for an exhibit
that, in his opinion, did not qualify as art and demeaned Catholicism. The
answer to all arguments of this type is clear: Individual taxpayers disagree
with many different government expenditures for many different reasons.
Doves might oppose high levels of military spending, libertarians may think
not a dime should go to safety net programs like Medicaid. But taxpayers do
not, and cannot, enjoy a line-item veto. Forcing someone to put a dollar in a
church's collection plate in the pursuit of legitimate public policy goals is

equivalent to forcing someone to put a dollar in Boeing's coffers to buy an F-14 fighter, or to send a dollar to Mexico for a government bailout.[26] If, of course, the faith-based funding initiative is held to be unconstitutional, then there *is* a legitimate difference between paying churches and paying Boeing. But a violation of the Establishment Clause cannot be established by a citizen's grievance at having to pay for something he doesn't believe in. That grievance is legitimate only if there is, in fact, a genuine constitutional violation.

Consider now the case for government funding of religion that the Israeli subjects advance. It is a simple but powerful point: equality demands equal treatment of all people, whether religious or not. Israelis give financial support to religious education, says Naomi, "not because we want to... but because we are duty-bound." "The state," says Ronit, "must respect every [educational] stream and give it funding." Sectarian education, according to Tanya, "is a kind of special education" the state is fully justified in subsidizing. "If the state funds opera and supports football," Rotem claims, "then there is no reason why it shouldn't support religious education." "One of the rules of democracy," says Shmuel, "is that you give people the ability to live their own way. And if there are people who want to be religious that's fine and they are entitled to have their own budget...."

There is a curious feature of the justification for government funding of religion suggested in these excerpts. None of the subjects cited in the previous paragraph is religious; three are secular, two are traditional. With the exception of Shmuel, who attended a *heder* (religious primary school) until age twelve (and then rejected orthodoxy), none of these subjects has gone to religious schools. None of them has sent or intends to send their children to religious schools. And all of them express various degrees of disdain for religious Israelis, particularly Haredim, and have complaints about the ways in which some religious schools operate or take more than their fair share of funds. So the position in favor of government funding is not what some economists would think of as rational, in the narrow sense of conducing to one's own ends. Nor is it rational in the wider sense that individuals take account of their families' and friends' welfare in their own utility calculations; many of Israel's secular Jews, we should recall, profess *hatred* for their Haredi brethren. No: the position seems to come from a sense of what counts as a fair allocation of state resources and thus is better described as *reasonable*—taking other people's interests as seriously as one's own interests and applying principles of justice in an even-handed manner. These liberal Jewish subjects stake out a position of political morality that is not only unconnected to, but possibly contrary to, their own interests and immediate values. This suggests that there may be real force behind the positions they take—a justification that looks toward the public interest and political justice rather than to the satisfaction of self-regarding preferences. We have good reason to take their views particularly seriously.

Theoretical support for the equality defense of government funding for religion that these Israelis offer is found in a notion of government impartiality toward the lives of its citizens that Bikhu Parekh advocates here:

> Just as we should allow religious citizens to speak in a religious language, we should also find other ways of valuing their presence and encouraging their contribution to collective life. The state could give them a charitable status as it generally does in all liberal societies, contribute towards their upkeep as it does in Germany, Sweden, the Netherlands, Britain, and elsewhere, encourage them to undertake philanthropic activities, and so forth. It might be argued that public funds should not be used to support sectional interests. If that were so, no public authority would be justified in supporting or giving a charitable status to museums, art galleries, universities, and operas, spending public funds to rescue mountain climbers or those lost in dangerous expeditions, or providing designated areas to anglers and ramblers. We rightly want it to support these activities because they are valuable, are shared by sizable sections of citizens, and add to the richness of collective life. Religion belongs to this category.[27]

Parekh's idea may gain even more support when we observe that, in most societies, significantly more citizens participate in religious life than climb mountains or go to the opera. A conception of "justice as evenhandedness," as Joseph Carens puts it, allows us to see liberalism as flexible and as responsive to a particular society's needs.[28] A liberal state is charged with providing citizens with the primary goods they need to attempt to realize their own conceptions of the good life. It is thus at least partially responsible for helping citizens of all religious and nonreligious beliefs and perspectives live full, rich lives. It might best achieve this goal through a relatively hands-off approach in which religious citizens are free to form their own communities, organize their own schools and other institutions and raise private contributions to pay for their institution. But this laissez-faire approach might be unsuited to the society in question and inadequate to its values, its people, its ethos. A hands-off approach might severely disadvantage certain elements of the population. And it might contradict state goals or constitutional principles to help religious citizens realize their spiritual and educational ends.

The provision of certain state benefits to religious citizens or religious groups, however, need not implicate the state in battles over religious truth. Religious services provided or funded by the state could be regarded as *social services* for those portions of the population for whom religion is a fundamental aspect of their lives. In an article defending a conception of liberal impartiality, Thomas Nagel argues that political disputes involving questions of coercion must be debated on terms open to a "common critical rationality."[29] In defining this standard, Nagel claims that convictions stemming from "personal faith or revelation" have no place in the forum of public justification. An interlocutor, he observes, does not *"have what you have"*—the knowledge gained through revelation—and therefore cannot engage the religious person in a debate. In clarifying his position, however, Nagel makes a crucial point, one I want to expand upon. A political order, he says, should extricate itself from disputes about the *truth* even as it takes close account of *how citizens interpret the truth,* and why and how this knowledge might be relevant politically:

> The fact that someone has certain religious or moral convictions
> has its own considerable importance, from an impersonal stand-
> point, in determining how he should be treated and what he
> should do, but it is not the same as the importance that the truth of
> those convictions would have, if it could be admitted as a premise
> in a political argument.[30]

A religious citizen, then, may not legitimately claim that something ought to be banned just because her religion (held by her to be the true religion) says so.[31] An ultra-Orthodox legislator in Israel cannot legitimately demand that turning on the lights in one's home on Saturdays should be criminalized on the grounds that this act is prohibited by traditional interpretations of Jewish law as a violation of the Sabbath-day proscriptions on work. The same legislator *may*, however, request that certain public streets in Haredi-dominated neighborhoods be closed to vehicular traffic on Saturdays in order to facilitate the Sabbath observance of those for whom driving on this day is regarded as a sin. The idea is not to prohibit the perceived "sin"—drivers would still be free to take their cars through the 90 percent of the city not dominated by the ultra-Orthodox—but to provide a more welcome environment for those for whom quiet, peaceful observance the Sabbath day is a fundamental value.

The relevant fact in this example is not that driving on Shabbat is sinful. The relevant fact is that the specified portion of the population believes Shabbat driving to be sinful, and suffers a harm when another portion of the population drives through their neighborhoods on Shabbat. This principle helps to explain why at least some kinds of government funding for religious services might be appropriate in a liberal framework. Funding, in fact, will usually constitute an easier case than the example just mentioned. For in the street-closing matter, there is the question of just how much harm a driver does to a Haredi person's Shabbat experience by entering his neighborhood. And there is the question of how much of an inconvenience a street's closing would have on the driver and whether the inconvenience should be seen as a denial of freedom of movement. These factors may well lead to a decision *against* closing a particular street. But in government funding of religious education, there are, we might say, only winners. The religious group gets to educate its youth according to its own values while non-religious and otherwise religious groups enjoy their parallel right of sending their children to schools matching their favored world views. The only coercion comes in the form of taxation: everyone pays, in part, for all of these educational streams. However, since each community pays taxes, the argument goes, each should also get its proper share of state educational monies. It would be unfair to make everyone pay equal rates of taxes and then to fund only secular schools, requiring religious schools to stand on their own bottoms. As many of my subjects claim, the Haredim "should get what they deserve" and should be allowed to pursue their own ways of life.

One Religious Zionist subject, Richard, opposes state funding for religious schools—for a revealing reason. His problem is not with state money going to religion, but with the balkanizing effects of a multiple-stream approach to primary and secondary education. Richard would forge the existing secular-public, religious-public and Haredi private streams into a single mandatory educational system that unites all portions of the Jewish Israeli public: "The fact that we have totally separate educational institutions from age three up means we are creating separate nations within the nation," he says. The alternative, for Richard, is one educational stream that teaches everything: citizenship, Judaism, and a complete secular curriculum. It would probably mirror Richard's Religious Zionist perspective, combining religious studies with secular studies and showcasing the state as a religiously Jewish entity. But such a unified curriculum would do violence to the broad diversity present within Israel's Jewish communities: secular Jewish students would have to sit through much more religious study than they or their parents would want, and Haredi students would be taught principles (such as the holiness of the state of Israel) that contradict their interpretation of Judaism in an environment that may lead them away from their religious roots and threaten their communities' viability. The benefits of a more unified Israeli society would thus be unlikely to be realized with such a revolution in Israel's education policy. The plan would institutionalize one perspective on Judaism—a minority view held by approximately 15 percent of Jews—and thereby do a disservice to both the majority perspective (secular and traditional) and those of other minorities (Haredi).

According to the impartiality view I have presented, a liberal state may decide to engage in funding for religious causes not out of a recognition that a particular religion is the true religion, and not out of a state endorsement of particular religious practices or beliefs, but out of an objective concern for the things that citizens themselves happen to value. If something is important to a citizen, then, it is potentially important to the state as well—not because that something has innate value, or because the state itself finds value in it, but because a *citizen* ascribes value to it. A certain disinterested approval for citizens enjoying success in their life plans leads states to fund a range of activities, from health care to university studies, from sports programs and scientific research to art and music. There is no *a priori* reason why religion should not be added to this list.[32]

Contextual factors, however, may lead to different conclusions about whether religion should be funded. In a state dominated by one religio-national group, such as Israel, funding for religion is both an expression of social solidarity and an accommodation of those portions of the population that benefit from subsidized religious services. The latter include both minority Jewish sects and the Muslim and Christian communities in the Arab sector. In the United States, however, where hundreds if not thousands of religious groups compete for adherents, the Constitution might be wise in keeping government a healthy distance from religious matters and institutions. Noah Feldman presents a strong case for why it might be important to preserve a policy of strict separation in the American context. National unity, he argues, would be undercut by policies involving even indirect funding of religious institutions.[33] The multiplicity of sects, and the polity's history and ethos, makes a difference in whether and how funding should be deemed appropriate.

In sum, vigilance is necessary in analyzing each proposed instance of state funding of religious services. Each such proposal, if it is to be approved, should meet the worthy objections with regard to the potential for discriminatory allocation, divisiveness and abuse. There is little reason, however, to fear an uncontrollable slippery slope from "three pence" to theocracy. Providing additional state funds for faith-based charities will not turn the United States into a Christian state that compels church attendance and launches an inquisition. Intermediate scrutiny is the appropriate standard in this case: If a government policy involving funding for religious institutions is thought to be closely linked to a significant (not simply legitimate) state interest, applied in an even-handed manner and in a way that takes seriously the interests of both religious and non-religious citizens, it may pass liberal muster.

Imposing Religion: Strict Scrutiny

In contrast to the prior two sections, where I argued that symbolic affiliations and financial ties between religion and state may at times be acceptable from the perspective of liberalism (with the latter being more problematic), here I claim that direct links between political and ecclesiastical bodies that threaten individual rights are very seldom, if ever, justifiable. In order to satisfy liberal demands, arrangements in this category must be necessary to serve a compelling state interest. They must be the only and best means available to solve a very urgent social problem.

The following are examples of religious affiliations that fit in this category: compulsory church attendance laws; the delegation of personal status issues such as marriage and divorce to religious courts; enforcement of religious gender roles (including dictates concerning dress, education and work) in private or public; and forced tithing to a religious authority.[34] In short, this third category includes both coerced observance of religious commandments and systematic discrimination against nonbelievers or adherents of rival faiths. State policies which entail or cause these types of harms to individuals are extremely unlikely to be acceptable according to liberalism.

The theoretical support for such a position is uncontroversial within liberalism. The principle of non-coercion is, on many accounts, the very heart of liberalism itself. As a theory that is built in large measure on the value of individual liberty, liberalism ought to regard government policies that turn the state into the enforcement branch of any religion's commandments with the highest degree of suspicion. Individual citizens' basic human and civil rights—including rights of bodily integrity, equal treatment, legal due process and political participation; and freedom of movement, occupation, speech, assembly, and religious exercise—are not subject to curtailment or control by any religious worldview. They are not to be denied by the state on the basis of a purely religious justification. And control over these rights is not to be delegated to religious authorities, in whose hands they are at risk of violation.

Still, in this category some questions are clearer than others. Subjecting citizens to violence or persecution on account of their religion; demanding the conversion of citizens to a particular religion; requiring or preventing attendance at a house of worship—all these are clear violations of liberalism's non-coercion principle and cannot be said to serve a legitimate—let alone a compelling—state interest. In Rawlsian terms, no suitably "public" reason could be summoned to justify any such impositions of the state on citizens' lives: the reason would have to rely solely on the *truth* of the religion in question, not a sense in which the proposal serves the general interest in a diverse polity. But other religiously motivated state infringements on liberty *could* be argued to have a legitimately public justification. The question is whether the public reasons behind such a policy are *compelling*, and whether the means chosen to pursue that compelling end are *necessary* to its realization.

Take the question of Israel's millet system, discussed in detail in chapter 6. Among my Jewish subjects, much consternation was voiced concerning the control that the rabbinical authorities wield over questions of marriage, divorce and burial. Complaints came from secular, traditional and Religious

Zionist Jews alike: secular Jews objected to the requirement that they marry in a religious ceremony; traditional Jews lamented that they could not use their own rabbis, whether Reform or Conservative, and that they could not adapt their ceremony and *ketuba* to reflect their understanding of Judaism; and some Religious Zionists resented the condescension and mistrust which the ultra-Orthodox-dominated rabbinate seemed to regard them. Many liberal Jews also pointed to hundreds of thousands of Israelis' inability to marry at all, due to their unclear Jewish origins; to the plight of *agunot* ("chained" women seeking to end their marriages but unable to secure a divorce due their husbands' failure to issue the document [a *get*] required by Jewish law); and the unsolicited intrusion of the rabbinical authorities when burying a loved one. The delegation of these personal status questions to the rabbinical authorities entails violations of fundamental human liberties including the right to marry and the right of free religious exercise. Nevertheless, an argument can be made that this arrangement is necessary either to ensure the continued existence of Israel as a Jewish state or to preserve the unity of the Jewish people as one nation—two values with a great deal of currency among all portions of Israel's Jewish population. Ultimately, I argued, these reasons fail to justify the policy. The purported values, while legitimate, do not rise to the level of compelling state interests given the contrasting senses in which different segments of the population regard "Israel as a Jewish state" and "Jews as a unified nation"—there is too little agreement on how these values should be understood and put into practice. And even if the goals, however vague, are to be regarded as compelling, the means employed are neither necessary nor even sufficient to satisfy them. The religious coercion of Jewish Israelis in matters of marriage, divorce and burial is not consistent with liberal justice.

The considerations might be different, however, when considering the millet system as it applies to non-Jews. The Arab subjects, it may be recalled, are divided on this question. Those opposing the power of Muslim and Christian religious courts over the faithful (and not so faithful) in their respective communities cite the same reason Jews give for rejecting similar control by the rabbinate: the injustice of demanding religious action without consent. But several of the subjects (Muhammad and Omer) support the delegation of state authority to the Muslim and Christian courts on the grounds of religious autonomy. And indeed this is the justification Israel could offer for pursuing this policy. Toleration of minority religious cultures could be said to depend on giving each community a certain degree of control over its adherents. Without such authority, the communities may risk weakness, division or even dissolution in a polity that is dominated by a single religio-national group. Empowering the minority religious leadership to lead, and to make rulings that apply to all members of the faith community, may be an effective way to keep the peace between the 80 percent Jewish majority and the 20 percent Arab minority. (Giving autonomy along not religious but national lines is another option—i.e., to Arabs as a whole or to local Arab communities rather than to Muslim, Christian and Druze religious groups—but one that would confront dicier questions, including those concerning the status of multiple sub-national authorities.) And another admittedly contingent reason to keep the millet system for Muslim and Christian Arabs is this: it has proven to be a workable local tradition. First implemented by the Turks when Palestine was part of the Ottoman Empire, the system was adopted seamlessly by the British after World War I and then by the Israelis in 1948. Consistency of policy has its virtues: it is what people are accustomed to, what they have come to rely on. It is on long deposit in the local bank of political ideas. So Israel's policy vis-à-vis its religious minorities clearly pursues a compelling state interest—accommodation of the Arab minority. And the means it employs toward this goal stem from local traditions may be necessary; there are no obvious ways to rework the arrangement in ways that would satisfy the minority and keep the tenuous peace between Israeli Arabs and Israeli Jews.

Although the policy is inherently suspicious in a liberal state—it locks individuals into their religious communities, which then exercise partial legal authority over their members—it does so in order to pursue a kind of religious toleration. So it would be a grievous violation of Israel's historically grounded commitment to the Arab minority to abolish the millet system. But liberalism is also committed to equality of citizenship and thus cannot envisage a situation in which, say, Jews have the right to avoid rabbinical courts while Muslims must continue to marry and divorce via Muslim Sharia courts. A compromise solution—while unlikely to completely satisfy everyone—would be to leave the millet system itself untouched but to give individuals of every religious faith a secular opt-out provision. According to this proposal, religious authorities are still empowered over members who seek to conduct their major life events religiously. But for those who do not choose such a life, there is a way out.

Conclusion

The analysis in this chapter suggests that liberal democracy allows some room for religious connections with the state; at the same time, it clarifies why certain connections are worrisome or even anathema to a liberal politics. The mistake of most general accounts of the relationship between liberalism and religion has been to regard *all* religious linkages with the state as coercive and to conclude that only a complete and strict separation of religion and state will suit a liberal polity. But not all religion is oppressive. Not all is coercive. Some connections between religion and state express support for a particular tradition, help define a state's ethos, or aid individuals in living meaningful lives, while doing no harm or only slight expressive harm to citizens affiliating with other traditions. These pose no more trouble than do any national symbols expressing a link between the state and its dominant culture. Public financial support for various kinds of religious institutions, including religious schools, involve a higher risk of abuse and social division and may lead to discrimination in favor of a majority religion and against minority faiths. They should thus be subject to stricter constraints and greater care than symbols but—in light of the liberal value of impartial regard for all citizens' chosen ways of life—not ruled out of bounds entirely. Finally, affiliations between state and religion that require unwilling citizens to conform to certain religious beliefs or performances are particularly worrisome in a liberal state and should nearly always be ruled out as violations of individual rights.

As Israel continues to steer a constitutional course through the thicket of religion and liberal democracy, its leaders and citizens must remember that all religious infusions into politics should be approached with caution. The wars of religion in Europe, the Islamic Revolution in Iran and the repressive Taliban regime in Afghanistan—among many other examples—illustrate the profound dangers to life and liberty that can be associated with attempts to integrate religion and state. The wrong religious infusions in politics can threaten, or thwart, liberal government. But strict separation is not the single solution that fits all societies. The challenge of determining the proper relationship between religion and democracy must be addressed with a nuanced, contextual eye that takes close account of local circumstances and the ways in which citizens interpret them. In the higher law of Israel and other societies, religion and liberal democracy may legitimately, and even fruitfully, converge.

Notes

1. Ludwig Wittgenstein, *Philosophical Investigations*, trans. G.E.M Anscombe, (Englewood Cliffs, NJ: Prentice Hall, 1958), § 114.

2. By an "expressive harm" I mean an injury inflicted through the communication of an idea (verbally or otherwise). An analysis and defense of the expressive interpretation of law, including applications to several constitutional questions in the United States, is found in Elizabeth S. Anderson and Richard H. Pildes, "Expressive Theories of Law: A General Restatement," *University of Pennsylvania Law Review* 148 (May 2000): 1503-75.

3. Ronald Dworkin, *Taking Rights Seriously* (Cambridge: Harvard University Press, 1977), 180.

4. My use of the term "plural" is therefore a bit problematic. In some cases, as in Israel's designation of both Hebrew and Arabic as official languages, or its concurrent use of the Hebrew and Roman calendars, what I am calling plural state affiliations explicitly make provisions for multiplicity. In other cases, as in its Sabbath policies, Israel sets Judaism as the standard and allows alternatives or exemptions from that standard for members of other religions. In all cases, it may be said, Israel expresses a preference for Jews and Judaism over non-Jews and other religions and so is not "pluralist" in the strong sense of respecting each religion equally.

5. As some passages from the interviews show, choices may be somewhat more nuanced: Arabs might show some respect to the Israeli national anthem by standing (but not singing) as it is played; or they might show contempt for it by hoisting anti-Israel placards or shouting down those who choose to sing.

6. This exclusivism is not unique, of course, to states with religious motifs in their flags or anthems: every state represents itself with single flag and a single official anthem.

7. See Flags of the World website, <http://www.crwflags.com/fotw/flags/gb.html> (8 August 2005) and the British Government's website, <http://www.royal.gov.uk/output/page398.asp> (8 August 2005).

8. France's blue, white and red vertical stripes represent, respectively, Saint Martin, the Virgin Mary (to whom France was consecrated by Louis XIII in the 17th century) and Saint Denis (the patron saint of Paris). Ukraine's horizontal light blue and yellow stripes signify an affiliation with Christianity. For France, see Flags of the World website, <http://www.crwflags.com/fotw/flags/fr.html> (8 August 2005); for Ukraine, <http://www.crwflags.com/fotw/flags/ua.html> (8 August 2005).

9. Costa Rica's flag has five horizontal stripes of red, white and blue, thought to represent unifying ideals such as intellectualism, perseverance, happiness, wisdom, freedom and generosity. See <http://www.costarica.com/Home/Culture/National_Symbols/National_Flag> (8 August 2005).

10. The U.N. General Assembly adopted the "Zionism is racism" principle, Resolution 3379, on November 10, 1975. It rescinded it in December 1991. See text of the resolution on the Jewish Virtual Library website, <http://www.us-israel.org/jsource/UN/unga3379.html> (8 August 2005). An attempt to pass a similar resolution (stating that the "Zionist movement...is based on racial superiority") at the August 2001 U.N. World Conference Against Racism in Durban, South Africa was unsuccessful.

11. Yael Tamir, "Commentary: A Jewish Democratic State," in Michael Walzer, Menachem Lorberbaum and Noam J. Zohar, eds., *The Jewish Political Tradition, Volume One: Authority* (New Haven: Yale University Press, 2000), 519.

12. The Avalon Project, Yale Law School, <http://www.yale.edu/lawweb/avalon/mideast/israel.htm> (8 August 2005).

13. The basic design for the flag was taken from the World Zionist Organization's flag (adopted in 1897 at the First Zionist Congress in Basel); "Hatikva" was written in the late 19th century and adopted as the Zionist anthem in 1905 at the Seventh Zionist Congress.

14. Anderson and Pildes, "Expressive Theories of Law," 1512-13.

15. They write that meanings cannot "be reduced…to the addressee's subjective reactions to what is said." Anderson and Pildes, "Expressive Theories of Law," 1574.

16. The International Red Cross and Red Crescent refuses to recognize Israel's equivalent organization, the Magen David Adom (Red Star of David), or include it as a member.

17. See Flags of the World website, <http://www.crwflags.com/fotw/flags/ch.html> (8 August 2005).

18. For those who would argue that the impact of particularist symbols is too slight to figure into a theory of liberal justice (as might defenders of the "expression does no harm" principle considered above, for example), a paradox arises that trivializes the problem. If the symbols do little good for the majority, and little harm to the minority, there is little reason for either opposing or approving of them. But if, as I have argued, expression can have meaningfully negative and positive implications, liberalism needs to say something about how to balance the costs and benefits.

19. Shahar Ilan, "An Anthem for all Nationals," *Ha'aretz*, 7 July 2005.

20. Mueller v. Allen, 463 U.S. 388 (1983) (upholding a Minnesota state tax deduction for educational expenses incurred in both public and parochial schools); Bowen v. Kendrick, 487 U.S. 589 (1988) (upholding federal funding for an educational program that benefited religious organizations); Zobrest v. Catalina Foothills School Dist., 509 U.S. 1 (1993) (upholding a school district-funded interpreter for a deaf child in a Catholic school); Rosenberger v. Rectors of the University of Virginia, 515 U.S. 819 (1995) (requiring public university funding of both secular and religious student publications on free speech grounds); Mitchell v. Helms, 530 U.S. 793 (2000) (upholding policy giving books and software to religious schools); Zelman v. Simmons-Harris, 536 U.S. 639 (2002) (upholding an Ohio school voucher program used primarily in Catholic schools but available on a neutral basis).

21. According to the much-critiqued "Lemon test" (which has been all but supplanted by Justice O'Connor's "endorsement" test) a state practice satisfies the Establishment Clause as long as it (1) reflects a clearly secular purpose, (2) has a primary effect that neither advances nor inhibits religion, and (3) avoids excessive government entanglement with religion. The test was articulated in Lemon v. Kurtzman 403 U.S. 602 (1971).

22. Available at <http://www.law.ou.edu/hist/remon.html> (8 August 2005).

23. See Noah Feldman, *Divided by God: America's Church-State Problem — and What We Should Do About It* (New York: Farrar, Straus and Giroux, 2005), 33-42.

24. Americans United for Separation of Church and State, "The Faith-Based Initiative: Churches, Social Services & Your Tax Dollars": <http://www.au.org/site/PageServer?pagename=resources_brochure_faithbased> (8 August 2005).

25. Dan Barry and Carol Vogel, "Giuliani Vows to Cut Subsidy Over Art He Calls Offensive," *New York Times*, 23 September 1999.

26. In an apropos comic by political cartoonist Tom Tomorrow, a penguin stands in an IRS office and declares: "I find our support of the Indonesian military highly offensive." The clerk replies: "I'm terribly sorry, sir. We'll replace your portion immediately!" <http://www.salon.com/comics/tomo/1999/10/18/tomo/index.html> (8 August 2005).

27. Bhikhu Parekh, "The Voice of Religion in Political Discourse," in *Religion, Politics and Peace*, ed. Leroy S. Rouner (Notre Dame, Ind.: University of Notre Dame Press, 1999), 77-78.

28. Joseph H. Carens, *Culture Citizenship, and Community: A Contextual Exploration of Justice as Evenhandedness* (Oxford: Oxford University Press, 2000).

29. Thomas Nagel, "Moral Conflict and Political Legitimacy," *Philosophy and Public Affairs* 16, no. 3 (Summer 1987): 232.

30. Nagel, "Moral Conflict," 236.

31. I develop a fuller case for this point in chapter 1.

32. A libertarian opposing all redistributive taxation will argue that *none* of these ought to be on the list of state responsibilities. There is no libertarian argument, however, as to why religion is a special case that is particularly unsuited for government funding. My argument is thus not with libertarians but with liberals who believe the state does have at least some role in providing basic resources to help its citizens pursue their own values and ideas of the good life.

33. Feldman, *Divided by God*, 244-49.

34. Forced tithing differs from taxation to support religion, which can, as I argued above, be consistent with liberalism. The latter supports even-handed distribution of state resources in ways determined by representative political institutions; its purpose is to serve the public at large. The former simply delivers private funds directly to the coffers of a church with no government control or oversight; it props up religion by subjecting citizens to religious law without their consent.

Appendix
Interview Guides

Questions for Jewish Subjects

Background and Religious Observance

Where do you live?
How old are you?
What is your occupation?
What is your educational background?
What does being Jewish mean to you?
How important is Judaism to you?
How would you describe your level of observance?
Do you keep a Kosher home?
Do you observe the Sabbath? In what ways?
Which Jewish holidays do you celebrate? How do you celebrate them?
Which other *mitzvot* do you observe?
How did your family practice Judaism when you were growing up?

Attitudes About Israel's Jewish Character

Do you think Israel is a Jewish state? Why or why not?
> *If yes:* is Israel Jewish enough, too Jewish, or not Jewish enough? Should
> Israeli political life, generally speaking, be conducted according to
> the Jewish religion?
> *If no:* why not? Should Israel be a Jewish state?
In what ways does the Jewish character of the state affect you personally?

Do you think there is a difference between a "Jewish state" and a "State for
the Jews"? What is that difference? Which ought Israel to be, if any?
Some people think that Israel should be a "state of all its citizens." Do you
agree? What would that mean?
Some people think that Israel should separate religion and state. Do you
agree? Do you think a complete separation of Judaism from the state
would be good or bad for Jews? For Judaism? For the state? How?

Attitudes Toward Democracy

Do you think Israel is a democratic state? Why or why not?
If yes: is Israel democratic enough, not democratic enough, or too de-
mocratic?
If no: why not? Should it be democratic?
What do you think of when you hear the word "Democracy"? What does it
mean to you?
Is democracy important to you?
Are you happy you live in a democracy (assuming you think Israel is a de-
mocracy)? Why or why not?

Assessing Links Between Judaism and Democracy

In the two most recent basic laws, there is a purpose clause which reads:
"This Basic Law is designed to anchor in a Basic Law the values of the
State of Israel as a Jewish and democratic state." What does that mean
to you? Do you see a conflict between Judaism and democracy? Or are
they compatible with each other?
Which ought to have priority in Israel: Judaism or democracy?
Are you personally more committed to Judaism or to democracy?
Is democracy a Jewish value?

Reactions to Specific Issues

For each of the following linkages between state and religion, please tell me
whether you approve or disapprove, and tell me why:

Law of return gives preference to Jews
Hebrew is the national language
The state's anthem ("Hatikva") speaks of the Jewish longing to return to
Zion
The state's flag has a Star of David

The state's official symbol is the menorah – the Jewish candelabrum
The state gives financial support to religious education
The state gives official recognition to the Chief Rabbinate
The state gives religious courts jurisdiction over marriage
The state gives religious courts jurisdiction over divorce
The state gives religious courts jurisdiction over burial
Most busses don't run on Shabbat
State kitchens observe *kashrut*
Many businesses don't operate on Shabbat
Many Yeshiva students receive deferrals from the military draft
Religious parties control 27 Knesset seats (of 120) (in 2000: Shas 17, United Torah Judaism 5, NRP 5)

In your opinion, should the orthodox retain its monopoly on matters of Jewish marriage, divorce, burial and conversion? Or do you think that non-orthodox options should be made available to Jews who are secular or reform or conservative? Why do you think so?

Have you heard about the 1998 Supreme Court decision on military draft deferrals for yeshiva students? Is it fair for the state to grant so many deferrals to the haredim? Should the Knesset set limits on the number of exemptions? Is it fair for the state to attempt any change in the status quo on this issue?

Have you heard about the Supreme Court decision in March concerning an Israeli Arab couple who wanted to buy a home in the town of Katzir? Chief Justice Barak wrote in his decision that it is illegal for the state (directly or by proxy) to discriminate against Arab citizens. He rejects the principle of "separate but equal" and says that the couple may purchase land in Katzir.

What was your reaction to this ruling? Does the Jewish character of the state give Jews a special claim to the land, and to buying property on the land, that Israeli Arabs do not have?

Would you want to live next door to an Israeli Arab? Would you move out of your home if an Arab moved in next door? Would you move out of the neighborhood if several Arab families started to enter it? Do you think that mixed communities pose a security risk to Israel?

Do you think that, in the event of a peace agreement with Syria, return of the Golan Heights should be conditional upon a national referendum? What do you think about the proposition that a large majority should be required to make sure that Arab votes do not determine the outcome?

Would you vote yes or no in a referendum to return the Golan Heights to Syria as part of a peace agreement?

On Their Dreams for Israel

Do you think Israel needs a constitution?
If you were writing Israel's constitution, if you could actualize your dreams, what would be the ideal relationship between Judaism and the state?
How do you think other groups of people in Israel would respond to your ideal state?
Do others in Israel share your view? Who?
Is it possible for all Israelis to agree to live under your ideal society?
    If yes: why would a (secular Jew, or haredi Jew, or reform Jew) agree to live in that kind of Israel? How would it appeal to everyone?
    If no: could Israel survive under those circumstances?
Who in Israeli society needs to learn how to compromise (if anyone)?

Attitudes on Religious Discourse in Politics, Supreme Court

Do you think that, in general, it is appropriate for Israelis to use arguments based in the Jewish religion when talking about political issues? Or should only secular reasons be used? Does it make a difference if the discussion is in Knesset, in the courts, or on the streets?
Do you think it is appropriate for rabbis to issue rulings on political questions? Or should they stay out of political disputes?
What is your opinion of the Israeli Supreme Court (on matters of religion and state)?
Have you ever participated in a demonstration concerning the Supreme Court? Which one? Why did you participate? What did you see as the main message of the rally in which you participated?

Attitudes Toward Other Religious Groups

How much of the difference among Israeli Jews do you consider cultural, and how much based on rival interpretations of religion?
Do you feel a kinship with Jews in groups other than your own? How strong is that kinship? What is it based upon?
How much contact do you have with groups other than your own?
Tell me things that you respect about haredi Jews . . . Religious Zionist Jews . . . Reform/Conservative Jews . . . secular Jews.
Tell me things that you find most offensive or problematic about haredi Jews . . . Religious Zionist Jews . . . Reform/Conservative Jews . . . secular Jews.

Do you think Israeli Arabs full citizens of Israel? Should they be? Are Jews from the Reform and Conservative branches full citizens? Should they be? Are haredi Jews full citizens? Should they be?

Questions for Arab Subjects

Background

Where do you live?
How old are you?
What is your educational background?
What is your occupation?
What is your religion?
How important is your religion to you?
Tell me about your family.
How important is religion to your family?
Please tell me the story of how you came to be a citizen of Israel.

Arabs as Israelis

When you speak Hebrew, how do you feel?
When you hear "Hatikva" being sung or played, how do you feel?
Do you think of yourself more as an Arab or more as an Israeli?
Do you think of yourself as a Palestinian?
Which is stronger, your Israeli identity or your Arab identity?
What does it mean to be an Israeli?
Do you want more or less integration into Israeli society?
If and when Palestine becomes an independent state, would you want to live there?

Attitudes About Israel's Jewish Character

Do you think Israel is a Jewish state? Why or why not?
In your opinion, is there a difference between Israel as a Jewish state and Israel as a Zionist state?
In what ways does the Jewish character of the state affect you personally?
Do you think there is a difference between a "Jewish state" and a "State for the Jews"? What is that difference?
If Israel were to be one of these, which do you think it should be?

Some people think Israel should be a "state of all its citizens"? Do you
   agree? How would that change things?
Some people think there should be a complete separation of Judaism from
   the state. Do you agree? Why or why not?

Attitudes Toward Democracy

Do you think Israel is a democratic state? Why or why not?
   If yes: is Israel democratic enough, not democratic enough, or too de-
      mocratic?
   If no: why not? Should it be democratic?
What do you think of when you hear the word "democracy"? What does it
   mean to you?
Is democracy important to you?
Are you happy you live in a democracy (assuming you think Israel is a de-
   mocracy)? Why or why not?

Assessing Links Between Judaism and Democracy

In the two most recent basic laws Basic Law: Human Dignity and Freedom
   and Basic Law: Freedom of Occupation, there is a purpose clause which
   reads: "This Basic Law is designed to anchor in a Basic Law the values
   of the State of Israel as a Jewish and democratic state." What does that
   mean to you? Do you see a conflict between Judaism and democracy?
   Or are they compatible with each other?
Do you think democracy is possible in a state which calls itself Jewish?

Reactions to Specific Issues

For each of the following, please tell me whether you approve or disapprove,
   and tell me why:

   Law of return gives preference to Jews
   Hebrew is the national language
   The state's anthem ("Hatikva") speaks of the Jewish longing to return to
      Zion
   The state's flag has a Star of David
   The state's official symbol is the Jewish candelabrum
   The state gives financial support to religious education
   The state gives official recognition to the Chief Rabbinate

The state gives Jewish, Christian and Muslim religious courts jurisdiction over marriage and weddings
The state gives religious courts jurisdiction over divorce
The state gives religious courts jurisdiction over burial
The State recognizes the Jewish sabbath and Jewish holidays
The State respects the laws of kashrut in public kitchens
Many Yeshiva students receive deferrals from the military draft
Religious parties control 27 Knesset seats out of 120 (Shas 17, United Torah Judaism 5, NRP 5)

Have you heard about the Supreme Court decision in March concerning an Israeli Arab couple who wanted to buy a home in the town of Katzir? Chief Justice Barak wrote in his decision that it is illegal for the state (directly or by proxy) to discriminate against Arab citizens. He rejects the principle of "separate but equal". What was your reaction to this ruling? Would you want to live next door to a Jewish Israeli?
Do you think that, in the event of a peace agreement with Syria, return of the Golan Heights should be conditional upon a national referendum? What do you think about the proposition that a large majority should be required to make sure that Arab votes do not determine the outcome?
Would you vote yes or no in a referendum to return the Golan Heights to Syria as part of a peace agreement?

On Their Dreams for Israel

Do you think Israel needs a constitution?
If you were writing Israel's constitution, if you could actualize your dreams, what would be the ideal relationship between Judaism and the state?
How do you think other groups of people in Israel would respond to your ideal state?
Do others in Israel share your view? Who?
Is it possible for all Israelis to agree to live under your ideal society?
   If yes: why would a (secular Jew, or haredi Jew, or reform Jew) agree to live in that kind of Israel? How would it appeal to everyone?
   If no: could Israel survive under those circumstances?
Who in Israeli society needs to learn how to compromise (if anyone)?

Attitudes on Religious Discourse in Politics, Supreme Court

Do you think that, in general, it is appropriate for Israelis to use arguments based in the Jewish religion when talking about political issues? Or should only secular reasons be used? Does it make a difference if the discussion is in Knesset, in the courts, or on the streets?

Do you think it is appropriate for rabbis to issue rulings on political questions? Or should they stay out of political disputes?

What is your opinion of the Israeli Supreme Court (on matters of religion and state)?

Have you ever participated in a demonstration concerning the Supreme Court? Which one? Why did you participate? What did you see as the main message of the rally in which you participated?

Attitudes Toward Other Religious Groups

How much contact do you have with groups other than your own?

Tell me things that you respect about haredi Jews . . . Religious Zionist Jews . . . Reform/Conservative Jews . . . secular Jews. Tell me things that you find most offensive or problematic about haredi Jews . . . Religious Zionist Jews . . . Reform/Conservative Jews . . . secular Jews.

Bibliography

English Sources

Adallah (The Legal Center for the Rights of the Arab Minority in Israel). *Legal Violations of Arab Minority Rights in Israel: A Report on Israel's Implementation of the International Convention on the Elimination of all Forms of Racial Discrimination.* Shfaram, Israel: Adalah, March 1998.

Americans United for Separation of Church and State. "The Faith-Based Initiative: Churches, Social Services & Your Tax Dollars." www.au.org /site/PageServer?pagename=resources_brochure_faithbased (8 August 2005).

Anderson, Elizabeth S. and Richard H. Pildes. "Expressive Theories of Law: A General Restatement." *University of Pennsylvania Law Review* 148 (May 2000): 1503-75.

Aristotle. *Nicomachean Ethics.* Translated by Terence Irwin. Indianapolis, Ind.: Hackett Publishing Company, 1985.

Avineri, Shlomo. *The Making of Modern Zionism: The Intellectual Origins of the Jewish State.* London: Weidenfeld and Nicholson, 1981.

Avnon, Dan. "Legislative Rights Talk in Israel: The Supreme Court as Interpreter of Israel's Jewish and Democratic Values." Paper prepared for delivery at the Second Workshop of Parliamentary Scholars and Parliamentarians, Oxfordshire, England, August 3-4, 1996.

Barak, Aharon. *Judicial Discretion.* New Haven: Yale University Press, 1989.

Barak-Erez, Daphne. "From an Unwritten to a Written Constitution: The Israeli Challenge in American Perspective." *Columbia Human Rights Law Review* 26 (Winter 1995): 309-55.

Beitz, Charles R. "Human Rights as a Common Concern." *American Political Science Review* 95 (June 2000): 269-82.

———. "Rawls's Law of Peoples." *Ethics* 110, no. 4 (July 2000): 669-96.

——. *Political Equality.* Princeton: Princeton University Press, 1990.

Bellah, Robert N., Richard Madsen, Anne Swidler, William W. Sullivan and Steven M. Tipton. *Habits of the Heart: Individualism and Commitment in American Life.* Berkeley: University of California Press, 1985.

Berman, Eli. "Sect, Subsidy and Sacrifice: An Economist's View of Ultra-Orthodox Jews." Discussion Paper No. 98.08. Jerusalem: Maurice Falk Institute for Economic Research in Israel & Jerusalem Institute for Israel Studies, 1998.

Birnbaum, Ervin. *The Politics of Compromise: State and Religion in Israel.* Rutherford, NJ: Fairleigh Dickinson University Press, 1970.

Bishara, Azmi. "Arab Citizens of Israel: Little to Celebrate." *Tikkun* 13 (July/August 1998).

Buchanan, Allen. "Rawls's Law of Peoples: Rules for a Vanished Westphalian World." *Ethics* 110, no. 4 (July 2000): 697-721.

Carroll, Lewis. *Alice in Wonderland.* New York: Grosset & Dunlap, 1946.

Carter, Stephen. *The Culture of Disbelief: How American Law and Politics Trivialize Religious Devotion.* New York: Anchor Books, 1994.

Constitution for Israel website. www.cfisrael.org//home.html (25 August 2005).

Donin, Hayim Halevy. *To Be a Jew: A Guide to Jewish Observance in Contemporary Life.* New York: Basic Books, 1972.

Don-Yehiya, Eliezer. "Jewish Messianism, Religious Zionism and Israeli Politics: The Impact and Origins of Gush Emunim." *Middle Eastern Studies* 23 (April 1987): 215-34.

Dowty, Alan. "Is Israel Democratic? Substance and Semantics in the 'Ethnic Democracy' Debate." *Israel Studies* 4, no. 2 (1999): 1-15.

Dworkin, Ronald. *Taking Rights Seriously.* Cambridge: Harvard University Press, 1977.

Edelman, Martin. *Courts, Politics and Culture in Israel.* Charlottesville: University Press of Virginia, 1994.

Elazar, Daniel, ed. *Constitutionalism: The Israeli and American Experiences.* New York: University Press of America, 1990.

Elazar, Daniel. Contribution to "The Jewish State: The Next Fifty Years (A Symposium)." *Azure* no. 6 (Winter 1999): 76-80.

Ezrahi, Yaron. *Rubber Bullets: Power and Conscience in Israeli Statehood.* Berkeley: University of California Press, 1998.

Feldman, Noah. *Divided by God: America's Church-State Problem – And What We Should Do About It.* New York: Farrar, Straus and Giroux, 2005.

Friedman, Menachem. "Jewish Zealots: Conservative Versus Innovative." In *Jewish Fundamentalism in Comparative Perspective: Religion, Ideology and the Crisis of Modernity,* ed. Laurence J. Silberstein. New York: New York University Press, 1994.

Galston, William. *Liberal Purposes: Goods, Virtues and Diversity in the Liberal State.* Cambridge: Cambridge University Press, 1991.

Gavison, Ruth. "Jewish and Democratic? A Rejoinder to the Ethnic Democracy Debate." *Israel Studies* 4, no. 1 (1999): 44-72.

Ghanem, As'ad, Nadim Rouhana and Oren Yiftachel. "Questioning 'Ethnic Democracy': A Response to Sammy Smooha." *Israel Studies* 3, no. 2 (1998): 253-67.

Gorenberg, Gershom. *The End of Days: Fundamentalism and the Struggle for the Temple Mount.* New York: Free Press, 2000.

Goodin, Robert E. Review of *Habits of the Heart,* by Robert N. Bellah et al. *Ethics* 96 (January 1986): 431-32.

Gross, George. "The Constitutional Question in Israel." In *Constitutionalism: The Israeli and American Experiences,* ed. Daniel J. Elazar. New York: University Press of America, 1990.

Gusfield, Joseph. "I Gotta Be Me." *Contemporary Sociology* 15 (January 1986): 7-9.

Ha'aretz (English version of Hebrew daily newspaper), 1998-2005.

Halpern, Ben and Jehuda Reinharz. *Zionism and the Creation of a New Society.* Oxford: Oxford University Press, 1998.

Hamburger, Philip. *Separation of Church and State.* Cambridge, Mass.: Harvard University Press, 2002.

Hartman, David. *Conflicting Visions: Spiritual Possibilities in Modern Israel.* New York: Schocken Books, 1990.

Hattis Rolef, Susan, ed. *Political Dictionary of the State of Israel.* New York: Macmillan Publishing, 1987.

Hazony, Yoram. *The Jewish State: The Struggle for Israel's Soul.* New York: Basic Books, 2000.

———. "Did Herzl Want a 'Jewish' State?" *Azure* 9, no. 2 (Spring 2000): 37-73.

Hegel, G. W. F. *Elements of the Philosophy of Right.* Translated by H. B. Nisbet. Edited by Allen W. Wood. Cambridge: Cambridge University Press, 1991.

Herzog, Don. *Happy Slaves: A Critique of Consent Theory.* Chicago: University of Chicago Press, 1989.

Hobbes, Thomas. *Leviathan.* Edited by Edwin Curley. Indianapolis, Ind.: Hackett Publishing Company, 1994.

Hochschild, Jennifer. *What's Fair? American Beliefs About Distributive Justice.* Cambridge, Mass.: Harvard University Press, 1981.

Hofnung, Menachem. "The Unintended Consequences of Unplanned Constitutional Reform: Constitutional Politics in Israel." *American Journal of Comparative Law* 44 (Fall 1996): 585-604.

Horowitz, Dan and Moshe Lissak. *Trouble in Utopia: The Overburdened Polity of Israel.* Albany: SUNY Press, 1989.

Hume, David. "Of the Original Contract." In *Hume's Political Essays*, ed. Knud Haakonssen, 186-201. Cambridge: Cambridge University Press, 1994.

Jerusalem Post (English-language daily newspaper), 1998-2005.

Kahane, Ariel, ed. "Proposal to Encourage Emigration." *Arutz Sheva News Service*, 26 July 2001.

Kramnick, Isaac and R. Laurence Moore. *The Godless Constitution: A Moral Defense of the Secular State*. New York: W. W. Norton & Company, 2005.

———. *The Godless Constitution: The Case Against Religious Correctness*. New York: W. W. Norton & Company, 1996.

Kuper, Andrew. "Rawlsian Global Justice: Beyond *The Law of Peoples*." *Political Theory* 28 (October 2000): 640-74.

Lahav, Pnina. "Rights and Democracy: The Court's Performance." Pp. 133-139 in *Israeli Democracy Under Stress*, edited by Larry Diamond and Ehud Sprinzak. Boulder: Lynne Rienner Publishers, 1993.

———. *Judgment in Jerusalem: Chief Justice Simon Agranat and the Zionist Century*. Los Angeles: University of California Press, 1997.

Leibowitz, Yeshayahu. *Judaism, Human Values, and the Jewish State*. Edited by Eliezer Goldman. Cambridge: Harvard University Press, 1992.

Levy, Shlomit, Hanna Levinsohn, and Elihu Katz. *Beliefs, Observances and Social Interaction Among Israeli Jews*. Jerusalem: Louis Guttman Israel Institute of Applied Social Research, 1993.

———. *Beliefs, Observances and Values Among Israeli Jews 2000*. Jerusalem: Israel Democracy Institute and AVI CHAI Foundation, 2002.

Levy, Jacob T. "State Symbols and Multiculturalism." *Report from the Institute for Philosophy and Public Policy* 20, no. 4 (Fall 2000): 16-22.

Lewittes, Mendell. *Religious Foundations of the Jewish State*. Northville, NJ: Jason Aronson, Inc., 1977.

Liebman, Charles S. and Eliezer Don-Yehiya. *Civil Religion in Israel: Traditional Judaism and Political Culture in the Jewish State*. Berkeley: University of California Press, 1984.

———. *Religion and Politics in Israel*. Bloomington: Indiana University Press, 1984.

Liebman, Charles S. and Elihu Katz, eds. *The Jewishness of Israelis: Reponses to the Guttman Report*. Albany, N.Y.: SUNY Press, 1997.

Locke, John. *A Letter Concerning Toleration*. Indianapolis, Ind.: Hackett Publishing Company, 1983.

Ma'oz, Asher. "Enforcement of Religious Courts' Judgments Under Israeli Law." *Journal of Church and State* 33, no. 3 (Summer 1991): 474-75.

Martin, Waldo E., ed. *Brown v. Board of Education: A Brief History with Documents*. New York: Bedford/St. Martin's, 1998.

Mazie, Steven. "Consenting Adults? Amish 'Rumspringa' and the Quandary of Exit in Liberalism." *Perspectives on Politics* 3, no. 4 (December 2005): 745-59.

———. "Rethinking Religious Establishment and Liberal Democracy: Lessons from Israel." *Review of Faith and International Affairs* 2, no. 2 (Fall 2004): 3-12.

———. "Importing Liberalism: Brown v. Board of Education in the Israeli Context." *Polity* 36, no. 3 (April 2004): 389-410.

Mazie, Steven and Patricia Woods. "Prayer, Politics and the Women of the Wall: The Benefits of Collaboration in Participant Observation at Intense, Multi-Focal Events." *Field Methods* 15, no. 1 (February 2003): 25-50.

Mishory, Alec. "The Flag and the Emblem." Israel Ministry of Foreign Affairs website, www.israel-mfa.gov.il/mfa/go.asp?MFAH0 cph0 (8 August 2005).

Monette, Duane R., Thomas J. Sullivan and Cornell R. DeJong. *Applied Social Research: Tools for the Human Services.* Fourth edition. New York: Harcourt Brace, 1998.

Monsma, Stephen V. and J. Christopher Soper, eds. *Equal Treatment of Religion in a Pluralistic Society.* Grand Rapids, Mich.: Eerdmans Publising Company, 1998.

———. *The Challenge of Pluralism: Church and State in Five Democracies.* Lanham, Md.: Rowman & Littlefield, 1997.

Nagel, Thomas. "Moral Conflict and Political Legitimacy." *Philosophy and Public Affairs* 16, no. 3 (Summer 1987): 215-40.

———. *Equality and Partiality.* New York: Oxford University Press, 1991.

Neuberger, Benyamin. "Religion and Democracy in Israel." Jerusalem: The Floersheimer Institute for Policy Studies, 1997.

Neuhaus, Richard. *The Naked Public Square: Religion and Democracy in America.* Grand Rapids, Mich.: Eerdmans Publishing Company, 1986.

New York Times, 1996-2005.

O'Brien, Conor Cruise. *The Siege: The Saga of Israel and Zionism.* New York: Simon and Schuster, 1986.

O'Brien, David. *Constitutional Law and Politics, Volume Two: Civil Rights and Civil Liberties.* New York: W.W. Norton & Company, 1991.

Oz, Amos. *In the Land of Israel.* Translated by Maurie Goldberg-Bartura. San Diego: Harcourt Brace, 1983.

Parekh, Bhikhu. "The Voice of Religion in Political Discourse." Pp. 63-84 in *Religion, Politics and Peace,* edited by Leroy S. Rouner. Notre Dame, Ind.: University of Notre Dame Press, 1999.

Parnass-Honig, Tikva. "The High Court Decision on Katzir: Nemystification [sic] of Its Claims for Equality." *News From Within* 14, no. 4 (April 2000), 3.

Plato. *Republic*. Translated by A.D. Lindsay. Edited by Terence Irwin. London: Everyman, 1992.

Prince-Gibson, Eetta. "Letter from Katzir: Won't You Be My Neighbor?" *Hadassah Magazine*, May 2001, 47-49.

Rabinowicz, Harry M. *Hasidism and the State of Israel*. East Brunswick, NJ: Associated University Presses, 1982.

Rackman, Emanuel. *Israel's Emerging Constitution 1948-51*. New York: Columbia University Press, 1955.

Rawls, John. *A Theory of Justice*. Cambridge, Mass.: Harvard University Press, Belknap Press, 1971.

———. *Political Liberalism*. New York: Columbia University Press, 1993.

———. *Collected Papers*. Edited by Samuel Freeman. Cambridge, Mass.: Harvard University Press, 1999.

———. *The Law of Peoples*. Cambridge, Mass.: Harvard University Press, 1999.

———. *Justice as Fairness: A Restatement*. Cambridge, Mass.: Harvard University Press, Belknap Press, 2001.

Raz, Joseph. *The Morality of Freedom*. Oxford: Oxford University Press, 1988.

Rejwan, Nissim. *Israel in Search of Identity*. Gainesville, Fla.: University Press of Florida, 1999.

Riley, Jonathan. "Interpreting Berlin's Liberalism." *American Political Science Review* 95, no. 2 (June 2001): 283-95.

Rorty, Richard. "Religion as Conversation-Stopper." *Common Knowledge* 3, no. 1 (1994): 1-6.

Rousseau, Jean-Jacques. *On the Social Contract*. Translated by Donald Cress. Indianapolis, Ind.: Hackett Publishing Company, 1987.

Sachar, Howard M. *A History of Israel: From the Rise of Zionism to Our Time*. Vol. 1. New York: Alfred A. Knopf, 1979.

Sandel, Michael. Review of *Political Liberalism*, by John Rawls. *Harvard Law Review* 107 (1994): 1765-95.

Scanlon, T.M. "Contractualism and Utilitarianism." In *Utilitarianism and Beyond*, ed. Amartya Sen and Bernard Williams, 103-28. Cambridge: Cambridge University Press, 1982.

———. *What We Owe to Each Other*. Cambridge, Mass.: Harvard University Press, Belknap Press , 1999.

Schiff, Gary. *Tradition and Politics: The Religious Parties of Israel*. Detroit: Wayne State University Press, 1977.

Schiffer, Varda. "The Haredi Education System: Allocation, Regulation and Control." Jerusalem: The Floersheimer Institute for Policy Studies, 1998.

Schwarzenbach, Sibyl A. "Rawls, Hegel and Communitarianism." *Political Theory* 19, no. 4 (November 1991): 539-71.

Sharfman, Daphna. *Living Without a Constitution: Civil Rights in Israel*. Armonk, N.Y.: M.E. Sharpe, 1993.

Shetreet, Shimon. *Justice in Israel: A Study of the Israeli Judiciary.* Amsterdam: Martinus Nijhoff Publishers, 1994.

———. "State and Religion: Funding of Religious Institutions—The Case of Israel in Comparative Perspective." *Notre Dame Journal of Law, Ethics and Public Policy* 13 (1999): 421-53.

Smooha, Sammy. "Ethnic Democracy: Israel as an Archetype." *Israel Studies* 2, no. 2 (1997): 198-241.

Sontag, Deborah. "Israel's Next Palestinian Problem." *New York Times Magazine,* 10 September 2000, 48-53.

Stegeby, E. Kenneth. "An Analysis of the Impending Disestablishment of the Church in Sweden." *Brigham Young University Law Review* (1999): 703-67.

Strong, S.I. "Law and Religion in Israel and Iran: How the Integration of Secular and Spiritual Laws Affects Human Rights and the Potential for Violence." *Michigan Journal of International Law* 19 (Fall 1997): 109-217.

Sullivan, Andrew. "This *Is* a Religious War." *New York Times Magazine,* 7 October 2001, 44-52.

———. "Right Turn: What Conservatives Should Learn from 9/11." *The New Republic,* 17 December 2001, 22-26.

Tamir, Yael. "Commentary: A Jewish Democratic State." Pp. 518-23 in *The Jewish Political Tradition, Volume One: Authority,* edited by Michael Walzer, Menachem Lorberbaum and Noam J. Zohar. New Haven: Yale University Press, 2000.

———. *Liberal Nationalism.* Princeton: Princeton University Press, 1993.

Teson, Fernando. *A Philosophy of International Law.* Boulder: Westview, 1998.

"The History of 'Hatikva': Israel's National Anthem." Our Jerusalem website, 1 May 2001, <http://www.ourjerusalem.com/history/story/history 20010501a.html> (8 August 2005).

Usher, Graham. "Exhausting the Dream." *Al-Ahram Weekly Online,* no. 375, 30 April–6 May 1998, <http://www.weekly.ahram.org.eg/1998/375/reg0.htm> (29 July 2005).

Vital, David. *The Origins of Zionism* (Oxford: Oxford University Press, Clarendon Press, 1975.

———. "The Afflictions of the Jews and the Afflictions of Zionism: The Meaning and Consequences of the 'Uganda' Controversy." In *Conflict and Consensus in Jewish Political Life,* ed. Stuart A. Cohen and Eliezer Don-Yehiya, 79-91. Jerusalem: Bar Ilan University Press, 1986.

Waldron, Jeremy. "Religious Contributions in Public Deliberation." *San Diego Law Review* 30 (Fall 1993): 817-48.

Walzer, Michael. *Spheres of Justice.* New York: Basic Books, 1983.

———. *On Toleration.* New Haven: Yale University Press, 1997.

Weiss, Robert S. *Learning from Strangers: The Art and Method of Qualitative Interview Studies.* New York: Free Press, 1994.

Williams, Carol J. "Sweden Ends Designation of Lutheranism as Official Religion." *Los Angeles Times*, 1 January 2000.

Wittgenstein, Ludwig. *Philosophical Investigations*. Translated by G. E. M. Anscombe. Englewood Cliffs, NJ: Prentice Hall, 1958.

Wooton, David, ed. *Political Writings of John Locke*. New York: Penguin Books, 1993.

Ynet News (online Israeli news source), 2003-2005.

Zamir, Itzhak and Allen Zysblat, eds. *Public Law in Israel*. Oxford: Oxford University Press, Clarendon Press, 1996.

Hebrew Sources

Barak, Aharon. "Mehaipcha hukatit: zechuiot yesod muganot" (A constitutional revolution: fundamental rights protected). *Mishpat U'Memshal* 1, no. 1 (August 1992): 9-35.

Bechor, Guy. *Huka le-yisrael: sipuro shel ma'avak* (A constitution for Israel: a story of conflict). Jerusalem: Keter Press Enterprises, 1996.

David, Yossi, ed. *Medinat Yisrael: bein yahadut ve-demokratia* (The state of Israel: between Judaism and democracy). Jerusalem: Israel Democracy Institute, 2000.

Divrei ha-Knesset (Knesset proceedings). Second Session of the 13th Knesset, 6431-32, 6434.

Divrei ha-Knesset (Knesset proceedings). Response of the Deputy Minister of Defense to Question No. 352, 14 March 2000, 417.

Elon, Menachem. "Derech hok ba-huka" (The way of law in the constitution: the values of a Jewish and democratic state in light of the Basic Law: Human Dignity and Freedom). *Iyyunei Mishpat* (Tel Aviv University Law Review) 17 (1993): 659-88.

Friedman, Menachem. "Ve-eleh toldot ha-status-quo" (And these are the origins of the status quo: religion and state in Israel). In *Ha-ma'avar mi-yishuv le-medinah 1947-1949: retzifut ve-tmurot* (The transition from settlement to state 1947-1949: continuity and change), ed. Varda Pichavsky, 47-77. Haifa: Herzl Institute of Haifa University, 1990.

Gavison, Ruth. *Yisrael ke-medinah yehudit ve-demokratit: metahim ve-sikuim* (Israel as a Jewish and democratic state: tensions and prospects). Tel Aviv: Van Leer Jerusalem Institute, Hakibbutz Hameuchad Publishing, 1999.

———. "Ha-omnam yehudit ve-demokratit? Mashmauto shel din Katzir" (Truly Jewish and democratic? The significance of the Katzir decision). *Kivunim Hadashim: Journal of Zionism and Judaism* no. 2 (April 2000): 21-29.

Ilan, Shahar. "Dehiat ha-gius shel bahurei yeshivot" (Draft deferment for yeshiva students: a policy proposal). Publication #4/10. Jerusalem: Floersheimer Institute for Policy Studies, December 1999.

Israel Ministry of Justice. *Hok Sha'ot Avodah U'menuha* (Hours of Work and Rest Law) (1951). In *Laws of the State of Israel*, vol. 5 (1950-51), 125-33; vol. 23 (1968-69), 60-61; vol. 35 (1980-81), 133-35.

———. *Pekudat Sidrei Ha'shilton Ve'ha'mishpat* (Law and Administration Ordinance) (1948). In *Laws of the State of Israel*, vol. 1 (1948), 18.

Margolin, Ron, ed. *Medinat Yisrael ke-medinah yehudit ve-demokratit* (The state of Israel as a Jewish and democratic state). Jerusalem: The World Association for Jewish Philosophy/AVICHAI, 1999.

Marmorstein, Mordechai. *Derekh hadashah yeshana* (Religious Zionism: a reappraisal). Tel Aviv: Mapik, 1993.

Mautner, Menachem, Avi Sagi and Ronen Shamir, eds. *Rav-tarbutiut be-medinah demokratit ve-yehudit* (Multiculturalism in a democratic and Jewish state). Tel Aviv: Ramot, 1998.

Ona, Moshe. *Be-derakhim nifradot* (On separate paths: the religious parties of Israel). Gush Etzion: Yad Shapira Press, 1983.

Preisler, Zvi H., ed. *Legislation in the State of Israel: Arranged by Subjects with Six Indexes*. Vol. 2. Jerusalem: Ketuvim Publishers, 2000.

Ravitsky, Aviezer. *Dat u'medinah ba-mahshevet Yisrael* (Religion and state in Jewish philosophy: models of unity, division, collision and subordination). Jerusalem: Israeli Democracy Institute, 1998.

Sapir, Gidon. "Gius shel talmidei yeshiva be-Yisrael" (Drafting yeshiva students in Israel: a proposed framework of relevant normative considerations). *Plilim* 9 (2000): 217-53.

Sheleg, Yair. *Ha-dati'im he-hadashim: mabat achshavi al ha-hevrah ha-datit be-yisrael* (The new religious Jews: recent developments among observant Jews in Israel). Jerusalem: Keter Press, 2000.

Shifman, Pinhas. *Mi mefahed mi-nisuin ezrahim?* (Who's afraid of civil marriage? The case for reform). Jerusalem: Jerusalem Institute for Israel Studies, 1995.

Tel Aviv University Law School. *Medinah yehudit ve-demokratit* (A Jewish and democratic state). Tel Aviv: Ramot, 1996.

Weinryb, Eliezer. *Dat u'medinah: heibetim philosophim* (Religion and state: philosophical aspects). Tel Aviv: Hakibbutz Hameuchad, 2000.

Court Cases: United States

Bowen v. Kendrick, 487 U.S. 589 (1988).

Brown v. Board of Education of Topeka, 347 U.S. 483 (1954).

Everson v. Board of Education, 330 U.S. 1 (1947).
Lemon v. Kurtzman 403 U.S. 602 (1971).
McGowan v. Maryland, 366 U.S. 420, 445-448 (1961).
Mitchell v. Helms, 530 U.S. 793 (2000).
Mueller v. Allen, 463 U.S. 388 (1983).
Olmstead v. U.S., 277 U.S. 438, 478 (1928).
Plessy v. Ferguson, 163 U.S. 538 (1896).
Roe v. Wade, 410 U.S. 113 (1973).
Rosenberger v. Rectors of the University of Virginia, 515 U.S. 819 (1995).
Walz v. Tax Commission of City of New York, 397 U.S. 664 (1970).
Wisconsin v. Yoder, 406 U.S. 205 (1972).
Zelman v. Simmons-Harris, 536 U.S. 639 (2002).
Zobrest v. Catalina Foothills School Dist., 509 U.S. 1 (1993).

Court Cases: Israel

Ka'adan v. Israel Lands Administration, H.C. 6698/95 (1995).
Kol Ha'am v. Minister of Interior, H.C. 73/53, 87/53 (1953) 7 P.D. 871.
Na'amat (Women's Labor Zionist Organization) v. Minister of Interior, H.C. 5070/95 (2002).
Rubinstein v. Minister of Defense, H.C. 3267/97, 715/98 (1998).
United Bank Mizrahi Bank Ltd. v. Migdal Assoc. Village, 49(4) P.D. 221 (1995).
Yehuda Ressler v. Knesset of Israel, H.C. 24/01 (2002).
Yuri Shmuckler et al. v. the Municipality of Ashkelon and the State of Israel 7182/98, 566 (3)99, (1999).

Interviews

Aaron [pseud.]. Interview by author, 19 April 2000, Ra'anana, Israel. Transcript of tape recording.
Avi [pseud.]. Interview by author, 15 May 2000, Jerusalem, Israel. Transcript of tape recording [Hebrew].
Chaim [pseud.]. Interview by author, 24 April 2000, Kibbutz Ketura, Israel. Transcript of tape recording [Hebrew].
Ganit [pseud.]. Interview by author, 14 June 2000, Jerusalem, Israel. Transcript of tape recording [Hebrew].
Majjed [pseud.]. Interview by author, 11 May 2000, Jerusalem, Israel. Transcript of tape recording [Hebrew].
Mina [pseud.]. Interview by author, 11 April 2000, Ramat Aviv, Israel. Transcript of tape recording [Hebrew].

Muhammad [pseud.]. Interview by author, 5 May 2000, Qualansuwa, Israel. Transcript of tape recording [Hebrew].

Nachman [pseud.]. Interview by author, 5 June 2000, Jerusalem, Israel. Transcript of tape recording [Hebrew].

Nadia [pseud.]. Interview by author, 5 April 2000, Jerusalem, Israel. Transcript of tape recording [Hebrew].

Naomi [pseud.]. Interview by author, 8 May 2000, Jerusalem, Israel. Transcript of tape recording [Hebrew].

Nehama [pseud.]. Interview by author, 11 June 2000, Jerusalem, Israel. Transcript of tape recording [Hebrew].

Nosson [pseud.]. Interview by author, 30 May 2000, Givat Ze'ev, Israel (West Bank). Transcript of tape recording [Hebrew].

Omer [pseud.]. Interview by author, 17 May 2000, Jerusalem, Israel. Transcript of tape recording [Hebrew].

Oren [pseud.]. Interview by author, 12 May 2000, Jerusalem, Israel. Transcript of tape recording [Hebrew].

Regev, Rabbi Uri, executive director of the Israel Religious Action Center [has since become director of the World Union for Progrssive Judaism]. Interview by author, 15 June 2000 and 21 June 2000, Jerusalem, Israel. Transcript of tape recording.

Richard [pseud.]. Interview by author, 11 May 2000, Jerusalem, Israel. Transcript of tape recording.

Rita [pseud.]. Interview by author, 19 May 2000, Ra'anana, Israel. Transcript of tape recording [Hebrew].

Rivka [pseud.]. Interview by author, 11 April 2000, Ramat Aviv, Israel. Transcript of tape recording.

Ronit [pseud.]. Interview by author, 29 May 2000, Jerusalem, Israel. Transcript of tape recording [Hebrew].

Rosen, Rabbi Mickey, founder and spiritual leader of the Yakar Center for Tradition and Creativity. Interview by author, 22 June 2000, Jerusalem, Israel. Transcript of tape recording.

Rosenblum, Jonathan, Jerusalem Post columnist. Interview by author, 22 June 2000 and 21 June 2000, Jerusalem, Israel. Transcript of tape recording.

Rotem [pseud.]. Interview by author, 17 April 2000, Jerusalem, Israel. Transcript of tape recording.

Shmuel [pseud.]. Interview by author, 12 April 2000, Haifa, Israel. Transcript of tape recording.

Shulamit [pseud.]. Interview by author, 13 April 2000, Jerusalem, Israel. Transcript of tape recording.

Tanya [pseud.]. Interview by author, 28 May 2000, Jerusalem, Israel. Transcript of tape recording [Hebrew].

Yehuda [pseud.]. Interview by author, 1 May 2000, Jerusalem, Israel. Transcript of tape recording [Hebrew].

Yeshayahu [pseud.]. Interview by author, 4 June 2000, Jerusalem, Israel. Transcript of tape recording [Hebrew].

Yoel [pseud.]. Interview by author, 18 May 2000, Ra'anana, Israel. Transcript of tape recording.

Yoram [pseud.]. Interview by author, 11 May 2000, Jerusalem, Israel. Transcript of tape recording [Hebrew].

Youssef [pseud.]. Interview by author, 12 May 2000, Jerusalem, Israel. Transcript of tape recording [Hebrew].

Zvi [pseud.]. Interview by author, 17 May 2000, Jerusalem, Israel. Transcript of tape recording [Hebrew].

Index

About the Author

Steven V. Mazie is Assistant Professor of Politics at Bard High School Early College in Manhattan, where he teaches political theory and public law. He has taught previously at Bard College, New York University and the University of Michigan. Mazie received a Ph.D. in Political Science from the University of Michigan in 2002 and is a 1993 graduate of Harvard College (*magna cum laude*). Mazie was a Raoul Wallenberg Scholar at the Hebrew University of Jerusalem in 1993-94 and has had affiliations with the Harry S Truman Research Institute for the Advancement of Peace in Jerusalem and CLAL—the National Jewish Center for Learning and Leadership in New York City. Mazie's recent articles have appeared in *Perspectives on Politics*, *Polity*, *Field Methods* and *Review of Faith and International Affairs*. He has been honored with numerous awards and fellowships, including a National Science Foundation research grant, the Beverly & Arnold Greenberg Dissertation Fellowship in Jewish Studies from the National Foundation of Jewish Culture, a Charlotte W. Newcombe Doctoral Dissertation Fellowship, and the 2003 Best Paper Award in Religion and Politics from the American Political Science Association. Mazie, a native of Des Moines, Iowa, lives with his wife and daughter in Brooklyn.